MONTEREY & CARMEL

ANN MARIE BROWN

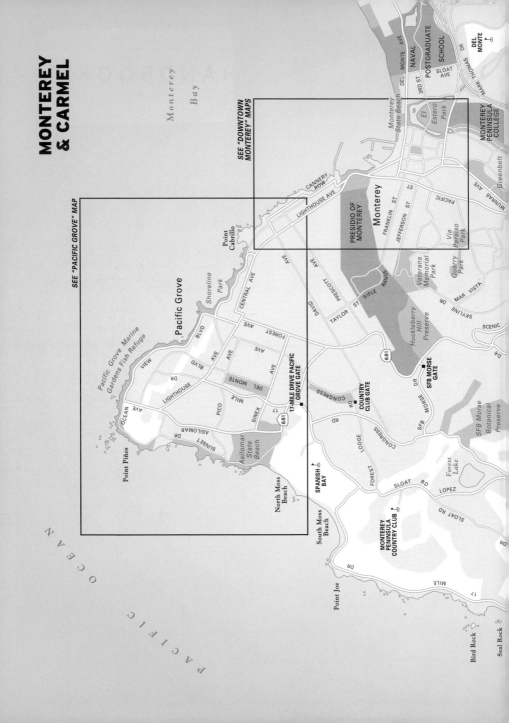

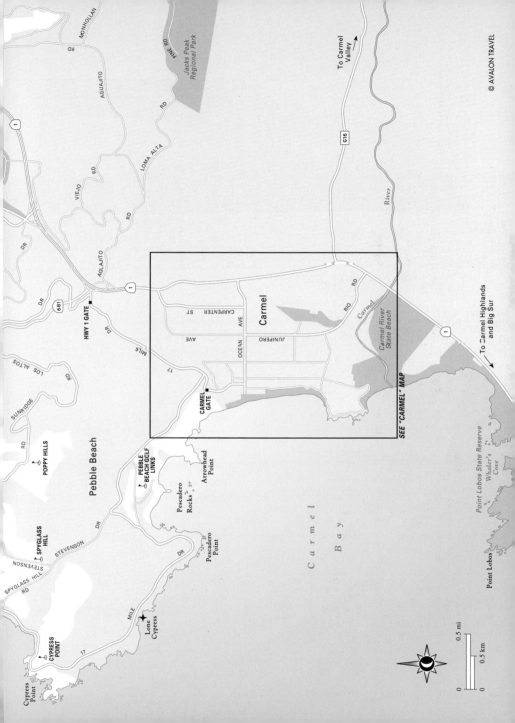

© AVALON TRAVEL

To Carmel
Valley

G16

River

Jacks Peak
Regional Park

MONHOLLAN RD
PINE RD
AGUAJITO RD
LOMA ALTA RD
VIEJO RD
RD
AGUAJITO DR
DR
DR
681
LOS ALTOS DR
SUNRIDGE RD
POPPY HILLS RD
SPYGLASS HILL
STEVENSON
SPYGLASS HILLS RD
DR
DR
17 MILE DR
17 MILE DR
MILE DR

HWY 1 GATE

Carmel

CARPENTER ST

OCEAN AVE

JUNIPERO AVE

RIO RD

Carmel

Carmel River
State Beach

SEE "CARMEL" MAP

CARMEL
GATE

Pebble Beach

PEBBLE BEACH GOLF LINKS

Pescadero Rocks

Arrowhead
Point

Pescadero
Point

Lone
Cypress

CYPRESS
POINT

Cypress
Point

C a r m e l

B a y

Point Lobos State Reserve

Whaler's
Cove

Point Lobos

To Carmel Highlands
and Big Sur

0.5 mi

0.5 km

0

Contents

Discover
Monterey & Carmel

The only remembered line of the native Ohlone people's song of world renewal, "dancing on the brink of the world," has a particularly haunting resonance around Monterey Bay. Here, in the hovering fog and ghostly cypress along the untamed coast, the indigenous "coast people" once danced. Like the area's vanished dancers, Monterey Bay is a mystery: Everything seen, heard, tasted, and touched only hints at what remains hidden.

The biggest mystery is magnificent Monterey Bay itself, almost 60 miles long and 13 miles wide. Its offshore canyons, grander than the Grand Canyon, are the area's most impressive feature — the bay's largest submarine valley dips to 10,000 feet. While much of this deep-sea canyon has never been explored, we do know that it is one of the most biologically prolific spots on earth, as evidenced by the wealth of marine life found here. Whales, dolphins, seals, sea lions, a wide variety of fish and sea birds, and Monterey's iconic sea otters all thrive. On the edge of the bay is a large peninsula fringed by shifting sand dunes, tidal mudflats teeming with life, and some of the state's most rugged, wild coastline, pocketed with rocky crags and aquamarine coves and framed by high bluffs dotted with wind-sculpted trees.

Further mysteries await at each of the towns lining Monterey Bay. The city of Monterey sits front and center, steeped in California history

and bursting with pride over its world-famous aquarium. Next door lies oceanfront Pacific Grove, a quaint, small town home to the annual monarch butterfly migration. The swank nearby enclave of Pebble Beach is accessible only via scenic 17-Mile Drive, which cruises past palatial homes, luxury resorts, seaside beaches, and prestigious golf courses. Then there's charming, cute Carmel, where the town's beaches are so lovely and its come-hither shops so alluring that they prove hard to resist. At Big Sur, California's seaside scenery is at its most photogenic, and the best of the coast is available to anyone with a pair of hiking boots or a car. Big Sur's gorgeous coastal eye candy winds 70 miles south to artsy Cambria and San Simeon, where William Randolph Hearst built his famous castle. Any exploration of Monterey's gems should begin north in sunny Santa Cruz, where leftist politics thrive, the beach and boardwalk rules, and surfers are the celebrities.

So put the top down on the convertible and pack your surfboard or hiking boots — a luxurious, tranquil coastal road trip awaits.

Planning Your Trip

▶ WHERE TO GO

Monterey

Monterey boasts California's first capital, first government building, first federal court, first newspaper, and first theater, as well as **Monterey Bay Aquarium**—one of the most fascinating aquariums in the world.

Right next door is peaceful **Pacific Grove,** where alcohol has been legal only since the 1960s, and where the annual monarch butterfly migration is big news. Inland from Monterey is agriculturally rich **Salinas,** boyhood stomping grounds of noted author John Steinbeck.

Carmel

Noted for its storybook cottages and spectacular crescent beach, Carmel was first populated by artists, writers, and other assorted bohemians, such as Henry Miller and Robinson Jeffers. Their legacy includes myriad art galleries and shops that cater heavily to the tourist trade, as well as unique and timeless landmarks, such as Jeffers' **Tor House.** Yet the founding of Carmel must be credited to the **Carmel Mission,** built here in 1771, the second Spanish mission in California.

A scenic cruise 10 miles inland, **Carmel Valley** greets visitors with boutique wineries, organic produce, and a century-old zen center complete with hot springs.

Big Sur

A favored spot for artists, romantics, and nature lovers, the coast of Big Sur is arguably the most beautiful in California. Its 75-mile stretch of sandstone cliffs and crashing waves is accessed via the winding, two-lane **Big Sur Scenic Byway,** which carves its course along

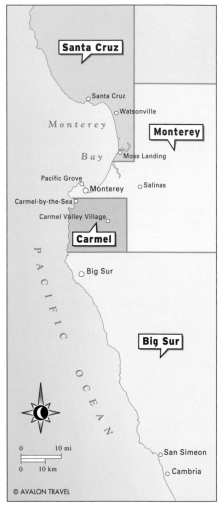

the edge of a dramatic meeting of land and sea. Along the way, the coastal beauty is collected in a series of state parks like **Pfeiffer Big Sur State Park.** On the south end of the coast are two charming coastal towns, **Cambria** and **San Simeon,** the latter where Hearst Castle stands sentinel over the Central Coast.

Santa Cruz

North of Monterey, Santa Cruz is worth exploring for its historic **Santa Cruz Beach Boardwalk,** sandy **beaches,** and world-class **surf** breaks. Just inland are the redwoods, waterfalls, and hiking trails of a handful of state parks such as **Big Basin Redwoods State Park.** To the south are miles of agricultural fields and the wildlife-rich waterways of **Elkhorn Slough National Estuarine Research Reserve.** To the north lie miles of unspoiled beaches, plus the **Año Nuevo State Reserve,** mating grounds for the northern elephant seal.

IF YOU HAVE...

- **ONE DAY:** Visit Monterey.
- **ONE WEEKEND:** Add Big Sur and Carmel.
- **ONE WEEK:** Add Santa Cruz and Pacific Grove.

▶ WHEN TO GO

The busiest season around the Monterey coast is **summer,** and that's when rates are highest at area lodgings, parking near the beach is hardest to come by, and traffic snarls along Highway 1 occur in the larger cities. Ironically, it's also when the weather can be the least appealing. Although it hardly ever rains, summer fog can move in for days, keeping the coast damp and cool. Fortunately, the climate along this stretch of coastline is mild enough year-round that travelers aren't limited to summer visits. Some of the warmest, driest weather of the year happens in **autumn** (Sept.–Oct.), when the fog pushes back from the coast. **Spring** also brings clear, dry weather, although it can be windy as well. The vast majority of the year's precipitation occurs November to April, but still, there are far more sunny days than rainy days in **winter,** and that's when rates at most area lodgings are at their lowest (excluding the winter holiday periods—Thanksgiving, Christmas, New Year's, and Presidents' Day). Also, if you are an animal lover, some of the best wildlife sightings of the year occur during the winter months—including the annual migrations of monarch butterflies, northern elephant seals, and gray whales.

▶ BEFORE YOU GO

Bring three things with you: **1) advance reservations for overnight lodging; 2) advance reservations for major attractions,** and **3) clothing for layering.** Year-round the weather is quite variable; a day that dawns foggy and cold can be dry and warm in the afternoon, then foggy and cold again in the evening.

If you are planning to drive the Big Sur coast, it's always wise to check on **road conditions,** as the precipitous Pacific Coast Highway does sometimes shut down. Most years, it closes during the winter for at least a few days due to landslides.

Explore Monterey & Carmel

▶ THE BEST OF MONTEREY AND CARMEL

Day 1

Get up early and fuel up with a big breakfast at **Trailside Café** or **Wild Plum Café,** because you have a big day ahead of you. Start with an early morning walk along Fisherman's Wharf before the crowds arrive, while it's still quiet enough to hear the seals bark and the waves crash against the piers. If you are visiting in the peak of whale-watching season (Dec.– Apr.), hop on a boat at the wharf and take a three-hour whale-watching tour, or one of the shorter sightseeing cruises. Even if you don't see whales, you are likely to spot dolphins, porpoises, sea otters, harbor seals, sea lions, and a good variety of marine birds.

From the wharf, you can walk directly to the **Monterey Maritime and History Museum,** about 100 yards distant. Watch the short video on Monterey's history, take a look at some of the museum's great nautical exhibits, and then walk out the door and pick up the signed **Path of History** at **Monterey State Historic Park** (look for the yellow tiled markers in the sidewalk).

Keep an eye on your watch as you visit the historical buildings along the Path of History, because you want to get to the **Monterey Bay Aquarium** by about 2:30 P.M., when the day's crowds begin to disperse. You'll need at least two hours to do a speed tour of the aquarium, and you'll definitely want to be here around 3 P.M. to see the afternoon feedings of sea otters and penguins. After your aquarium visit, you'll have just enough time to stroll through some of the

Fisherman's Wharf, Monterey

HISTORICAL ARCHITECTURE

Monterey was prominent in the early days of California settlement. The city became the first capital of Alta California in 1775 and remained California's capital until 1845. Gaspar de Portolá and Father Crespi, together with Father Junípero Serra, founded both Monterey's presidio and mission, the latter of which was eventually relocated to Carmel. In 1791, Santa Cruz became the site of Misión Exaltación de la Santa Cruz and a military garrison on the north end of Monterey Bay.

The early days of California's history are best explored through Monterey and Carmel's wealth of historic architecture and buildings. From missions to lighthouses, the exciting path of California's transformation can be traced up and down the Monterey coast.

- **Carmel Mission.** The 1771 mission is California's second, and the onetime headquarters and favorite foreign home of Father Junípero Serra. The stunning Baroque stone church, with its four-bell Moorish tower and arched roof, was completed in 1797. Most of the buildings are reconstructions, but the mission gardens are evocative and inviting, featuring some rare plants.

- **Presidio of Monterey.** The only surviving building from Monterey's Royal Presidio is the 1791 San Carlos Cathedral on Church Street (near Figueroa). Now a parish church and a National Historic Landmark, the chapel's interior walls are decorated with Native American and Mexican folk art.

- **Mission Santa Cruz.** The Santa Cruz mission, founded in 1791, was California's 12th mission. Destroyed in an 1857 earthquake, the Santa Cruz Mission Adobe holds the last of the original adobe structures.

- **Mission San Juan Bautista.** Located by San Juan Bautista

State Historic Park, just north of Salinas, California's 15th mission was founded in 1797. Although not architecturally spectacular, it is one of the largest. Movie fans may remember Jimmy Stewart and Kim Novak in the mission scenes from Alfred Hitchcock's *Vertigo*, filmed here.

- **Custom House.** At the heart of Monterey's Custom House Plaza is this fine adobe structure, the oldest government building in California. It was used by the Mexican government from 1822 to 1846 to collect tariffs imposed on foreign merchants.

- **Point Piños Lighthouse.** Pacific Grove's lighthouse is the oldest in continuous operation on the Pacific coast. Its beacon and foghorn have been warning seagoing vessels away from the northernmost tip of the Monterey Peninsula since February 1, 1855.

- **Point Sur Light Station.** Atop Point Sur, south of Carmel and north of Big Sur, stands this 1889 stone sentinel presiding over the shipwreck site once known as the "Graveyard of the Pacific."

Mission San Juan Bautista

shops along **Cannery Row** and decide which seaside restaurant will get your dinner business. For waterfront views, it's hard to beat **The Fish Hopper** on Cannery Row, or **Abalonetti** or **Café Fina** at Fisherman's Wharf.

Hopefully you made advance reservations to stay at one of Cannery Row's ocean-front resorts, like the top-drawer **InterContinental the Clement Monterey** or the equally elegant **Monterey Plaza Hotel & Spa.** You'll sleep like the righteous while you listen to the waves spill upon the shore. Rest well—you have a busy schedule tomorrow.

Day 2

Head over to Pacific Grove, just down the road from Cannery Row, to see what small-town coastal California is all about. Fuel up with java from **The Works** or a full breakfast at **Toastie's Café,** then, in the winter months, pay a visit to the monarch butterfly grove off Lighthouse Avenue. Here, thousands of orange and black lepidoptera cling to the eucalyptus trees and flit about the town's gardens in search of nectar. If the butterflies aren't in town, stop by the **Pacific Grove Museum of Natural History** to learn about these colorful insects as well as sea otters, seabirds, and other local wonders. Afterwards, mix natural history with nautical history by touring the town's historic **Point Piños Lighthouse,** the oldest in continuous operation on the Pacific coast, shining its beacon since 1855.

Getting hungry? Stop in for a burrito or tacos to go at **Peppers MexiCali Cafe** or **Zocalo** and head to **Asilomar State Beach** for a picnic. The beach is a great place for tide-pool exploring, beachcombing, flying kites, and surfing, with long stretches of soft, white sand punctuated by shifting sand dunes.

Most out-of-town visitors choose to drive the infamous **17-Mile Drive** into **Pebble Beach,** and you can do so from the Pacific Grove gate near Asilomar. Plan on 2–3 hours for a leisurely drive with plenty of time for photo opportunities. A sunset cocktail at **Roy's Restaurant** is a must. As the sun sinks into the Pacific, take a seat next to the outdoor fire pits and listen to the bagpiper play on **The Links at Spanish Bay.**

A bagpiper plays each evening at The Links at Spanish Bay.

a bounty of organic produce at Earthbound Farms

Carmel's Fountain of Woof

If you'd rather save nine bucks (the 17-Mile Drive's entry fee), then cruise your car or ride your bike along Pacific Grove's **Three-Mile Drive** (Ocean View Blvd.) instead. Lining this waterfront road is a string of small public parks and large parking turnouts—ample spots to pull over and admire the surging surf, or wave at the kayakers or sea otters as they float past.

With any luck, you were able to book a room at one of Pacific Grove's charming bed-and-breakfasts (try **Seven Gables, Green Gables,** or **Inn at 17-Mile Drive**), so tonight you'll enjoy sweet dreams and cozy comfort in this peaceful Victorian village by the sea.

you're on a tight schedule. After lunch, drive over to the **Carmel Mission** and take a look at one of California's most beautiful historic buildings, complete with a four bell Moorish tower, arched roof, and classic mission-style gardens. You should still have plenty of time in the afternoon to head to **Point Lobos State Reserve** and walk along its dramatic, rocky coastline. Don't forget your camera so you can capture the park's ubiquitous pounding surf, aquamarine coves, and cypress-lined bluffs.

For dinner, head back to downtown for a romantic meal at **Bouchée Bistro, Anton**

Day 3

Start your day in downtown Carmel by poking your head into some of the town's beguiling art galleries and upscale shops. If you aren't the shop-till-you-drop type, take a walk on the soft, white sands of **Carmel Town Beach** instead (a short walk down the hill from downtown Carmel), or drive a few miles up Carmel Valley Road to visit the organic **Earthbound Farms,** or one of the Valley's notable wineries, like **Château Julien.**

When lunchtime rolls around, head to a Carmel institution, the **Hog's Breath Inn,** once owned by the town's ex-mayor, actor Clint Eastwood. The back patio, made of bricks and cobblestones and warmed by a huge outdoor fireplace, is the kind of place where you'll want to linger all afternoon, but remember,

bell tower at Carmel Mission

and Michel, or Casanova. And it wouldn't be a true Carmel day unless you spent the night in one of the town's intimate inns, such as the Carmel Country Inn or Sea View Inn. If

B&Bs aren't your bag, plan to lay your head at the Asian-style The Tradewinds at Carmel, the hip Carmel Mission Inn, or the Western-country-style Mission Ranch.

► COASTING THE PACIFIC COAST

The Pacific Coast Highway, or Highway 1, is one of the most spectacular feats of road building to be found anywhere in the western United States. Fill up your tank with gas, pull on your driving gloves, crank up the satellite radio, and get ready for a classic road trip, California-style.

Day 1

Plenty of California towns lay claim to the title of "Surf City, U.S.A.," but Santa Cruz has bragging rights that few can match. Jack O'Neill, inventor of the wet suit, got his start here. The Surfing Museum at Lighthouse Point interprets 100 years of surfing history. Below the point lies Steamer Lane, the Holy Grail of Santa Cruz surfing spots.

Highway 1 passes right through the center of this beach-hip, eco-friendly college town. Relive your youth by spending a few hours cruising the Santa Cruz Beach Boardwalk. Ride its classic wooden roller coaster and rediscover the teeth-aching pleasures of cotton candy. Take a surfing lesson on Cowell Beach. From October to mid-February, marvel at the thousands of monarch butterflies that gather at Natural Bridges State Beach.

If you want to get away from the hustle and bustle, head to the north or south of town, where there are miles of unspoiled beaches. Tops among them are Bonny Doon (to the north) and Sunset (to the south). As you drive south along Highway 1 from Santa Cruz, be sure to turn off at the seaside hamlet of Moss Landing, where sea otters play in

sandstone arch at Natural Bridges State Beach

BEST BEACHES

With so many fine stretches of sand running along the Monterey-area coast from north of Santa Cruz to south of Big Sur, you simply can't see them all. So how do you decide which ones *must* make contact with the bare soles of your feet? Here are some favorites, by region:

MONTEREY

- **Marina State Beach,** for its silky coastal dunes and great hang-gliding conditions

- **Asilomar State Beach,** for its shifting sand dunes, wind-sculpted forests, and tidepools (in Pacific Grove)

- **Fanshell Beach,** for its azure waves lapping upon Pebble Beach's ultra-exclusive shoreline (in Pebble Beach)

CARMEL

- **Carmel Town Beach,** for its white sands framing the aquamarine waters of Carmel Bay and annual sandcastle-building contest

- **China Cove,** for being swimmer friendly and incredibly photogenic (at Point Lobos State Reserve)

BIG SUR

- **Pfeiffer Beach,** for its soft, white sand streaked with mauve and black, and its offshore rock formations riddled with caves and arches

- **Sand Dollar Beach,** for its large, horseshoe-shaped cove and consistently good weather (32 miles south of Big Sur)

- **Moonstone Beach,** for its tidepools at Leffingwell Landing and plentiful white agates, jasper, chert, and jade (in Cambria)

SANTA CRUZ

- **Panther Beach** and neighboring **Hole-in-the-Wall Beach,** for their exclusivity (in Davenport, north of Santa Cruz)

- **Natural Bridges State Beach,** for its dramatic rock arch, tidepools, and fine crescent of sand

- **Sunset Beach,** for its spectacular sunsets and 200-foot-tall sand dunes (south of Santa Cruz)

- **Moss Landing State Beach,** for its proliferation of sea otters (in Moss Landing)

From north of Santa Cruz to south of San Simeon, the Monterey coastline lures beach lovers.

the calm harbor waters, birders and kayakers flock to **Elkhorn Slough,** and seafood restaurants serve up flapping-fresh fish.

Day 2

You can't go to **Monterey** without visiting its world-famous **aquarium,** so pull off Highway 1 at the Del Monte exit and spend at least a few hours ogling jellyfish, sea otters, blue-fin tuna, and penguins. Take a whale-watching boat tour from **Fisherman's Wharf** and walk a mile or two of the **Path of History** to visit some of Monterey's oldest buildings. Be sure to eat lunch or dinner at one of dozens of restaurants perched right next to the sea at **Cannery Row.**

Point Lobos State Reserve

Day 3

Highway 1 bypasses the quaint downtown area of **Carmel,** so make sure you take the Ocean Avenue turnoff and spend some time touring its myriad art galleries and boutiques. For strolling or a picnic on the sand, it's hard to beat **Carmel Town Beach,** and for spectacular Old California architecture, the **Carmel Mission** is well worth a tour. Stop in for take-out sandwiches at one of the stores in the Crossroads shopping center at Highway 1 and Rio Road; then head south and pull off at **Point Lobos State Reserve,** where there are a bounty of seaside overlooks that will inspire a picnic.

Day 4

Trade in your rental minivan for a convertible; you are about to drive the finest stretch of coastline Highway 1 has to offer. Get an early morning start to avoid sharing this curvaceous road with too many other drivers, and

be sure to have good walking shoes or hiking boots packed in the trunk. You'll need them for exploring the **Big Sur** coast. A half-dozen parks filled with redwoods, waterfalls, and miles of sparkling oceanfront real estate will entice you out of your car.

Start with an easy stroll to Soberanes Point at **Garrapata State Park;** you can climb to the top of 280-foot Whale Peak and watch for the spouts of whales. As you head south, pause briefly to admire the graceful arch of the **Bixby Bridge,** the unofficial entrance to Big Sur.

Next stop: the redwood-guarded path to 60-foot Pfeiffer Falls at **Pfeiffer Big Sur State Park.** Giant trees and verdant ferns decorate the one-mile trail to the waterfall. Be sure to stop in at the park's excellent bookstore/gift shop as well and browse its fantastic collection of natural history books and local arts and crafts. While you're here, it's tempting to have lunch at the park's **Big Sur Lodge Restaurant,** but you might want to save your appetite. An absolute must while driving this stretch of highway is a stop for a meal at **Nepenthe,** where the coastal views are divine. Better stay away from the bar's signature South Coast margaritas, though; they don't mix well with a day behind the wheel.

For a chance to see the work of some of Big Sur's local artists, stop in at the **Coast Gallery,** across the street from (and slightly south of) Nepenthe, or visit Nepenthe's own **Phoenix Shop,** filled with artistic treasures from the Central Coast and around the world. A few miles south is **Julia Pfeiffer Burns State Park,** where **McWay Falls** drops to the sea. The wheelchair-accessible trail to the waterfall overlook takes only about 10 minutes to walk; don't miss it.

As you head south beyond Big Sur proper, you'll find much less in the way of services,

McWay Cove at Julia Pfeiffer Burns State Park

so make sure you have all your needs taken care of before you leave town. If all this hiking and driving has taken its toll on you, stop at **Sand Dollar Beach,** a large, horseshoe-shaped cove across the highway from Plaskett Creek Campground, 32 miles south of Big Sur. A short walk will take you to the widest expanse of sand found along the Big Sur coast.

Day 5

The Pacific Coast Highway didn't exist when William Randolph Hearst built his monolithic monument to his own ego, Hearst Castle, in San Simeon, and elephant seals didn't start colonizing the beaches here until 1990—but now travelers come from around the world to witness these two unusual attractions.

Hearst Castle, the layman's moniker for **Hearst San Simeon State Historical Monument,** today ranks right up there with Disneyland as one of California's premier tourist attractions. The "ranch," as Hearst called it, is filled with a dizzying array of furnishings, art, and antiques collected (some would say pilfered) from around the world. Choose from one of four daytime tours or an evening tour of Hearst Castle; advance reservations are recommended in the summer and during holiday periods.

Four miles north of the entrance road to Hearst Castle, right alongside Highway 1, is the roadside parking area for the **Piedras Blancas elephant seals** colony. Although the elephant seals are most plentiful from November to March, some can usually be seen any day of the year. All you have to do is drive up, park, and walk a few yards to the overlook area on a bluff above the beach.

If there is any time left in your day, head south a few more miles to **Cambria,** where you can stroll its shops, browse its antique stores, and walk along the boardwalk on the bluffs above **Moonstone Beach.**

▶ THE GREAT OUTDOORS

Hiking

Some 20 miles up-canyon from Santa Cruz via Highways 9 and 236 is **Big Basin Redwoods State Park.** Hiking is sublime, especially in autumn when the days are sunny and the crowds have scattered. The park features 80 miles of trails. Shorter, easy paths lead from park headquarters through groves of 2,000-year-old giant trees, while longer treks travel to the park's "big three" waterfalls—Berry Creek, Silver, and Golden. Many visitors choose to revel in this spectacular place by staying the night, either in the park's campground or in the neighboring tent cabins. Backpackers head for the 30-mile Skyline-to-the-Sea Trail, where they can sleep trailside (reservations required for trail camps).

For ease of access, it's hard to beat **Henry Cowell Redwoods State Park,** just six miles from Santa Cruz. The 0.8-mile, wheelchair-accessible Redwood Grove Nature Trail meandering through the old-growth redwood grove in dark San Lorenzo Canyon is this park's showpiece, but much longer hikes are possible to more remote redwood groves and swimming holes on the San Lorenzo River.

The park's northern Fall Creek section—another 2,300 acres of public land, just a few miles distant from the park's main entrance—offers more hiking trails.

Another great hiker's park is **The Forest of Nisene Marks State Park** in Aptos, comprising some 10,000 acres of hefty second- and third-growth redwoods on the steep southern slopes of the Santa Cruz Mountains. Leave the main fire road (Aptos Creek Rd.) to the mountain bikers and set off on the hikers-only single-tracks, like the Loma Prieta Grade and Bridge Creek Trail to Maple Falls.

To the south in Big Sur, more parks wait to be explored on foot. During the spring wildflower season, there may be no better spot along the Central California coast to see a huge variety of blossoms than on the seven-mile Soberanes Canyon and Rocky Ridge Loop across the inland hills of **Garrapata State Park.** Just about everybody stops to take the short walk to see McWay Falls tumble to the sea at **Julia Pfeiffer Burns State Park,** but more serious hikers will want to walk a 4.3-mile loop on Ewoldsen Trail through the redwoods to a spectacular high vista of the coast.

Aptos Creek in The Forest of Nisene Marks State Park

GOOD EATS

How best to combine those notable earthy assets of the Monterey Bay area, fine wines and local farms? Visit area wineries to purchase primo fruit of the vine – the bottled edition – and complete your meal with some seasonal produce. Follow it up with a fine picnic and your own private tasting.

Outstanding in the Field is a program of events in which local organic farmers and winemakers pair up with renowned chefs to offer organic farm tours and prepare and serve multicourse meals – on well-laden tables that do, in fact, stand out in the farmer's field. The national event was started by Santa Cruz chef Jim Denevan, and several dinners are held each year in the greater Monterey Bay area.

MONTEREY

To taste the rich agricultural heritage of Monterey, plan your trip around local certified farmers markets.

- **Old Monterey Market Place,** in historic downtown Monterey, is held every Tuesday.

- **Monterey Peninsula College** hosts a smaller farmers market that takes place on Thursday afternoon.

- **Marina,** north of Monterey, is known for its certified organic farmers market every Sunday.

- **Pacific Grove,** Monterey's charming southern neighbor, has its own farmers market, held every Monday afternoon.

- **Oldtown Salinas Farmers Market** in "old town" Salinas is held on Saturday, across the street from the National Steinbeck Center.

- **Salinas Farmers Market** is another Salinas farmers market held at Hartnell College on Sunday.

- **Alisal Community Farmers Market** is yet another Salinas farmers market, held on summer Thursdays.

- **The Farm,** on Highway 68 just west of Salinas, sells certified organic fruits and vegetables (seasonal).

CARMEL

Carmel Valley is another outpost of organic produce.

- **Earthbound Farms** is a 60-acre showcase with just-picked local produce, including veggies, fruits, herbs, and flowers from other locales. The farm's organic kitchen can pack a picnic basket with gourmet goodies.

Vineyards also do quite well in Carmel Valley, particularly with chardonnay and pinot noir, but also with cabernet sauvignon, merlot, syrah, and sauvignon blanc. The region's winning wineries include:

- **Château Julien Wine Estate**

- **Heller Estate Organic Vineyards**

- **Bernardus Winery**

- **Jouillian Vineyards**

- **Parsonage**

SANTA CRUZ

In Santa Cruz, three farmers markets take place weekly.

- **Downtown Santa Cruz Market** is held Wednesday year-round.

- **Westside Market** is held on Saturday year-round.

- **Live Oak Market** is held on Sunday in summer and fall only.

- Since the late 1800s, the Santa Cruz mountains have been well known for vineyards. Regional winemaking got a big boost in 1981, with official recognition of the Santa Cruz Mountains appellation. More than 70 small wineries now produce Santa Cruz Mountains wines, including:

- **Bonny Doon Vineyard** (in Bonny Doon)

- **Hallcrest Vineyards** and **The Organic Wine Works** (in Felton)

- **Zayante Vineyard** (in Felton)

driftwood-laden beach at Andrew Molera State Park

Andrew Molera State Park offers a wide choice of trails, but for a quick taste, hike the 1.25-mile trail to the windswept promontory at Molera Point and enjoy up-close oceanfront views. An eight-mile loop on River Trail, Hidden Trail, Ridge Trail, Panorama Trail, and Bluffs Trail leads to redwood groves, big views of the coast from the park's high ridge, and a "secret" beach.

And if you are looking for one more spot to stretch your legs, try the Limekiln Trail at **Limekiln Creek State Park,** 2.5 miles south of Lucia. This one-mile path leads through a dense forest of coastal redwoods to a set of 1880s wood-fired kilns used for making bricks. A fork off the main trail leads to 100-foot Limekiln Falls, spectacular in the wet season.

Surfing

There is no better place to learn to surf in Northern California than in Santa Cruz, where the water is relatively warm (compared to points farther north) and the waves at many beaches are gentle and consistent. Beginners can haul out their big sticks and get wet at **Cowell Beach** on the north side of the Santa Cruz Wharf and at **Capitola Beach,** near its small rock jetty.

Experienced surfers head directly to the most famous surf spots in Santa Cruz: **Steamer Lane,** just off Lighthouse Point on West Cliff Drive, and **Pleasure Point,** at East Cliff Drive and Pleasure Point Drive.

Diving

Monterey is world famous for its cold, nutrient-rich waters and undulating kelp forest teeming with sea life. A few great spots for beginning divers are **San Carlos Beach, McAbee Beach,** and **Breakwater Cove,** all near Cannery Row. To the south in Carmel, more experienced divers head to Bluefish Cove and Whaler's Cove at **Point Lobos State Reserve,** where only a limited number of diving permits are available each day. Nearby **Monastery Beach,** just outside the reserve, is also a great spot for diving, but with its steep dropoffs and unstable sand, this spot is for experts only.

Biking

The epicenter of mountain biking in Santa Cruz are the miles of trails on the inland side of Highway 1 at **Wilder Ranch State Park,** but there's plenty more pedaling possibilities among the redwoods at **The Forest of Nisene Marks State Park** and **Henry Cowell Redwoods State Park.**

Over in Monterey, mountain bikers throng to the 7,000 acres of grasslands and oaks at **Fort Ord,** a former military base. Skinny-tire riders covet the 18-mile-long **Monterey Peninsula Recreation Trail,** a paved biking path that stretches from Asilomar State Beach in Pacific Grove to Castroville, passing by world-famous sights like the Monterey Bay Aquarium and Cannery Row. Also in Pacific Grove is the easy and scenic Three-Mile Drive (Ocean View Blvd.), which is level enough so that you can ride your single-speed beach cruiser. If you enjoy a little hill climbing, ride your bike along the world-famous **17-Mile Drive** (and save yourself $9, the current tariff for automobile drivers).

► GOOD MIGRATIONS

In the Monterey Bay Area, it's easy to tour nature, or, more accurately, to participate vicariously in nature's grand, ongoing tours of California. From birds traveling the Pacific Flyway to gray whales cruising past the coast, there's a whole lot of migrating going on in the greater Monterey area, especially during the winter months. Here's the calendar in brief: In December and January, gray whales migrate south to Mexico. In March and April, gray whales migrate north to the Arctic. From December through March, northern elephant seals appear on the beaches. From October through February, monarch butterflies cluster at their wintering sites. And in September, peak numbers of birds migrate through the Monterey area. Pull up a chair and watch the show.

Monarch Butterflies

Monarchs are the only butterflies known to make annual round-trip migrations. These beautiful orange and black insects travel from as far north as northern Canada to wintering spots on either the Pacific coast or the mountains of Michoacan, in central Mexico. They fly 30 miles per day over thousands of miles—all in the desire to reach a spot where a winter freeze is unlikely. They seek out dense groves of trees, usually native Monterey pines or Monterey cypress, or nonnative eucalyptus groves. Because these types of trees are common in the Monterey area, it is estimated that as much as 35 percent of the western monarch butterfly population (as many as 200,000 individuals) may spend their winters in Monterey County.

In **Santa Cruz, Pacific Grove,** and elsewhere up and down the coast, adult monarch butterflies arrive in late October and early November, their delicate paperlike wings sometimes tattered and torn from traveling. Yet they still have that urge to merge, first alighting on low shrubs, then meeting at certain local "butterfly trees" to socialize, sun themselves, and mate. They tend to pick the exact same sites year after year. In the spring, they head back north to recolonize their summer territory. No single butterfly travels the entire migration; it takes several generations to complete a round-trip. The monarch's offspring—actually, its offspring's grandchildren—eventually make their way back to the California coast, without ever having been here.

Monarch Butterfly Grove Sanctuary at Pacific Grove

In Santa Cruz, the best spot for butterfly watching is at the eucalyptus grove at **Natural Bridges State Beach,** where the winter population is often more than 10,000 butterflies. Visitors can walk the 0.25-mile wheelchair-accessible trail to the grove's observation deck on their own, or attend a free, docent-led butterfly tour. Warm, sunny days are the best times to view the monarchs as they flit about the trees.

Pacific Grove so loves its butterflies that the town has nicknamed itself Butterfly City, U.S.A. Town laws threaten a big fine and/or a sentence of six months in jail for "molesting" monarch butterflies. From October to February the most popular destination in "P.G." is the **Monarch Butterfly Grove Sanctuary** at the eucalyptus grove on Ridge Road, off Lighthouse Avenue. The rest of the year, stop by the **Pacific Grove Museum of Natural History** to see the facsimile butterfly tree and various exhibits on the colorful monarchs.

Birds

September marks the peak of the autumn bird migration around Monterey Bay, with wintering shorebirds arriving in the area en masse. Out at sea, jaegers, shearwaters, and alcids are present in great numbers in the fall. The first waves of wintering ducks and other waterfowl begin to show up as well. In the peak of the migration season (usually late Sept.), more than 20,000 individual birds per day congregate

GREAT WRITERS

A few moments standing on the shores of Monterey Bay, a first glance off the edge of the world from Highway 1 in Big Sur – that's all it takes to understand why writers would be drawn to this area.

Robert Louis Stevenson lived for several months at the French Hotel adobe boardinghouse on Houston Street, now included in Monterey State Historic Park. He collected material, including grand landscapes, real and imagined, which would later appear in *Treasure Island*.

Pulitzer and Nobel Prize-winner **John Steinbeck,** author of *The Grapes of Wrath* and *Of Mice and Men,* was born and raised in Salinas. Today, two must-see destinations – the National Steinbeck Center and the Steinbeck House – pay suitable homage.

Poet **Robinson Jeffers,** who wrote volumes of long, narrative blank verse that shook up the national literary scene in the 1920s and 1930s, settled in Carmel. Jeffers' controversial poems covered dark subjects like incest and murder, but he was also known for being a tough outdoorsman and a great champion of the environmental movement. Visitors can tour Jeffers' Carmel home.

Big Sur attracted its own bohemians – the Beat-generation variety. **Lawrence Ferlinghetti,** who published Allen Ginsberg's poetic anthem *Howl* and later founded San Francisco's City Lights Books, owned a cabin beneath the Bixby Bridge, the focus of the 1962 novel *Big Sur,* by Jack Kerouac.

Even more famous as a Big Sur literary icon was **Henry Miller,** author of *Tropic of Cancer* and *Tropic of Capricorn,* who made his home there from 1944 to 1963. Today, visitors can stop by the Henry Miller Memorial Library and pay tribute to the great writer.

at Steinbeck Plaza on Monterey's Cannery Row

great blue heron in the marshes of Monterey Bay

Elephant Seals

The annual arrival of northern elephant seals on the beaches of Año Nuevo, north of Santa Cruz, and at Piedras Blancas, north of San Simeon, is as eagerly anticipated as the passing of the gray whales. The huge males can weigh up to 5,000 pounds and put on a tremendous show as they bellow, roar, and fight each other for the best spots on the beach. When there is nothing to fight about, the seals lie like slugs on the beach, every few minutes flipping sand over their backs.

Nearly hunted to the edge of extinction, northern elephant seals numbered only 20–100 at the turn of the 20th century. All these survivors lived off the west coast of Baja California. Their descendants eventually began migrating north to California in winter, and now show up in vast numbers every year along the California coast.

Male northern elephant seals start arriving at the **Año Nuevo State Reserve** in December, followed in January by the females, ready to bear offspring conceived the previous year. The males battle over status, with the successful alpha bulls fighting to protect harems of 50 or so females from marauders. Public access to the reserve is allowed only on guided tours from mid-December to the end of March. Visit the beaches without a tour guide in spring and summer, when many elephant seals—and other types of pinnipeds—return here to hang out on the beaches.

Another significant "e-seal" colony can be observed right along Highway 1 just south of **Piedras Blancas,** four miles north of Hearst Castle. In fact, nowhere else in California can you get so close to so many of the blubbery creatures. Although the elephant seals are most plentiful from November to March, a few can be seen any day of the year. All you have to do is drive up, park, and walk a few yards to the overlook area on a bluff above

at Moss Landing's **Elkhorn Slough National Estuarine Research Reserve.** Year-round at the slough, it is possible to spot many endangered and threatened birds such as the brown pelican, California clapper rail, peregrine falcon, and California least tern. Farther south in Carmel, the lagoon at **Carmel River State Beach** is a bird sanctuary for hawks, kingfishers, cormorants, herons, pelicans, sandpipers, snowy egrets, and migrating ducks and geese. North of Santa Cruz, head to **Wilder Ranch State Park** and walk the Old Cove Landing Trail along the bluff tops to an overlook above Wilder Beach, a prime nesting area for snowy plovers. Peregrine falcons hunt the grasslands and agricultural fields. Gazing out to sea, birders can watch for shearwaters, marbled murrelets, jaegers, sea ducks, and loons.

Other great birding spots in the Santa Cruz area are **Schwann Lake** at Seabright Beach, **Rancho del Oso** and Waddell Beach north of Davenport, and the **Arboretum at U.C. Santa Cruz.**

the beach. The seals are often less than 30 feet away. The nonprofit group Friends of the Elephant Seal also runs an information center and gift shop in San Simeon.

Whales

Most famous of the year's whale migrations is the annual sojourn of the gray whale. Once endangered by whaling, the grays are now swimming steadily along the comeback trail. Early in October, the fat and sassy gray whales are carrying an extra 6–12 inches of blubber on board, following months of dining in rich Arctic seas. They head south, taking a 6,000-mile journey to winter in the warmer waters of Baja, Mexico. Pregnant females leave first, traveling alone or in small groups. Larger groups make up the rear guard, with the older males and nonpregnant females engaging in highly competitive courtship and mating rituals along the way. Most of the grays pass by the Monterey area on their southward journey in December and January. Males, newly pregnant females, and young gray whales head north from February to June, followed by cows and calves. On their northward migration, the greatest numbers pass by Monterey in March and April.

To watch migrating whales from land, there are prime "whale vistas" all along the Santa Cruz, Monterey, and Big Sur coastlines, starting near **Año Nuevo** and continuing south to **Point Lobos** and **Big Sur.** Any high point of land along the coast is a good place to search for the distinctive "puffs of smoke" from spouting whales, especially on calm days when the spouts are not obscured by whitecaps and choppy water. Oceangoing, commercial whale-watching tours are also readily available; the easiest place to get on a whale-watching boat is at Fisherman's Wharf in **Monterey,** where tours are offered daily.

And if you miss the December–April migration of the gray whale, you always have a chance at spotting other species of whales. In the summer months (June–Oct.), blue whales—the largest animal on earth, weighing about 40 tons—are sometimes spotted along the Monterey coast. Humpback whales are on the same schedule as the blues, although their season begins a little earlier and runs a little later.

California gray whale

MONTEREY

In his novel by the same name, local boy John Steinbeck described Monterey's Cannery Row as "a poem, a stink, a grating noise, a quality of light, a tune, a habit, a nostalgia, a dream," and also as a corrugated collection of sardine canneries, restaurants, honky-tonks, whorehouses, and waterfront laboratories. The street, he said, groaned under the weight of "silver rivers of fish." The local chamber of commerce liked his description so much that they eventually put it on a plaque and planted it in today's touristy Cannery Row.

Local promoters claim that the legendary writer would be proud of what the visitor dollar has wrought here, but this seems unlikely. When Steinbeck returned in 1961 from his self-imposed exile, he noted that "the canneries that once put up a sickening stench are gone, their places filled with restaurants, antique shops, and the like. They fish for tourists now, not pilchards, and that species they are not likely to wipe out."

An early port for California immigrants and the site of California's first pier, Monterey is now a bustling tourist mecca that tries hard to hang onto its once-cloistered charm. This city-by-the-sea is still a fisherman's town. Although the sardine industry went out with Steinbeck, squid fishing remains big business (you must eat calamari while in Monterey). The justifiably popular Monterey Bay Aquarium is often blamed for the city's hopeless summer traffic

© ANN MARIE BROWN

HIGHLIGHTS

(Monterey Bay Aquarium: This world-class cluster of fish tanks, built into Cannery Row's converted Hovden Cannery, is now the number-one aquarium in the United States, and a leading conservation advocacy organization (page 28).

(Monterey Maritime and History Museum: Here you'll find the bells and whistles of Monterey history, along with compasses, fabulous photography, ship models, a scrimshaw collection, and the original Fresnel lens from the Point Sur lighthouse (page 35).

(Monterey State Historic Park: This "pathway of history" in California's first capital city protects and preserves a variety of fine historic adobes, many of which exemplify the Monterey colonial style (page 35).

(Monterey Museum of Art: Enjoy this excellent collection of regional, California, and Western art before adjourning to the exquisite Monterey-style adobe La Mirada, home to the museum's Asian art and artifacts collection (page 41).

(Three-Mile Drive: This jaunt along Pacific Grove's Ocean View Boulevard offers notable community parks, crashing surf, craggy shorelines, picnicking, and wildlife watching. And, unlike the more famous 17-Mile Drive, this one's free (page 72).

(Pacific Grove Museum of Natural History: Another great Pacific Grove freebie, the natural history museum showcases local wonders, from sea otters and seabirds to rare insects and native plants. Kids especially love *Sandy*, the gray whale sculpture right out front (page 76).

(National Steinbeck Center: This high-tech museum celebrates Salinas native John Steinbeck, the first American to win both the Pulitzer and Nobel Prizes for literature (page 90).

(Pinnacles National Monument: Exploring these 26,000 acres of volcanic spires atop the San Andreas Fault is a little like rock climbing or hiking on the moon (page 96).

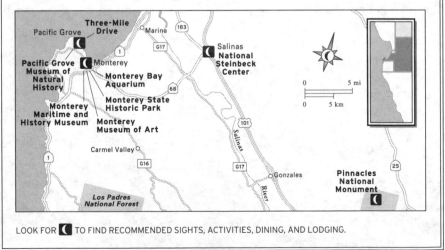

LOOK FOR (TO FIND RECOMMENDED SIGHTS, ACTIVITIES, DINING, AND LODGING.

snarls, but the real culprit is a too-rapid increase in the population base throughout the Monterey Peninsula.

The centerpiece of Monterey is the magnificent bay itself, almost 60 miles long and 13 miles wide. Its waters contain one of the richest marine life zones in the world, with 100 species of sea birds, 345 species of fish, and four species of sea turtles, in addition to abundant whales, dolphins, seals, sea lions, and otters. The bay's offshore canyons dip as deep as 10,000 feet, creating a near-shore environment that is one of the best places in the United States to view a wide variety of marine animals. The cute-and-comical sea otter—the unpaid marketing icon of Monterey Bay—is the most famous of the bay's creatures, but even deep-water species such as orcas and blue whales are often seen.

PLANNING YOUR TIME

If you are planning to visit the world-famous Monterey Bay Aquarium and neighboring attractions in Cannery Row and Fisherman's Wharf, you'll need at least one day just to devote to that. Add on another couple days to explore some of the region's "living" history at Monterey State Historic Park and take a whale-watching boat tour of Monterey Bay, and you'll need a minimum of two to three days in the region.

During peak summer months, you can avoid the infamous traffic by using Monterey's free public trolleys whenever possible, or parking your car in one spot and then riding a bike or walking to the town's famous sites—the aquarium, Fisherman's Wharf, Cannery Row, and Monterey State Historic Park. All are in close proximity.

HISTORY

In addition to being the main port city for both Alta and Baja California, from 1775 to 1845, Monterey was the capital of the Spanish-ruled

Alta California—and naturally enough, the center of much political intrigue and scheming. Spared the devastating earthquakes that plagued other areas, Monterey had its own bad times, which included being burned and ransacked by the Argentinean revolutionary privateer Hippolyte Bouchard in 1818. In 1822, the Spanish reign ended in California, and Mexico took over. In 1845, Monterey lost part of its political prestige when Los Angeles temporarily became the territory's capital city. In July 1846 when the rancheros surrendered to Commodore John D. Sloat, commander of the U.S. Navy, the area became officially American, although the town's distinctive Spanish tranquility remained relatively undisturbed until the arrival of farmers, fishing fleets, fish canneries, and whalers. California's first constitution was drawn up in Monterey's Colton Hall in 1849, during the state's constitutional convention.

© ANN MARIE BROWN

Fisherman's Wharf is no longer used by fishermen, but it manages to retain its salty charm.

MONTEREY

Sights

CANNERY ROW

In the early 20th century, Cannery Row's 16 canning plants and 14 reduction plants processed a quarter million tons of silver sardines every year, culled from the depths of Monterey Bay just offshore of the Row. By 1950, the fish were depleted and the canneries shut down, leaving Cannery Row a ghost town. But largely because of the popularity of John Steinbeck's 1945 prize-winning novel *Cannery Row,* which detailed the exploits of the characters who lived and worked on the Row, within a decade the cannery buildings were restored and refurbished, then filled with shops and restaurants. In 1984, the world-famous Monterey Bay Aquarium was added to the Row, giving it top-notch status as a tourist destination.

© ANN MARIE BROWN

In addition to more than 20 restaurants and myriad jewelry and apparel stores, Cannery Row also has its own Wax Museum.

Today's Cannery Row (www.canneryrow .com) is host to myriad jewelry and apparel stores, a wax museum, more than 20 restaurants, and shops selling ice cream and cinnamon rolls. But there are still a few truly unique venues, such as **A Taste of Monterey** (700 Cannery Row, 831/646-5446 or 888/646-5446, www.tastemonterey.com, daily 11 A.M.–6 P.M., free admission, $10 for wine tasting), which offers samplings of more than 50 Monterey-area wines in its seaside tasting room. The shop's panoramic view of Monterey Bay is worth a special trip by itself. Nearby, the **Culinary Center of Monterey** (625 Cannery Row, 831/333-2133, www.culinarycenterof monterey.com) offers hands-on cooking classes taught by resident and visiting celebrity chefs.

Those seeking outdoor adventures such as kayaking, stand-up paddling, surfing, or bicycling can find rentals and guided-tour opportunities at **Adventures by the Sea** (299 Cannery Row, 831/372-1807, www.adventures bythesea.com, daily 9 A.M.-sunset). And if your muscles are sore from so much seaside recreation, stop in at one of the Row's day spas for a little pampering. The best of the lot is **Vista Blue at the Monterey Plaza Hotel and Spa** (400 Cannery Row, 831/646-1700 or 800/334-3999, www.montereyplazahotel .com). In addition to a wide array of pampering treatments, the penthouse spa boasts an ocean-view sundeck with an outdoor fireplace.

◖ MONTEREY BAY AQUARIUM

The Monterey Bay Aquarium is a world-class cluster of oversized fish tanks built into the converted Hovden Cannery on the edge of Monterey Bay. Visitors get to view, and

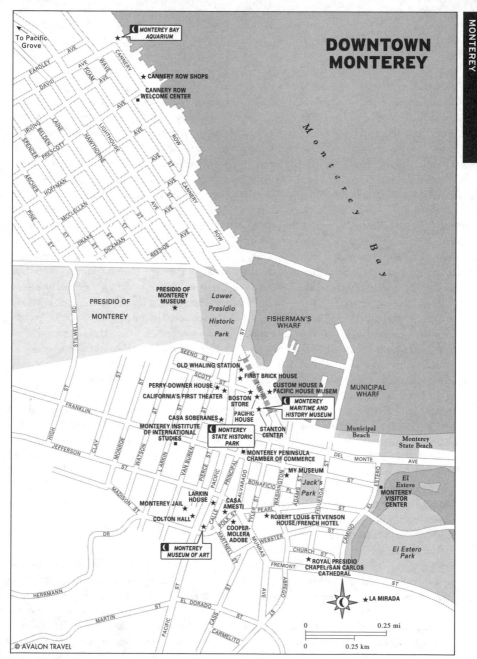

DOWNTOWN MONTEREY

MONTEREY BAY AQUARIUM

To Pacific Grove

CANNERY ROW SHOPS

CANNERY ROW WELCOME CENTER

Monterey Bay

PRESIDIO OF MONTEREY MUSEUM

PRESIDIO OF MONTEREY

Lower Presidio Historic Park

FISHERMAN'S WHARF

SEENO ST

OLD WHALING STATION

FIRST BRICK HOUSE

PERRY-DOWNER HOUSE

CUSTOM HOUSE & PACIFIC HOUSE MUSEM

CALIFORNIA'S FIRST THEATER

BOSTON STORE

MONTEREY MARITIME AND HISTORY MUSEUM

MUNICIPAL WHARF

CASA SOBERANES

PACIFIC HOUSE

MONTEREY INSTITUTE OF INTERNATIONAL STUDIES

MONTEREY STATE HISTORIC PARK

STANTON CENTER

Municipal Beach

Monterey State Beach

MONTEREY PENINSULA CHAMBER OF COMMERCE

MY MUSEUM

Jack's Park

El Estero

MONTEREY VISITOR CENTER

LARKIN HOUSE

CASA AMESTI

MONTEREY JAIL

COLTON HALL

COOPER-MOLERA ADOBE

ROBERT LOUIS STEVENSON HOUSE/FRENCH HOTEL

MONTEREY MUSEUM OF ART

El Estero Park

ROYAL PRESIDIO CHAPEL/SAN CARLOS CATHEDRAL

LA MIRADA

0   0.25 mi

0   0.25 km

© AVALON TRAVEL

sometimes touch, many of the bay's creatures in the context of their natural habitat. More than 300,000 animals and plants representing 571 species—including fish, invertebrates, mammals, reptiles, birds, and plant life—are on display. In addition to the permanent galleries and exhibitions of live creatures, the aquarium's auditorium shows short films several times each day featuring past exhibitions such as "Jellies: Living Art," and detailing current research programs sponsored by the Monterey Bay Aquarium Research Institute ("Mysteries of the Deep"). The aquarium's attractions are not all indoors, either. Several outdoor observation decks are lined with telescopes for bay watching. Here you might spot an occasional otter slipping into the aquarium over the seawall, or catch sight of gray whales spouting.

The aquarium first opened in 1984, thanks to the financial backing of David Packard, cofounder of Hewlett-Packard. His daughter, marine biologist Julie Packard, is the aquarium executive director. The building and its exhibit have been vastly expanded and improved upon in the last 25 years. Among its many achievements, the Monterey Bay Aquarium is perhaps best known for having the first great white shark ever successfully kept in captivity. After nearly 200 days, that shark was released to the open ocean. A few other great white sharks have since been on exhibit at the aquarium for short periods of time, then released. Although the sea otters have long been the most popular crowd pleasers at the aquarium, the penguin exhibit that opened in spring 2008 is holding a close second. Amazingly, the aquarium manages to walk the delicate tightrope of cultural attractions by appealing equally to adults as well as kids.

The aquarium is also well known for its "Seafood Watch" education program, which publishes guides for responsible seafood purchasing and consumption. The guides take into account not just what fish and seafood choices are becoming scarce in the ocean, but also whether those creatures are caught or farmed in a sustainable manner.

The aquarium is a huge draw for Monterey visitors, attracting almost two million people per year, so plan ahead. Allow yourself at least three hours to tour the aquarium; many visitors spend a whole day, or go for a few hours two days in a row. The least crowded days of the week are Tuesday, Wednesday, and Thursday, and the least busy times of day are afternoons 2–6 P.M. (after the school groups have departed). Fall and winter are always less crowded than spring and summer (except for the winter holidays). Advance tickets are highly recommended, especially in summer; purchase at www.mbayaq.org or 800/756-3737. For information only, phone 831/648-4800. If you have purchased advance tickets, you can avoid long lines at the entrance gate. In the winter months, except for holiday periods, it is possible to just show up and take your chances.

The Monterey Bay Aquarium is open daily 10 A.M.–6 P.M. (closed Dec. 25). In summer (May 26–Sept. 1), the aquarium opens earlier at 9:30 A.M.; and is open slightly later on summer weekends (July–Sept. 1) until 8 P.M. Admission is $24.95 adults, $22.95 seniors, youth, and college students with ID, and $15.95 for children ages 3–12.

Sea Otters

Just inside the aquarium's entrance is the 55,000-gallon, split-level Sea Otter Tank. The sea otters, who are brought to the aquarium as rescued animals and are no longer able to live in the wild, are constantly eating, playing, or grooming themselves, putting on a nonstop

© DARREN MURTHA

The Monterey Bay Aquarium is housed in the old Hovden Cannery buildings, perched on piers above Monterey Bay.

show for visitors. The first-floor windows of the exhibit give visitors an underwater view of the otters; on the second floor, you can watch them playing on the surface. At 10:30 A.M., 1:30 P.M., and 3:30 P.M. daily, you can watch aquarists train and feed the sea otters. Their food is usually stuffed into toys like balls and rings, which forces the otters to pound on them to remove it, as they would in the wild (the show lasts about 15 minutes). Although the otter is the smallest marine mammal in North America, it has a huge effect on the ecosystem because of its eating habits. These sleek aquatic clowns consume 25 percent of their body weight in seafood daily.

Outer Bay

For a pure show of speed and power, you can't beat watching the giant bluefin tunas in the Outer Bay exhibit. Hammerhead sharks, green and black sea turtles, and other marine life also share this 1.2-million-gallon exhibit with its floor-to-ceiling window, but it's the huge tunas, some weighing more than 300 pounds, that steal the show with their rocketlike speed and maneuverability. The giant ocean sunfish, a prehistoric-looking creature that lumbers along at the speed of a glacier, is also a big hit with viewers. On Tuesday, Thursday, Saturday, and Sunday at 11 A.M., you can watch the tunas, barracuda, and bonito as they are fed (feeding lasts about 15 minutes). Even the slow-moving sunfish manages to snag a few morsels before the torpedolike tunas devour the rest. No matter how crowded it is at feeding time, you'll have no trouble seeing the action, thanks to the exhibit's 15-foot-tall, 54-foot-long window, one of the largest windows that exists in the world.

The Outer Bay exhibit also features the

THREATENED SEA OTTERS

Southern sea otters range north along the San Mateo County Coast and south all the way to Santa Barbara. Their greatest numbers appear to be in and around the region of Monterey Bay – Santa Cruz, Monterey, and San Luis Obispo counties – and near the Channel Islands. Few creatures put on such a delightful show for onlookers; simply watching sea otters swim and feed themselves is mesmerizing entertainment. Otters dive as deep as 250 feet into the ocean to dislodge abalone, sea urchins, crabs, clams, mussels, and other shellfish. After staying underwater for as long as four minutes, they return to the surface, float on their backs, and eagerly smash the shellfish with rocks held in their paws. They feed heartily, each otter consuming about 20-25 pounds of seafood per day – two and a half tons per year – much to the dismay of commercial shellfish interests. (Sea otters often eat so many purple sea urchins that their teeth and nails are stained purple.) When an otter finishes a meal, it licks its paws and vigorously scrubs its belly, which serves as both kitchen counter and dining table.

Such scenes are still fairly common, yet the population numbers of the California sea otter, listed as a threatened species under the federal Endangered Species Act, are not what they should be. In 1995, the U.S. Fish and Wildlife Service counted 2,377 sea otters. By 1998, the population had dropped to 1,937 – and some 200 dead otters washed ashore on area beaches, for reasons unknown. In the next decade, the population increased to about 3,000 otters, but by 2008, it was clear that the increase had slowed. During the 2008 census, observers counted 2,760 California sea otters, 8.8 percent fewer than the 2007 spring count of 3,026.

For southern sea otters to be considered for delisting by the U.S. Fish and Wildlife Service (meaning their species would no longer be called "threatened"), their population would have to exceed 3,090 for three continuous years, according to the agency's Southern Sea Otter Recovery Plan.

Ongoing hazards to sea otters include coastal pollution, infectious disease, natural toxins (such as red tide algae), entrapment in fishing nets or wire fishing pots, and occasional shark attacks. Recent research suggests parasitic disease is a primary culprit for sea otter deaths, causing fatal disease in the brains and nervous systems of sea otters and other animals. Two primary parasites have been discovered – *Toxoplasma gondii*, its spores introduced by cat feces flushed into sewage systems through the disposal of cat litter, and *Sarcocystis neurona*, spread through opossum feces.

In centuries past, an estimated population of almost 16,000 sea otters along the California coast was decimated by eager fur hunters. A single otter pelt was worth upward of $1,700 by 1910, when it was generally believed that sea otters were extinct here. But a small pod survived off the coast near Carmel, a secret well guarded by biologists until the Big Sur Highway opened in 1938.

© ANN MARIE BROWN

The cute and comical sea otter is the unpaid marketing icon of Monterey Bay.

© DARREN MURTHA

The jellyfish at the Monterey Bay Aquarium mesmerize visitors with their diaphanous beauty.

largest permanent collection of jellyfish species in the United States. It's almost impossible not to become mesmerized by the gentle, pulsing action of egg-yolk jellies, sea nettles, and comb jellies as they seem to drift to the beating baton of some unseen conductor, but if that doesn't do it for you, try walking underneath the glass dome filled with thousands of silver anchovies. This swirling mass of glittering fish dances the most beautifully choreographed ballet you've ever seen.

Giant Octopus

If you've ever read Jules Verne, you won't want to miss the Giant Octopus exhibit, where you can witness these eight-legged masters of camouflage as they change skin color and texture to blend in with their surroundings and to communicate emotion. The giant octopus is the largest species of octopus in the world,

growing to nearly 30 feet long and weighing nearly 100 pounds. It's easy to discount the octopus because it is not nearly as active and entertaining as other animals in the aquarium, but this is one of the ocean's most intelligent creatures, capable of solving complex problems like unscrewing jar lids. It is also a deadly predator, able to catch and devour four-foot-long sharks.

Splash Zone and Penguins

This is far and away the most popular exhibit for families with young children, with nearly 50 interactive exhibits in English and Spanish allowing children to experience sea life close at hand. In the 40-foot-long touch pool, kids can see and touch plants and animals that live in the kelp forest, including sea stars, abalones, sea urchins, and kelp crabs. Nearby, families can walk through a glass-enclosed tunnel of kelp. But the biggest crowd pleaser is the African black-footed penguin colony; the highly animated, tuxedo-clad birds swim, waddle around, stare out the exhibit windows at the watching humans, and generally charm the pants off everybody. Penguin feedings take place daily at 10:30 A.M. and 3 P.M., and unlike the feeding in the Outer Bay exhibit, this show is heavily geared toward the under-six set. For a brief time, grown-ups will enjoy watching the waddling birds line up to be hand-fed fish, but eventually the kid-oriented narration—delivered by bubbly hosts who are even more perky than the flightless birds—will drive the adults toward other exhibits.

Kelp Forest

The nearly three-story-tall Kelp Forest, the aquarium's centerpiece and the first underwater forest ever successfully established as a display, offers a diver's-eye view of the undersea world. This giant fish tank with acrylic walls more than seven inches thick holds 343,000 gallons of seawater. Visitors can essentially look through a window into Monterey Bay. It took three years to construct this exhibit (1981–1984), which is maintained by a complicated series of tunnels and pumps that continually recirculate water back into the bay (2,000 gallons per minute are on the move), and a wave machine at the top of the tank that creates the water movement necessary for kelp to survive.

At 28 feet high, the Kelp Forest is also one of the tallest aquarium exhibits in the world, and it has to be: exposed to direct sunlight, the kelp continues to grow at a rate of more than four inches per day. Sardines, leopard sharks, anchovies, wolf-eels, and myriad other fishes swim among the fronds. At 11:30 A.M. and 4 P.M. daily, you can watch a diver hand-feed the sharks, fishes, and other animals in this exhibit (feeding lasts about 15 minutes).

Sandy Shore and Aviary

Monterey Bay is home not only to critters such as fish, crustaceans, and marine mammals, it's also a critical habitat for birds. At the Sandy Shore and Aviary exhibit, visitors get a close-up look at the many bird species of Elkhorn Slough, just north of Monterey, one of the largest coastal wetlands in the state. Watch as long-billed curlews and sandpipers forage in the sand and black-necked stilts and phalaropes wade along the edge of the waves. For birders, it's a bit strange—but also very exciting—to see so many different species sharing a 15-foot stretch of beach. Other wetland and sandy shore creatures shown in this exhibit include clams, crabs, ghost shrimp, sea pens, pipefish, and bat rays (you can touch their velvetlike skin in the bat ray pool). If you're lucky, you'll get to see one of the 10-pound sea hares (they look like big slugs) release its dark-colored ink against a perceived threat.

Rocky Shore

In the Rocky Shore gallery, the secrets of the Monterey Bay intertidal zone are revealed. In the indoor Touch Pool, visitors can pet the colorful sea stars or feel the bumpy texture of a sea cucumber. Walk through the acrylic tunnel that allows you to experience the power of waves crashing overhead. The outdoor Great Tidepool exhibit is surrounded by the aquarium itself on three sides, and on the fourth by artificial rock. Waves crash on the rocky shore, which is home to sea stars, anemones, barnacles, monkeyface eels, and small fish, plus visiting sea otters and harbor seals that occasionally shimmy up the stairs for a better look at the people.

FISHERMAN'S WHARF

Tacky and tawdry, beat up by years of wind and waves, the 1845 pier at Fisherman's Wharf (831/649-6544, www.montereywharf.com) is no longer used by fishermen, but it has a salty, ramshackle charm about it. The wharf is full of cheap souvenir shops, food stalls, restaurants, and stand-up bars indiscriminately frosted with gull guano. Built of stone by enslaved Native Americans, convicts, and military deserters when Monterey was Alta California's capital, Fisherman's Wharf was originally a pier for cargo schooners. Later used by whalers and Italian American fishing crews to unload their catches, the wharf today is bright and bustling with entrepreneurs of all kinds hawking their wares. You'll hear a constant clamor from salespeople proffering samples of clam chowder. Come early in the morning to beat the crowds, and then launch yourself on a sightseeing tour of Monterey Bay or a whale-watching cruise. The wharf is located off Del Monte Avenue at the foot of Alvarado Street; leave your car in one of four gated lots ($0.75 per hour or $5 all day). Parking here also provides you access to the neighboring Monterey State Historic Park and Monterey Maritime and History Museum.

◖ MONTEREY MARITIME AND HISTORY MUSEUM

There's so much Western history in Monterey, it's hard to wrap your mind around it. Get an overview of the story of the former capital of Spanish and Mexican California by watching the 16-minute film "A Glimpse of the Past" at the Monterey Maritime and History Museum in the Stanton Center (5 Custom House Plaza, 831/372-2608, www.montereyhistory .org). Then wander through the museum's exhibits, which include almost 6,000 nautical artifacts—compasses, bells, ship models, the original two-story-high Fresnel lens from the Point Sur lighthouse, and even an underwater research vessel that performed deep-diving duties in Monterey Bay. The museum's permanent exhibits, many interactive, cover local maritime history, from the first explorers and cannery days to the present.

The museum is open 10 A.M.–5 P.M. daily, closed Thanksgiving, Christmas, and New Year's Day. Admission is $8 for adults, $5 for seniors and youth, and free for children under 12. Guided group tours are available by reservation.

◖ MONTEREY STATE HISTORIC PARK

Monterey State Historic Park (20 Custom House Plaza, 831/649-7118, www.parks .ca.gov) protects and preserves more than two dozen historic buildings that tell the stories of

© ANN MARIE BROWN

Fisherman's Wharf

© ANN MARIE BROWN

To take a walk on the Path of History, just follow the round yellow tiles in the sidewalk which are marked in several languages.

the early days of California. If you didn't go to high school in California, or if you slept during history class, you may be surprised to learn that Monterey served as California's capital under Spanish, Mexican, and U.S. military rule. The U.S. flag was first officially raised in California here on July 7, 1846, bringing 600,000 square miles of land to the United States. Even if you aren't a history buff, this state historic park offers much to peak your interest.

Most of the park's buildings and museums are open 10 A.M.–4 P.M. daily and closed Christmas, Thanksgiving, and New Year's Day. Admission to all buildings is free. A 2.5-mile self-guided walking tour called the **Path of History** can be entered at any point, although most visitors begin at Custom House Plaza. Just look for the yellow tiled markers in the sidewalk, and pick up a free walking tour

map before setting out. Available at most of the park's buildings and elsewhere around town, the brochure describes dozens of historic structures; several of these are detailed below. If you don't have time to visit them all, at least be sure to see the Custom House and Pacific House Museums, and the Cooper-Molera Adobe. For years, **California's First Theater** was the most popular attraction on the Path of History; it was built as a saloon and boarding house and then used to showcase minstrel shows and plays in the 1840s. The building has been closed due to structural problems and may not reopen until 2010 at the earliest.

Also free are guided tours of particular buildings, as are general guided walking tours along the Path of History. Tours begin at the Pacific House Museum and are offered on Monday, Tuesday, Wednesday, and Friday at

10:30 A.M. and last about 45 minutes. Wear comfortable walking shoes. Schedules for all tours can change, so be sure to call to verify current tour times on the day you plan to visit the park.

Pacific House Museum

Start your exploration at the Pacific House Museum (20 Custom House Plaza, 831/649-7118, daily 10 A.M.–4 P.M., free admission), located a stone's throw from Fisherman's Wharf. Built in 1847, this two-story adobe building functioned over the years as a hotel, courthouse, army barracks, and tavern. The wheelchair-accessible Pacific House is filled with exhibits that interpret 150 years of Monterey's history, focusing primarily on the period when the city was the capital of Spanish and Mexican California. Don't miss

the Native American exhibits on the second-floor **Monterey Museum of the American Indian,** including an extensive collection of baskets, beadwork, and pottery. Behind the museum is the outdoor Memory Garden, a white-walled courtyard retreat filled with lush greenery and flowers, which once served as the corral for the army's horses and was the site of bear and bull fights. Today the lovely garden is a popular spot for weddings.

Custom House

Across the plaza is the adobe Custom House (daily 10 A.M.–4 P.M., free admission), the oldest government building in California—it is designated as State Historic Landmark #1—which was used by the Mexican government from 1822 to 1846 to collect tariffs imposed on foreign merchants. It was here that Commodore John

© ANN MARIE BROWN

Right across from Fisherman's Wharf, the Pacific House Museum is the place to start your exploration of Monterey State Historic Park.

MONTEREY

© ANN MARIE BROWN

The Custom House is the oldest government building in California and State Historic Landmark #1.

Sloat raised the American flag in 1846, claiming California for the United States. Today the Custom House is filled with goods that 19th-century sea captains might have brought into Monterey and tried to pass through customs, such as barrels of flour, fine china, and dried cowhides that were used as currency. For decades the most popular exhibit here was a colorful talking parrot named Sebastiana, but alas, she flew up to bird heaven in 2007, after 50 long years of entertaining visitors. A small exhibit focuses on one of the more famous sailors who passed through these doors in 1835, Richard Henry Dana, author of *Two Years Before the Mast*. From an upstairs room, visitors can watch for ships arriving from sea, just as custom agents did more than 150 years ago.

Larkin House and Sherman Quarters

Built of adobe and wood in 1835 by Yankee merchant Thomas Oliver Larkin, the two-story Larkin House (510 Calle Principal at Jefferson and Pacific Sts., 831/649-7118, free 45-minute guided tours on Tues., Wed., Sat., and Sun. at 2 P.M.) served first as a general store, then later as the American consulate, then still later as the military headquarters for generals Kearny, Mason, and Sherman. Thomas Larkin was the first and only U.S. Consul to Alta California under Mexican rule, serving during President Polk's administration. He also played a role in building Monterey's first wharf, as well as San Francisco's first wharf. A fine pink Monterey mud adobe that became the model for the local Monterey Colonial style, Larkin House is furnished with more than $6 million in antiques and 19th-century period furnishings from around the world. It was one of the first adobe homes in California to be built with two stories, and one of the most luxurious of its time, with features such as multiple fireplaces, an interior staircase, and a verandah wrapped around its second floor.

The tiny adobe home and headquarters of William Tecumseh Sherman (that's General Sherman of Civil War fame) is next door. This is where Sherman lived while briefly assigned to Monterey as a lieutenant in 1847, a position which he abhorred. Known as the Sherman Quarters, the museum focuses on both Larkin and Sherman (Larkin built this small structure in 1834). The Sherman Quarters are open daily for viewing, 10 A.M.–4 P.M.

Cooper-Molera Adobe

The Cooper-Molera Adobe (525 Polk St., corner of Polk, Alvarado, and Munras Sts., 831/649-7118 or 831/649-7111) is a two-story Monterey Colonial adobe constructed in 1829. The 2.5-acre complex, which includes a neighboring home, two barns, a small visitor center, colorful gardens filled with blossoming lavender and jasmine, and a few farm animals, was fully restored in the 1980s to its 19th-century authenticity. John Rogers Cooper was a wealthy ship captain who made his fortune by trading in sea otter pelts, tallow, and hides. The expansive grounds are available for self-guided tours Monday–Saturday 10 A.M.–4 P.M. and Sunday 1–4 P.M. Guided tours of the adobe home are offered Monday–Wednesday and Friday–Saturday at 3 P.M. and Sunday at noon and 3 P.M. Stop by the **Cooper Museum Store** here, run by the Old Monterey Preservation Society, to sample the wares—unique books, antique reproductions, and other specialty items representing the mid-1800s, like wooden whirligigs and tin boxes of tiddledywinks. There's also an extensive collection of books on Monterey and California cultural and natural history. (The store is usually open Mon.–Sat. 10 A.M.–4 P.M. and Sun. 1–4 P.M.)

Stevenson House

The two-story Stevenson House (530 Houston St., 831/649-7118) adobe boardinghouse, also known as the French Hotel, was the home of the Scottish storyteller and poet Robert Louis Stevenson for a few months in autumn 1879, while he was in frail health and courting his American love (and later wife) Fanny Osbourne. In a sunny upstairs room is the small portable desk at which he reputedly wrote parts of *Treasure Island*. Several upstairs rooms are dedicated to Stevenson memorabilia, including paintings and first editions. The boardinghouse also housed hundreds of artists, fishermen, government officials, and the like, but none quite as famous as the great Scottish writer. Guided tours of the building are offered on Monday and Friday at 2 P.M. and Saturday and Sunday at 10:30 A.M. On Saturday the building is open for self-guided tours from 11:30 A.M.–2 P.M.

© ANN MARIE BROWN

The colorful Cooper-Molera Adobe features more than two acres of grounds and gardens for exploring.

Casa Soberanes was also known as The House of the Blue Gate.

The gardens at Casa Soberanes are bordered by century-old wine bottles buried bottoms up.

Casa Soberanes

Casa Soberanes (336 Pacific St., corner of Del Monte Ave. and Pacific St.) is an 1840s Mediterranean-style adobe with a tile roof and cantilevered balcony, perched on a hillside overlooking the bay. Also known as the House of the Blue Gate for reasons that become obvious when standing at its garden entrance on Pacific Street, Casa Soberanes was home to the Soberanes family from 1860 to 1922 and is furnished with an intriguing combination of Mexican folk art and period pieces from China and New England. The Soberanes were just one of many families who lived here over the years; the house was originally constructed by Rafael Estrada in the mid-1840s. The outdoor gardens feature whalebone-and-abalone-bordered flowerbeds, some encircled by century-old wine bottles buried bottoms up. Guided tours are available on weekdays except Thursday at 11:30 A.M., and weekends at noon.

Casa del Oro

Built by Thomas O. Larkin as part of his business empire, this two-story chalk-rock and adobe building, built in 1845 and once known as Casa del Oro (House of Gold), served a number of purposes. At one time or another, it was a barracks for American troops, a general store (Joseph Boston & Co.), a saloon, and a private residence. Rumor has it that this "house of gold" was also once a mint or, when it functioned as a saloon, that it accepted gold dust in payment for drinks—hence the name. Since the store boasted Monterey's first safe, which is still on display, it's more likely that during the California gold rush, miners stored their wealth here. These days, it's been re-created as the **Boston Store** (at the corner of Scott and Olivier, 831/649-3364, Thurs.–Sun. 11 A.M.–3 P.M.) once more, operated by the nonprofit Historic Garden League of Monterey. The wares inside look to be straight out of the 1850s—antiques and reproductions, including handcrafted Russian toys and games, are for sale. Be sure to visit the herb garden adjacent to the building.

Old Whaling Station

The 1847 two-story adobe Whaling Station (391 Decatur St., 831/375-5356) near the Custom House, now maintained and operated by the Junior League of Monterey County, was a flophouse for Portuguese whalers in the 1850s. It was built by David Wright, with its design based on Wright's ancestral home in Ayton, Scotland. The Wright family lived there for a few years until 1855, when the Old Monterey Whaling Company took over the home and used it as a headquarters for its whaling operations and as an employee residence. Visitors can still see the large iron pots that rendered the whale blubber into oil. The garden is open 10 A.M.–4 P.M. daily for self-guided tours. Showcasing an extensive planting of heirloom roses, it is a popular spot for weddings. Whale lovers, walk softly—the walkway in front of the house is made of whalebone (vertebrae), cut into diamond patterns. Sidewalks built of whalebone were once a common sight in the United States and are now quite rare, most having deteriorated over time.

First Brick House

This nearby building (351 Decatur St., 831/649-7118, daily 10 A.M.–4 P.M.) was constructed by Gallant Duncan Dickenson in 1847, built with clay bricks fashioned and fired in Monterey. Dickenson is credited with being the first to bring the art of making bricks from clay (instead of mud adobe) to California. Fired clay was much stronger than adobe, allowing for walls to be built to normal widths (adobe walls were often as much as three feet thick). Clay bricks were also much less susceptible to damage from winter rains. Dickensen left for the Sierra foothills gold country before his Monterey house was finished, so the first brick house in California and 60,000 unused bricks were auctioned off by the sheriff in 1851 for just over $1,000. Today the building's main room houses exhibits on Monterey history.

COLTON HALL

The Reverend Walter Colton, Monterey's first American alcalde, or local magistrate, built this pillared stone structure as a schoolhouse and public hall. Here at Colton Hall (351 Pacific St. btw. Madison and Jefferson Sts., 831/646-5640, www.monterey.org, daily 10 A.M.–4 P.M., free admission), Colton and Robert Semple published the first American newspaper in California, cranking up the presses on August 15, 1846. California's constitutional convention took place here in 1849, and the first state constitution, which gave property rights to women and forbade slavery, was drafted upstairs. Don't miss the small stone jail behind the building; it was used from 1854 to 1956, and no prisoner ever escaped from it.

【 MONTEREY MUSEUM OF ART

The Monterey Museum of Art (559 Pacific St., 831/372-5477, www.montereyart.org, Wed.–Sat. 11 A.M.–5 P.M., Sun. 1–4 P.M., closed holidays, $5), across the street from Colton Hall, showcases a fine collection of California and Western art, including bronze cowboy-and-horse statues by Charles M. Russell. Photography fans will be pleased

the La Mirada adobe of the Monterey Museum of Art

with the number of Ansel Adams and Imogen Cummingham works on display here. Admission also gets you into **La Mirada** (720 Via Mirada, 831/372-3689, www.montereyart .org, Wed.–Sat. 11 A.M.–5 P.M., Sun. 1–4 P.M., closed holidays), an impressive Monterey-style adobe that is home to the museum's Asian art collection. Changing exhibits are displayed in four contemporary galleries that complement the original estate. The home is located in one of Monterey's oldest neighborhoods. The original adobe portion was the residence of Jose Castro, one of the most prominent citizens in California during the Mexican period. Purchased in 1919 by Gouverneur Morris— author/playwright and descendant of the same-named Revolutionary War figure who signed the Declaration of Independence and authored much of the U.S. Constitution—the adobe was restored and expanded, with the addition of a two-story wing and a huge drawing room, to host artists and Hollywood stars (Charlie Chaplin was a guest in Morris's home). The Dart Wing, added in 1993, was designed by architect Charles Moore.

The house is exquisitely furnished in antiques and early California art, and surrounded by 2.5 magnificently landscaped acres, with a walled rose garden, traditional herb garden, and rhododendron garden with more than 300 camellias, azaleas, rhododendrons, and other flowering perennials and trees.

MY MUSEUM

If you have kids in tow, don't miss a visit to MY Museum (Monterey County Youth Museum, 425 Washington St., 831/649-6444, www.my museum.org, children over 2 and adults $7, children under 2 free) near Cannery Row. This 2,700-square-foot gallery is the polar opposite of a traditional "look but don't touch" museum. The concept here is to allow curiosity to flourish in a place where adults and children can learn together by doing, not just looking.

The museum is packed with a variety of hands-on exhibits like the Creation Station, which features 75 bins filled with recyclable and non-recyclable arts and crafts materials. Visitors of all ages can create whatever they like and take their projects home with them. Another popular exhibit is Body Works, a mini–medical office with real crutches, neck braces, dental equipment, and more. And when the little ones get hungry, head to MY Pizzeria, where children make, bake, and serve their own pizzas.

And speaking of kid-oriented fun, children go ape over Monterey's **Dennis the Menace Park** (Pearl St. and Camino El Estero), designed by the creator of the famous comic strip. This is no run-of-the-mill playground; the park is filled with creative play structures, like a train locomotive, a climbing wall, slides of all shapes and sizes, and a mini-maze for kids to "get lost" in.

MONTEREY INSTITUTE OF INTERNATIONAL STUDIES

This prestigious, private, and nonprofit graduate-level college (460 Pierce St., 831/647-4100, www.miis.edu, visitors welcome by appointment only Mon.–Fri. 8:30 A.M.–5 P.M.) specializes in foreign-language instruction. Students prepare for careers in international business and government, and in language translation and interpretation. The school's 200-seat auditorium is set up for simultaneous translations of up to four languages. Most of the institute's programs—including guest lectures—are open to the public. Tours of the campus are led by current students and usually begin at 1 P.M.; call the admissions office at 831/647-4123 for an appointment.

PRESIDIO OF MONTEREY

One of the nation's oldest military posts, the Presidio of Monterey (bwtn. Hwy. 68 and Lighhouse Ave., www.monterey.army.mil) is the physical focal point of most early local history. The original complex, now gone, was founded by Gaspar de Portolá in 1770 to protect the Spanish mission (later moved to Carmel) and was located in the area defined these days by Webster, Fremont, Abrego, and El Estero Streets. The current Presidio of Monterey can be traced to 1846, when the United States seized Monterey, annexed California, and began construction of Fort Mervine as part of the Civil War. During its early history, this fortification had many names, including Fort Halleck, Fort Savannah, and the Monterey Redoubt. Today the Presidio is an active U.S. Army installation and the home of the Defense Language Institute Foreign Language Center.

History buffs, head for 26-acre **Lower Presidio Historic Park,** which traces Monterey's military history through the Spanish, Mexican, and American periods. On-site are commemorative monuments to Portolá, Junípero Serra, Sebastian Vizcaíno, and Commodore John Sloat, plus acknowledgment of native peoples. (When Lighthouse Avenue was widened through here, most of what remained of a 2,000-year-old Rumsen village was destroyed, leaving only a ceremonial rain rock, a rock mortar for grinding acorns, and an ancient burial ground marked by a tall wooden cross.) The 31-foot-tall granite Sloat Monument sits at the base of the Civil War–era Fort Mervine, a diamond-shaped fortress. The fort's forward ravelin is all that remains. Also here: panoramic views of Monterey Bay and the Presidio of Monterey Museum, a museum that was once the fort's ammunitions store.

Presidio of Monterey Museum

The Presidio of Monterey Museum (Building 113, Corporal Ewing Rd., just off Artillery

© ANN MARIE BROWN

A statue of Father Junípero Serra overlooks the bay at Lower Presidio Historic Park.

St., 831/646-3456, www.monterey.org/museum/pom, Mon. 10 A.M.–1 P.M., Thurs.–Sat. 10 A.M.–4 P.M., Sun. 1–4 P.M., free admission), located at the base of the bluff beneath the Sloat Monument, was once a tack house. So, it seems appropriate that it's now filled with artifacts, uniforms, pistols, cannons, historic photos, posters, and dioramas about the U.S. Cavalry and local history, beginning with Native Americans and the arrival of the Spanish, and continuing into Monterey's Mexican, then American, periods. Children are naturally drawn to the life-size horse with a lieutenant in full uniform riding in its saddle. To get an idea of the life of a common soldier in the Presidio, watch the museum's video *Year on a Cavalry Post.*

Royal Presidio Chapel

Originally built as a mission by Father Junípero Serra in June 1770, this building (550 Church St., near Figueroa, 831/373-4345, www.historic

monterey.org) became the Royal Presidio Chapel of San Carlos Borromeo when the mission was relocated to Carmel. This is the oldest building on the Monterey Peninsula and the oldest church in continuous use in California. A national historic landmark, the chapel was originally wood, but after suffering extensive fire damage in 1789, it was rebuilt with stone and adobe, and reopened in 1795. After 1835, it became the San Carlos Cathedral, a parish church. The cathedral's interior walls are decorated with Native American and Mexican folk art. Above, the upper gable facade is the first European art made in California, a chalk-carved Virgin of Guadalupe tucked into a shell niche. Visitors are welcome any time the church is open, but please do not disturb scheduled church services. To get here, turn onto Church Street just after Camino El Estero ends at Fremont—a district once known as Washerwoman's Gulch.

Recreation

BEACHES

Stretching from the Municipal Wharf north almost to Seaside, **Monterey State Beach** (Del Monte. Ave. at Park Ave., 831/649-2836, www.parks.ca.gov) is one of the safest swimming beaches on Monterey Bay, with soft sand shelves that slope gently downhill. The state beach consists of three separate beaches, each about a mile apart, accessed off Del Monte Avenue. Surfing, beachcombing, and fishing are popular. Beach volleyball courts, kayak and canoe rentals, snack bars, and restrooms are available. Free parking is available off Del Monte Avenue, but during the busy summer season, it is easiest to park in the pay lots between Fisherman's Wharf and Wharf #2. To access the beach, take the Seaside exit off Highway 218, west of Highway 1.

Ten miles north of downtown Monterey, **Marina State Beach** (Reservation Rd. in Marina, 831/384-7695, www.parks.ca.gov) is comprised of 170 acres of coastal dunes and sandy beaches. It's usually windy here, making it a great place for kite flying. Swimming is not recommended because of dangerous surf. Boardwalk trails lead across the photogenic dunes, and surf anglers set their lines from the sand. Marina State Beach is a designated hang gliding landing site, so don't be surprised if you see colorful paragliders or hang gliders soaring overhead. To access the beach, take the Reservation Road exit off Highway 1 in Marina.

BIKING

The 18-mile-long **Monterey Peninsula Recreation Trail** is a paved biking and walking path that stretches from Asilomar State Beach in Pacific Grove to Castroville. Most visitors

The 18-mile-long Monterey Peninsula Recreation Trail provides blue-water views and is a great place to pedal, run, or walk.

don't pedal the entire thing, but rather stick to the stretch near Monterey's most popular attractions. Scenic ocean and bay views are free for the taking as the trail saunters past landmarks that include the Monterey Bay Aquarium, Cannery Row, Fisherman's Wharf, Custom House Plaza, and Del Monte Beach. All your senses are involved in the experience of this ride, but most of all your olfactory sense—Monterey smells wonderfully fishy. To get away from the omnipresent crowds near the aquarium, ride the path north toward Marina or south toward Pacific Grove and Asilomar. There are myriad places to park your car and get on the 18-mile-long trail, but some of the more obvious starting points include the junction of Del Monte Boulevard and Lapis Road in Marina, Laguna Grande Park in Seaside, the Fisherman's Wharf parking lot in Monterey, or the trail's southern terminus at Lover's Point Park in Pacific Grove. Bring your own bike or rent one at **Wheel Fun Rentals at Bay Bikes** (three locations at Cannery Row, Fisherman's Wharf, and the Embassy Suites in Seaside, 831/655-2453, www.baybikes.com) or **Adventures by the Sea** (299 Cannery Row, 831/372-1807, www.adventuresbythesea.com).

Mountain bikers flock to the hills and dales of **Fort Ord,** once a military base and now a world-class recreation area for outdoor recreationists. More than 7,000 acres belonging to the old Army base, just east of Monterey, are managed by the Bureau of Land Management's Fort Ord Office (831/394-8314), including 50 miles of tight single-track and wide multi-use roads that wind through grassland hills, dense oaks, and coastal chaparral. No matter how foggy and cool the Monterey coast may be, it is usually sunny and warm at Fort Ord. There are numerous places to access Fort Ord's trails, but one of the best for fat-tire riders is the dirt

parking lot off Highway 68, three miles west of the junction with Reservation Road and 10 miles east of Highway 1 (near the junction with San Benancio Rd.). Pick up a map at the trailhead and pedal along Toro Creek Road from the parking area, and then put together a loop or an out-and-back of any length you please.

HIKING

Most visitors head south to Carmel or Big Sur or north to Santa Cruz for hiking opportunities, but Monterey boasts two lovely parks just a few miles outside of town, both of which are great places to stretch your legs. At **Jacks Peak County Park** (25001 Jacks Peak Park Dr., 831/372-8551, www.co.monterey.ca.us), Jacks Peak towers 1,068 feet above the ocean and is the highest point on the Monterey Peninsula. The Skyline Nature Trail is an easy 1.2-mile loop around the summit, and from it, you can branch off onto Jacks Peak Trail to head to the top of the peak. On clear days, views of the Carmel Valley, Monterey Peninsula, Point Lobos, and Pacific Ocean are divine. If it's foggy, you can still enjoy the lovely forest of Monterey pines through which these two trails travel. To get to the park, take Highway 68 east from Highway 1 for 1.7 miles. Turn right on Olmsted Road and drive 1.5 miles to Jacks Peak Drive. Follow Jacks Peak Drive to the park entrance.

Toro County Park is a bit farther out of town but worth the drive if you are seeking a longer and more challenging hike, and if the weather is cool. It's eight miles round-trip to the top of Ollason Peak (elevation 1,800 feet), with many steep sections along the route. Spring brings an amazing display of wildflowers, and the summit offers lovely views of Monterey Bay and the Central Valley. The park is found 13 miles east of Highway 1 via

Highway 68. Take the Portola Drive exit and follow the signs to Toro County Park. The Ollason Peak trailhead is found at the Quail Meadow Group Picnic Area.

FISHING

If your dream is to catch a deep-sea monster like a big salmon (Apr.–Oct.) or albacore (Aug.–Dec.), sign up for a fishing charter with **Randy's Fishing Trips** (66 Fisherman's Wharf #1, 831/372-7440 or 800/251-7440, www.randysfishingtrips.com) or **Chris' Fishing Trips** (48 Fisherman's Wharf #1, 831/375-5951, www.chrisfishing.com). Trips leave very early in the morning and typically run until mid-afternoon; rates are $55–65 per person plus rod rental ($10) and a one-day fishing license ($13).

KAYAKING

A great way to explore Monterey Bay is by getting right into it—in a kayak. **Monterey Bay Kayaks** (693 Del Monte Ave., 831/373-5357 or 800/649-5357, www.montereybaykayaks.com, $30–60 per person for three-hour tours) offers guided family tours suitable for kids ages three and up, bay tours, sunset tours, and full-moon tours. Or, if you just want to paddle on your own, kayak rentals are available for $30 per person per day, with a choice of sit-on-top, recreational, or closed deck kayaks. Wetsuits, paddling jackets, life jackets, water shoes, and a half hour of on-land instruction are included in the rental price; no experience is necessary for sit-on-top kayaks, although good swimming skills are required. **AB Seas Kayaks** (32 Cannery Row #5, 831/647-0147 or 866/824-2337, www.montereykayak.com) and **Adventures by the Sea** (299 Cannery Row, 831/372-1807, www.adventuresbythesea.com) offer similar services at similar prices.

Surf kayakers consider their options before paddling out into the whitewater at Monterey Bay.

© ANN MARIE BROWN

SAILING

Carrera Sailing Charters (66 Fisherman's Wharf at Randy's Fishing Trips, 831/375-0648, www.sailmontereybay.com) offers the comfortable 32-foot sloop *Carrera* for nature tours, sunset cruises, and private charters. With a six-passenger maximum, this offshore racing cruiser provides an intimate sailing experience. Most cruises last about 90 minutes; rates are typically $45 per person. Another possibility for photo and nature outings, dinner cruises, and sunset sails is **Monterey Bay Sailing and Diving** (Old Fisherman's Wharf #1, 831/372-7245, www.montereysailing.com). If you want to learn how to sail instead of just being a passenger, **Monterey Sailing Academy** (32 Cannery Row, 831/372-9463, www.montereysailing.org) is an American Sailing Association Training Center. Complete

MONTEREY

their course and you will be able to charter sailboats all around the world.

The Monterey Bay Aquarium also offers a sailing program called **Science Under Sail** (866/963-9646, www.montereybayaquarium.org, daily in summer, $49 for youths ages 10–17 and $59 for adults) on board a 65-foot sailboat. On this three-hour cruise, passengers get to work alongside an aquarium naturalist as he or she studies Monterey Bay, and take a turn at the helm of the vessel. Ninety-minute "sunset sails" with wine and light refreshments are also offered every evening in summer.

SCUBA DIVING

Monterey is world famous for its cold, nutrient-rich waters and undulating kelp forest teeming with sea life—octopi, anemones, sea otters, seals, and a mixed bag of whatever fish swim by. Many visitors come to Monterey specifically to learn to scuba dive. One of the best spots for beginning divers is **San Carlos Beach** (near the Coast Guard pier at Wave and Drake Sts.) at the end of Cannery Row. Here divers can explore the remains of sunken cannery equipment just offshore. Bathrooms and showers are located on the pier. Two more great beginner dive sites are **McAbee Beach** near Cannery Row (in front of the Spindrift Inn), and **Breakwater Cove** at the intersection of Cannery Row and Foam Street. Typical dive depths at these sites are about 10–60 feet.

Several in-town dive shops can set you up with lessons, equipment rentals, and local knowledge, including up-to-the-minute dive conditions. The most convenient is **Glenn's Aquarius II Dive Shop** located right on the water at Breakwater Cove (32 Cannery Row, 831/375-6605 or 866/375-6605, www.aquarius2.com, Mon.–Fri. 9 A.M.–6 P.M., Sat.–Sun. 7 A.M.–6 P.M.). If you don't have a dive buddy,

Glenn's local dive guides can accompany you on shore dives, or take you out to sea to dive from a boat ($80 fee includes two dive sites, two rental tanks, and snacks and drinks).

If you'd like to get certified in SCUBA (either PADI or SDI), head to the heated training pool at **Monterey Dive Center** (598 Foam St. near Cannery Row, 831/373-4831, www.themontereydivecenter.com). The typical instruction rate for open-water diver certification is $350 per person, including all equipment (six people maximum per class). For divers who are already certified, equipment rentals, air fills, and guided tours are also available.

Other dive shops in town include **Aquarius Dive Shop** (2040 Del Monte Blvd., 831/375-1933, www.aquariusdivers.com, Mon.–Fri. 9 A.M.–6 P.M., Sat.–Sun. 7 A.M.–6 P.M.), **Bamboo Reef** (614 Lighthouse Ave., 831/372-1685, www.bambooreef.com, Mon.–Fri. 9 A.M.–6 P.M., Sat.–Sun. 7 A.M.–6 P.M.), or **Monterey Bay Dive Company** (225 Cannery Row, 831/656-0454, www.mbdcscuba.com).

A great map of dive sites in the Monterey Bay area (including Point Lobos State Reserve, Santa Cruz, and Big Sur) is available from **Franko's Maps** (808/625-7728, www.frankosmaps.com) and can be purchased at most dive shops.

SKYDIVING

If you've always wanted to try skydiving, Monterey is as good a place as any to do so. At least you'll be able to enjoy some beautiful scenery as you plummet toward the earth at 120 miles per hour. **Skydive Monterey Bay** (3261 Imjin Rd., Marina, 831/384-3483, www.skydivemontereybay.com, $159–259 per person) makes the experience possible for first timers by offering tandem jumps with experienced "jump masters." Wannabe skydivers simply show up at the Marina Airport 20 minutes before their prearranged jump time wearing comfortable clothes; the instructors do the rest. Skydive Monterey Bay claims to offer the highest tandem jump anywhere in the United States—that means you'll walk out the door of an airplane at 18,000 feet in altitude. You'll experience an entire 90 seconds of freefall before your jumpmaster opens the parachute. Then, providing everything goes as it should, you'll have another five minutes of floating gently toward earth. Shorter jumps from 10,000 and 15,000 feet are also available.

WHALE-WATCHING AND BOAT TOURS

Because Monterey Bay's submarine canyon lies so close to shore, deep-water species of whales and dolphins can be seen year-round and much closer to land here than elsewhere in California. Gray whales are most commonly seen from December through April as they migrate from the Bering Sea to Baja and back again; humpback whales and blue whales (the largest animal on earth, weighing about 40 tons) can be seen in the summer months; and smaller whale species such as fin, minke, and killer whales (orcas) can be seen sporadically at any time of year. Thousands of dolphins and porpoises frolic in the bay year-round. Numerous companies on Fisherman's Wharf offer whale-watching tours; as a general rule, avoid tours that are offered by fishing-boat operators and stick to companies that specialize in whale watching.

Monterey Bay Whale Watch (84 Fisherman's Wharf, 831/375-4658, www .gowhales.com) offers boat tours led by marine biologists; whale sightings are guaranteed or you are given a credit for another trip. Gray whales are typically seen from mid-December through April on three-hour tours ($32 adults,

Whale-watching boat trips leave several times a day from Fisherman's Wharf.

$21 children 12 and under); humpbacks and blue whales are spotted May through mid-December on three- to five-hour tours ($34–43 adults, $23–33 children 12 and under). Dolphins, porpoises, sea otters, harbor seals, and sea lions can be seen at any time of year. Tours are offered daily but advance reservations are required. Remember to dress warmly for these trips, even in the middle of summer.

If you didn't reserve in advance, you can sign up for a last-minute whale watching tour with **Princess Monterey Whale Watching** (96 Fisherman's Wharf, 831/372-2203, www.bay watchcruises.com). Three-hour tours depart daily at 10 A.M. and 1:30 P.M. (also 4:30 P.M. in summer and fall).

A less time-intensive way to tour Monterey Bay is on a glass bottom boat, the **Little Mermaid** (90 Fisherman's Wharf, 831/372-7151, www.baywatchcruises.com, $10 adults, $8 children under 12). These 25-minute tours stick much closer to shore and depart daily every half hour from 11:30 A.M. until sunset from June to October; weekends and holidays only in winter. Sea otters, sea lions, and marine birds are common sightings. Although you probably won't see whales and deep-water creatures on these cruises, you won't get seasick, either.

Entertainment and Shopping

NIGHTLIFE
Bars and Clubs

For varied entertainment every night of the week, head to **The Planet Ultralounge** (2110 Fremont St., 831/373-1449, www.theplanet monterey.com, daily 7 P.M.–2 A.M.), where the bill ranges from comedy to live music to dinner-and-dancing. Sunday nights are "salsa night" with the house band Rumba Café (dance lessons start at 8 P.M.) and Thursday nights have a country-Western theme, while Friday and Saturday are usually reserved for stand-up. Two bars and a dinner menu are available.

Since 1971, **Doc Rickett's Lab** (1803 E. Franklin St., 831/649-4241, www.docricketts lab.com, daily 5 P.M.–2 A.M.) has been entertaining locals and visitors alike with DJs spinning rock 'n' roll, country, and top-40 music, plus live comedy. It is located just one block up from Cannery Row.

The slightly more upscale dance club **Hippodrome** (321 Alvarado St., 831/646-9244, www.hippclub.com, daily 9 P.M.–2 A.M.) has four dance floors, four bars, DJs, go-go cages, video projectors, an outdoor patio, live music, and views of the bay from its second-floor windows. DJs typically mix techno, hip-hop, and other music geared toward the 20-something crowd. In an attempt to class up the place, tennis shoes and casual clothing are not permitted on weekends. In its previous incarnation, this nightspot was called Club Octane.

Plenty of British ex-pats call Monterey home, and plenty more British tourists visit the city, which is probably why this relatively small town has not one but five British-style pubs. **Brittania Arms** (444 Alvarado St., 831/656-9543, www.britanniaarms.com, daily 11 A.M.–1:30 A.M.) is popular for all-you-can-eat fish-and-chips on Monday nights, plus 24 beers and ales on top, a wide array of single-malt scotches, and live soccer from England on the big-screen TV on Saturday mornings. Happy hour is 4–7 P.M. on weekdays.

Occasionally the place features live music on weekend nights.

Another Brit-style pub serving bangers-and-mash, cottage pies, and beef Wellington along with its vast array of international beers and ales is **The Mucky Duck** (479 Alvarado St., 831/655-3031, www.muckyduckmonterey.com, daily 2 P.M.–2 A.M.). The outdoor fire pits on the patio are a big selling point, plus 70 different whiskeys and happy hour six days a week (Mon.–Sat. 4–7 P.M.).

Still can't get enough of those dark stouts and malt scotches from across the pond? There's always the **Crown & Anchor** (150 West Franklin St., 831/649-6496, www.crownandanchor.net, daily 11 A.M.–2 A.M.), which wins hands down for the coolest-looking pub, complete with models of old sailing ships surrounding its dark green, wood-paneled bar.

Live Music

For live jazz, blues, and classic rock on weekend nights and most weekdays, make a nighttime trip to the Cannery to take in the show at **Sly McFly's Refueling Station** (700 Cannery Row, 831/372-3225, www.slymcflys.com, daily 11 A.M.–2 A.M.). The dance floor is big enough to accommodate all comers, and those usually include tourists dressed in T-shirts and shorts as well as Monterey locals in business clothes stopping by after work. The cocktails and beer flow like an endless river, and although the bar-style food (seafood, steak, pasta, sandwiches) is nothing to write home about, it will fill you up while you wait for the evening's band to start. And although you've probably never heard of the musicians taking the stage—especially on weekday nights when local bands perform—you are probably going to enjoy them. Somebody in charge here knows how to pick live acts. Sly's is also the place to catch

Sunday- and Monday-night football games. Stained glass windows give the place a historic look, keeping with the Cannery Row theme. If you visit in the daytime, you can enjoy a stellar Monterey Bay view.

Cibo Ristorante Italiano (301 Alvarado St., 831/649-8151, www.cibo.com, Tues.–Sun. 5 P.M.–1:30 A.M.) is well known for both cutting-edge Sicilian fare and live jazz six nights a week. There's free wireless Internet access in the lounge area, and the martinis come highly recommended. On Sunday nights the music accompanies the dinner hour, but Tuesday to Saturday the sounds of jazz, soul, funk, and Latin dance music don't begin until 9:30 or 10 P.M. You might want to dress up a bit for a night here; there are usually lots of pretty people here.

PERFORMING ARTS

The intimate, club-style **Monterey Live** theater (414 Alvarado St., 831/373-5483, www.montereylive.org) operates inside an original adobe in downtown Monterey. It offers live music (usually acoustic because of the theater's small size), live theater, dance performances, spoken word, and comedy nightly. The Live Wired Café has a full bar, serves light fare, and features a 5 P.M. happy hour Monday to Friday, with live music as well as food and drink specials. With only 100 seats, you won't be watching the action on a big-screen television—everything is up close and very real.

The **Bruce Arris Wharf Theater** (Fisherman's Wharf #1, 831/372-1373, www.mctaweb.org) performs upstairs in a wooden building near the end of Fisherman's Wharf. Shows tend to be on the "lite" side (musicals, comedies, and radio and Broadway reviews), and are geared more toward casual tourists than true theatergoers. The theater, named

MONTEREY

after an artist and friend of John Steinbeck, has been in operation continuously since 1976.

The **Paper Wing Theatre Company** (320 Hoffman Ave., 831/675-0521, www.paper wingtheatreco.com) off Lighthouse Avenue presents live plays and musicals with a little more of an edge (*The Rocky Horror Picture Show* is a common offering).

CINEMA

The **Cannery Row 3-D IMAX theater** (640 Wave St., 831/372-4629, www.bellacinema .com) features films geared toward the young and young at heart, such as *Batman the Dark Knight, Dinosaurs Alive,* and *Sea Monsters 3D.*

When the **Golden State Theatre** (417 Alvarado St., 831/372-4555, www.golden statetheatre.com) opened in 1926, it was the largest theater between San Francisco and Los Angeles. Designed to look like a Moorish castle, Golden State Theatre had what were then such modern amenities as a Mighty Wurlitzer pipe organ and an internal and external telephone system. Today this restored historical theater showcases classics films, and patrons can still hear the Wurlitzer play during intermission.

If you're an indie film fan, or would rather read subtitles than see the latest blockbuster schlock, head to **Osio 6 Cinema** (350 Alvarado St., 831/644-8171, www.osiocinemas.com). The venue is small, so be sure to arrive early to get a prime seat.

FESTIVALS AND EVENTS
Spring
Spring starts off by whistling Dixie in early March at **Dixieland Monterey** (888/349-6879, www.dixieland-monterey.com), held at various venues in downtown Monterey and along Fisherman's Wharf. Jazz bands, swing bands,

and of course Dixieland bands make an appearance here.

In mid-April, the "Bikestock" of North America takes place at the **Sea Otter Classic Cycling Festival** at Laguna Seca Recreation Area (831/755-4899, www.seaotterclassic .com). This huge cycling event attracts all kinds of cyclists, including Olympic champions. Mountain bike racing is the main event, but there are also noncompetitive "fun rides," road races, and a trade show featuring the latest cycling clothing and hardware.

For something less aerobically challenging, head to the mid-May **Marina International Festival of the Winds** (www.marinafestival .com), where you can fly a kite or just watch the experts do so. The festival also includes kite-making workshops, hang gliding demonstrations, wind-related craft workshops for kids, and live music and entertainment.

Summer
Music lovers flock to the **Monterey Bay Blues Festival** at the Monterey Fairgrounds (831/394-2652, www.montereyblues.com), an event that has been rocking the county for more than 20 years. Blues greats such as Taj Majal, B.B. King, and Keb Mo perform on three separate stages. More than 50 acts strut their stuff each year over the course of the three-day event.

Those with a literary bent are sure to enjoy Monterey's **Annual Steinbeck Festival** in Salinas (National Steinbeck Center, 831/775-4721, www.steinbeck.org), held in early August. The four-day event features films, talks, and bus and walking tours celebrating the most famous son of Monterey County and the literary light of Cannery Row.

And Steinbeck himself would probably applaud the **Annual Winemaker's Celebration**

(831/375-9400, www.montereywines.org) held in early to mid- August at Custom House Plaza. The event includes educational seminars, wine- barrel building, live music, and the tasting of wines from more than 40 Monterey County wineries. Another popular wine event held earlier in the summer (usually June) is the **Monterey Wine Festival** (888/814-WINE, www.montereywine.com), which takes place at various locations throughout the county. This festival includes tastings, wine talks, and cooking and wine pairing demonstrations.

The biggest event of August is the **Monterey County Fair** (831/372-5863, www.monterey countyfair.com), held for a week in mid-month at the fairgrounds. Fairgoers get a look at the county's finest-looking sheep, cows, and other livestock, plus taste lots of homemade food and locally grown produce. If you're lucky, you might win yourself a stuffed animal on the amusement midway.

Autumn

Autumn brings the sunniest weather and the peak of the festival season to Monterey, beginning with the world-famous **Monterey Jazz Festival** (Monterey County Fairgrounds, 925/275-9255, www.montereyjazzfestival.org), happening every year since 1957 and hosting such jazz greats as Wynton Marsalis and Herbie Hancock. Typically staged in the third week of September, this is the oldest continuously held jazz festival in the world. In addition to the music, there is food, art, gifts, and music-related seminars and talks.

Often held the same weekend as the jazz festival, the **Monterey Bay Birding Festival** (831/763-5600, www.montereybaybirding.com) celebrates the incredible diversity of birds in the Monterey area. During the course of this three-day event, birders travel to Pinnacles National Monument, Big Sur, Elkhorn Slough, and other areas of Monterey County to look for birds and listen to talks by noted avian biologists.

In mid-October, Mazda Raceway at Laguna Seca plays host to Le Mans racing in the **Monterey Sports Car Championships** (800/327-7322, www.laguna-seca.com), an event in which the stars of sports-car racing drive BMWs, Porsches, and Corvettes.

Winter

What better way to enjoy winter than with a glass of wine in hand, and an easy way to obtain one (or more) is to attend the **Wine Passport Weekend** in mid-February (831/375-9400, www.calwineries.com). This county-wide event allows participants to purchase a "passport" ($50) to taste vintages at wineries throughout Monterey. At each winery, your passport is stamped and you become eligible to win wine-related prizes. In case you sip a few too many vintages, shuttle transportation is available.

SHOPPING
Cannery Row

Cannery Row is the obvious starting point for most visiting shoppers searching for gifts, apparel, jewelry, and the like. More than 150 stores are located along the six-block stretch of the Row between Reeside and David Avenues. **A Taste of Monterey** (700 Cannery Row, 831/646-5446 or 888/646-5446, www.taste monterey.com, daily 11 A.M.–6 P.M., free admission, $10 for wine tasting) offers wine samplings of local Monterey Bay Area wines. The lovely seaside location is only complemented by its panoramic view of the bay.

American Revival Company (711 Cannery Row, 831/372-3567, www.americanrevival.net, daily 9 A.M.–9 P.M. except Sun. and Mon. until 8 P.M.) sells really great stuff from the past, or at least replicas of it, like Route 66 memorabilia, Betty Boop posters, reproductions of dime-store novel covers from the 1930s to 1960s, and authentic-looking one-million-dollar bills (okay, those never really existed). It's easy to while away an hour just looking at all the stuff in this store.

Another good spot to be entertained as you shop is at **Island Soap and Candle Works** (685 Cannery Row, 831/644-9425, www.monterey soap.com, daily 10 A.M.–8 P.M. in summer, until 6 P.M. in winter). First there is the satisfying olfactory experience upon entering the front door; then there is the fascination of watching soaps and candles being made the old-fashioned way. Employees cook up a traditional South Pacific soap using pure coconut oil, as well as a line of specialty soaps with coconut, olive, palm, macadamia, and kukui nut oils combined with herbs. A variety of soaps and beeswax candles are available for purchase.

Foodies flock to **For Garlic Lovers** (700 N. Cannery Row, 800/745-3221, www.forgarlic lovers.com, daily 10 A.M.–8 P.M. in summer, until 6 P.M. in winter) for salsas, marinades, barbecue sauces, salad dressings, mustards, and all things garlic related. The store has cookbooks and gadgets galore.

When the kids get bored with shopping, take them to **Beach Bear and Co.** (700 Cannery Row D1, 831/372-5810, www.beachbearco .com, daily 11 A.M.–6 P.M.), where they can make their own stuffed teddy bear and take him or her home. With choices of hundreds of bear "forms" and accessories, each bear made here is unique. And adults can join in on the fun, too—there's no age discrimination when it comes to making teddy bears.

Don't forget about the shop at the **Monterey Bay Aquarium** (886 Cannery Row, 831/648-4800, daily 10 A.M.–6 P.M.), which

has a wonderful selection of educational and "eco" items. You need to pay an admission fee to the aquarium to visit this shop, but if you don't want to do so, you can always shop online at www.mbayaq.org.

Just down the street from Cannery Row and the Aquarium lies the **American Tin Cannery Premium Outlet** (125 Ocean View Blvd., 831/372-1442, www.americantincannery.com, daily 10 A.M.–6 P.M.), where outlet stores include Carole Little, Carter's Children's Wear, Nine West, and Woolrich.

Fisherman's Wharf

There isn't much in the way of serious shopping on Fisherman's Wharf, but if you want to satisfy your sweet tooth, you can easily do so at **Carousel Candies** (31 Fisherman's Wharf, 831/372-5520, www.carouselcandies.com, daily 10 A.M.–6 P.M.). The folks at Carousel have been handmaking saltwater taffy in Monterey for nearly 50 years, and they also do a bustling trade in chocolate turtles, English toffee, haystacks, fudge, caramel apples, and caramel corn. It's all high enough quality that it's worth the extra trip to the dentist.

If you're looking for a new strand of pearls, try **Morning Star Pearls** (95 Fisherman's Wharf, 831/373-8105, daily 10 A.M.–6 P.M.), where you can purchase those delicate treasures from the sea in every imaginable form—in rings, necklaces, bracelets, or even just loose.

Since it is usually much cooler in Monterey than most visitors expect it will be, almost every other shop on Fisherman's Wharf sells sweatshirts, sweaters, and fleece jackets. Several gift/trinket shops are also found on the wharf, hawking wares such as lighthouse figurines, model ships, crystals, and seashells. Just remember, if you buy them, eventually you will have to dust them.

Monterey State Historic Park

Located near Fisherman's Wharf, Monterey State Historic Park has a few interesting shops that operate out of park buildings to help generate funds for historic preservation, garden development, and other improvements. Worth a look along Monterey's Path of History is the **Cooper Museum Store** (in the Cooper-Molera Adobe at Polk and Munras Sts., 831/649-7118, Mon.–Sat. 10 A.M.–4 P.M., Sun. 1–4 P.M.), which offers quality 1800s-vintage reproductions, from toys to furniture. There's also an extensive collection of books on Monterey and California cultural and natural history.

The **Boston Store** (Scott and Olivier Sts., 831/649-3364, Thurs.–Sun. 11 A.M.–3 P.M.) is run by the nonprofit Historic Garden League and offers antiques, ribbons, linens, crockery, preserves, soaps, potpourri, tea, and herbs, all representative of items used in early California, including an interesting collection of Russian toys and dolls. A lovely herb garden flanks the property.

Munras Avenue

For all-purpose shopping, an upscale mall is conveniently installed astride Monterey's motel row, Munras Avenue. At the **Del Monte Shopping Center** (1410 Del Monte Center off Munras Ave., 831/373-2705, www.delmonte center.com) you'll find the usual coffee, food, apparel, books, and movie theater, plus the mall's anchor store, Macy's. Del Monte Shopping Center is open Monday–Friday 10 A.M.–9 P.M., Saturday 10 A.M.–7 P.M., and Sunday 11 A.M.–5 P.M.

Downtown Monterey

A rarity in this day and age, the independent bookstore is alive and well in downtown Monterey. **Carpe Diem Fine Books** (245 Pearl St., 831/643-2754, www.carpediem finebooks.com, daily noon–5 P.M. or by appt.) is the place to find out-of-print, collectible, and rare books, as well as a few of the more common variety. First editions and fine art books are their specialty, but bibliophiles can also shop for a wide range of books covering topics on the American West, the California missions, and the Monterey Peninsula. The shop is set in a historic stone building near the Robert Louis Stevenson house.

In a similar vein is the **Old Monterey Book Company** (136 Bonifacio Place, 831/372-3111, Tues. 3–7 P.M., Wed.–Sat. 11 A.M.–5 P.M.) and **The Book Haven** (559 Tyler St., 831/333-0383, Mon.–Sat. 10 A.M.–6 P.M.), both specializing in antiquarian, rare, and out-of-print books.

Home furnishing shops also abound in downtown Monterey. For the romantic, **Palazzo** (631 Cass St., 831/641-0575, www .palazzo-ub.com, Tues.–Fri. 10:30 A.M.–6 P.M., Sun. 10:30 A.M.–4:30 P.M.) offers a wide range of furniture and wares that appear to have been pilfered from a crumbling Tuscan villa. There's plenty of home and garden decor, most with a European vintage flair, but also smaller gift items like textiles, dishes, bath products, and fine stationery.

And if you are looking for something to put on your walls, head to one of downtown Monterey's many art galleries, most featuring the work of local artists. One of the most interesting is that of the **Youth Arts Collective** (472 Calle Principal, 831/375-9922, www.yacstudios.com, Tues.–Fri. 3–7 P.M. and Sat. noon–4 P.M.), a nonprofit organization that provides equipment and supplies to young Monterey artists between the ages of 14–22. Art of a more commercial sort can be found at the **Venture Gallery by the Bay** (260 Alvarado Mall, 831/372-6279, www.venturegallery.com, daily 10 A.M.–6 P.M.), off the lobby of the Portola Hotel, which specializes in paintings, sculpture, and ceramics depicting the Monterey landscape.

Accommodations

CAMPING

Tent campers will find slim pickings in Monterey, although there are plenty of options farther north in Santa Cruz and south in Big Sur. **Laguna Seca Recreation Area** (1025 Hwy. 68, 831/758-3604, www.co.monterey.ca.us/parks, $22–30 per night), six miles east of Monterey on Highway 68, has 172 sites for tents or RVs up to 40 feet long. If you want to visit the Laguna Seca Raceway, it's practically next door, and all the sights and activities in Monterey are about 15 minutes away. RVers can also find a spot near the beach at **Marina Dunes RV Park** off Reservation Road in Marina (831/384-6914, www.marinadunesrv.com, $45–65 per night).

HOSTELS

Thanks to the Monterey Hostel Society, budget travelers can bunk at the old Carpenter's Union Hall, now a 45-bed hostel just four blocks from Cannery Row. Among its other features, the HI-USA **Monterey Hostel** (778 Hawthorne St., 831/649-0375, www.montereyhostel.org, $28–59 per person) offers a choice of dorm-style rooms or private rooms, a big lounge with Internet access, games, and a piano, and a kitchen where you can cook your own meals. Do-it-yourself pancakes are available from the self-serve breakfast bar each morning. The nightly rate includes a pillow, sheets, and a blanket (no sleeping bags allowed). Unlike at many hostels, the curfew here is 1 A.M., so you can go out for an evening on the town without getting locked out too early.

HOTELS AND MOTELS
Under $150

The attractive and accommodating **Colton Inn** (707 Pacific St., 831/649-6500 or 800/848-7007, www.coltoninn.com, $125–175) offers all the basics at an affordable rate, plus extras like a dry sauna and sundeck, in-room DVD players, free wireless Internet, and an expansive continental breakfast. Some rooms have fireplaces, whirlpool tubs, balconies, microwaves, and refrigerators. The inn is within walking distance of the restaurants and shops of downtown Monterey.

The **Best Western de Anza Inn** (2141 North Fremont St., 800/780-7234, www.book.bestwestern.com, $129–169) is a terrific value in Monterey, located just minutes from all the attractions. Pay no attention to the bland chain-motel look; everything you need is right here and affordable. The motel has big rooms, high ceilings, comfortable beds, and a complimentary continental breakfast. Parents, take note: the kids are always happy when there's a pool, and this Best Western has a nice one. Even if it's foggy and cool in Monterey, the under-12 crowd always wants to go swimming.

There's nothing fancy about the **Sand Dollar Inn** (755 Abrego St., 831/372-7551 or 800/982-1986, www.sanddollarinn.com, $79–199), but for an affordable stay in Monterey, it's a safe bet. Some rooms have king-size beds and gas fireplaces; a pool and hot tub are on-site. Guests can easily walk to Cannery

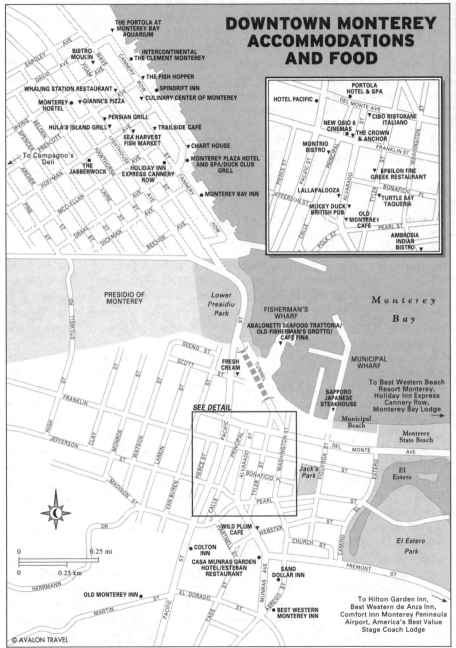

DOWNTOWN MONTEREY ACCOMMODATIONS AND FOOD

THE PORTOLA AT MONTEREY BAY AQUARIUM

BISTRO MOULIN

INTERCONTINENTAL THE CLEMENT MONTEREY

THE FISH HOPPER

WHALING STATION RESTAURANT

SPINDRIFT INN

MONTEREY HOSTEL

GIANNI'S PIZZA

CULINARY CENTER OF MONTEREY

PERSIAN GRILL

HULA'S ISLAND GRILL

TRAILSIDE CAFÉ

SEA HARVEST FISH MARKET

CHART HOUSE

To Compagno's Deli

THE JABBERWOCK

HOLIDAY INN EXPRESS CANNERY ROW

MONTEREY PLAZA HOTEL AND SPA/DUCK CLUB GRILL

MONTEREY BAY INN

HOTEL PACIFIC

PORTOLA HOTEL & SPA

DEL MONTE AVE

NEW OSIO 6 CINEMAS

CIBO RISTORANE ITALIANO

THE CROWN & ANCHOR

MONTRIO BISTRO

FRANKLIN ST

EPSILON FINE GREEK RESTAURANT

LALLAPALOOZA

BONAFICIO PL

TURTLE BAY TAQUERIA

MUCKY DUCK BRITISH PUB

OLD MONTEREY CAFÉ

PEARL ST

AMBROSIA INDIAN BISTRO

PRESIDIO OF MONTEREY

Lower Presidio Park

FISHERMAN'S WHARF

Monterey

Bay

ABALONETTI SEAFOOD TRATTORIA/ OLD FISHERMAN'S GROTTO/ CAFÉ FINA

MUNICIPAL WHARF

FRESH CREAM

TUNNEL

SAPPORO JAPANESE STEAKHOUSE

To Best Western Beach Resort Monterey, Holiday Inn Express Cannery Row, Monterey Bay Lodge

SEE DETAIL

Municipal Beach

Monterey State Beach

Jack's Park

El Estero

WILD PLUM CAFÉ

WEBSTER

El Estero Park

COLTON INN

CASA MUNRAS GARDEN HOTEL/ESTEBAN RESTAURANT

SAND DOLLAR INN

0   0.25 mi

0   0.25 km

OLD MONTEREY INN

BEST WESTERN MONTEREY INN

To Hilton Garden Inn, Best Western de Anza Inn, Comfort Inn Monterey Peninsula Airport, America's Best Value Stage Coach Lodge

© AVALON TRAVEL

Row, the aquarium, and Fisherman's Wharf. A free continental breakfast is provided.

Located just 15 few minutes away from Cannery Row and the Monterey Bay Aquarium, the budget-minded **Comfort Inn Monterey Peninsula Airport** (1200 Olmsted Rd., 831/372-2945, www.comfortinn.com, $99–149) provides comfy rooms and a free continental breakfast. All rooms have free high-speed Internet access, microwaves, refrigerators, flat-screen televisions, and irons and ironing boards. A few rooms have balconies and/or fireplaces.

America's Best Value Stage Coach Lodge (1111 10th St., 831/373-3632, www.americasbestvalueinn.com, $90–125) may be part of a large chain, but it feels more like a small mom-and-pop establishment. With only 25 rooms on two floors, the lodge manages to maintain a family-run feel, right down to the model stage coach parked out front, and well-tended flowers surrounding the swimming pool and grounds. Rooms come equipped with microwaves and refrigerators, free high-speed Internet, and cable television. A continental breakfast gets you going in the morning. Rates are often well below 100 bucks in the off-season, and that's hard to beat.

$150-250

If you want to be able to walk right onto the sand from your hotel room, or listen to the sea lions barking as the sun sinks in the west, the **Best Western Beach Resort Monterey** (2600 Sand Dunes Dr., 831/394-3321, www.montereybeachresort.com, $169–249) can provide that. The biggest selling point of a stay here at Monterey's only full-service beachfront hotel is the proximity of Del Monte Beach and the stunning coastal views from the oceanside rooms (rooms on the other side of the hotel are cheaper, but nowhere near as enjoyable). An on-site restaurant makes it possible for you to spend an entire day here without ever driving your car. Like so many hotels in Monterey, this one charges an extra fee for parking ($10).

Staying true to the Hilton brand of service and amenities, the **Hilton Garden Inn Monterey** (1000 Aguajito Rd., 831/373-6142, www.monterey.stayhgi.com, $160–220) is a good choice for an overnight in Monterey, with a stylish, comfortable lobby and neighboring bar, large guest rooms with microwaves, refrigerators, and free high-speed Internet access, and an on-site pool, spa, and fitness center. A few little touches make your stay special, like fresh-baked cookies at the front desk and a generous breakfast in the morning. There's nothing of interest within walking distance of this hotel, but a few minutes' drive will get you to the aquarium and Cannery Row.

What you pay for at the **Holiday Inn Express Cannery Row** (443 Wave St., www.ichotelsgroup.com, $199–249) is its stellar location on Cannery Row. You can park your car here and spend the rest of your time in Monterey walking to the city's best sights. Otherwise, this Holiday Inn is about what you'd expect from any Holiday Inn—clean and comfortable rooms with fairly bland decor, free breakfast in the morning, and high-speed Internet access. Nothing much to write home about, but you won't spend much time in your room anyway.

It's just a basic, standard motel, but the **Monterey Bay Lodge** (55 Camino Aguajito, 831/372-8057, www.montereybaylodge, $199–279) is a relatively affordable option just 150 steps from Monterey State Beach and a 10-minute walk from the wharf and downtown. The lodge's 45 rooms are arranged around its outdoor pool and spa. A stay here is all about convenience: there's an on-site restaurant, complimentary high-speed Internet access, and free parking. Kids will get a kick out of the fountain that sprays upward from the depths of the pool.

The 171-room **Casa Munras Garden Hotel** (700 Munras Ave., 831/375-2411 or 800/222-2446, www.hotelcasamunras.com, $189–259) is conveniently located close to Monterey's historic downtown and is set amid four acres of lovely gardens. All guest rooms have free wireless Internet access and DVD players; many of the rooms have fireplaces. The hotel's restaurant, Esteban, serves Mediterranean cuisine for lunch and dinner. Many guests spend their summer evenings around the bar's outdoor fire pit.

The downtown **Best Western Monterey Inn** (825 Abrego St., 831/373-5345 or 877/373-5345, www.montereyinnca.com, $179–259) is what you might call a "high-end" Best Western, located about six blocks from Fisherman's Wharf. The inn has 80 spacious rooms—some with fireplaces, all with in-room coffeemakers and refrigerators. Be sure to ask for one of the rooms on the higher floors with a downtown and/or bay view. The heated pool and hot tub are a welcome sight after a long day of sightseeing.

Over $250

Overlooking Monterey Bay in the heart of Cannery Row, the **(InterContinental the Clement Monterey** (750 Cannery Row, 831/375-4500, www.ichotelsgroup.com, $350–550) offers magnificent panoramic coastal views, luxurious room decor, and the sights and sounds of the surf and sea. Many of the 208 rooms and suites, spread out over

four floors, boast fireplaces, balconies, and ocean views. The property features over 15,000 square feet of indoor/outdoor meeting space, a restaurant and bar, a spa, a health club, and a swimming pool. One of many highlights of a stay here: watching the sea otters frolic while enjoying an after-dinner drink on the oceanfront patio.

For an upscale stay in Monterey, book a room at the **(Monterey Bay Inn** (242 Cannery Row, 831/373-6242 or 800/424-6242, www.montereybayinn.com, $280–350), which offers contemporary accommodations right on the bay. The inn's 47 mostly bay- or harborview rooms have private balconies with an expansive view of the water, and are decorated with a stylish mix of cherry wood furniture and colorful artwork. You'll sleep well in the plush king-sized beds. A continental breakfast for two is brought to your room each morning, and fresh-baked cookies are available in the lobby in the afternoon.

Just a few blocks away and even more luxurious is the four-story, 300-room, Craftsman-style **(Monterey Plaza Hotel & Spa** (400 Cannery Row, 831/646-1700 or 800/334-3999, www.montereyplazahotel .com, $299–399). The Plaza's elegant rooms and suites are decked out in Italian Empire and 18th-century Chinese furnishings, and each has a large marble bath with a separate vanity area. You'll find every amenity you could possibly want, including a complete fitness center and 10,000-square-foot full-service spa located on the rooftop, and exceptional food service. Rental bikes and kayaks are available. The Plaza has been lauded by both *Conde Nast* and *Travel and Leisure* as one of the top hotels in the world. Be sure to have at least one dinner at the Monterey Plaza's restaurant, the **Duck Club Grill** (400 Cannery

Row, 831/646-1706, www.montereyplaza
hotel.com, breakfast daily 6:30–11 A.M., dinner daily 5:30–9:30 P.M., $28).

Also deluxe and downtown is the four-dia-
mond, Spanish-style **Hotel Pacific** (300 Pacific
St., 831/373-5700 or 800/554-5542, www
.hotelpacific.com, $249–319). The hotel's 105
suites have hardwood floors, feather beds, balconies or decks, gas fireplaces, refrigerators, in-
room coffeemakers, and televisions. Bathrooms
come equipped with telephones, an extra television, terrycloth bathrobes, and hand-milled
soaps. Bonuses include a continental breakfast,
afternoon tea, and free underground parking.
History buffs who choose to walk Monterey's
Path of History will appreciate that the hotel
is adjacent to Casa Soberanes.

The seven-story **Portola Hotel and Spa at
Monterey Bay** (2 Portola Plaza, 831/649-4511
or 888/222-5851, www.portolaplazahotel.com,
$300–400) boasts 369 rooms and 10 suites and
is popular with business travelers and vacationers seeking luxury and location. Freshly baked
cookies are provided when you check in. The
on-site Peter B's Microbrewery Pub is well
loved by those who crave handcrafted beers
and sports television. The hotel is a five-minute walk to Fisherman's Wharf and less than
a mile from the aquarium and Cannery Row.
Once you are here, you probably won't need
your car for a couple days.

The beachfront **Spindrift Inn** (652 Cannery
Row, 831/646-8900 or 800/841-1879, www
.spindriftinn.com, $239–299) was once a bor-
dello but today is a European-style hotel. The
rooftop patio garden offers panoramic views
of Monterey Bay. Rooms feature hardwood
floors, wood-burning fireplaces, second telephones in the tiled bathrooms, marble tubs,
featherbeds with goose-down comforters,
all-cotton linens, and terry bathrobes. In the
morning, a continental breakfast and the daily
newspaper are delivered to your room on a silver tray. Wine and cheese are served in the
lobby in the afternoon. If you want to stay
right in Cannery Row and have easy access to
the aquarium, this is a great spot.

BED-AND-BREAKFASTS

Monterey's showcase country inn is the gorgeous ivy-covered 1929 English Tudor **C Old
Monterey Inn** (500 Martin St., 831/375-8284
or 800/350-2344, www.oldmontereyinn.com,
$240–415), featuring 10 elegant rooms and
suites, most with fireplaces. All have sitting
areas, featherbeds, CD players, a whirlpool tub
for two, and special touches such as skylights
and stained glass. As if the inn isn't appealing
enough, the colorful gardens and strategically
positioned fountains and outdoor seating areas
are sure to win you over. Those who enjoy con-
tainer gardening will be suitably impressed by
more than 200 pots of impatiens. Guests enjoy
marvelous breakfasts, homemade cookies, and
a sunset wine hour, plus wonderful hospitality
24 hours a day.

The **Jabberwock** (598 Laine St.,
831/372-4777 or 888/428-7253, www.jabber
wockinn.com, $165–295) is a seven-room
Craftsman-style inn just five blocks from
Cannery Row, with common rooms and gardens that offer lovely views of the bay. The
guest rooms are decorated in a Victorian style,
with lace-trimmed sheets, goose-down pillows
and comforters, and fresh flowers. Some rooms
have fireplaces and whirlpool tubs. Rates include a big gourmet breakfast plus cookies and
milk at night.

Food

FARMERS MARKETS

Tuesday is the day for Monterey's weekly Farmer's Market, also known as the **Old Monterey Market Place** (Alvarado St., 831/655-8070, www.oldmonterey.org), held in the historic downtown area from 4–8 P.M. April–October and 4–7 P.M. November–March. The market covers more than three city blocks, running the entire length of Alvarado Street, and is held rain or shine. More than 130 vendors sell fresh produce and flowers from the local area, arts and crafts, handmade jewelry, furniture, and clothing. Food stalls offer tantalizing international cuisine, and in "Baker's Alley" you can shop for fresh pastries, baklava, and European-style bread. Produce vendors come from all over California to sell certified and organic certified fruits and vegetables.

A similar but smaller event is held every Thursday from 2:30–6 P.M. at **Monterey Peninsula College** (970 Fremont St., North Side Lower Level Parking Lot, 831/728-5060,

© MONTEREY COUNTY CVB

The Old Monterey Market Place is held each Tuesday throughout the year.

www.montereybayfarmers.org). Additionally, every Sunday from 10 A.M.–2 P.M., the town of **Marina,** 10 miles north of Monterey, hosts a certified farmers market (215 Reservation Rd., Marina Village Shopping Center, 831/384-6961, www.everyonesharvest.org).

CASUAL DINING
Breakfast and Lunch

For breakfast or lunch, the **Trailside Cafe** (550 Wave St., 831/649-8600, www.trailsidecafe .com, daily 8 A.M.–3 P.M., $8) is a welcoming spot serving fresh and simply prepared foods. The café gets its name from the Monterey Peninsula Recreation Trail which runs right past it, meaning you'll be sipping lattes and munching eggs Benedict in the company of cyclists, joggers, and walkers. In the morning, heaping plates of huevos rancheros are carried out from the kitchen. For lunch, be sure to try a grilled artichoke, or the Baja-style fish tacos. The outdoor patio has a lovely view of Monterey Bay, and pets are welcome.

The **Old Monterey Cafe** (489 Alvarado St., 831/646-1021, www.cafemonterey.com, daily 7 A.M.–2:30 P.M., $10) serves all kinds of omelettes at breakfast, plus unusual choices like calamari and eggs, linguica and eggs, and pigs in a blanket. Just about everything is good at lunch, too, from homemade soups, hearty shrimp Louie, and an Athenian Greek salad (with feta cheese, Greek olives, shrimp, and veggies), to the three-quarter-pound burgers and steak or calamari sandwiches. Fresh-squeezed juices and espresso and cappuccino are featured beverages. For late risers, breakfast is served until closing.

At the (**Wild Plum Café and Bakery** (731 B Munras Ave., 831/646-3109, www.thewildplumcafe.com, Mon.–Sat. 7 A.M.–5 P.M., $5–9) you are just as likely to run into locals grabbing a cappuccino and a bran muffin before work as visitors killing time before the aquarium opens. This colorful, city-style café is the kind of place where you could easily hang out for a few hours, noshing on a Mediterranean scramble, vegetarian quesadilla, free-range chicken salad, or fresh-baked whole grain breads. Most everything is made with organic ingredients, and there are plenty of sweet treats to go with a cup of coffee.

There is no better place in Monterey to get a sandwich than at **Compagno's Market and Deli** (2000 Prescott Ave., 831/375-5987, Mon.–Fri. 9 A.M.–6 P.M., Sat.–Sun. 10 A.M.–6 P.M., $6–10). One sandwich can practically feed your whole family, which is why the line is often trailing out the door at lunchtime. Salads, cakes, and pies are great, too (try the peanut butter chocolate pie), and beer lovers will appreciate the huge selection of micro-brews. There is no way you can leave this legendary spot and still be hungry. Don't expect any ambience here—it's really just an unassuming corner market with a few tables and lots of military memorabilia on the walls—but you can always pick up a sandwich to go and find any scenic spot in Monterey to eat it.

Greek

Along with everything else, the pita bread is handmade at **Epsilon Fine Greek Restaurant** (422 Tyler St., 831/655-8108, www.epsilon restaurant.com, daily 5–9:30 P.M., $15–20). Having been in business in Monterey for the last 20 years, this restaurant has achieved mastery of all the Greek favorites: avgolemono soup, gyros, dolmades, suvlaki, musaka, and the like. A wide variety of seafood is also available, prepared as it might be on the Greek islands.

SAY CHEESE

Not every town can brag of having a cheese named after it, but Monterey can. Monterey Jack cheese is said to be the only cheese truly native to California, although cheese historians insist that the first Jack-style cheeses really came from Spain. In the early 1700s, when Spanish Franciscan monks settled in the Monterey area, they brought with them a style of soft, white, creamy cheese, which may have later became known as Jack cheese. It is possible that the name derived from the "housejack," a vice-like contraption that was used to apply pressure to the cheese. But proud Monterey natives link the name to David Jacks, an entrepreneur who arrived in Monterey County in the late 1800s and started a dairy operation. Jacks' dairy produced a creamy white cheese, which he marketed as "Jacks' cheese." As the cheese became popular and was exported out of the county, the name was shortened to Jack cheese.

Hawaiian

Hula's Island Grill and Tiki Room (622 Lighthouse Ave., 831/655-4852, www.hulas tiki.com, dinner daily from 5 P.M., $20) is an island party near Cannery Row with great Hawaiian food and a tiki bar serving custom concoctions like the Hula's Hurricane (three rums infused with pineapple and vanilla and topped with tropical juices) and the Pink Bikini Martini (vodka infused with pineapple and watermelon). If you can think beyond the drinks and order dinner, pick your favorite fish and choose from a variety of preparations, such as Hula's pan-fried version with shiitake mushrooms, or blackened Cajun style with fresh mango salsa, or macadamia-encrusted with a mango papaya sauce. There's also island-style cioppino, pulled pork, burgers, steaks, wraps, and rice bowls—all served up in a festive, funky environment. Portions are large, so bring your appetite.

Indian

Ambrosia India Bistro (565 Abrego St., 831/641-0610, www.ambrosiaib.com, lunch daily 11:30 A.M.–2:30 P.M., dinner daily 5–10 P.M., $9–27) specializes in what they call "Indian Frontier Cuisine," a blend of authentic, regional flavors incorporating both curry and tandoori cooking methods. Chef Bhupender Singh creates Indian delicacies like kebabs of chicken, lamb, or fish, and serves them with fresh house-made Indian breads. The exotic spices and flavors will leave your tastebuds tingling. If you are new to Indian food, the buffet-style lunch allows you to sample a full range of offerings and, on the weekends, it's served with champagne. Diners can sit inside or in the outdoor courtyard garden.

Iranian

If you've never tried Iranian food, you can have your chance at the **Persian Grill** (675 Lighthouse Ave., 831/372-3720, www.persiangrill.com, lunch Wed.–Mon. 11:30 A.M.–2:30 P.M., dinner Wed.–Mon. 5:30–9:30 P.M., $12–18). The foods of ancient Persia (as Iran was called until the 1930s) include aromatic stews (khoresht) flavored with mint and other spices, stuffed fruit and vegetables (dolmeh) and roasted meats (kabob). Belly dancers perform on the first and third Saturday of every month.

Italian

There are several exceptional Italian fine-dining restaurants in Monterey, but for a casual Italian meal, and pizza in particular, **Gianni's Pizza** (725 Lighthouse Ave., 831/649-1500, Mon.– Thurs. 3:30–10 P.M., Fri.–Sun. 11 A.M.–10 P.M.,

$10–20) is the place. At dinner hour, the restaurant is likely to be packed with big families and local sports teams devouring large quantities of thick-crust pizza loaded with prodigious portions of cheese and toppings, and foot-long bread sticks dipped in ranch dressing. There's nothing gourmet about the place, and that's just fine with those who prefer their pizza on the hearty side.

Japanese

For Japanese food accompanied by a lovely ocean view and showy sleight of hand performed by your chef, head to **Sapporo Japanese Steakhouse** (3 Fisherman's Wharf #2, 831/333-1616, Mon.–Thurs. 11:30 A.M.–10 P.M., Fri.–Sat. 11:30 A.M.–10:30 P.M., Sun. 11:30 A.M.–10 P.M., $20). Lots of families come here because the kids are always entertained by the Benihana-style showmanship as the food is prepared over hot flames at your table. All the basics are here—steak, shrimp, chicken, rice, and vegetables. It's not haute cuisine, but it's fun. Sushi lovers also have plenty to choose from.

Mexican

◖ **Turtle Bay Taqueria** (431 Tyler St., 831/333-1500, www.turtlebay.tv, 11 A.M.–9 P.M., $9) is a sibling to the region's popular Fishwife restaurant, and serves fast, reasonably priced coastal Mexican fare, utilizing citrus-grilled meat and seafood served with a little Caribbean flare. Wraps, quesadillas, burritos, and tacos are made to order while diners watch. Ingredients are very fresh and usually local, which is why everything tastes so good. Meals are served in the colorful, beach house–style dining room, which is lined with 14-foot palm trees. There's another Turtle Bay in Seaside at 1301 Fremont Street, 831/899-1010.

Seafood

The Monterey Fish House (2114 Del Monte Ave., Seaside, 831/373-4647, lunch 11:30 A.M.–2:30 P.M., dinner 5–9:30 P.M., $15–25) dining experience usually starts with a jam-packed wait in the door. You'll be rubbing up against Seaside locals who know where to get the best in great seafood, served in generous portions at reasonable rates. After you are finally seated, the small dining room means you can keep on socializing with your neighbors. Fish House fans rave about the cioppino, blackened salmon, oak-grilled fish, and oysters. If you want to skip the wait, get here right when the restaurant opens.

The world-famous **Old Fisherman's Grotto** (39 Fisherman's Wharf, 831/375-4604, www.oldfishermansgrotto.com, daily 11 A.M.–10 P.M., $15–35) sits on Monterey's touristy waterfront and distinguishes itself from the crowd with great food and a family legacy dating from the 1950s. The restaurant serves a multitude of seafood entrées, steaks, pastas, and children's meals, so you will probably find yourself in a quandary, flipping through the multi-paged menu trying to decide. Fresh

---

SEAFOOD WATCH

Much of the work done by the Monterey Bay Aquarium is not necessarily visible to visitors. Since the mission of the aquarium is to "inspire conservation of the oceans," public education and scientific research are high priorities.

Particularly useful for seafood fans, and accessible via the aquarium's website (www.mbayaq.org), is its *Seafood Watch* guide, a regularly updated list designed to help us make enlightened choices about the fish and other seafood we eat at restaurants and purchase at stores. Separate guides are available for each region of the United States. On the aquarium's "avoid" list for the West Coast, for example, are various tunas (bluefin, albacore, bigeye, and yellowfin); Chilean sea bass; Atlantic cod; orange roughy; imported king crab; mahi mahi; Caribbean spiny lobster; farmed salmon; mid-Atlantic sea scallops; imported shrimp; and imported swordfish. Some of these fish are not only caught in an environmentally unfriendly manner, they may also contain high levels of mercury or other contaminants.

Fish lovers, take heart: there are plenty of good choices on the Aquarium's "Good Alternatives" and "Best Choices" lists, as well. Many types of fish that are caught in U.S. waters make the good or best lists: Pacific cod; king crab and snow crab from Alaska; Dungeness crab; Maine lobster; wild Pacific and Alaska salmon; Pacific sanddabs; squid; and U.S. farmed tilapia, shrimp, striped bass, clams, mussels, abalone, and oysters.

Consumer guidance in support of sustainable fisheries worldwide is also available as a wallet-sized card, which can easily be printed from the website, and is handed out at the aquarium and many local restaurants, including Passionfish and Fishwife in Pacific Grove, and Old Fisherman's Grotto and The Duck Club Grill in Monterey. A separate wallet card that lists only sushi choices is also available. If you have a Blackberry or other mobile device, you can simply log on to mobile.seafoodwatch.org, and you will automatically be directed to the most up-to-date seafood guide for your area.

Specific research initiatives sponsored by the Monterey Bay Aquarium include the Sea Otter Research and Conservation Program (SORAC) and the Tuna Research and Conservation Center (TRCC), the latter in conjunction with Stanford University's Hopkins Marine Station. The Monterey Bay Aquarium Research Institute (MBARI) at Moss Landing initiates dozens of bay-related projects each year, and is also a full research partner in the Monterey Bay National Marine Sanctuary's Research Program. More information on all of these organizations and their programs is available via the aquarium's website.

Dungeness crab is served year-round, and their famous Monterey-style clam chowder (a strictly guarded family recipe) is a must.

Named for tender squid, breaded and then sautéed in butter, **Abalonetti Seafood Trattoria** (57 Fisherman's Wharf, 831/373-1851, www.abalonettimonterey.com, daily 11 A.M.–9 P.M., $14–22) is best known for its calamari (abalonetti, if you will), which is prepared eight different ways, including barbecued. Plenty of other crowd-pleasing favorites are available, like salmon, Dungeness crab, fish-and-chips, and a few red meat items for the iron deficient. The antipasti bar is outstanding. Considering that it's right on the wharf, the restaurant is fairly inexpensive, and of course it offers that classic ocean/harbor view. A children's menu is available. Get a seat on the outside terrace on a sunny day, and you can enjoy your meal to the tune of barking sea lions.

It takes the better part of a day to visit the Monterey Bay Aquarium, and during that time you are likely to work up an appetite. Thanks to **The Portola** (866 Cannery Row, 831/648-4870, www.montereybayaquarium.org, lunch daily 11 A.M.–3 P.M., restaurant bar daily 11 A.M.–5:30 P.M., $10–15 plus admission to the aquarium) you don't have to leave the premises to fill your belly. The Portola has both a full-service restaurant and casual café/bar, so you can dine as you like depending on your time and inclination. The menu changes seasonally, but you can expect to find plenty of organic produce and seafood, such as line-caught Alaskan salmon, Monterey Bay calamari, and Pacific halibut. In addition, given its location within the aquarium, the Portola offers one of the best ocean views on Cannery Row.

Naturally enough, seafood is the predominant dinner theme along Cannery Row. The casually elegant **Chart House** (444 Cannery Row, 831/372-3362, www.chart-house.com, dinner daily 5–9:30 P.M., $25) brings its trademark nautical-themed decor to the Row. This Chart House serves the same cuisine that you'll find at waterfront Chart House restaurants all over California—seafood, steaks, prime rib, and a meal-in-itself salad bar—and it's predictably tasty and reasonably priced. Plus, there is always something happening right outside the window, whether it is kayakers paddling by, sea otters frolicking, or the sun sinking into the sea. The hot chocolate lava cake is a winner for dessert.

If you've been to the big island of Hawaii, you may have eaten at Kona's **The Fish Hopper,** and this is Monterey's version of the same restaurant (700 Cannery Row, 831/372-8543, www.fishhopper.com, daily 10:30 A.M.–10 P.M., $18–35). Both locations offer panoramic views of the Pacific Ocean, but sadly, the water is a wee bit colder in Monterey. Specialty cocktails are a big deal here—fruit daiquiris, mai tais, planters punch, and so on—and it's fun to sip one while watching the sun sink over the Pacific and sea otters playing in the water a few feet from your table. But the food is also notable; all of the Fish Hopper's seafood is harvested by sustainable methods that do not harm the environment. You won't find a lot of deep-fried fish on the menu, but for traditionalists, the ubiquitous clam chowder is available. Seafood pasta entrées play heavily, including the Ultimate Seafood Pasta, consisting of lobster meat, scallops, prawns, and Dungeness crab combined with a rich cream sauce and served over fresh spinach fettuccine.

FINE DINING
American
The relaxed, all-American ◖ **Montrio Bistro** (414 Calle Principal, 831/648-8880, www.montrio.com, dinner Sun.–Thurs. 5–10 P.M.,

Fri.–Sat. 5–11 P.M., $8–18), set in a one-time firehouse with brick-lined walls, is one of Monterey's favorite restaurants. Patrons might start their meal with fire-roasted artichokes, an eggplant terrine, or Dungeness crab cakes, then move on to grilled gulf prawns, lamb tenderloins, Moscovy duck confit, or Black Angus New York steak. Vegetarians can dig into the oven-roasted portobello mushroom over polenta and veggie ragout. In true bistro style, if you don't want a big meal, you can order from the "small bites" menu or try a salad or sandwich. Montrio also features exquisite desserts, a full bar, and an extensive wine list.

Lallapalooza (474 Alvarado St., 831/645-9036, www.lalla-palooza.com, dinner from 4 P.M., $15–25) is an upscale dinner house that serves 21 different martinis, including a few that are nonalcoholic. The double chocolate version is sure to insult the sensibilities of shaken-not-stirred purists, but it's served in an airy, lively atmosphere that is popular with the after-work crowd. Lallapalooza's cuisine is classically American—gourmet burgers, premium steaks, pastas, and grilled salmon—but there is enough on the two available menus (dinner and bar) that even salad eaters will be happy.

Contrary to its name, (**Tarpy's Roadhouse,** three miles off Highway 1 (on Hwy. 68 at Canyon del Rey, 831/647-1444, www.tarpys.com, daily 11:30 A.M.–10 P.M., $25–35), is not to be confused with some cheap-eats-and-beer joint. The point here is to reinterpret American classics with entrées like Dijon-crusted lamb loin, baby back ribs, and grilled vegetables with succotash. The menu usually includes some wild game choices, as well as a surprising amount of vegetarian entrées. It's a something-for-everyone kind of place. Plus, the setting can't be beat. Seven separate dining rooms are located in a

historic stone house on five beautifully landscaped acres.

At the Monterey Plaza Hotel is the renowned **Duck Club Grill** (400 Cannery Row, 831/646-1706, www.montereyplazahotel .com, daily breakfast 6:30–11 A.M., dinner 5:30–9:30 P.M., $28), which delivers outstanding Monterey Bay views and superb American regional cuisine. Wood-roasted specialties include oak-broiled steaks, Colorado lamb chops, and duck. This is the sort of restaurant where meat lovers are in their element, but since this is Monterey, you'll also find Dungeness crab cakes and other seafood entrées on the bill. Valet parking is complimentary—a real plus in this neighborhood.

You might think that a place called **The Whaling Station** (763 Wave St., 831/373-3778, www.pisto.com, dinner daily from 5 P.M., $25–50) would serve primarily seafood, but this John Pisto–owned restaurant is best known as the place to go for steak—and it is graded USDA prime, not choice. Television chef Pisto has a handful of restaurants in his Monterey-area food empire, but this is the only one where red meat is the star of the show. There are many different cuts to choose from, plus a wide range of salads, appetizers, and desserts, and yes, even a few fish entrées. In classic steakhouse style, many diners order the Caesar salad served tableside for two. After dinner, ask to see the house selection of premium cigars.

French

(**Fresh Cream** (99 Pacific St., 831/375-9798, www.freshcream.com, dinner daily 5:30–10 P.M., $25–35) is rarely found by casual Monterey visitors, but for people who live here, this is the place to dine for special occasions like anniversaries and birthdays. Fresh Cream is classy, it's French, and it manages to feel unpretentious while still providing an upscale dining experience. The menu blends classics like rack of lamb, filet mignon, lobster bisque, and escargots with more cutting-edge Monterey-style cuisine, such as plum-glazed prawns with Asian vegetables, and pan-seared ahi tuna with pineapple rum sauce. The location is a bit odd—the restaurant is upstairs in what looks like an office building—but once inside, the harbor views are divine. Fresh Cream has been pleasing diners since 1979 and has received numerous awards, including the AAA Four Diamond and *Wine Spectator* Award of Excellence. Come with high expectations; they will be met.

Another great choice for French food is **Bistro Moulin** (867 Wave St., 831/333-1200, www.bistromoulin.com, lunch Mon.–Sat. 11:30 A.M.–2 P.M., dinner Mon.–Sat. 5 8:30 P.M., $25), which looks so Parisian on the inside you'll expect the wait staff to speak French. All the standards are prepared well here—French onion soup, escargots, moules frites (steamed mussels and French fries), duck confit, boeuf Bourguignon, and chocolate mousse for dessert. The chef who is the talent behind this warm and charming restaurant spent 25 years at the award-winning Casanova in Carmel. There are only about 10 tables, so make sure you have reservations.

Italian

For a memorable Italian meal, consider **Cibo Ristorante Italiano** (301 Alvarado St., 831/649-8151, www.cibo.com, dinner daily 5–10 P.M., $15–20), which serves stylish Sicilian fare in an even more stylish dining room. Expect a fairly dressy crowd in this sculpture-and-painting-infused restaurant and bar, where live jazz is featured several nights a week. The menu includes plenty of gourmet-style pizzas

and pastas, plus grilled meats and fowl. The bay shrimp in pesto, vodka, and cream sauce is a house specialty, and the martinis come highly recommended. "Cibo" means food in Italian, and it's pronounced "chee-bo."

The question of where to eat on Fisherman's Wharf inevitably brings up the name **Café Fina** (48 Fisherman's Wharf, 831/372-5200, www.cafefina.com, lunch daily 11:30 A.M.–2:30 P.M., $17–29), a great choice for Italian-style seafood. In addition to myriad fish entrées, the café serves handmade pasta, raviolis stuffed with crab or smoked salmon, and seasonal organic homegrown vegetables from chef/owner's Dominic Mercurio's ranch. A wood-burning brick oven prepares excellent crisp-crust pizza, and for those not inclined toward the fruits of the sea, there are mesquite-grilled lamb chops, or "brick chicken" (marinated in rosemary and cooked under the weight of bricks). And of course, no matter what you order, there's always that compelling view of Monterey Bay from on top of the wharf.

Mediterranean

For an elegant evening of mixing it up with tapas-style small plates, **Esteban** (700 Munras Ave., 831/375-0176, www.estebanrestaurant.com, daily 11:30 A.M.–10 P.M., $10–20) provides a cool hangout in the Casa Munras Hotel. Start off with tender baby squid and Spanish chorizo. It's so good that next you'll be ordering pan-fried barramundi, crispy-skinned organic salmon, and slow-roasted organic beets. Since most of the "small plate" and "mini plate" dishes are under ten bucks, you can sample a lot of different flavors and still not break the bank. For dessert, don't miss the meringue-topped Meyer lemon tart or the Spanish fig cake. Order coffee and it's served in a mini–French press.

Practicalities

INFORMATION AND SERVICES

Tourist Information

The **Monterey Visitor Center** (Lake El Estero at the junction of Camino El Estero and Franklin, 831/657-6400) is staffed by the Monterey County Convention and Visitors Bureau and offers personal expertise as well as reams of flyers on just about everything in and around the region. From April to October, it's open Monday–Saturday 9 A.M.–6 P.M., Sunday 9 A.M.–5 P.M.; from November to March, Monday–Saturday 9 A.M.–5 P.M., Sunday 10 A.M.–4 P.M. For additional area information, including a current visitor guide, call 877/666-8373 or go to www.montereyinfo.org. You can download the visitor guide directly from the website, or order it and have it mailed to you.

Media and Communications

The **Monterey County Herald** (www.montereyherald.com) is the mainline community news source. For an alternative view of things, pick up the free **Monterey County Weekly** (www.montereycountyweekly.com), which also offers entertainment (including clubs) and events information. Monterey's main **post office** (565 Hartnell St., 831/372-4063) is open Monday–Friday 8:30 A.M.–5 P.M. and Saturday 10 A.M.–2 P.M.

Emergency Services

The **Community Hospital of the Monterey Peninsula** (23625 Holman Hwy./Hwy. 68, Monterey, 831/624-5311, www.chomp.org) is just north of the junction of Highway 1 and Highway 68. The main office of the **Monterey Police Department** (351 Madison St., 831/646-3914 or 911) is open 24 hours daily.

GETTING THERE AND AROUND

Air

Monterey Peninsula Airport (831/648-7000, www.montereyairport.com) provides service to and from San Francisco, Los Angeles, Phoenix, Denver, Las Vegas, Long Beach, Ontario, and San Diego. United Airlines, Allegiant, American Eagle, and American West service this airport. Taxi service is available through Central Coast Taxi (831/626-3333). Limousine service is available through Arrow Luxury Transportation Company (831/646-3175). Rental cars are available at the airport through the following companies: Alamo (800/327-9633, www.alamo.com), Avis (800/831-2847, www.avis.com), Budget (800/527-0700, www.budget.com), Enterprise (800/736-8222, www.enterprise.com), Hertz (800/654-3131, www.hertz.com, and National (800/227-7368, www.nationalcar.com).

A much larger airport is located about 90 minutes from Monterey in San Jose, CA. **San Jose International Airport** (408/501-7600, www.sjc.org) is served by all major U.S. airlines and also provides flights to and from Mexico. The Monterey-Salinas Airbus (831/373-7777, www.montereyairbus.com) provides 14 trips daily to the San Jose and San Francisco international airports from downtown Monterey ($30–40 per person one-way).

Train

Amtrak's Coast Starlight train stops in Salinas each day on its route between Seattle and Los Angeles. Free bus service is provided from Salinas to downtown Monterey, a 30-minute ride. Otherwise, the closest you can get to Monterey by Amtrak train is San Jose or

Merced. From there, you would need to transfer to a motor coach (bus) for the last 90–100 miles to Monterey. An Amtrak motor coach travels from Merced to Monterey; a Monterey-Salinas Transit bus travels from San Jose to Monterey. The Monterey Transit Plaza is located at Jules Simoneau Plaza at the intersection of Munras Avenue, Pearl Street, and Tyler Street near the southern end of Alvarado Street in downtown Monterey. Tickets may be purchased from an Amtrak travel agent, over the telephone from Amtrak at 800/872-7245 or on the web at www.amtrak.com.

Bus

Greyhound Bus service (800/231-2222, www.greyhound.com) is not available in Monterey but it is available in nearby Salinas, a half hour away. Greyhound also serves nearby Santa Cruz.

To get around on public buses otherwise, **Monterey-Salinas Transit** (831/899-2555 or 888/678-2871, www.mst.org) serves the entire area (275 square miles of Monterey County and southern Santa Cruz County), including Pacific Grove, Carmel, and Carmel Valley, from Watsonville south to Salinas. An express bus (#55) runs daily to and from San Jose. Local buses can get you just about anywhere, but some run sporadically. Pick up the free Rider's Guide schedule at the downtown **Transit Plaza** (where most buses stop and where Alvarado, Munras, Pearl, and Tyler Sts. converge). The standard single-trip fare (one zone) is $2; exact change required; free transfers. Some longer routes traverse multiple zones and cost more. Seniors, the disabled, and children can ride for $1 with the transit system's courtesy card. Children under age five ride free. A regular adult day pass costs $4.50, and a super day pass (valid on all routes and all zones) is $9; seniors and students pay half price.

Car

Direct driving access to Monterey is provided from San Jose and San Francisco via Highway 156 off Highway 101. Access from Los Angeles is easiest via Highway 101 and Highway 68. The Coast Highway, or Highway 1, runs from San Francisco to Los Angeles and also provides access to Monterey via Highway 68.

Getting around Monterey by car in the summer months can be a problem; even finding streets is confusing due to missing signs, complex intersections and traffic signals, and one way routes. Local traffic jams can be horrendous. So save yourself some headaches and avail yourself of local public transportation. Park your car at the 12-hour meters or in the pay lots near Fisherman's Wharf, and then walk (or bike) elsewhere, or take the shuttle or bus.

Trolley

Once parked, from Memorial Day through Labor Day and other major holidays throughout the year, you can ride Monterey-Salinas Transit's **MST Trolley** (831/899-2555 or 888/678-2871, www.mst.org), a free rubber-tired trolley system connecting the Tin Cannery shopping center (at the edge of Pacific Grove), the Monterey Bay Aquarium, Cannery Row, Fisherman's Wharf, and the town's historic downtown adobes with the downtown conference center, nearby motels and hotels, and parking garages. The free trolleys depart every 10–12 minutes weekdays 10 A.M.–7 P.M. and weekends 10 A.M.–8 P.M. A separate MST trolley route serves adjacent Pacific Grove Tuesday–Saturday 10 A.M.–7 P.M.

Tours

All of the must-do tours in Monterey take place

on Monterey Bay. But if you would rather keep your feet on dry land, there are several good tour choices available.

Ag Venture Tours in Monterey (831/761-8463, www.agventuretours.com) specializes in winery tours in Monterey, Carmel Valley, Salinas Valley, and the Santa Cruz Mountains. A typical daylong tour includes tasting at three different wineries, a vineyard walk, and a picnic lunch ($75–120 per person). Half-day tours cost $50–80 per person. Included in the tour price is pickup and return at your residence or hotel.

For a spooky adventure, take a tour on the **Ghost Trolley** (527 Hartnell St., 831/624-1700, www.toursmonterey.com, $28 adults, $9 children 12 and under). This 90-minute tour begins at one of Monterey's most notoriously haunted buildings, the Stokes Adobe, then travels the Path of History visiting locations of recent and historical ghost sightings. The Ghost Trolley is a close cousin to the Wine Trolley (in fact it's the exact same vehicle), which travels daily from Portola Plaza to the vineyards of Carmel Valley for a day of wine tasting ($49 per person for five-hour tour and tastings). Tours leave every day at 11 A.M., but advance reservations are required.

Film buffs shouldn't miss the three-hour tour with **Monterey Movie Tours** (2 Serrano Way, 831/372-6278 or 800/343-6437, www.montereymovietours.com). Passengers travel in a 32-seat motorcoach as the tour travels past famous movie locations throughout Monterey, Pacific Grove, and Carmel, including the 17-Mile Drive. The bus is equipped with overhead video screens and personal headsets so you can watch and listen to actual scenes from classic movies as the bus rolls past the places where they were filmed.

Pacific Grove

Between Carmel and Monterey lies peaceful Pacific Grove, where alcohol has been legal only since the 1960s, and the annual monarch butterfly migration is big news. Many tourists glimpse Pacific Grove only as they enter the gates of the world-famous 17-Mile Drive, but the small town is worth a closer look, with a plethora of colorful Victorians converted to bed-and-breakfasts and antique shops, a string of bucolic beachfront parks, an excellent natural history museum, and a historic lighthouse that stands sentry over Asilomar State Beach.

Pacific Grove began in 1875 as a prim, proper tent city founded by Methodists who, Robert Louis Stevenson observed, "come to enjoy a life of teetotalism, religion, and flirtation." No boozing, waltzing, zither playing, or reading Sunday newspapers was allowed. In the early 1900s, the dedicated inebriate John Steinbeck lived here, but he had to leave town to get drunk. Pacific Grove was the last dry town in California; only since 1969 has alcohol been legal. The first Chautauqua in the western states was held here—bringing "moral attractions" to heathen Californians—and the hall where the summer meeting tents were stored still stands at 16th and Central Avenues. For more information about Pacific Grove's history, and/or to get a good look at some of its most impressive gingerbread-trimmed Victorian buildings, stop in at the Chamber of Commerce office downtown at Forest and Central Avenues and pick up a brochure for the town's historic walking tour.

The city limits of Pacific Grove extend from

PACIFIC GROVE

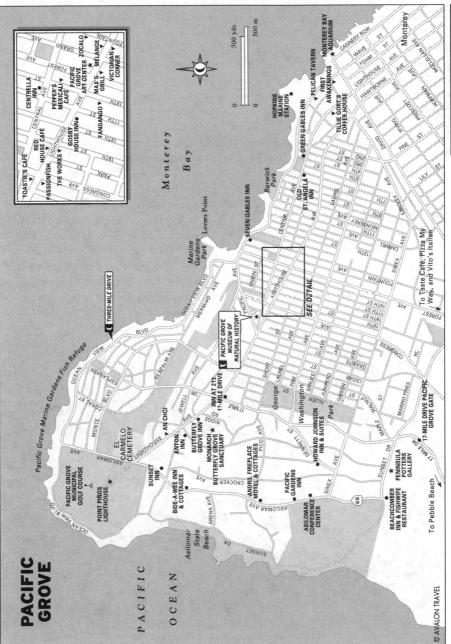

500 yds

500 m

MONTEREY

Monterey

CANNERY ROW

MONTEREY BAY AQUARIUM

WAVE ST

FOAM AVE

LIGHTHOUSE AVE

HAWTHORNE AVE

PELICAN TAVERN

FIRST AWAKENINGS

MONTEREY AVE

MCCLELLAN AVE

HOFFMAN AVE

PRESCOTT

IRVING AVE

PINE ST

LILY

HOPKINS MARINE STATION

TILLIE GORT'S COFFEE HOUSE

GREEN GABLES INN

SEVEN GABLES INN

Berwick Park

OLD ST. ANGELA INN

4TH ST

3RD ST

2ND ST

5TH ST

6TH ST

7TH ST

9TH ST

11TH ST

13TH ST

LAUREL AVE

CENTRAL AVE

MONTEREY AVE

CARMEL AVE

SINEX AVE

To Taste Café, Pizza My Way, and Vito's Italian

LIGHTHOUSE

SEE DETAIL

UNION ST

FOUNTAIN

17TH ST

18TH ST

19TH ST

FOREST

Monterey Bay

Marine Gardens Park

Lover's Point

OCEAN VIEW BLVD

MERMAID AVE

PACIFIC GROVE MUSEUM OF NATURAL HISTORY

SHORT ST

LAUREL AVE

PINE AVE

SPRUCE AVE

ALDER ST

JUNIPERO AVE

GRANITE ST

CONGRESS

CEDAR ST

GIBSON AVE

WALNUT ST

MARINO PINES

17-MILE DRIVE PACIFIC GROVE GATE

THREE-MILE DRIVE

PACIFIC

OCEAN

Pacific Grove Marine Gardens Fish Refuge

OCEAN VIEW BLVD

ESPLANADE

SEA PALM AVE

JEWELL AVE

17 MILE DRIVE

George

Washington Park

MARBLE ST

CORAL ST

MONTE AVE

LIGHTHOUSE AVE

ASILOMAR AVE

EL CARMELO CEMETERY

AN CHOI

RIDGE RD

ANTON INN

BUTTERFLY INN

MONARCH

BUTTERFLY GROVE INN

BUTTERFLY GROVE SANCTUARY

INN AT 213 17-MILE DRIVE

CROCKER AVE

PICO AVE

DENNETT ST

HOWARD JOHNSON INN & SUITES

PACIFIC GARDENS INN

SINEX AVE

SUNSET DR

PENINSULA POTTERS GALLERY

17 MILE DR

To Pebble Beach

PACIFIC GROVE MUNICIPAL GOLF COURSE

POINT PIÑOS LIGHTHOUSE

SUNSET INN

BIDE-A-WEE INN & COTTAGES

ARENA AVE

ANDRIL FIREPLACE MOTEL & COTTAGES

ASILOMAR AVE

ASILOMAR CONFERENCE CENTER

BEACHCOMBER INN & FISHWIFE RESTAURANT

68

Asilomar State Beach

SUNSET DR

© AVALON TRAVEL

DETAIL INSET (upper left)

GRAND AVE

FOUNTAIN AVE

FOREST AVE

ZOCALO

PACIFIC GROVE ART CENTER

MÉLANGE

MAX'S GRILL

VICTORIAN CORNER

CENTRELLA INN

CENTRAL AVE

PEPPER'S MEXICALI CAFÉ

FANDANGO

16TH ST

17TH ST

18TH ST

19TH ST

RED HOUSE CAFÉ

GOSBY HOUSE INN

LIGHTHOUSE AVE

TOASTIE'S CAFÉ

PASSIONFISH

THE WORKS

PARK ST

CONGRESS AVE

the Monterey Bay Aquarium to the gate of the 17-Mile Drive. Nicknamed "Butterfly City U.S.A." in honor of migrating monarchs who spend the winter here, Pacific Grove dazzles with its rocky shoreline, abundant parks, more than 1,200 colorful Victorians and historic homes, and well-deserved community pride. Both *Life* and *Time* magazines have called Pacific Grove "the most romantic city in the U.S.," and a view of the sunset from Lover's Point may convince you that it's true.

SIGHTS
◖ Three-Mile Drive

From Pacific Grove, you could embark on the 17-Mile Drive, which tours the homes of the rich and famous in adjacent Pebble Beach. But less crowded and hoity-toity, and just as spectacular, is a drive (or better yet, a walk or bike ride) along Pacific Grove's Ocean View Boulevard, which becomes Sunset Boulevard

in Asilomar. Pacific Grove is one of the few cities in California that owns its own beaches and shores, all dedicated to public use. Along Ocean View Boulevard are a string of small public parks and large parking pullouts, all of which offer spectacular sunsets, crashing surf, craggy shorelines, rich tidepools, flower-carpeted cliffs, and a wealth of possible wild-life sightings: whales, dolphins, sea otters, sea lions, seals, and shorebirds. Have a picnic at enchanting **Lover's Point** (near 17th St.), a granite-lined headland backed by manicured lawns and punctuated by a couple of interesting sculptures—one depicting a butterfly and another a child pointing to the sea. Wade or swim at the relatively safe beach at **Perkins Point.** Stop anywhere you please and watch sea lions poke their heads out of the water, pelicans dive into the waves, kayakers paddle by and wave, and sea otters float by on their backs, munching on shellfish.

Three generations enjoy a seat on a bench by the sea along Pacific Grove's Three-Mile Drive.

© ANN MARIE BROWN

The 17-Mile Drive

You have to pay a $9 fee to cruise the 17-Mile Drive (800/654-9300, www.pebblebeach .com), but most agree that it's worth it for the chance to ogle Pebble Beach's world-famous golf courses, the palatial homes of the rich and famous, and nearly nonstop views of the Monterey coast framed by windswept cypress trees. The 17-Mile Drive is open for touring from dawn to dusk year-round; motorcycles are not permitted, but bicyclists get in for free. Five gates access the drive, including the Pacific Grove gate at Highway 68/Sunset Drive just east of Asilomar. (You can also enter the drive at the junction of Hwy. 68 and Hwy. 1, or at the Carmel gate off Ocean Ave. in Carmel.) The gate attendant takes your money and hands you a map of the route, which travels through evergreen Del Monte Forest and skirts dozens of ritzy homes, including the Byzantine castle of the banking/railroading Crocker family. (The estate's private beach is heated with underground pipes.)

More natural highlights include **Shepherd's Knoll,** which offers a great panoramic view of both Monterey Bay and the Santa Cruz Mountains; and **Point Joe,** a treacherous, turbulent convergence of conflicting ocean currents that is wet and wild even on calm days. "Joe" has been commonly mistaken by mariners as the entrance to Monterey Bay, so countless ships have gone down on these rocks. Many tourists have their picture taken with the centuries-old **Lone Cypress** tree, the unofficial botanical mascot of the 17-Mile Drive and probably the world's only copyrighted tree, which stands sentinel on a rocky promontory. **Fanshell Beach** is a secluded spot and perfect for picnics, but swimming can be dangerous. If you need to pick up picnic supplies, head to the Pebble Beach Market adjacent to The

The centuries-old "Lone Cypress" on the 17-Mile Drive stands sentinel above the crashing Pacific.

© DARREN MURTHA

Lodge at Pebble Beach (1700 17-Mile Drive). If you make only short stops, plan on about three hours to cruise the 17-Mile Drive.

Point Piños Lighthouse

Built of local granite in 1855 and rebuilt in 1906, Point Piños is the oldest continuously operating lighthouse on the Pacific coast, listed on the National Register of Historic Places. The beacon here and the mournful foghorn have been warning seagoing vessels away from the northernmost tip of the Monterey Peninsula since February 1, 1855. The original French third-order Fresnel lenses and prisms are still in use, although the lighthouse is now powered by electricity and a 1,000-watt lamp instead of whale oil. The light is located a mere 89 feet above sea level, but when amplified by the lenses and prisms, it can produce

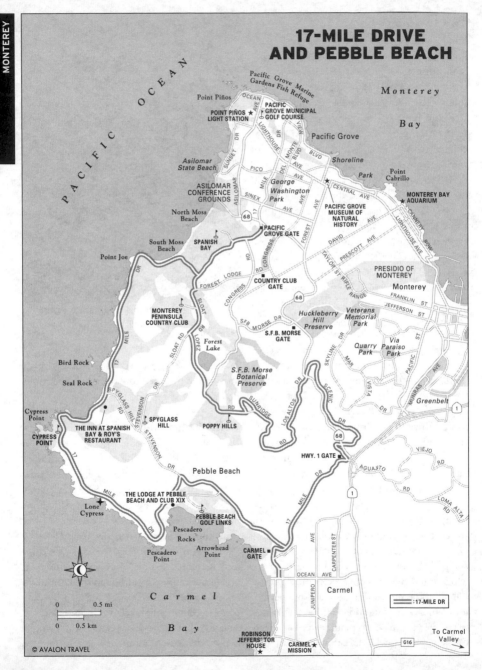

17-MILE DRIVE
AND PEBBLE BEACH

Monterey

Bay

PACIFIC   OCEAN

Pacific Grove Marine
Gardens Fish Refuge

Point Piños

**POINT PIÑOS
LIGHT STATION** ★

**PACIFIC
GROVE MUNICIPAL
GOLF COURSE**

Pacific Grove

Shoreline

Park

Point
Cabrillo

**MONTEREY BAY
AQUARIUM** ★

*Asilomar
State Beach*

**ASILOMAR
CONFERENCE
GROUNDS**

George
Washington
Park

**PACIFIC GROVE
MUSEUM OF
NATURAL
HISTORY** ★

North Moss
Beach

South Moss
Beach

**SPANISH
BAY**

**PACIFIC
GROVE GATE**

Point Joe

**COUNTRY CLUB
GATE**

**PRESIDIO OF
MONTEREY**

Monterey

**MONTEREY
PENINSULA
COUNTRY CLUB**

Forest
Lake

*Huckleberry
Hill
Preserve*

*Veterans
Memorial
Park*

**S.F.B. MORSE
GATE**

*Quarry
Park*

*Via
Paraiso
Park*

*S.F.B. Morse
Botanical
Preserve*

Bird Rock

Seal Rock

**SPYGLASS
HILL**

POPPY HILLS

Greenbelt

Cypress
Point

**CYPRESS
POINT**

**THE INN AT SPANISH
BAY & ROY'S
RESTAURANT**

VIEJO

HWY. 1 GATE ■

AGUAJITO

Pebble Beach

LOMA ALTA

Lone
Cypress

**THE LODGE AT PEBBLE
BEACH AND CLUB XIX**

**PEBBLE BEACH
GOLF LINKS**

Pescadero
Rocks

Pescadero
Point

Arrowhead
Point

**CARMEL
GATE** ■

Carmel

Carmel

Bay

0   0.5 mi

0   0.5 km

**ROBINSON
JEFFERS' TOR
HOUSE** ★

**CARMEL
MISSION** ★

**To Carmel
Valley**

═══ :17-MILE DR

© AVALON TRAVEL

© ANN MARIE BROWN

The Point Piños Lighthouse stands guard over Asilomar State Beach and the rugged northern tip of the Monterey Peninsula.

© ANN MARIE BROWN

From October to February, a visit to the Monarch Butterfly Grove Sanctuary is a highlight of a trip to Pacific Grove.

a 50,000 candlepower beam visible up to 15 miles distant.

Robert Louis Stevenson wrote of visiting lightkeeper Allen Luce in 1879, and remarked on Luce's sociability, piano playing, ship models, and oil paintings. The most famous lightkeeper was Mrs. Emily Fish, who served from 1893 to 1914. She was called the "Socialite Keeper" due to her love of entertaining guests at the lighthouse. Visitors today can tour the lighthouse, which has a small visitor center/museum and a few rooms decorated in period furniture. **Doc's Great Tidepool,** yet another Steinbeck-era footnote, lies near the foot of the lighthouse. Point Piños Lighthouse (831/648-5716, www.pgmuseum.org, Thurs.– Mon. 1–4 P.M., $2) and the **U.S. Coast Guard Museum** inside are located two blocks north of Lighthouse Avenue on Asilomar Boulevard.

Monarch Butterfly Grove Sanctuary

From October to February, the monarchs reign over Pacific Grove, much to the delight of residents and visitors. You may see these festive-looking orange-and-black butterflies flitting about anywhere there are flower-filled gardens, but to see them in their greatest numbers, head to the eucalyptus grove on Ridge Road off Lighthouse Avenue, about a mile from downtown Pacific Grove. On cool days, the butterflies cluster in large masses in the trees to conserve their body heat. They look like bunches of dead leaves. As soon as the temperature gets above 55 degrees and the sun warms their bodies, the butterflies start to move about, seeking out nectar. They always return to the grove as the shadows fall in the late afternoon. These hardy insects will spend the winter in this mild coastal climate, then head north and east in the early spring to hunt for milkweed plants on which to lay their eggs. The grove is open from dawn till dusk and admission is free. A walk of about 100 feet will bring you to the largest concentration of butterflies. For more information on the butterfly grove, contact the Pacific Grove Museum of Natural History (165 Forest Ave., 831/648-5716, www.pgmuseum.org, Tues.–Sat. 10 A.M.–5 P.M.).

❮ Pacific Grove Museum of Natural History

Pacific Grove's Museum of Natural History (165 Forest Ave., 831/648-5716, www.pg museum.org, Tues.–Sat. 10 A.M.–5 P.M., free admission) showcases local wonders of nature, including sea otters, seabirds (a huge collection with more than 400 life-mounted specimens),

rare insects, and native plants. This is a great place to learn all about the rare California condor. If you have never seen one of these gigantic birds with their nine-foot wing spans, the photos of the Big Sur condors will amaze you. A fine array of Native American artifacts, about half of which are from Monterey County tribes, is also on display, as well as a huge relief map of Monterey Bay. Youngsters will make a beeline for *Sandy,* the gray whale sculpture right out front. If you aren't visiting Pacific Grove during the October–February monarch butterfly season and can't see the real thing, be sure to watch the video and check out the exhibit on these beautiful lepidoptera.

Asilomar

The Young Women's Christian Association's national board of directors coined the Spanish-sounding nonword "Asilomar" from the Greek

Asilomar State Beach is ideal for long walks and beachcombing.

© ANN MARIE BROWN

asilo (refuge) and the Spanish *mar* (sea) when they established Asilomar as a YWCA retreat in 1913. Many of Asilomar's buildings were designed by architect Julia Morgan (best known for Hearst's San Simeon estate) and are now historical landmarks. Today Asilomar is a non-profit unit of the California state park system and serves primarily as a conference center, offering meeting rooms and accommodations for large groups. But the general public can also stay here at the **Asilomar Conference Center** (800 Asilomar Blvd., 831/372-8016 or 831/642-4242, www.asilomarcenter.com, $169 199), and even better, can enjoy the adjacent **Asilomar State Beach** off Sunset Drive (parking free).

RECREATION
Beaches
Asilomar State Beach (free parking along Sunset Dr.) is well loved by surfers and is a great place for tidepool exploring, beachcombing, flying kites, and building sand castles, with long stretches of soft white sand punctuated by shifting sand dunes, wind-sculpted forests, and spectacular sunsets. Wooden boardwalks trace paths over the coastal dunes while protecting the fragile dune vegetation. You can walk right onto the gated enclave of Pebble Beach from Asilomar; a boardwalk connects the beach with the 17-Mile Drive and The Links at Spanish Bay golf course.

Lover's Point Beach Park (Ocean View Blvd. near 17th St., www.ci.pg.ca.us) is home to divers, kayakers, surfers, volleyball players, and sightseers. This 4.4-acre community park has a large lawn, beach volleyball court, children's swimming pool, concrete pier, and snack bar. Unlike at Asilomar, there isn't much sand at this beach park; however, there are rocky outcrops and tidepool-lined coves that beg

One of the many public parks along the Three-Mile Drive or Ocean View Boulevard is seaside Lover's Point.

to be photographed. Experienced divers and snorkelers brave the cold water here, as the underwater terrain has prolific kelp forests and marine life. Snorkel and wetsuit rentals are available at the beach in the summer months. Lover's Point's scenic backdrop of crashing surf and wind-sculpted Monterey pines makes it a popular spot for weddings.

Biking
The northern end of the **Monterey Peninsula Recreation Trail** winds along the shoreline in Pacific Grove. The official northern terminus of the trail is Lover's Point, but many cyclists choose to continue riding along the bike lane that follows the Asilomar coastline and then enters the gates of the 17-Mile Drive. Bicyclists do not have to pay a fee to ride the 17-Mile Drive, but unlike pedaling along the mellow

MONTEREY

recreation trail, riding the 17-Mile Drive is an up-and-down affair, with a few steep sections providing moderate aerobic challenges. Rent a bike at **Adventures by the Sea** (299 Cannery Row, 831/648-7236, www.adventuresbythesea .com, $7 per hour, $20 half-day, $25 all day).

Kayaking

In the summer months, kayaks can be rented from **Adventures by the Sea** (www.adventures bythesea.com, 9 A.M.–5 P.M., $30 per person for single or double kayaks) at Lover's Point, located on the sand below the volleyball courts. Splash paddling suits or wetsuits are provided with all rentals, plus dry bags so you can keep your camera and other personal belongings dry. Guided 2.5-hour tours are also available (regularly scheduled at 10 A.M. and 2 P.M. daily in summer, $50 per person). From November–April, contact Adventures by the Sea's main shop (299 Cannery Row, 831/273-1807 or

831/648-7236, www.adventuresbythesea.com) for kayak tours and rentals.

ENTERTAINMENT AND SHOPPING
Performing Arts

The sidewalks roll up early in Pacific Grove, but if you're looking for something to do past sunset, head to **Lighthouse Cinema** (525 Lighthouse Ave., 831/643-1333, www.sr entertainmentgrp.com) to catch a first-run movie on one of four screens. Otherwise, you might get lucky and find some culture happening at the **Pacific Grove Performing Arts Center** (835 Forest Ave., 831/241-2771, http://performingartscenterpg.org), a 674-seat venue which occasionally hosts the local Ensemble Monterey Chamber Orchestra (www .ensemblemontery.org) and Lovers Point Jazz Production (www.loverspointjazz.com). There are sometimes free exhibits, concerts, poetry

Visitors can rent kayaks at Lover's Point in Pacific Grove and paddle alongside the sea otters.

© DARREN MURTHA

readings, and lectures at the **Pacific Grove Art Center** (568 Lighthouse Ave., 831/375-2208, www.pgartcenter.org).

A more certain bet for live acoustic music, poetry readings, or book signings is **The Works** (667 Lighthouse Ave., 831/372-2242, www .theworkspg.com, Mon.–Sat. 7 A.M.–6 P.M., Sun. 8 A.M.–5 P.M.), a combination bookstore/ coffeehouse that occasionally hosts evening programs.

Festivals and Events

In Pacific Grove, a handful of hometown-style events happen year-round. The renowned Pacific Grove **Wildflower Show,** an exhibit of more than 600 native species in bloom (150 outdoors) at the Pacific Grove Museum of Natural History (165 Forest Ave., 831/648-5716, www.pgmuseum.org) is held the third week in April.

In March or April, the **Good Old Days** (831/373-3304, www.pacificgrove.org) celebration is touted as Monterey County's largest arts and crafts show; more than 250 vendors make their wares available, and some 50,000 visitors come to meander among the aisles of booths. Four stages host live music over the course of the weekend. Highlights of the festival include a parade and police motorcycle demonstration and competitions.

In late July, come for the annual **Feast of Lanterns** (www.feast-of-lanterns.org), a traditional boat parade and fireworks ceremony that began when Chinese fishermen lived at China Point (their village was torched in 1906). For many years, the event was celebrated as the ceremonial end to Pacific Grove's Chautauqua Assembly with a lantern parade to the beach and fireworks over the bay. Today, there are street dances, flag ceremonies, children's activities, and sand castle contests. High school girls wearing colorful Chinese garb are selected to reign over the festival as the Royal Court, and they receive scholarships for their participation.

Pacific Grove's biggest party comes in November with **Monarch Madness.** This native, naturalistic, and noncommercial community bash heralds the return of the migrating monarchs and includes the Butterfly Parade, carnival, and bazaar, all to benefit the PTA. Not coincidentally, from October to February, the most popular destination in town is the Monarch Butterfly Grove Sanctuary (Pacific Grove Museum of Natural History, 165 Forest Ave., 831/648-5716, www.pgmuseum.org, Tues.–Sat. 10 A.M.–5 P.M., free admission).

Shopping

Pacific Grove boasts more than 50 local art galleries, enough to keep any art fan busy. The most famous of these is the **Thomas Kinkade National Archive** (361 Lighthouse Ave., 831/655-5520, www.kinkadegalleries.com, daily 10 A.M.–5 P.M.), featuring strangely mystical fairy-tale-style paintings from the self-proclaimed "Painter of Light." Even if you think Kincade's paintings are New Age schlock, it's worth a trip just to see the mansion in which the gallery is set. The 1886 Victorian was built of clear-heart redwood in a Moorish style, rather than the "gingerbread" mode of so many buildings of the same era. The mansion and its gardens are open for visitors to explore.

Peninsula Potters Gallery (2078 Sunset Dr., 831/372-8867, www.penpots.com, Tues.–Sun. 11 A.M.–4 P.M.) is the place to appreciate handmade stoneware and porcelain pottery in traditional and contemporary styles. At the **Artisana Gallery** (309 Forest Ave., 831/655-9775, Tues.–Sun. 10 A.M.–4 P.M.), shoppers can find unique handmade jewelry, fine art by California artisans, statuary, organic candles, lamps, incense, music, and textiles.

Also worth a stop is the excellent **Pacific Grove Art Center** (568 Lighthouse Ave., 831/375-2208, www.pgartcenter.org, Wed.–Sat. noon–5 P.M. and Sun. 1–4 P.M.), featuring continually changing exhibits of contemporary California artists.

ACCOMMODATIONS

To maintain its "hometown America" aura, Pacific Grove has limited its motel development, and in general its lodgings tend to be on the pricier side. One look at the town's spectacular coastal scenery and you'll understand why. Bed-and-breakfast inns are popular; the town has a larger concentration of these inns than anywhere else south of San Francisco and north of Los Angeles.

Hotels and Inns

$100-150

Guests enjoy all the modern amenities at the **Howard Johnson Inn and Suites** (660 Dennett St., 831/373-8777 or 800/221-9323, www.montereyhojo.net, $115–165), from free high-speed Internet service to an extended continental breakfast and morning newspaper. All rooms are equipped with televisions with DVD players, refrigerators, and microwaves, but the big selling point here is that you can walk to Asilomar Beach. If you are traveling with your family, the hotel has several suites available that are large enough for four people.

The **Beachcomber Inn** (1996 Sunset Dr., 831/373-4769 or 800/634-4769, www.montereypeninsulainnns.com, $125–165) is a value-priced, older-style seaside motel, perfect for families or couples who aren't looking to stay at the poshest hotel in town. Sure, the decor is dated, but budget-minded travelers aren't going

to quibble about it, especially when off-season rates are as low as $100. The beach is a short walk away and the popular Fishwife restaurant (1996-1/2 Sunset Dr., 831/375-7107, www.fishwife.com, daily 11 A.M.–9 P.M., $10–20) is right next door. The owners have bikes available for guests to borrow (yes, they are free) and provide a generous continental breakfast.

$150-250

Sunset Inn (133 Asilomar Blvd., 831/375-3529, www.gosunsetinn.com, $175–245) is a 21-room boutique hotel with wood floors, modern decor, plush beds, flat-screen televisions, and a great location in a quiet neighborhood near Asilomar State Beach (the sand is within easy walking distance) and Pacific Grove's golf course. A few rooms come equipped with fireplaces and jetted tubs. Complimentary high-speed Internet access and a very basic continental breakfast round out the amenities.

A stone's throw away are the 1930s-style cottages at **Bide-a-Wee Inn & Cottages** (221 Asilomar Blvd., 831/372-2330, www.bideawee inn.com, $199–249). This pet-friendly lodging is a favorite of dogs and their people, who enjoy the fact that it is only a three-minute walk to the ocean and/or the Point Piños Lighthouse. Some of the cottages have kitchenettes and/or fireplaces. If you like peace and quiet on your vacation, you'll love this place. The nearby **Andril Fireplace Motel & Cottages** (569 Asilomar Blvd., 831/375-0994, www.andrilcottages.com, $210–270) is a similar property, offering cottages and rooms in a wide range of sizes and configurations. Most cottages have full kitchens and private decks; some have wood-burning fireplaces. As at Bide-a-Wee, pets are welcome here.

The state-owned **Asilomar Conference Center** (800 Asilomar Blvd., 831/372-8016 or 831/642-4242, www.asilomarcenter.com,

$169–199) enjoys an incredible 60-acre setting on the Pacific Ocean, complete with swimming pool, volleyball nets, horseshoe pits, and miles of beaches to stroll. When it's not completely booked with businesspeople, conferences, and other groups, the center is a reasonably priced choice for leisure travelers. Accommodations include 313 rooms located in 30 cottage-style buildings sprinkled around the large property; some units have fireplaces. All are on the rustic side and blissfully free of telephones or televisions. From the deer roaming the property to the ease of a dawn run on the beach, everything about a stay here is peaceful and relaxing. Rates include a full country breakfast in the Crocker Dining Hall.

If you're visiting Pacific Grove to see the monarch butterflies, the **Butterfly Grove Inn** (1073 Lighthouse Ave., 831/373-4921 or 800/337-9244, www.butterflygroveinn.com, $199–249) is perfectly situated right next to the butterfly grove. In fact, those orange-and-black winged beauties are likely to be flying around the door of your motel room. The inn is just fine but unremarkable in every other way, offering the typical amenities of the average Best Western. Many rooms are set up with an extra bed or a futon, making this is good choice for families. Rates drop as low as $99 in the winter season.

Bed-and-Breakfasts
$100-150
The **Anton Inn** (1095 Lighthouse Ave., 888/242-6866, www.antoninn.com, $135–270) provides a surprisingly affordable B&B stay in Pacific Grove, complete with all the services and amenities that you would hope for—evening wine and hors doeuvres, a generous breakfast, and gracious service. Expect a few unique charms, like electric fireplaces in each room and original art by local artists on the walls. The inn is close to everything in downtown Pacific Grove and only two blocks from the beach.

$150-250
Near Asilomar and hidden in the pines is the **Pacific Gardens Inn** (701 Asilomar Blvd., 831/646-9414 or 800/262-1566, www.pacific gardensinn.com, $169–239), where 28 contemporary rooms feature wood-burning fireplaces, refrigerators, TVs, phones, and even popcorn poppers and coffeemakers. Suites feature full kitchens and living rooms. A complimentary continental breakfast and evening wine and cheese are offered. This is a B&B stay at a motel price, and unlike many B&Bs, this is not just a couples place. Families will feel welcome here, too.

A national historic landmark, the **Centrella Inn** (612 Central Ave., 831/372-3372 or 800/233-3372, www.centrellainn.com, $175–275) offers 26 elegant rooms and suites, including attic suites, five private cottages with fireplaces, and a romantic garden room with a whirlpool tub for two. All of the rooms have private baths and are appointed with Victorian-era antiques and colorful floral fabrics. Many rooms have old-fashioned claw-foot tubs; some have ocean views. Breakfast is buffet style, and fresh-baked cookies are available daily. You can walk to restaurants and almost everything else in Pacific Grove.

The Cape Cod–style **Old St. Angela Inn** (321 Central Ave., 831/372-3246 or 800/748-6306, www.oldstangelainn.com, $180–220) is a converted 1910 country cottage featuring eight guest rooms decorated with antiques, quilts, and other homey touches. Each room has a private bath, and, in true B&B style, there are no televisions (but wireless

Internet service is available). Amenities include a garden hot tub, a redwood-and-glass solarium, complimentary breakfast, and afternoon wine or tea and hors d'oeuvres. The inn is only a block from the coastline; Lover's Point is a short walk away.

The lovely **(Green Gables Inn** (104 Fifth St., 831/375-2095 or 800/722-1774, www.greengablesinnpg.com, $190–270) is a gabled Queen Anne Victorian. This seaside "summer house" offers marvelous coastal views from five rooms upstairs, a suite downstairs, and five rooms in the carriage house. Of these, seven feature private bathrooms. Like most B&Bs in Pacific Grove, the inn's walls are lined with flowered wallpaper and the guest rooms are filled with antiques and teddy bears—a decorating style that you either love or hate. People who stay here generally love it. A member of the Four Sisters family of inns, everything is done to the highest caliber, including breakfast, which includes hot dishes as well as pastries, breads, and fresh fruit. Even the orange juice is fresh squeezed.

The **Gosby House Inn** (643 Lighthouse Ave., 831/375-1287 or 800/527-8828, www.gosbyhouseinn.com, $190–255) is another of the Four Sisters chain of inns. This one is a charming yellow Queen Anne Victorian that offers guests fine antiques, a restful garden, and fresh flowers. Most of the 22 rooms have private bathrooms; some have fireplaces, whirlpool tubs, and TVs. All the usual Four Sisters amenities and features apply, including the Grandma's-house decor and teddy bears snuggled on the guest beds. You'll either love this stuff or feel suffocated, but everybody enjoys the view and the Pacific Grove location.

OVER $250

Victoriana is particularly popular in Pacific Grove. The most famous Victorian inn in town is the elegant **(Seven Gables Inn** (555 Ocean View Blvd., 831/372-4341, www.pginns.com, $255–305), which offers ocean views from all 25 rooms (located in seven different bright yellow buildings) and an abundance of European antiques and Victorian finery. King- and queen-sized beds are covered in fine linens and down comforters. Rates include a big gourmet breakfast, afternoon wine and cheese, and cookies and milk at bedtime. Rooms with the best ocean views come with the highest price tag, but even Seven Gables' lowest-priced rooms come with fabulous hospitality and a perfect Pacific Grove location.

(The Inn at 213 Seventeen Mile Drive (213 17-Mile Dr., 831/642-9514, www.innat17.com, $255–325) is located in a sprawling 1920s Craftsman-style house and has been the recipient of many B&B honors. Innkeepers Charlie and Diana have the perfect touch—they are accessible and friendly, without being intrusive. They know exactly what B&B hospitality should be, from chocolate on the pillows, to chef-prepared delicious breakfasts, to wine and cheese in the evening and afternoon snacks. Guests have a choice of 14 rooms with private baths, some located in the main house and others in cottages nestled in the oak and redwood trees throughout the property. If you're "allergic" to quaint Victoriana, you'll like the simpler, more contemporary furnishings at this inn.

FOOD
Farmer's Market

In summer 2008, after much discussion and political hand-wringing, Pacific Grove finally approved their Farmer's Market. This small weekly event (Lighthouse Ave. btw. Forest Ave. and 18th St., Mon. 4–8 P.M., 831/384-6961, www.everyonesharvest.org) hosts about a dozen vendors offering all types of vegetables, fruits, and flowers for sale, plus another half-dozen restaurant booths selling hot food. There are also a few requisite arts and crafts booths, and a couple of bands playing music on the sidewalk around the market. While this farmer's market is nowhere near as large as the weekly markets in Monterey, it has a friendly, intimate ambience that is just right for Pacific Grove.

Breakfast

A short stroll from the Monterey Bay Aquarium, **First Awakenings** (125 Oceanview Blvd., 831/372-1125, www.firstawakenings.net, daily 7 A.M.–2 P.M., $10) in the American Tin Cannery is a great place to fill up on bluegerm pancakes (blueberry with wheat germ), omelettes, and savory and sweet crepes at breakfast. Sandwiches such as the chicado (grilled chicken, avocado, and cheese) star at lunch. Salad lovers will find a huge variety here. The restaurant has been serving happy eaters since 1993. Dine inside or out.

There's usually a line on weekend mornings at **Toastie's Café** (702 Lighthouse Ave., 831/373-7543, Mon.–Sat. 6:30 A.M.–3 P.M., Sun. 7 A.M.–2 P.M., $7–12), and that's because breakfast here is dependably delicious. The kitchen serves up dozens of plates of eggs Benedict, plus pancakes, waffles, and plenty of other egg dishes. Lunch consists of hefty burgers and sandwiches. There's nothing fancy about this place, but the food is good and the service is fast and friendly.

If all you want is coffee and a muffin, the place to go is **The Works** (667 Lighthouse Ave., 831/372-2242, www.theworkspg.com, Mon.–Sat. 7 A.M.–6 P.M., Sun. 8 A.M.–5 P.M.), a combination bookstore/coffeehouse with plenty of tables for reading the morning paper and big windows for looking out on Pacific Grove's

main drag. The back room is filled with books you will surely want to read and/or buy, so don't plan on getting out of here quickly.

American

The **Pelican Tavern** (125 Ocean View Blvd., 831/647-8200, www.thepelicantavern.com, daily 11 A.M.–11 P.M., $10–15) is a casual, family-friendly place located in the American Tin Cannery outlet center. It's the kind of place where you go to watch Monday night football and munch on a Cajun shrimp salad, a half-pound hamburger, or fish-and-chips. The Pelican Tavern has great views of the coast and the Monterey Peninsula Recreation Trail, and yes, pelicans are often seen gliding past.

Asian

For contemporary Asian cuisine served in a serene setting, **An Choi** (1120 Lighthouse Ave., 831/372-8818, www.anchoirestaurant .com, lunch Tues.–Fri. noon–2:30 P.M., dinner daily 5–9 P.M., $10–12) is a local favorite. The food is a mix of Vietnamese, Thai, Chinese, Japanese, and Korean, so diners can select from a diversity of items such as beef Pho noodle soup, Hanoi crispy crab rolls, pad thai, or clay-pot fish. The chef, who is Vietnamese by birth, does everything well, and he and his wife are two of the friendliest restaurant owners in Pacific Grove.

California-French

Melange (542 Lighthouse Ave., 831/333-0301, www.melangerestaurant.com, Wed.–Sat. 11:30 A.M.–2 P.M., daily 5:30–10 P.M., $19–28) delivers on its name with a mixture of often incongruous elements they call "fusions." The result is incredible food and great wine pairings. Those open to culinary experiments will delight in the Chef's Tasting Menus, with small plates that might include Maine lobster hand roll or veal sweet breads. If you prefer, try the big plates with offerings like fettuccini with wild mushrooms or filet mignon with a veal-Madeira demi-glace. You can order wine by the "taste," by the glass, or by the bottle.

Chef/owner Max Muramatsu of **Max's Grill** (209 Forest Ave., 831/375-7997, www.maxgrill .com, Tues.–Sun. 5–9 P.M., $16–23) trained as a classic French chef and spent much of his career in Tokyo, but since moving to Pacific Grove he has hit his stride creating innovative California-French cuisine. The menu is filled with dishes you think you've had before, but Max's version of tempura ahi tuna rolls, cioppino, grilled sand dabs, and braised lamb shank are prepared with creative Pacific Rim–style twists that make the old favorites new again. All of the breads and desserts are prepared in-house and are well worth the extra calories. Bargain hunters will enjoy the lower-priced sunset menu, served Tuesday–Sunday 5–6 P.M.

Continental

For nearly 20 years, **Taste Café & Bistro** (1199 Forest Ave., 831/655-0324, www.tastecafe bistro.com, daily 11:30 A.M.–9 P.M., $16–24) has been satisfying diners with its medley of Continental-Californian cuisine laced with a distinct French accent. Diners can watch chef/owner Bill Karaki as he prepares herb-roasted chicken, grilled rabbit, fresh soups, eggplant Napoleon, and escargots. Bill's wife Sue is in charge of desserts, and her creations include brioche bread pudding, apple galette, and a decadent chocolate torte. Many regular customers come here for the addictive au gratin potatoes, served with many of the entrées. And here's a surprise for a restaurant of this caliber—children are welcome here, and can choose from their own menu.

The **Red House Café** (662 Lighthouse Ave., 831/643-1060, www.redhousecafe.com, Sat.–Sun. 8:30–11 A.M., lunch Tues.–Sun. 11 A.M.–2:30 P.M., dinner Tues.–Sun. 5 P.M. to closing, $15) is set in a bright red Victorian in downtown Pacific Grove. It's a fine place for a casual Continental-style dinner (filet mignon, salmon, roasted chicken, seafood pasta) or lunch (warmed eggplant sandwich, portabello mushroom sandwich), and also for breakfast on the weekends. Tea lovers will enjoy the fact that the Red House is the only place on the Monterey Peninsula that serves Mariage Frères tea from France.

Italian

Victorian Corner (541 Lighthouse Ave., 831/372-4641, www.victoriancornerpg.com, Mon.–Thurs. 7:30 A.M.–3 P.M. and 5–9 P.M., Fri.–Sat. until 10 P.M., $10–21) features Sicilian specialties created from old family recipes interspersed with traditional American fare such as salads, chicken, steaks, and hamburgers. Four generations of the Aliotti family bring you breakfast, lunch, and dinner in this Pacific Grove landmark building, built in 1893. Grandma Aliotti is responsible for making the cannoli and tiramisu daily, and as it is with most grandmas, portions are very generous.

Not just ordinary pizza but gourmet pizza is on the menu at **Pizza My Way** (1157 Forest Ave., 831/643-1111, www.pizza-myway .com, Mon.–Thurs. 4–9:30 P.M., Fri.–Sat. 11 A.M.–10 P.M., Sun. noon–9:30 P.M., $15–25). Try the Mediterranean Treat (fresh garlic, chopped basil, mushrooms, tomatoes, feta cheese, mozzarella cheese), Chicken Masterpiece (white sauce, mozzarella cheese, fresh garlic, mushrooms, onions, tomatoes, marinated grilled chicken, fresh cilantro), or the Shrimp Lovers (white sauce, mozzarella cheese, Alaskan shrimp, lemon, black pepper, and fresh garlic), and select your crust style: too-thin, regular, or thick crust. Traditionalists can order pepperoni and sausage—yes, they make that kind, too.

Sitting down to a meal at **Vito's Italian Cuisine** (1180 Forest Ave., 831/375-3070, daily 5–9:30 P.M., $15–25) you can be assured of two things: first, enjoying authentic Sicilian favorites like veal marsala, fettucine alla puttanesca, and pollo picatta; and second, not going away hungry. Portions are plentiful, so much so that it may be hard to make room for tiramisu at the end of the evening. But you should indulge in it anyway, as this light-as-air dessert is made with Vito's secret family recipe.

Mediterranean

For boisterous Basque/Mediterranean food, try **Fandango** (223 17th St. off Lighthouse Ave., 831/372-3456, www.fandangorestaurant .com, Mon.–Sat. 11:30 A.M.–2:30 P.M. and 5–9:30 P.M., Sun. 10 A.M.–2 P.M. and 5–9:30 P.M., $25). One of the best restaurants on the Monterey Peninsula, Fandango serves hearty country fare—mesquite-grilled seafood, grilled rack of lamb, osso bucco, North African couscous, boullabaisse, and seafood paella—in four separate dining rooms warmed by fireplaces and brightened by colorful curtains and fresh flowers. Each of the uniquely decorated rooms is dripping with Tuscan country charm, so it's hard to choose a favorite. This is the kind of comfortable place where you'll want to dine with your sweetie while holding hands across the table. The Caesar salad is a house specialty, as is the chocolate nougatine pie for dessert. Dressy attire prevails at dinner, but since this is Pacific Grove, it's not *too* dressy.

Mexican

The homemade chiles rellenos at immensely popular **Peppers MexiCali Cafe** (170 Forest Ave., 831/373-6892, Mon.–Thurs. 11:30 A.M.–9 P.M., Fri.–Sat. 11:30 A.M.–10 P.M., Sun. 4–9 P.M., $10) are some of the best on the Monterey Peninsula. But you can't go wrong ordering any of the Mexican specialties here, including grilled seafood tacos, Jamaican curry prawns, or seafood fajitas. Full bar service is available, including the real McCoy—100 percent blue agave tequila, which makes terrific margaritas. You'll probably have to spend some time in the bar, because there is often a wait for tables.

Zocalo (162 Fountain Ave., 831/373-7911, daily 11:30 A.M.–8:30 P.M., $8–17) is the place for an authentic Mexican meal. You don't go here for the atmosphere (although the dining room is a pleasant enough space with lots of windows looking out on a Pacific Grove side street), you go here for the food. The homemade tortillas are to die for. In fact, all of the dishes are house-made in the traditional style—plates of tamales, fish tacos, enchiladas, burritos, and more—and served up with unpretentious service and honest-to-goodness authenticity. Zocalo can have a wait, but generally you don't need reservations.

Seafood

A great choice for seafood, served here with a Caribbean flare, is the relaxed, reasonably priced, and family-friendly **Fishwife** at Asilomar Beach (1996-1/2 Sunset Dr., 831/375-7107, www.fishwife.com, daily 11 A.M.–9 P.M., $10–20). Depending on what is in season and fresh, entrées might include salmon, halibut, sand dabs, or mahi mahi. Regardless of the season, diners can always count on Boston clam chowder, crab cakes, steamed mussels, and golden-fried cala-mari. Mango cheesecake and key lime pie are long-standing favorites for dessert. A second Fishwife is located in Seaside at 789 Trinity Ave., 831/394-2027.

Passionfish (701 Lighthouse Ave., 831/655-3311, www.passionfish.net, daily from 5 P.M., $25) is another seafood hot spot, serving only fish that is currently considered sustainable, such as spot prawns, which are caught at depths of up to 900 feet with traps that minimize harm to other species. The restaurant's menu changes almost daily, but typical entrées might include wild Monterey Bay salmon, tilapia in sweet-roasted red pepper vinaigrette over veggie risotto, oysters in a ginger vinaigrette, and a few nonfishy items like New York steak and slow-cooked duck confit. Wine is an affordable adventure here, since most bottles are priced almost at retail—a rarity at restaurants anywhere. You can order by the glass, bottle, or half-bottle from an ever-changing international selection. No wonder Passionfish has won numerous *Wine Spectator* awards and received raves in the December 2006 issue of *Bon Appetit* magazine. It's also the only certified "green" restaurant in Monterey County. The only downer here is that the sparsely decorated dining room is far from cozy, with tables too closely spaced, so this isn't the best choice for a romantic dinner.

Vegetarian

Try the vegetarian and vegan dishes at **Tillie Gort's Coffee House** (111 Central Ave., 831/373-0335, www.tilliegortscafe.com, daily 8 A.M.–9 P.M.) and art gallery, just a stroll from Cannery Row. The Mediterranean frittata, cinnamon raisin French toast, and tofu and various other scrambles shine at breakfast. Meat lovers will be happy to know that sides

of chicken apple sausage, bacon, and Canadian bacon are available. Lunch and dinner consists of pastas, salads, veggie burgers, and a few Mexican items. Tillie Gort's is locally famous for decadent black-bottom cupcakes, too.

PRACTICALITIES
Information and Services

For information on Pacific Grove, stop by the **Pacific Grove Chamber of Commerce** (Forest and Central Aves., 831/373-3304 or 800/656-6650, www.pacificgrove.org). The main **post office** in town is located at 680 Lighthouse Avenue (831/373-2271, Mon.–Fri. 7:30 A.M.–4:30 P.M., Sat. 10 A.M.–1 P.M.). There is no local newspaper in Pacific Grove; the best source for area news is the **Monterey County Herald** (www.montereycountyherald.com).

The Pacific Grove **police** department is located at 580 Pine Avenue (831/648-3143, www.ci.pg.ca.us). The nearest **hospital** is in Monterey (Community Hospital of the Monterey Peninsula, 23625 Hwy. 68, 831/624-5311, www.chomp.org).

Getting There and Around

To get to Pacific Grove from Highway 1 on the Monterey peninsula, take Highway 68 (Holman Hwy.) northwest until it becomes Sunset Drive near Asilomar. Sunset Drive turns into Asilomar Avenue, which junctions with Lighthouse Avenue and Ocean View Boulevard in Pacific Grove.

Alternatively, from Cannery Row or the Monterey Bay Aquarium, follow Lighthouse Avenue northwest for less than a mile into Pacific Grove. Access to Pebble Beach is possible only by following the 17-Mile Drive (all automobile drivers must pay a fee of $9 to enter the area). Five gates access the famous drive, including the Pacific Grove gate at Highway

68/Sunset Drive just east of Asilomar. (You can also enter the drive at the junction of Hwy. 68 and Hwy. 1, or at the Carmel gate off Ocean Ave. in Carmel.)

PEBBLE BEACH

The poshest town on the Monterey Peninsula, Pebble Beach is located on the peninsula's tip between Pacific Grove and Carmel-by-the-Sea, accessed only by the spectacular 17-Mile Drive. This swank enclave is best known for its world-famous golf courses set alongside the dramatic Pacific coastline. The town hosts a variety of big-name golf tournaments, including the U.S. Open and the annual AT&T Pebble Beach National Pro-Am. It is also home to the annual Concours d'Elegance (831/622-1700, www.pebblebeachconcours.net), considered to be one of the most prestigious showcases of the world's finest classic automobiles. The vast majority of visitors to Pebble Beach come only for short stays of a part of a day, as a typical overnight at one of the village's three lavish resorts starts at about $600.

Golf

The very exclusive Pebble Beach area has several world-class golf courses made famous by the **AT&T Pebble Beach National Pro-Am** (ww.attpgolf.com) golf tournament, which is held each year in late January or early February, and hosted by **Spyglass Hill Golf Club** (831/624-3811, www.pebblebeach.com). Designed by Robert Trent Jones Sr. in the 1960s as part of the master plan for the Pebble Beach waterfront, Spyglass Hill is reputed to be one of the toughest courses in the world, boasting a course rating of 75.5 and a slope rating of 147. The course, which is located one mile west of The Lodge at Pebble Beach, gets its name from Robert Louis Stevenson's classic

novel *Treasure Island*. The 18 holes at Spyglass are named after the book's characters, such as "Black Dog" and "Billy Bones."

Just a stone's throw away is **Pebble Beach Golf Links** (831/624-3811, www.pebblebeach .com), which is consistently rated the number-one public golf course in America by *Golf Digest*. Only guests at the ultraupscale Pebble Beach Resort can reserve tee times more than 24 hours in advance, and some guests reserve as far as 18 months in advance. This world-famous course, which hugs the craggy, wave-crashing coastline, was built in 1919.

For beginners or the budget-minded, a better bet is the nearby **Peter Hay Golf Course** (831/624-3811, www.pebblebeach.com), a par-three, nine-hole course next to Pebble Beach Lodge. For an all-day fee of $25, you can tell your friends you played golf at Pebble Beach.

Traditionalists who want to play golf in the old Scottish manner insist the only place to heft a club is **The Links at Spanish Bay** (831/624-3811, www.pebblebeach.com), a true links-style golf course near Asilomar State Beach, which features a bounty of sand dunes and ocean-borne northwest wind.

Pacific Grove has its own golf course, with oceanfront scenery that rivals that of Pebble Beach. **Pacific Grove Golf Links** (77 Asilomar Ave., 831/648-5775, www.ci.pg.ca.us) is known as the "Poor Man's Pebble." Its first nine holes are set in a forest of Monterey pines and cypress; the back nine are all oceanview. Reservations to play can be made seven days in advance; the cost of playing nine holes is $20–25, and 18 holes runs a mere $40–45. Discounted twilight rates are available after 2 P.M. in winter and 4 P.M. in summer.

Horseback Riding

If golf isn't your thing, sign up for a horseback

MONTEREY

ride on the beach instead. The trusty steeds at **Pebble Beach Trail Rides** (Portola Rd. and Alva Lane, 831/624-2756, www.ridepebblebeach.com) trot along the beach four times daily at 10 A.M., noon, 2 P.M. and 3:30 P.M.; make reservations at least one day in advance ($65 per person). The guided 80-minute beach rides, which lead past Cypress Point and onto the sand near Seal Rock, are open to anyone over the age of 12; no riding experience is necessary. Additional rides are offered through the woods of Del Monte Forest ($55 per person). Young children ages 3–6 can ride ponies on the grounds of the Pebble Beach Equestrian Center.

Accommodations

The superswank lodging choices in adjacent Pebble Beach are definitely beyond the reach of most people's pocketbooks. But if you win the lottery, book a stay at **The Inn at Spanish Bay** (2700 17-Mile Dr., 831/647-7500 or 800/654-9300, www.pebblebeach.com, $580–750). Rooms are ultradeluxe, with gasburning fireplaces, patios, and balconies with views. Amenities include the usual first-class luxuries plus beach access, a pool, saunas, whirlpools, a health club, tennis courts, and a putting green. Considering the rate, the complimentary water, soda, and candy in the rooms are a nice touch. Several restaurants are on-site, but the inn's casual Roy's Restaurant (831/647-7423, www.pebblebeach.com, daily 6 A.M.–11 P.M., $35–50) is a favorite of many guests—a great spot for a meal before or after a round of golf. The Inn at Spanish Bay's lobby alone is worth the price of admission, with spectacular views, inviting couches in front of the fireplace, and an open-air patio. An unexpected bonus: the bagpiper that plays at sunset every night while guests sip cocktails on the terrace.

A bagpiper plays every evening at The Inn at Spanish Bay.

Another outpost of luxury is **The Lodge at Pebble Beach** (1700 17-Mile Dr., 831/624-3811 or 800/654-9300, www.pebblebeach.com, $675–825). It's not uncommon for guests to drop a thousand dollars a night to stay in one of The Lodge's suites, so this is an "if you have to ask, you can't afford it" kind of place. Then again, it costs $500 just to play a round of golf at Pebble Beach (but a mere $350 at Spyglass). In addition to the "regular" lodge rooms and suites are the elegant, estate-style cottages at the Lodge's 24-room **Casa Palmero** (1518 Cypress Dr., 831/624-3811 or 800/654-9300, www.pebblebeach.com, $890–1,100), near the first fairway of the Pebble Beach Golf Links. For still more pampering, the lodge's **Spa at Pebble Beach** (daily 8 A.M.–8 P.M., 831/649-7615) is a full-service spa facility, offering every kind of luxurious body and facial service you can imagine.

Food

A favorite of Pebble Beach visitors is **Roy's Restaurant** at the Inn at Spanish Bay (2700 17-Mile Dr., 831/647-7423, www.pebblebeach.com, daily 6 A.M.–11 P.M., $35–50). Some say that Roy's earns its popularity more by hype than by substance, but a meal here delivers a true Pebble Beach experience—great food, a fabulous ocean view, and an ounce (or sometimes a pound) of pretention. Roy's is open for three meals each day, and it's certainly a good idea to show up before dark so you can enjoy the spectacular Pebble Beach scenery. This is a good place to bring someone you are trying to impress, like a first date or an important client. At dinner, seafood is featured prominently on the Hawaiian fusion–style menu (sushi, crab cakes, blackened ahi, butterfish), but so are meaty classics like filet mignon, rack of lamb,

and barbecue ribs. Try to avoid peak times on weekends as the dining room can get noisy, especially if there are big groups seated near you (and this is fairly common). For drinks before dinner, take a seat next to the outdoor fire pits, listen to the bagpiper play on The Links at Spanish Bay, and watch the sun put on its end-of-the-day magic show. After your meal, you can hang out in the lobby and listen to live jazz.

Over at The Lodge at Pebble Beach, **Club XIX** (1500 Cypress Dr., 831/625-8519, www.pebblebeach.com, daily 6–10 P.M., $70) is the place where every serious golfer must dine at least once in his or her life. The restaurant overlooks Pebble Beach's legendary 18th hole. Well-heeled diners enjoy contemporary California cuisine with a strong French accent—sautéed veal sweetbread, roasted quail, seared foie gras tarte tatin, and grand marnier souffle. Many choose to go with the prix fixe menu, with or without wine pairings, but à la carte choices are available as well. To finish off your meal, don't miss the port and cheese plate, or the extensive selection of cognacs. No matter what you order, it's all fabulous, and fabulously expensive.

For a more casual dinner, lunch, or late-night supper at The Lodge at Pebble Beach, pay a visit to **The Tap Room** (1500 Cypress Dr., 831/625-8535, www.pebblebeach.com, daily 11 A.M.–1 A.M., $35–50), a prime steak house serving fine cuts of prime beef, seafood, and classic American bar–style favorites—potato skins, buffalo wings, fried calamari, Caesar salad, and meatloaf. There's usually some kind of sporting event on television, and a cluster of golfers sitting at the bar enjoying the huge selection of microbrews. Be sure to check out The Tap Room's collection of Pebble Beach golf photos and memorabilia.

Salinas and Vicinity

The 100-mile-long Salinas Valley, with its fertile soil and lush lettuce fields, is often referred to as the nation's Salad Bowl, as it produces 50 percent of the United States' cauliflower and mushrooms, 25 percent of its celery, 60 percent of its broccoli, and 90 percent of its artichokes. Additionally, Salinas grows more lettuce than any other city in the U.S.—80 percent of this country's total production.

Salinas was also the blue-collar birthplace of novelist John Steinbeck, who chronicled the lives and hard times of California's down-and-out. Some things don't change. Almost 70 years after the 1939 publication of Steinbeck's Pulitzer Prize–winning *The Grapes of Wrath,* the United Farm Workers (UFW) are still attempting to organize the primarily Hispanic farm laborers and migrant workers here.

Salinas is a scenic 17-mile drive from Monterey, and worth a look for its historic Victorian buildings, charming downtown complete with antique stores, galleries, and a strollable Saturday farmers market, as well as the fascinating National Steinbeck Center, a tribute to Salinas's most famous native son.

STEINBECK'S LEGACY

The Grapes of Wrath didn't do much for John Steinbeck's local popularity. What began as a photojournalism project chronicling the "Okie" Dust Bowl migrations to California during the Depression later became Steinbeck's most famous work of fiction. The entire book was a whirlwind, written between June and October 1938. After publication, it became a bestseller and remained one through 1940. Steinbeck was unhappy about the book's incredible commercial success; he believed there was something wrong with books that became so popular.

Vilified in Monterey County as a left-winger and Salinas Valley traitor during his lifetime, Steinbeck never came back to Salinas. (The only way the town would ever take him back, he once said, was in a six-foot wooden box. And that's basically how it happened. His remains are at home at the local Garden of Memories Cemetery.) Most folks here have long ago forgiven their local literary light for his political views, so now you'll find his name and book titles at least mentioned, if not prominently displayed, all around town.

SIGHTS AND RECREATION
◖ National Steinbeck Center

The $15-million National Steinbeck Center (1 Main St., 831/775-4721, www.steinbeck.org, daily 10 A.M.–5 P.M., $10.95 adults, $8.95 seniors over 62 and students, $7.95 youths 13–17, $5.95 children 6–12, children 5 and under free), located in historic Old Town Salinas, opened to the public in 1998. A visit here is an interactive way to explore literature, history, agriculture, and art, especially as it relates to Monterey County and John Steinbeck, one of America's greatest novelists. In addition to changing exhibits, seven permanent galleries incorporate the use of sight, sound, and scent as they introduce Steinbeck's life and work in settings ranging from Doc Rickett's Cannery Row laboratory to a replica boxcar of ice-packed lettuce. For those unfamiliar with Steinbeck's writings, seven theaters show clips from famous films derived from his work (*East of Eden, The Grapes of Wrath, The Red Pony,* etc.).

Also on display is Steinbeck's trusty green truck and camper, Rocinante (named after

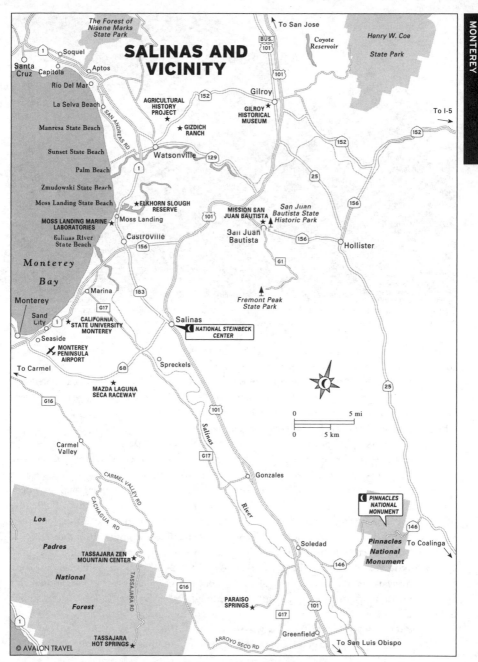

SALINAS AND VICINITY

The Forest of Nisene Marks State Park

To San Jose

Coyote Reservoir

Henry W. Coe State Park

Soquel

Santa Cruz Capitola   Aptos

Rio Del Mar

La Selva Beach

Manresa State Beach

Sunset State Beach

Palm Beach

Zmudowski State Beach

Moss Landing State Beach

MOSS LANDING MARINE LABORATORIES

Salinas River State Beach

Watsonville

AGRICULTURAL HISTORY PROJECT

★ GIZDICH RANCH

Gilroy

GILROY HISTORICAL MUSEUM

To I-5

ELKHORN SLOUGH RESERVE

Moss Landing

Castroville

MISSION SAN JUAN BAUTISTA

San Juan Bautista State Historic Park

San Juan Bautista

Hollister

Monterey Bay

Monterey

Marina

Sand City

Seaside

CALIFORNIA STATE UNIVERSITY MONTEREY

MONTEREY PENINSULA AIRPORT

To Carmel

Fremont Peak State Park

Salinas

NATIONAL STEINBECK CENTER

Spreckels

MAZDA LAGUNA SECA RACEWAY

Salinas

0   5 mi

0   5 km

Carmel Valley

CARMEL VALLEY RD

CACHAGUA RD

River

Gonzales

Los

Padres

TASSAJARA ZEN MOUNTAIN CENTER

National

TASSAJARA RD

Soledad

PINNACLES NATIONAL MONUMENT

Pinnacles National Monument

To Coalinga

Forest

PARAISO SPRINGS

ARROYO SECO RD

Greenfield

To San Luis Obispo

TASSAJARA HOT SPRINGS

© AVALON TRAVEL

© ANN MARIE BROWN

Salinas's pride and joy is the state-of-the-art National Steinbeck Center, which celebrates one of the West's most famous authors and the agricultural history of Monterey County.

Don Quixote's horse), in which the writer sojourned while researching *Travels with Charley*. The **Art of Writing Room** touches on the themes of Steinbeck's art and life, and allows visitors to explore their own creativity. The 30,000-piece **Steinbeck Archives** (open only to researchers by appointment) includes original letters, first editions, movie posters, and taped interviews with local people who remember Steinbeck. Some of the locals' barbed remarks, made decades after the publication of *The Grapes of Wrath,* make it clear that wrath at Steinbeck still runs at least as deep as the Salinas River. The highly interactive **Valley of the World Gallery** showcases the history, innovations, and technology of the agricultural industry in Monterey County's Salinas Valley.

The **museum store** (831/775-4721, www .steinbeckstore.org) features a good selection of books in addition to gift items. To visit some of the actual places Steinbeck immortalized in his fiction, be sure to pick up the booklet *Steinbeck Country: A Guide to Exploring John Steinbeck's Monterey County.*

Steinbeck House

Steinbeck described his family home—a jewel-box Queen Anne Victorian, located just two blocks from the National Steinbeck Center—as "an immaculate and friendly house, grand enough, but not pretentious." And so it still is. As both a dining and historic destination, the Steinbeck House (132 Central Ave., 831/424-2735, www.steinbeckhouse.com, public tours Sun. only 1–3 P.M. Memorial Day through Labor Day) offers private and public tours of the author's birthplace.

The Salinas Valley Guild also serves up gourmet lunches for Steinbeck fans and

© ANN MARIE BROWN

Author John Steinbeck was born in this Queen Anne Victorian, where visitors today can enjoy a gourmet lunch served by volunteers in period costumes.

literary ghosts alike, featuring Salinas Valley produce and Monterey County wines and beers. Lunches are served Tuesday–Saturday 11:30 A.M.–2 P.M. The menu changes weekly, and food is served by volunteers dressed in Victorian period costumes. Steinbeck House is also open for afternoon teas on occasional Saturdays (call for a current schedule). The house's basement serves as the **Best Cellar** gift shop (831/757-0508, daily 11 A.M.–3 P.M.), which sells Steinbeck books (of course), culinary items, and crafts. All proceeds support the Steinbeck House and local charities.

A Taste of Monterey

Located in the heart of Oldtown Salinas in the 1894 Pia Building is the Taste of Monterey Wine Visitors Center (127 Main St., 831/751-1980, www.tastemonterey.com, Mon.–Sat. 11 A.M.–5 P.M., free admission,

$10 for wine tasting), which offers samplings and sells the wares of more than 75 Monterey-area wines. This is a great spot for gift buying, with an extensive selection of gourmet foods, kitchen and home decor items, art, and wine accessories. The center is just steps away from the National Steinbeck Center, so it's easy enough to combine a visit to both attractions.

Wild Things

For a chance to see more than 100 exotic animals without going on safari, pay a visit to Wild Things (400 River Rd., 831/455-1901 or 800/228-7382, www.visionquestranch.com), a facility that supplies professionally trained animals for Hollywood movies and commercials. Visitors can attend daily one-hour tours (1 P.M. year-round except Christmas and Thanksgiving, also at 3 P.M. June–Aug., $10

elephants at Wild Things

is an outstanding example of a Mexican-era Monterey colonial adobe. Built between 1844 and 1848 by Jose Eusebio Boronda and virtually unaltered since, the tiny structure has been refurbished and now features museum displays and exhibits, including a few handsome original furnishings. Note the wood shingles, a considerable departure from traditional red-clay tiles.

California Rodeo

A Salinas tradition since 1911, the four-day California Rodeo (1034 N. Main St., 831/775-3100 or 800/771-8807, www.ca rodeo.com, $7–20) is held on the third weekend in July. It is one of the world's largest rodeos, with bronco busting and bull riding, roping and tying, barrel racing, a kiddie parade, cowboy poetry, and a big western dance on Saturday night. The rowdiness here rivals New Orleans' Mardi Gras, except it's all cowboy style, of course.

adult, $8 child 14 and under, no reservations needed). Private tours for families or groups are also available with advance reservations (eight-person minimum). The residents at Wild Things include a wide variety of creatures, from spiders to big cats to African elephants. The facility also maintains a full-time educational program and a sanctuary for retired and older animals, and operates a bed-and-breakfast for overnight guests (Vision Quest Ranch Bed & Breakfast, 400 River Rd., 800/228-7382, www.visionquestranch.com, $200–250).

Boronda Adobe

The Boronda Adobe (333 Boronda Rd. at W. Laurel, 831/757-8085, ww.mchsmuseum. com, tours Mon.–Fri. 10 A.M.–2 P.M., donation requested), headquarters for the Monterey County Historical Society (www.mchs museum.com or www.borondaadobe.com),

ACCOMMODATIONS

For budget travelers, Salinas has a nice array of inexpensive motels, including the usual Days Inn, Motel 6, and Super 8. Most other motels lining Highway 101 are a bit more upscale, but still priced lower than similar lodgings in Monterey. The three-story **Best Western Salinas Valley Inn and Suites** (187 Kern St., 831/751-6411, www.bestwesterncalifornia .com, $80–100) offers all the modern comforts plus a free continental breakfast. It's located just two miles from the National Steinbeck Center. The hotel features an outdoor pool, spa tub, steam room, and fitness room.

Right next door to Best Western is the **Comfort Inn and Suites Salinas** (181 Kern St., 831/770-1400, www.comfortinn.com, $120–160), where guests have access to similar amenities plus an indoor pool and hot tub, a real bonus if you want to swim on cooler winter days. Like the Best Western, this 60-room hotel is just off the freeway.

For a stay that is far from ordinary, book one of the four tent cabins at the **Vision Quest Ranch Bed & Breakfast** (400 River Rd., 800/228-7382, www.visionquestranch.com, $200–250). Home to over 100 exotic animals as well as E.A.R.S., a non-profit elephant sanctuary, Vision Quest is the B&B arm of Wild Things, an animal rental company. Many of the resident animals are actors in Hollywood films and commercials, or are in retirement after a lifetime of doing so. Human guests enjoy a continental breakfast delivered by an African elephant or one of the other talented animals, and get to meet with the facility's trainers as they make their evening rounds. The ranch's tent cabins are fairly luxurious, with wood floors, bathrooms, standard furniture, small refrigerators, and televisions with a selection of educational wildlife videos. This is an experience you won't forget.

FOOD

A wonderful coffee stop just a couple blocks from the Steinbeck Center is the **Cherry Bean Gourmet Coffee House & Roastery** (332 Main St., 831/424-1981, daily 6 A.M.–6 P.M.). All kinds of fancy coffee concoctions are available here, as well as the plain old black stuff (they roast their own beans), but it's worth breaking habit and trying one of their memorable hot chai drinks.

For breakfast downtown, see the specialists at **First Awakenings** (171 Main St., 831/784-1125, www.firstawakenings.net, daily 7 A.M.–2 P.M., $10), where the pancakes and French toast are reputedly the best in the county. Try the blueberry with wheat germ, or the raspberry, coconut, and granola. Omelettes, crepes, and scrambles keep the egg eaters happy, and at lunch, sandwiches, burgers, and salads round out the menu.

If you are going to eat barbecue anywhere in California, a rodeo town is the place to do it, and Salinas fits that bill. **Smalley's Roundup** (700 W. Market, 831/758-0511, www.smalleysroundup.com, lunch Tues.–Fri. 11:30 A.M.–1:30 P.M., dinner Tues.–Sun. 4–8 P.M., $10–25) is an icon, well-loved for its oakwood barbecue and other cowboy-style fine dining. Their famous tangy sauce is a source of local pride, whether it is slathered over beef ribs, pork ribs, or chicken. Portions are huge, and you'll need a lot of napkins.

The best bet for burgers and a long-running Salinas tradition is the unassuming **Toro Place Café** (665 Monterey-Salinas Hwy., 831/484-1333, daily 6:30 A.M.–2 P.M., $8–12), which has been serving classic French dips and sloppy chili burgers since 1945. Weather permitting, take your lunch out to the patio, which is dotted with round wooden picnic tables shaded by bright-colored umbrellas. The café works just fine for breakfast, too, as long as you like your morning repast greasy-spoon style (think biscuits and gravy, ham and eggs, or chicken-fried steak). And yes, that's a real bull's head on the wall.

For something a little more refined, pick up a copy of *The Grapes of Wrath* and sit down for a literary lunch at the historic **Steinbeck House** (132 Central Ave., 831/424-2735, www.steinbeckhouse.com, Tues.–Sat. 11:30 A.M.–2 P.M., $12–15, reservations suggested), just two blocks from the National Steinbeck Center. These gourmet lunches feature Salinas Valley produce and Monterey County wines and beers. The food is served by volunteers dressed in period Victorian costumes.

Reservations are suggested. Steinbeck House is also open for afternoon teas on occasional Saturdays (call for a current schedule).

Farmers Markets

Sample the famed Salinas Valley produce at the **Oldtown Salinas Farmers Market** (Main St., www.oldtownsalinas.com, Sat. 9 A.M.–2 P.M. year-round, 831/776-5540, www.oldtownsalinas.com), across from the National Steinbeck Center. The market features 60 vendors hawking certified organic vegetables and fruits, flowers, baked good, arts, crafts, and jewelry. There's plenty of family-oriented entertainment, too, so even the kids will enjoy a visit here. The most convenient parking is in the garage at the corner of Monterey and Market Streets.

For more weekend produce shopping, head to the **Salinas Farmers Market** (Hartnell College, 156 Homestead Rd., 831/728-5060, www.montereybayfarmers.org, Sun. 8 A.M.– noon year-round). Founded in 1977 and held for many years at the Northridge Mall, this market features about two dozen farmers and vendors. If you like exotic Asian vegetables, you'll find them here, along with more traditional American fare like broccoli, artichokes, cauliflower, mushrooms, leeks, and the like. If you're in town on a Thursday, take a stroll through the **Alisal Community Farmers Market** (632 E. Alisal St., 831/796-2861, Thurs. 9 A.M.–5 P.M., July–Oct.).

Another possible stop for an agricultural adventure is **The Farm** (831/455-2575, www.thefarm-salinasvalley.com, Mar. 10–Dec. 20, Mon.–Sat. 9 A.M.–6 P.M., until 5 P.M. in winter, free admission), on Highway 68 just west of Salinas, off the Spreckels exit (just look for the giant, mural-like sculptures of farmers by John Cerney). The Farm sells certified organic fruits and vegetables, field-grown flowers, and agricultural memorabilia, and offers visitors the opportunity to get out in the fields and commune with the vegetables. Farm tours are available by reservation, and there's a small farm-animal zoo for the kiddies.

PRACTICALITIES
Information and Services

The **Salinas Valley Chamber of Commerce** (119 E. Alisal St., 831/424-7611, www.salinaschamber.com) offers information on accommodations and sights. The Salinas chamber is also an official Monterey County Convention & Visitor Bureau outpost— and headquarters for the **Old Town Salinas Association** (831/758-0725, www.oldtownsalinas.com, Mon.–Fri. 8:30 A.M.–5 P.M., Sat. 9 A.M.–3 P.M.)—so stop here for any downtown event and business information or general Monterey County visitor information.

Getting There and Around

Salinas has an **Amtrak** station (11 Station Place, 831/422-7458 or 800/872-7245, www.amtrak.com); call or visit the website for fare and schedule information. There's no train station in Monterey, but you can connect from here to there via **Monterey-Salinas Transit** (1 Ryan Ranch Rd., Monterey, 831/424-7695 or 831/899-2555, www.mst.org) bus 20 or 21, or via the Amtrak Thruway bus as part of your train fare. **Greyhound** (19 W. Gabilan St., 831/424-4418 or 800/231-2222, www.greyhound.com) is also here, and the **Salinas Municipal Airport** (831/758-7214) is on Airport Boulevard.

PINNACLES NATIONAL MONUMENT

It was Teddy Roosevelt who first utilized presidential decree on behalf of the Pinnacles,

© DAVID GUBERNICK / MONTEREY COUNTY CVB

Geological oddities are the main attraction at Pinnacles National Monument.

protecting it as a national monument in 1908. The rocky landscape of the park had its origin as a volcanic eruption that occurred about 195 miles south of its present location. The lava formation slowly traveled northward along the San Andreas Fault, and currently moves at a rate of about 2–3 centimeters per year. Exploring these 26,000 acres of volcanic spires and ravines is a little like scrambling around on the moon. The weird rocks are bizarrely eroded, forming gaping gorges, dark caverns, and odd-shaped terraces. A rock climbers' heaven—but not for beginners—this stunning old volcanic formation also offers excellent hiking trails, two sets of talus caves, a campground, and a chance to see one of California's rarest birds, the California condor. Summer in the monument is usually too hot, but spring is the best time to visit, when a colorful array of wildflowers brighten up the chaparral. Fall and winter are also very pleasant.

There are two distinct regions of Pinnacles National Monument (5000 Hwy. 146, Paicines, 831/389-4485, www.nps.gov/pinn, year-round)—west and east—and it is not possible to drive from one to the other; only hiking trails connect the park's east and west sides. The park **Visitor Center** (formerly at Bear Gulch) is located in Pinnacles Campground (877/444-6777, www.recreation.gov, $23–36), on the east side of the park. The **Bear Gulch Nature Center** is located at the east entrance of the park. The vehicle entry fee is $5, and the walk-in fee is $3 (each valid for seven days). If you are entering the park's west side, the **Chaparral Ranger Station** is usually staffed. If you plan to spend the day at Pinnacles, bring everything you need with you (water or beverages, food, hiking equipment, and flashlights if you plan to explore the talus caves) as supplies are limited at the park. A few basics are available at the Pinnacles Visitor Center and camp store on the east side; nothing is available on the west side.

Talus Caves

There are two talus caves at Pinnacles that are open for self-guided exploration: Bear Gulch Cave is closer to the east entrance, and Balconies Cave is closer to the west entrance. **Bear Gulch Cave** is a tunnel-like jumble of boulders formed by thousands of years of water erosion. A visit to this special place requires a little advance preparation; bring a flashlight and good walking shoes. As you travel through the cave, you'll wedge under clefts in the rock, duck your head under ledges, and squint in the darkness to locate painted arrows pointing the way through the rocky maze. The adventure is easy enough for children to accomplish but equally fun for visitors of all ages. Most people walk through the cave in about 10 minutes, but it's so much fun, you won't want to hurry.

In 1998, it was discovered that Bear Gulch Cave was home to some very special residents— a colony of Townsend's big-eared bats—and the Park Service closed the cave to visitors for several years in order to protect the rare creatures. Today at least part of the cave is open for 10 months every year (mid-July through mid-May). During a few weeks in October and March, when the bats leave their home, the entire cave is open to visitors. If you have your heart set on exploring Bear Gulch Cave, call the park (831/389-4485) or visit its website (www.nps.gov/pinn) to check on the current closure status before making the long drive to the park.

Over on the park's west side, **Balconies Cave** is usually open year-round, but it is subject to flooding during heavy rains. As with Bear Gulch Cave, visitors should come

© ANN MARIE BROWN

A wide array of hiking trails crisscross Pinnacles National Monument.

prepared with a flashlight and sturdy walking shoes. Accessing Balconies Cave requires a 0.7-mile walk on the Balconies Trail from Chaparral trailhead parking area. At a junction with Balconies Cliffs Trail, bear right to enter the cave. After about 10 minutes of climbing on rocky staircases, ducking under boulders, and squeezing around constrictions in the rock, you'll emerge back into the sunlight. To return to your car, turn left and follow the Balconies Cliffs Trail, which travels up and over the top of the cave, offering many lovely views of the park's rocky, jumbled landscape.

Bird-Watching

Since 2003, Pinnacles National Monument has taken part in the California Condor Recovery Program, and more than 19 juvenile condors have been released in monument lands.

Currently, 16 condors are thriving in Pinnacles. One of the most likely place to spot the giant birds is from the High Peaks trail in the early morning or early evening.

Fall and winter are great times to see the park's other resident and visiting raptors: golden eagles, red-tailed hawks, sharp-shinned hawks, Cooper's hawks, American kestrels, and prairie falcons. At night, great-horned owls and Western screech owls can often be heard calling. Pinnacles National Monument is also home to six species of woodpeckers—acorn woodpeckers, hairy woodpeckers, downy woodpeckers, red-breasted sapsuckers, northern flickers, and Nuttall's woodpeckers.

Ranger Programs

On Saturdays in spring, summer, and fall, a ranger is often stationed at Bear Gulch Reservoir to provide information to visitors about wildlife, geology, the reservoir, and Bear Gulch Cave. Free evening programs are occasionally offered on Friday or Saturday nights, including full-moon and dark-sky hikes, bat viewings, and astronomy programs. Reservations are strongly suggested as space is limited; phone 831/389-4486 ext. 243.

Hiking

Of Pinnacles' 26,000 acres, nearly 16,000 are protected as wilderness. Some trails are fairly easy, while others are more rugged. Various interconnecting trails encourage creativity on foot. The fit, fast, and willing can hike east to west and back in one (long) day. The easiest cross-park route is the gentle Old Pinnacles Trail, rather than the steeper High Peaks and Juniper Canyon trails. No matter where you travel, be sure to pack plenty of water. Temperatures in summer and early fall can often top 100°F, and there is very little shade.

The best hiking weather occurs in the cooler months of the year.

From Bear Gulch on the east side of the park, a variety of trails are available. The **Moses Spring Trail** connects with the Rim Trail for a 2.2-mile loop that takes in the Bear Gulch talus caves and scenic Bear Gulch Reservoir, where rock climbers are often seen plying their trade on the canyon walls.

A major highlight of the park is the **High Peaks Trail,** which crawls along the 2,700-foot peaks of the Pinnacles and provides scenic views stretching out across multiple counties. The High Peaks Trail can be accessed from the Condor Gulch trailhead (across from the Bear Gulch Nature Center) for a 5.3-mile loop. The trail climbs immediately and relentlessly as it travels past wild black sage and colorful lichen-colored rocks to a railing-lined viewpoint that takes in the High Peaks. Continuing upward, you'll reach the High Peaks Trail and turn left. Before long you'll be traveling through narrow rock passageways and over and under the steep formations of the High Peaks. In places, the trail is merely a series of steps and handrails that have been carved into the rock, and the near-vertical drop-offs can be daunting. When you reach 2,605-foot Scout Peak, you'll find a bench, a restroom, and a fine view to the west. From there, continue along High Peaks Trail to return to Bear Gulch. You'll have to walk down Moses Spring Trail a short distance to get back to your starting point.

The longest hike from the east side of the park is the trek up the **North Chalone Peak Trail.** It is 8.6 miles round-trip, passes fantastic rock formations, and provides a great view of the Salinas Valley from the top of North Chalone Peak (elevation 3,304 feet). A decommissioned fire lookout tower sits atop its summit. To get there, follow the Moses Spring

Some trails in Pinnacles are just handrails and steps that have been carved into the rock.

Trail from Bear Gulch, then ascend the stairs to Bear Gulch Reservoir. Continue across the dam until you see the signed trail for North Chalone Peak; by taking this path you'll leave the vast majority of park visitors behind. At just shy of four miles from the start, you'll join up with a fire road leading to the summit. The last half-mile is the steepest stretch of the whole trip, but the reward at the top is a fine view of the Salinas River curving through its valley, the Santa Lucia Mountains, and all of Pinnacles National Monument. On rare, crystal-clear days, you can see all the way to the Pacific Ocean.

Visitors who drive into the park on its west side will wind up at the Chaparral trailhead and parking area. From there, you can follow a 0.7-mile trail to the **Balconies Cave,** which meanders along the often-dry west fork of Chalone Creek. Loop back on Balconies Cliffs Trail for a 2.4-mile round-trip. You can also access the spectacular High Peaks from the Chaparral trailhead by following Juniper Canyon Trail for 1.8 miles to Scout Peak, then turning left on High Peaks Trail. Loop back to your starting point on Tunnel Trail and Juniper Canyon Trail for a great 4.4-mile aerobic workout.

Camping

Pinnacles Campground (5000 Hwy. 146, Paicines, 877/444-6777, www.recreation.gov, $23–36) is officially a part of the national monument and is operated by the National Park Service. The 103-site campground is quite nice, featuring flush toilets, coin-operated showers, water, fire rings, picnic tables, a swimming pool, some RV hookups, and group facilities. Ranger programs are offered during the spring and summer in the campground amphitheater, and the park's main Visitor Center is located at the camp entrance.

Getting There

The east entrance of Pinnacles is open 24 hours daily and can be reached via Highway 25, then Highway 146 heading west. From Hollister, it's about 30 miles south, then about five miles west to the park entrance.

The west entrance is reached via Highway 146 heading east for 14 miles (exit Hwy. 101 just south of Soledad). Note that the west road becomes narrow and is not recommended for campers and trailers. The west entrance is open from 7:30 A.M.–8 P.M., when the gate closes.

SAN JUAN BAUTISTA

Three miles east of Highway 101, the tiny town of San Juan Bautista is charming and charmed, as friendly as it is sunny. (People here say the weather in this pastoral valley is "salubrious.") Named for John the Baptist, the 1797 Spanish mission of San Juan Bautista is central to this serene community at the foot of the Gabilan Mountains. But the historic plaza, still bordered by old adobes and now a state historic park, is the true center of San Juan—rallying point for two revolutions, onetime home of famed bandit Tiburcio Vasquez, and the theatrical setting for David Belasco's *Rose of the Rancho.* Movie fans may remember Jimmy Stewart and Kim Novak in the mission scenes from Alfred Hitchcock's *Vertigo,* which were filmed here.

San Juan Bautista State Historic Park

Surrounding the town's main plaza are the lovely old buildings of San Juan Bautista State Historic Park (Second St. btw. Washington and Mariposa Sts., 831/623-4526, www.parks.ca.gov, daily 10 A.M.–4:30 P.M., $3), a national historic landmark. The oldest of these is the **Plaza Hotel** (Second and Mariposa Sts.), originally barracks

the old Plaza Hotel at San Juan Bautista State Historic Park

© ANN MARIE BROWN

built in 1813 for Spanish soldiers. In horse and buggy days, San Juan Bautista was a major stage stop between San Francisco and Los Angeles and the largest town in central California, and the Plaza Hotel was famous statewide. (Note the two-story outhouse out back.) Eventually the railroad was built elsewhere and the local economy lost its luster.

Next door to the Plaza Hotel is the **Castro-Breen Adobe,** which was the home of Patrick and Margaret Breen, who were survivors of the ill-fated Donner Party. This group of pioneers tried to cross the Sierra during the unforgiving winter of 1846–1847, and in a horrible twist of history, some of the survivors were forced to resort to eating the flesh of their dead traveling companions in order to stay alive. The Castro-Breen building now serves as a museum and has lovely gardens in the back. Alongside the plaza is the stable building, packed with an

© ANN MARIE BROWN

The stable building at San Juan Bautista State Historic Park is filled with an impressive collection of horse-drawn wagons and carriages.

impressive collection of horse-drawn wagons and carriages, the tools used by wagonwrights, and a dozen or more saddles. An "Instructions for Stagecoach Passengers" plaque includes plenty of useful tips like "spit on the leeward side," "don't lop over neighbors when sleeping," and "don't point out where murders have been committed, especially if there are women passengers."

Mission San Juan Bautista

Partly destroyed by earthquakes in 1800 and 1906 (the San Andreas Fault is just 40 feet away), **Mission San Juan Bautista** (406 Second St., 831/623-4528, www.oldmission sjb.org, daily 9:30 A.M.–4:30 P.M.) has been restored many times. The 15th and largest of the Franciscan settlements in California, the mission here is not as architecturally spectac- ular as others in the Catholic chain, although

its 40-foot-high walls are the tallest of all the California missions. Visitors can tour Mission San Juan Bautista's gardens (beautiful heirloom roses frame the front entrance) and museum, which sits adjacent to, but is not technically a part of, the state historic park. Note the old dirt road beyond the wall of the mission cem- etery; this is an unspoiled, unchanged section of the 650-mile El Camino Real, the "royal road" that once connected all the California missions. Archaeological excavations at the mission by CSU Monterey, Hartnell College, and Cabrillo College students unearthed the foundations of the mission's original quad- rangle, tower, well, and convent wing (which many historians previously believed had never existed). Students also cleared the 1799 Indian Chapel of debris and restored it; inside is an ornate altar built in the 1560s and moved to the chapel for the Pope's visit in 1987. Many

MONTEREY

© ANN MARIE BROWN

Extensive rose gardens frame the bell tower of Mission San Juan Bautista.

of the students' other discoveries are on display in the mission's museum, along with artifacts such as priest vestments and hand-illustrated choir books.

Fremont Peak State Park

In March 1846, Gen. John C. Frémont and Kit Carson built a fort here in defiance of the Mexican government, unfurled their flags on Gabilan Peak (now Fremont Peak), and waited for the supposedly imminent attack of Californio troops. When no battle came, they broke camp and took off for Oregon. Fremont Peak State Park (831/623-4255, www.parks

.ca.gov, $4 per vehicle), a long, narrow, isolated strip in the Gabilan Mountains northeast of Salinas, is made up of rolling hills lined with oaks, madrones, Coulter pines, and spring wildflowers that attract hundreds of hummingbirds. The park offers a few walking trails and great views from the top of Fremont Peak (elevation 3,169 feet). A mere 0.6-mile hike will bring you to its radio transmitter–covered summit, where you'll find a divine panorama of Monterey Bay, Santa Cruz, Salinas, Watsonville, Hollister, and the Santa Lucia Mountains.

Another attraction at Fremont Peak is its observatory (831/623-2465, www.fpoa.net) with a 30-inch Challenger reflecting telescope. The observatory is open to the public on some weekends (Apr.–Oct.) for free astronomy programs, including lectures and observation.

Getting to the park requires negotiating a long and winding drive of 11 miles from San Juan Bautista (trailers are not recommended). From Highway 156, turn south on Alameda and then right on San Juan Canyon Road. The road ends at the state park.

Camping (800/444-7275, www.reserve america.com, $11–15 per night) at Fremont Peak State Park is available in about 25 primitive campsites and a group camp for up to 50 people.

Getting There

To get to San Juan Bautista, from U.S. 101 head east on Highway 156 for three miles. Turn left at the stoplight at Highway 156 and Alameda.

CARMEL

The name "Carmel-by-the-Sea" distinguishes this postcard-pretty coastal village from its similarly named neighbors—sun-baked Carmel Valley, 10 miles inland, and seaside Carmel Highlands, just south of Point Lobos State Reserve on the way to Big Sur. What the three Carmels have in common is one thing: money. Although the town's beginnings were bohemian in nature—artists, poets, writers, and other oddballs were the first to establish a community here, most of them shaken out of San Francisco after the 1906 earthquake—the Carmel of today carefully guards its quaintness while cranking up its commercialism. Shopping is the town's major attraction, and that means Tiffany & Co., not T-shirt shops. Still, the beautiful city beaches are free, and a tour of the elegant old Carmel Mission costs only a few bucks.

Carmel hasn't always been so uppity. Upton Sinclair, Sinclair Lewis, Robinson Jeffers, and Jack London were some of the literary lights who once twinkled in this town. Master photographers Ansel Adams and Edward Weston were more recent residents. But, as often happens in California, land values shot up, and the original bohemians were priced right out of the neighborhood. Still, Carmel is proud of its artistic heritage; its downtown boasts more than 60 art and photography galleries, and a

© ANN MARIE BROWN

HIGHLIGHTS

❰❰ Carmel Mission: California's second mission features an evocative 1797 baroque stone church, one of the state's most graceful buildings, complete with a four-bell Moorish tower, arched roof, and star-shaped central window (page 108).

❰❰ Robinson Jeffers' Tor House: Now a national historic landmark, this medieval-looking granite retreat presides over Carmel Bay. Tor House was built by the famed California poet Robinson Jeffers, who helped haul the huge stones up from the beach below with horse teams (page 110).

❰❰ Point Lobos State Reserve: A jewel in the crown of California's state parks, Point Lobos, just south of Carmel, offers miles of pounding surf and a dramatic, cypress-fringed, rocky coastline (page 111).

❰❰ Tassajara Zen Mountain Center: There's no better way to get back to nature than at the first Soto Zen monastery outside of Asia. Soak in the famous hot springs, explore the surrounding wilderness, and escape civilization for a while (page 133).

❰❰ Earthbound Farms: The roadside farm stand is still alive and well in Carmel Valley. At Earthbound Farms, you can purchase (or just admire) organic heirloom potatoes, pumpkins, squash, raspberries, and flowers, and enjoy a snack made at the farm's certified organic kitchen (page 135).

❰❰ Wine-Tasting: Day-trip through lovely Carmel Valley to explore some of the valley's hidden yet premium wineries. Better yet, sign up for the Grapevine Express or Wine Trolley and leave the driving to others (page 136).

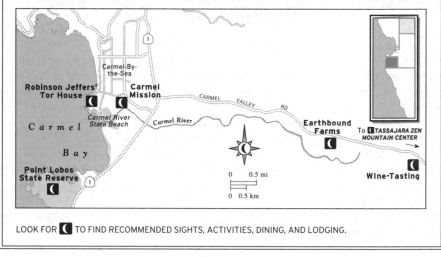

LOOK FOR **❰❰** TO FIND RECOMMENDED SIGHTS, ACTIVITIES, DINING, AND LODGING.

certain eccentricity still reigns in this town of 4,200 residents. City laws prohibit parking meters, high rises, street lights, neon signs, numbered street addresses, and plastic plants in the downtown area. And although you are unlikely to be ticketed for it, it's also against the law to wear high heels (but if you must have those extra inches, you can get a special permit from City Hall).

One other thing about Carmel: It's gone to the dogs. Dogs can run free on Carmel Town Beach. Dogs have their own special drinking fountain at Carmel Plaza—the Fountain of Woof. Dogs are not only welcome but

CARMEL

© ANN MARIE BROWN

Carmel is a very dog-friendly place, as evidenced by the Fountain of Woof in Carmel Plaza.

pampered at many hotels and eateries around town. Shopkeepers pass out doggie treats without prompting. And for dogs who like to shop, there are even a few upscale doggie boutiques.

PLANNING YOUR TIME

If you are a serious shopper or gallery hopper, you'll want at least two days to spend in Carmel, where you can browse or buy to your heart's content. Nature lovers and hikers will want an additional day to explore beautiful Point Lobos State Reserve, just south of town. Wine aficionados will need a full day to explore the boutique wineries and taste the vintages of Carmel Valley. If you are none of the above, you can visit this town's best sights—the Carmel Mission and Robinson Jeffers' Tor House—plus stroll through downtown Carmel and take a walk along the white sands of Carmel Town Beach, all in one day.

HISTORY

Carmel-by-the-Sea was established in 1903 by real estate developers who vowed to create a cultured community along the sandy beaches of Carmel Bay. To do this, they offered "creative people" such incentives as building lots for as little as $50. As a result of such irresistible inducements, Carmel was soon alive with an assortment of tents and shacks, which eventually gave way to cottages and mansions.

Tourism grew right along with the art colony; the public had a passion for travel during the early days of automobile adventuring. Quaint Carmel, home to "real bohemians," also offered tourists the chance to view (and buy) artwork—a prospect happily encouraged by the artists themselves. Carmel's commitment to the arts and its artists was formalized by the establishment of the Carmel Art Association in 1927. Still going strong, this artists' cooperative is a cultural focal point in contemporary Carmel.

CARMEL

Pebble
Beach

PEBBLE BEACH
GOLF COURSE

Carmel

Bay

Carmel Beach City Park

ROBINSON JEFFERS'
TOR HOUSE

*Carmel
River
State
Beach*

MISSION RANCH RESORT/
RESTAURANT AT MISSION
RANCH

CARMEL
MISSION

*Carmel River
State Beach*

To Tickle Pink Inn, Highlands Inn
Hyatt, Pacific's Edge, Big Sur and
POINT LOBOS STATE RESERVE

Detail inset (SEE DETAIL):

KURT'S CARMEL
CHOP HOUSE

CLARION
COLLECTION
CARMEL BY
THE SEA

5TH AVE

HOG'S
BREATH
INN

CASANOVA
LE COQ D'OR

FORGE IN
THE FOREST

PIATTI
RISTORANTE

GRASING'S

6TH AVE

*Devendorf
Park*

FLYING FISH GRILL

OCEAN AVE

OCEAN AVE

PORTABELLA

TOURIST
INFORMATION
CENTER

BOUCHÉE
BISTRO

CANTINETTA LUCA

ANTON &
MICHAEL

LITTLE
NAPOLI

7TH AVE

Map labels:

- DEL CIERVO RD
- 17 MILE DR
- 17 MILE DR
- 1ST AVE
- HORIZON INN
  AND OCEAN
  VIEW LODGE
- 2ND AVE
- CARMEL
  GATE
- THE TRADEWINDS
  AT CARMEL
- 3RD AVE
- CARMEL COUNTRY INN
- DOLPHIN INN
- CARMEL WAYFARER INN
- VAGABOND'S HOUSE INN
- L'ESCARGOT
- 4TH AVE
- 5TH AVE
- SEE DETAIL
- HAPPY LANDING INN
- LOBOS LODGE
- 6TH AVE
- OCEAN AVE
- L'AUBERGE CARMEL
- CARMEL VILLAGE INN
- 7TH AVE
- 8TH AVE
- COBBLESTONE INN
- 9TH AVE
- *Carmel
  Bay*
- SAN ANTONIO AVE
- CARMELO AVE
- CAMINO REAL
- MONTE VERDE ST
- LINCOLN ST
- DOLORES ST
- SAN CARLOS ST
- MISSION ST
- JUNIPERO
- 10TH AVE
- 11TH AVE
- SEA VIEW INN
- 12TH AVE
- COLONIAL
  TERRACE INN
- 13TH AVE
- *Mission
  Trails
  Park*
- SCENIC RD
- SANTA LUCIA AVE
- BAY VIEW AVE
- OCEAN VIEW AVE
- 14TH AVE
- 15TH AVE
- DOLORES ST
- LASUEN DR
- ATHERTON DR
- To Carmel Valley
- G16
- FROM SCRATCH
  & ROBATA GRILL
- RIO RD
- OLIVER RD
- Carmel River
- RIO RD
- RIO GRILL
- CARMEL
  MISSION
  INN
- ST
- ST
- ST
- DOLORES
- LINCOLN
- SAN CARLOS
- MISSION
- JUNIPERO

0   500 yds

0   500 m

© AVALON TRAVEL

Sights

CARMEL WALKS

To get oriented, take a walk through downtown. Carmel's shops and galleries are an easy day-long distraction for true window-shoppers, but local architecture is also intriguing. The area between 5th and 8th Streets, Junipero Avenue, and the city beach is packed with seacoast cottages, Carmel gingerbread-style houses, and adobe homes typical of the area. If you'd like to have a guide, sign up for a two-hour tour with Carmel Walks (831/642-2700, www.carmelwalks.com, $25). Tours lead past the town's original fairy-tale Tudor cottages designed by Hugh Comstock, famous movie locations, buildings designed by Bernard Maybeck, Julia Morgan, and Frank Lloyd Wright, and oddities such as a house made entirely of doors and another built from pieces of old ships. The tour also visits actress Doris Day's pet-friendly hotel and includes tales of locally famous dogs. Tours are offered Saturday at 10 A.M. and 2 P.M. and Tuesday–Friday at 10 A.M. Reservations are advised, or just show up at the outdoor courtyard of the Pine Inn on Lincoln Street at Ocean Avenue.

☾ CARMEL MISSION

If you are going to visit only one of California's 21 Spanish missions, the beautiful Carmel Mission (3080 Rio Rd., 831/624-3600, www.carmelmission.org, Mon.–Sat. 9:30 A.M.–5 P.M., Sun. 10:30 A.M.–5 P.M., $5 adults, $4 seniors, $1 children under 17) is the one to see. Properly called Mission San Carlos Borromeo del Rio Carmelo, it was California's second mission, and was originally established at the Monterey

Mission San Carlos Borromeo del Rio Carmelo

© DEBORAH JESCH

Presidio in 1770, then moved here the following year. It was the onetime headquarters and favorite foreign home of Father Junípero Serra, whose remains are buried at the foot of the altar in the sanctuary.

The mission's magnificent vine-draped cathedral is the first thing to catch the eye. The romantic Baroque stone church, one of the state's most graceful buildings, was completed in 1797, and features a four-bell Moorish tower, arched roof, and star-shaped central window. Visitors can tour the mission on their own; a self-guided brochure is provided with your entrance fee. Most of the buildings here are reconstructions since the Carmel Mission fell into ruins in the 1800s. These "new" old buildings, painstakingly rebuilt and restored in the 1930s, fail to capture the size and complexity of the original bustling mission complex: an odd-shaped quadrangle with a central fountain, gardens, a kitchen, carpenter and blacksmith shops, soldiers' housing, and priests' quarters. The native peoples attached to the mission— a labor force of 4,000 Christian converts— lived separately in a nearby village. More than 3,000 "mission Indians" are buried in the silent, simple cemetery, their graves decorated with abalone shells. The gardens themselves are fabulous, with old-fashioned plant varieties including bougainvillea, bird-of-paradise, and fuchsia.

The Carmel Mission contains five small museums. The book museum holds California's first unofficial library—the 600 volumes Father Serra brought to California in 1769. The silver altar furnishings are also originals, as are the ornate vestments, Spanish and native artifacts, and other mission memorabilia. Father Serra's simple priest's cell is a lesson by contrast in modern materialism.

CARMEL

© ANN MARIE BROWN

Father Junípero Serra's remains are buried at the Carmel Mission.

◖ ROBINSON JEFFERS' TOR HOUSE

A medieval-looking granite retreat on a rocky knoll above Carmel Bay, Tor House (26304 Ocean View Ave., 831/624-1813 or 831/624-1840, www.torhouse.org) was built by poet Robinson Jeffers, who hauled its huge stones up from the beach below with horse teams. The manual labor, he said, cleared his mind, and "my fingers had the art to make stone love stone." California's dark prince of poetry, Jeffers is known for being a tough outdoorsman, a great environmentalist, and a poet who wrote about the Central Coast in classic narrative and epic form. In April 1932, at the height of his career, he was featured on the cover of *Time* magazine. Jeffers generally remained aloof from the Monterey Peninsula's other "seacoast bohemians," but nonetheless, Tor House was visited by many

© ANN MARIE BROWN

The medieval looking Tor House and Hawk Tower were built by Robinson Jeffers.

A LITERARY LEGACY

A Bohemian group of poets, artists, and writers founded the Carmel that we know and love today, many having made their way here after the 1906 San Francisco earthquake and fire forced them out of that arts-friendly metropolis. Some of the writers were already friends before they moved to Carmel; others formed alliances during all-night beach parties at Carmel Town Beach, where they gathered around blazing bonfires and feasted on gin and abalone. Following is a short roundup of a few of Carmel's literary masters who populated the town in the first quarter of the 20th century.

Mary Austin: One of the West's greatest female environmentalists and writers, Mary Austin (1868-1934) is best known for authoring *Land of Little Rain,* an intimate study of the California desert. A bold feminist and an expert on American Indian affairs, she was consulted by President Theodore Roosevelt

on how to manage Western lands. Austin came to Carmel in the early 1900s to do research for her novel *Isidro* at the Carmel Mission. Both she and George Sterling had their works performed at the Carmel Arts and Crafts Club, the town's first cultural center and theater. In 1910 she was instrumental in the building of Carmel's Forest Theater, which was the first outdoor theater west of the Rocky Mountains.

Robinson Jeffers: Carmel's most famous poet, Robinson Jeffers, built his home on the headlands above Carmel Town Beach. Two structures of his stone-built residence – Tor House and Hawk Tower – can be visited today on guided tours. Jeffers is considered to be the "dark prince of poetry," his works echoing the tragedies of human existence. In 1947 he adapted *Medea* for the Broadway stage, and Dame Judith Anderson starred in the production. Many celebrities came to visit the brood-

of the 20th century's most creative minds—Joseph Campbell, Charles Lindbergh, George Gershwin, Edna St. Vincent Millay, Charlie Chaplin, and many others.

You can only begin to appreciate Tor House from the outside (it's just a short walk up from Carmel River Beach, on Ocean View Ave. btw. Scenic Rd. and Stewart Way), where its granite tower stands out among the other more traditional homes in this upscale seaside neighborhood. ("Tor" is a Celtic term describing a large outcropping of rock.) Jeffers built the three-story Hawk Tower, complete with a secret passageway, for his wife, Una, and twin sons. A steep and narrow staircase leads to the top, which reveals an inspiring view of the coast. The mellow redwood paneling, warm Oriental rugs, and lovely gardens here soften the impact of the home's bleak stone exterior—the overall effect somehow symbolizing Jeffers' hearth-centered life, seemingly far removed from the world's insanity. A national historic landmark, Tor House is open for guided tours Friday and Saturday only, 10 A.M.–3 P.M., advance reservations required (adults $7, college students $4, high school students $2). Tours are limited to six people; no children under 12 are allowed.

The Tor House Foundation also offers a full schedule of events, from its annual poetry prize, readings, and sunset garden parties to the Robinson Jeffers Seminars, Jeffers Country Bus Tour (of Big Sur), and Jeffers Poetry Walk.

◖ POINT LOBOS STATE RESERVE

One of the crown jewels of California's state parks, Point Lobos State Reserve (831/624-4909 or 831/624-3407, www.pointlobos.org or www.parks.ca.gov, daily 8 A.M.–sunset, $10 parking fee) is a 1,250-acre coastal wonderland

ing poet at his Carmel home, including Sinclair Lewis, Charles Lindbergh, Ansel Adams, and Charlie Chaplin.

Sinclair Lewis: The first American to be awarded the Nobel Prize in literature, Sinclair Lewis was a novelist, short story writer, and playwright who was famous for creating memorable characters and making fun of the insular life of small-town residents. He is best known for his novels *Babbitt* and *Main Street*, both of which criticized conventional American society and commercial capitalist values. His novel *Arrowsmith* garnered him a Pulitzer prize, an honor which he refused.

Jack London: Author of *The Sea-Wolf, The Call of the Wild, White Fang,* and dozens of other novels and short stories, including the classic *To Build a Fire,* Jack London came into his own in the Carmel artists' colony. He even wrote about it in his novel, *The Valley of the Moon* (in which his friend George Sterling is depicted as one of the characters). London was also a world traveler and adventurer, and one of the first Americans to make a substantial living as a writer.

George Sterling: The so-called King of Bohemia, Sterling was considered by many to be one of the greatest poets of the early 1900s, although he was not well known outside of California. Serving as the hub of a wheel of well-known writers, Sterling was responsible for bringing many of his literary contemporaries to Carmel. He was mentored by Ambrose Bierce and Ina Coolbrith, and later became a mentor to Robinson Jeffers. Jack London was one of his best friends. In 1926, Sterling committed suicide at his home at the San Francisco Bohemian Club. His most lasting legacy was a poem that called San Francisco the "cool, grey city of love."

located off Highway 1, three miles south of Carmel. Pack a picnic; this is the most scenic stretch of coastline the Monterey/Carmel area has to offer. The relentless surf and wild winds have pounded these reddish shores for millennia, sculpting six miles of shallow aquamarine coves, rocky tide pools, intimate beaches, and jutting points: Granite, Coal, Chute, Cannery, Pinnacle, Pelican, and Lobos itself. From here, look to the sea, as Santa Cruz poet William Everson did, "standing in cypress and surrounded by cypress, watching through its witchery as the surf explodes in unbelievable beauty on the granite below."

But get an early start; Point Lobos is an incredibly popular park. Park rangers limit the number of visitors allowed into the park at one time, so arrive very early in the day, especially in summer, to avoid long lines at the entrance station. You can also avoid the entrance fee by walking or biking onto the reserve grounds (no trail riding). Guided walking tours are also available; check at the ranger station for details.

Point Lobos can be enjoyed by hikers and nonhikers alike; much of the beauty of this park can be seen right from your car window, or from a picnic table near the ocean. Just by glancing out to sea, visitors have a near-guarantee of spotting sea lions, seals, and sea otters. Over 250 different animal and bird species, and over 350 plant species have been identified at the reserve. In the winter months (December to May), migrating gray whales are often spotted. In late summer, humpbacks and blue whales are sometimes seen feeding offshore. Transient pods of orcas (killer whales) also occasionally make an appearance.

© ANN MARIE BROWN

Relentless surf and wild winds have sculpted the craggy shoreline at Point Lobos State Reserve.

© ANN MARIE BROWN

the secluded China Cove at Point Lobos
State Reserve

© ANN MARIE BROWN

The Whalers Cabin Museum is a great place
to bone up on local history.

CARMEL

Visitors on land see only a portion (about half) of the reserve. The underwater world just offshore is one of the richest marine habitats in California. Only certified scuba divers are able to explore the watery world of 70-foot-high kelp forests, where animals without backbones and plants without roots create a world of vibrant color. Lingcod, cabezone, and rockfish swim in and out of view. In the summer months, swimmers and snorkelers can get a small taste of this world by descending a long flight of wooden stairs to **China Cove.** The cove boasts clear, emerald green water and a series of hollowed-out tunnels to float through. During low or minus tides (most common in the winter months), visitors head to the tide pools at Weston Beach, where the edge of the

underwater world is revealed for a few hours, until the seawater rushes back in.

Head to Whalers Cove to bone up on local history. The **Whalers Cabin Museum,** a shack overlooking Whalers Cove, was built by Chinese fishermen and tells the story of Point Lobos and vicinity. Exhibits focus on shore whaling along California's central coast and display everything from harpoons and whale-oil barrels to historic Monterey Peninsula whaling photos. The museum is open as staffing allows, usually 9 A.M.–5 P.M.

Hikers can follow crisscrossing trails through groves of Monterey cypress and pines accented by colorful spring wildflowers (more than 300 species bloom in this park; best viewing is in April).

Recreation

BEACHES

The sloping, mile-long crescent of **Carmel Town Beach,** also known as Del Mar Beach, is breathtakingly beautiful, with blinding-white sands framing the aquamarine waters of Carmel Bay, but the ocean is too cold and dangerous for swimming. Located just a short walk from downtown Carmel at the end of Ocean Avenue, this "city beach" is a tourist zoo in summer, but perfect for sunset strolls in winter. There is no parking or entrance fee, and dogs are permitted to run free (no leashes required). An annual sandcastle-building contest is held on these sands each summer. South of 10th Street, fires can be built on Carmel Town Beach—a great way to stay warm while watching the sunset. Bring a guitar and some friends.

A less-crowded alternative is to take Carmelo Street off Rio Road to **Carmel River State Beach** (831/649-2836, www.parks.ca.gov), which is fringed with eucalyptus and cypress trees. This is where the locals go to get away. The river-fed lagoon is a bird sanctuary, providing habitat for hawks, kingfishers, cormorants, herons, pelicans, sandpipers, snowy egrets, and sometimes flocks of migrating ducks and geese. The lagoon formed by the Carmel River is a good place for children to wade in the water; it's much safer than the open surf. Look up on the hill on the south side of the river and you'll see a cross that marks the spot where Gaspar de Portolá erected his own cross to signal passing ships in 1769.

Just south of the main part of the beach are **Middle Beach,** a curving sandy crescent on the south side of the Carmel River, and **Monastery Beach** at San Jose Creek, 2.5 miles south of Carmel. Monastery Beach, which is also known as San Jose Creek Beach, is named

Silky fine white sand carpets the beaches on both sides of the Carmel River.

© ANN MARIE BROWN

for the Carmelite Monastery on the hill above it. These beaches are accessible year-round from right alongside Highway 1, but there is limited parking near the highway (the sign on the beach that you see from the road reads Carmel River State Beach). Another access to these beaches is from the trailhead at the end of Ribera Road off Highway 1 (also very limited parking). In summer or fall, you can also walk across the dry riverbed at Carmel River State Beach. While beautiful, both beaches are extremely hazardous for swimming, with steep drop-offs and a deadly undertow. Monastery Beach is very popular with scuba divers, but because of the treacherous surf and strong currents, it's only for the highly experienced.

Point Lobos State Reserve (Hwy. 1, 831/624-4909 or 831/624-3407, www.point lobos.org or www.parks.ca.gov, daily 8 A.M.–sunset, $10 parking fee) is known for its beautiful pocket beaches, especially photogenic and swimmer-friendly **China Cove.** But if you want to get away from the crowds, head to the park's **Gibson Beach,** accessible by a steep set of wooden stairs.

HIKING

Hikers can choose from numerous easy walking trails in the Carmel area. To get a good taste of the region, start with the one-mile hike from **Carmel Meadows** to **Monastery Beach.** From Highway 1 south of Rio Road, turn west on Ribera Road and drive 0.7 mile to its end. Follow the bluff top and beachside trail past Middle Beach to San Jose Creek and Monastery Beach. At low tide, there are numerous tide pools to explore, but beware of wading or swimming, as the surf is extremely dangerous here.

Point Lobos State Reserve (831/624-4909, www.pointlobos.org, $10 parking fee) is laced

with hiking trails. Two lovely pathways start from the **Sea Lion Point** parking area and you can connect them to make a three-mile round-trip hike. Start hiking on **Cypress Grove Trail,** which shows off the park's windswept Monterey cypress trees, one of only two remaining native Monterey cypress groves. The trail loops around and heads back toward the parking area, but just before you reach it, turn left on **North Shore Trail** and ascend to the right turnoff for Whaler's Knoll Trail. Follow the switchbacks uphill to the top of **Whaler's Knoll,** which delivers what is arguably the best view in the whole park. The knoll was the spot where early-20th-century whalers would watch for whales, then hang a signal flag when they spotted them.

Or follow the paved road in Point Lobos all the way to its end and the trailhead at **Bird Rock.** From here you can explore the south

Monterey cypress line the Cypress Grove Trail at Point Lobos State Reserve.

CARMEL

shore of the park on an easy two-mile out-and-back hike. **South Shore Trail** skirts the jagged coastline from China Cove to Sand Hill Cove, passing four tiny beach coves along the way: Hidden Beach, Weston Beach, The Slot, and Sand Hill Cove. Be sure to take the side trails to each of these secluded coves, where you are likely to spot sea otters frolicking about in the calm waters.

SCUBA DIVING

Point Lobos State Reserve (Hwy. 1, 3 miles south of Carmel, 831/624-4909, www.pointlobos.org, daily 8 A.M.–sunset, $10 parking fee) is one of the state's designated "underwater parks" in recognition of its aquatic beauty and diversity. Scuba and free diving are popular in the waters near Bluefish Cove and Whalers Cove, but diving permits are required. Only a limited number of permits are

available each day; make reservations online or call for information. Point Lobos is a great spot for divers of all ability levels, but rangers aren't kidding when they mention "treacherous cliff and surf conditions," so think first before scrambling off in search of bigger and better reefs.

Monastery Beach (2.5 miles south of Carmel, near San Jose Creek) is another area popular with divers, but it, too, can be dangerous even in the most serene surf. There's a steep offshore drop-off into submarine Carmel Canyon within a few hundred yards of shore, and unstable sand underfoot. Divers can drop down hundreds of feet very quickly on the north end of the beach. The locals call this beach "Mortuary Beach" because almost every year someone dies here, often from the strong current and/or dense kelp beds. Even experienced divers should make sure they are

Scuba divers use kayaks to carry their gear to dive spots in Whalers Cove at Point Lobos State Reserve.

mentally and physically prepared before going into the water.

To rent equipment, you'll need to head over to Monterey. Several shops can set you up with everything you need: **Glenn's Aquarius II Dive Shop** (32 Cannery Row, 831/375-6605 or 866/375-6605, www.aquarius2.com, Mon.–Fri. 9 A.M.–6 P.M., Sat.–Sun. 7 A.M.–6 P.M.), **Aquarius Dive Shop** (2040 Del Monte Blvd., 831/375-1933, www.aquariusdivers.com, Mon.–Fri. 9 A.M.–6 P.M., Sat.–Sun. 7 A.M.–6 P.M.), **Bamboo Reef** (614 Lighthouse Ave., 831/372-1685, www.bambooreef.com, Mon.–Fri. 9 A.M.–6 P.M., Sat.–Sun. 7 A M –6 P.M.), or **Monterey Bay Dive Center** (225 Cannery Row, 831/656-0454, www.mbdcscuba.com).

SURFING

Carmel's coastline offers myriad spots for hauling out your "big stick" and getting wet. If you don't know how to surf, or just want to get some local knowledge, contact **Carmel Surf School** (831/915-4065, www.carmelsurflessons.com). Owner Noah Greenberg has been teaching surfing for more than 20 years; he offers two-hour lessons with all equipment for $100.

SPAS

For a little pampering, head to the **Garden Spa at the La Playa Hotel** (Camino Real and 8th, 831/277-3279, www.laplayahotel.com, Sun.–Thurs. 9 A.M.–5 P.M., Fri.–Sat. 9 A.M.–7 P.M.) for a Swedish massage, a facial, foot reflexology, or something more exotic, like a Tibetan "raindrop technique massage," in which 11 different essential oils are dropped onto your back and massaged along your vertebrae (not for the ticklish). A variety of antiaging treatments are also available. The rates for most one-hour treatments are $125–155.

Over at the Crossroads Shopping Center, **Yon-Ka Signature Day Spa** (118 Crossroads Blvd., 831/625-4410 or 831/625-4497, Mon.–Sat. 10 A.M.–6 P.M., Sun. noon–5 P.M.) offers a range of massage, facial, and body treatments, as well as waxing, aromatherapy, microdermabrasion for the face (an exfoliation or minisanding technique in which the skin surface is gently abraded to stimulate new cell growth), and lymphatic drainage treatments (utilizing gentle pumping and stoking techniques to drain away pockets of water retention). The rates for most one-hour treatments are $95–120.

Entertainment and Shopping

NIGHTLIFE

Visitors don't come to Carmel to go clubbing. In general, the sidewalks roll up early in this quiet, gentrified town (live entertainment in bars or restaurants was against the law until 2006), but today there are a few spots where you might find something happening after 9 P.M. At **Jack London's Bar & Grill** (Su Vecino Court, Dolores St. btw. 5th and 6th Aves., 831/624-2336, www.jacklondons.com, Sun.–Thurs. 11:30 A.M.–11 P.M., Fri.–Sat.

11:30 A.M.–midnight) you can order food until midnight on Friday and Saturday nights, and there is usually a blues or jazz band playing for some portion of the evening (by law, the music has to stop at 10 P.M.) If you can't stay up that late, the Friday Happy Hour blues program (6:30–8:30 P.M.) means discounted appetizers, beers, and early-bird dinners accompanied by local blues musicians.

Live music is often on the weekend bill at **Baja Cantina** (7166 Carmel Valley Rd.,

CARMEL

831/625-2252, www.bajacantinacarmel.com, daily 11:30 A.M.–11 P.M.), three miles from downtown Carmel. This Mexican restaurant is also known for its fascinating collection of automobile memorabilia, mango enchiladas, and Baja fajitas.

It's not exactly a wild party scene, but at the **Mission Ranch Inn** (26270 Dolores St., 831/625-9040, www.missionranchcarmel .com, daily 5–11:30 P.M.) movie-star icon and owner Clint Eastwood occasionally shows up and jams with whoever is tinkling the ivories at the piano bar. This is a great place for an evening cocktail.

PERFORMING ARTS

Sunsets from the beach or from craggy Point Lobos are entertainment enough. But for human drama, the 500-seat outdoor **Forest Theater** (831/626-1681, www.foresttheater guild.org), on the north side of Mountain View between Santa Rita and Guadalupe, hosts light drama and musicals, Shakespeare, and concerts. Attending an outdoor evening concert here is part of the ultimate Carmel experience. Bring a picnic and sit by the blazing stone fireplaces on either side of the stage.

Something is almost always happening at the **Sunset Cultural Center** (San Carlos at 9th, 831/620-2040, www.sunsetcenter.org), whether it is ballet, opera, or live music. The **Pacific Repertory Theatre** at the 300-seat Golden Bough Theater (Monte Verde St. btw. 8th and 9th Aves., 831/622-0100, www.pac rep.org) is the only professional theater company on the Monterey Peninsula. Underneath the Golden Bough theater is the 100-seat Circle Theater, a theater-in-the-round, used for Pacific Rep's more experimental, cutting-edge plays.

Classical music is alive and well in Carmel thanks to the **Carmel Music Society** (831/625-9938, www.carmelmusic.org), which was founded in 1927 and still hosts concerts each year from October to May, and the **Monterey Symphony,** whose concert season also runs from October to May (831/624-8511 or 800/698-1138, www.carmelmusic.org).

FESTIVALS AND EVENTS
Spring
In May, the **Carmel Art Festival** (831/642-2503, www.carmelartfestival.org) celebrates the beauty and freedom of plein air painting with this three-day event, in which painters fan out all over the Monterey Peninsula to paint in the natural light outdoors. There's also a youth art show and a sculpture show.

Summer
If you think you know your way around a plastic bucket and a handheld shovel, you might want to try your hand at Carmel's **Annual Great Sand Castle Contest** (831/620-2020) held every September on the white sands at Carmel Town Beach. For the competitors, it's a stressful day that begins with fast and furious construction efforts at 8 A.M. and ends at the 2 P.M. judging, but for spectators, it's a fun day on the beach. By afternoon, Carmel Town Beach is dotted with a wide variety of sand-sculpted whimsical creatures and architectural marvels.

For something a little more highbrow, show up in July or August for the town's three-week-long **Bach Festival** (831/624-2046, www .bachfestival.org), with candlelight and twilight concerts presented at various venues, including the Carmel Mission. Fans of Johann Sebastian Bach will delight in this world-class classical music celebration, which includes lectures and recitals as well as formal concerts.

© ANN MARIE BROWN

CARMEL

Art lovers will be pleased to know that plein air painting is alive and well in Carmel.

Autumn

In September, food lovers flock to the Quail Lodge Resort in Carmel Valley for the **Carmel Tomato Fest** (www.tomatofest.com), a one-day celebration that heralds the bright red fruit that everyone thinks is a vegetable. More than 350 heirloom tomatoes are on display, and many types of seeds are available for purchase. Plus 60 of California's finest chefs serve up gourmet tomato dishes. Attendees can also sample wines from more than 50 local wineries and taste dozens of different tomato-based salsas.

SHOPPING

Downtown Carmel-by-the-Sea boasts some very upscale shops, including Tiffany & Co., Wilkes Bashford, Cole Hahn, and Louis Vuitton. Everything in town is within walking distance, but for power shopping in a concentrated area, head to **Carmel Plaza** (Ocean Ave. and Mission St., 831/624-1385, www .carmelplaza.com, Mon.–Sat. 10 A.M.–6 P.M., Sun. 11 A.M.–5 P.M.), a three-story open-air shopping plaza where you can enjoy the splash of fountains and the sweet smell of flower gardens. This is where Carmel's Fido-famous "Fountain of Woof" is located (on the ground floor), plus 40 shops, including the aforementioned heavy hitters.

If you tire of the crowds in downtown Carmel, head across Highway 1 to **Barnyard Shopping Village** (Hwy. 1 and Carmel Valley Rd., 831/624-8886, www.thebarnyard.com, Mon.–Sat. 10 A.M.–6 P.M., Sun. 11 A.M.–5 P.M.), which has apparel and jewelry stores, home decor and gift shops, half a dozen salons and day spas, and a variety of restaurants serving everything from fondue to sushi. A similar shopping experience can be found about 300 yards south at **The Crossroads Shopping Village** (Hwy. 1 and Rio Rd., 831/625-4106, www.crossroads shoppingvillage.com, Mon.–Sat. 10 A.M.–6 P.M.,

Sun. noon–5 P.M.). The Crossroads also has a few very practical stores, like a Safeway grocery store and Longs Drugs.

Antiques

Antique shopping in Carmel is not for bargain hunters, but if you are looking for high-quality, big-ticket items, there are plenty of downtown shops to choose from. The **Anderle Gallery** (Lincoln St. btw. Ocean and 7th Aves., 831/624-4199, www.anderle gallery.com, daily 10 A.M.–6 P.M.) specializes in tribal arts from Africa, New Guinea, India, Indonesia, and Thailand, including antique palace and temple doors made of teak and rosewood, furniture made from petrified wood, totems, and one-of-a-kind lamps with mica shades. A walk through this shop is like a visit to a museum.

For American and European antiques, head to **Tresors Antiques** (7th Ave. btw. Dolores and San Carlos Sts., 831/624-1115, www .tresorsantiques.com, daily 11 A.M.–5 P.M.), purveyors of 18th- and 19th-century Continental antiques, fine and decorative arts, and estate jewelry for more than 30 years. Check out their fascinating collection of antique clocks and barometers, silver candelabras, inkwells and inkstands, and gilded scent bottles.

Lily's Chance Discoveries (Su Vecino Ct. btw. 5th and 6th Aves., 831/622-9530, www.lilyschancediscoveries.com., daily 10 A.M.–6 P.M.) offers smaller-sized antique items, such as mirrors, dinnerware, out-of-print books, vintage jewelry, Oriental rugs, and objets d'art. For gift buyers and souvenir seekers, Lily's also has some nonantique items, including specialty soaps from France.

Art Galleries

Carmel Village boasts nearly 100 art galleries

in a one-square-mile area. A great place to start gallery hopping is the **Carmel Art Association Gallery** (Dolores St. btw. 5th and 6th Aves., 831/624-6176, www.carmelart.org, daily 10 A.M.–5 P.M.), founded here in 1927. The art association features more than 120 local artists and regularly presents an impressive selection of their painting, sculpture, and graphic arts. The **Weston Gallery, Inc.** (6th Ave. btw. Dolores and Lincoln Sts., 831/624-4453, www .westongallery.com, daily 10:30 A.M.–5:30 P.M.) offers 19th- and 20th-century photographs by namesake local photographers Edward Weston and Brett Weston, as well as Ansel Adams, Michael Kenna, Rod Dresser, and Chip Hooper. For more contemporary Monterey Peninsula photography, head to **Gallery Sur** (Dolores and 6th St., 831/626-2615, www .gallerysur.com, daily 10 A.M.–6 P.M.), or the **Center for Photographic Art** in the Sunset Cultural Center (San Carlos St. and 9th Ave., 831/625-5181, www.photography.org, Tues.– Sun. 1–5 P.M.).

Over at the **Winfield Gallery** (Dolores St. btw. Ocean St. and 7th Ave., 831/624-3369 or 800/289-1950, www.winfieldgallery.com, Mon.–Sat. 11 A.M.–5 P.M., Sun. noon–5 P.M.) the focus is on sculpture, painting, and ceramics by established artists such as Jack Zajac, Bruce Beasley, Dan Corbin, Gwynn Murrill, Nicolas Africano, Mel Schuler, Russell Chatham, Helen Frankenthaler, and Richard Diebenkorn.

Sculpture fans will also want to visit **Highlands Sculpture Gallery** (Dolores St. btw. 5th and 6th Aves., 831/624-0535, www.highlands-gallery.com, Thurs.–Tues. 11 A.M.–5 P.M.), where the emphasis is on modern and contemporary works of outdoor, indoor, wall, and kinetic sculptures. It's the kind of place where you will be tempted to touch the art, and here, you are allowed to.

Plein air painting is alive and well in Carmel. On almost any sunny day you can find painters in the gardens of the Carmel Mission, or along the coast at Point Lobos, working quickly to capture the natural sunlight at a certain moment in time. To see a sampling of these colorful impressionistic works conceived and created alfresco, go to **Galerie Plein Aire** (Dolores St. btw. 5th and 6th Aves., 831/625-5686, www.galeriepleinaire.com).

Clothing and Jewelry

If the saying is true that "everyone should own something from Tiffany's," you can make that happen (for yourself or someone else) at **Tiffany's** (Ocean Ave. and Mission St., 831/624-1385, www.shopcarmelplaza.com, Mon.–Sat. 10 A.M.–6 P.M., Sun. 11 A.M.–5 P.M.) at Carmel Plaza in downtown Carmel Village. Neighboring Tiffany & Co. in the Plaza are several other high-end apparel and accessory chains: Wilkes Bashford, Cole Hahn, Louis Vuitton, and Tommy Bahama.

But for one-of-a-kind clothing, several unique apparel shops that you won't find elsewhere are also located in downtown Carmel. At **Zebaah Gizelle** (San Carlos Square, 831/620-1199, www.zebaah.com, daily 11 A.M.–7 P.M.) you'll find a selection of handmade women's boots, shoes, and handbags made of 100 percent Italian leather. **Sylvie Unique Boutique** (Carmel Plaza, 831/620-0980, www.carmeluniqueboutique .com, Mon.–Sat. 10 A.M.–6 P.M., Sun. 11 A.M.–5 P.M.) specializes in apparel collections from Italy, France, Germany, Israel, Japan, and America. For upscale intimate apparel (ideal for brides or the hard to fit), **Intima European Lingerie** (Mission St. btw. Ocean St. and 7th Ave., 831/625-0599, www .intimacarmel.com, Mon.–Sat. 10 A.M.–6 P.M.,

Sun. 11 A.M.–5 P.M.) is a shop that raises undergarments to high art.

After you've been dressed to the nines, you'll need to accessorize with some fabulous jewelry, so head to **Cayen Collection** (W. Mission St. btw. 5th and 6th Aves., 831/626-2722, www .cayencollection.com, daily 11 A.M.–5 P.M.), which showcases the original works of over 20 jewelry artists and has an amazing collection of gemstones from around the world.

Gift and Home

Elsewhere in Carmel Village, there are dozens of shops to capture your interest. Although Ocean Avenue is the central shopping street, many great boutiques are located just a block or two from the main drag. For something different to tote home as a souvenir, **It's Cactus** (Mission St. btw. Ocean and 7th Aves., 831/626-4213, www.itscactus.com, daily 10 A.M.–6 P.M.) offers colorful indigenous folk art from Guatemala, Indonesia, and other places around the globe. A great spot for home furnishings is **Homescapes** (Dolores St. and 7th Aves., 831/624-6499, www.homescapes carmel.com, daily 10 A.M.–6 P.M.), which offers an impressive import selection, including personally selected furniture and antiques from China, Korea, Japan, England, and Europe. The store has a dizzying array of items—from plantation chairs and teak dining tables to steel bells and bubbling fountains for the garden. There are plenty of live plants, too, including a gorgeous selection of orchids.

For a nod to traditional gift giving, head to **Bittner** (Ocean and San Carlos, 888/248-8637, www.bittner.com, daily 10 A.M.–6 P.M.), the shop for fine pens, stationery, journals, and datebooks. Sure, it may seem old school, but there's nothing like writing checks with a $500 pen to make you feel like somebody special.

Pets

Carmel being a pet-pampering town, there is plenty of four-footed browsing to do around town. **Diggidy Dog** (Mission St. and Ocean Ave. across from the Carmel Plaza, 831/625-1585, www.diggidydogcarmel.com, daily 10 A.M.–6 P.M.) offers all the essential mutt merchandise, from toys and treats to well-stuffed beds. A few token cat items are available too. If your dog or cat is hungry, take him or her to **The Raw Connection** (6549 Carmel Rancho Blvd., 831/626-7555, www.therawconnection.com, Mon.–Sat. 9 A.M.–6 P.M., Sun. 11 A.M.–5 P.M.) where the two of you can select from a range of raw-food diets, healthy treats, and natural supplements to keep your pet in tip-top shape. To help less-fortunate creatures, buy gently used clothing, jewelry, art, books, collectibles, and antiques at the **Monterey County SPCA Benefit Shop** (26364 Carmel Rancho Ln. near Barnyard Shopping Village, 831/624-4211, www.spca mc.org, Mon.–Sat. 10 A.M.–4 P.M., Sun. noon–4 P.M.).

Accommodations

HOTELS AND INNS $100-200

The "best value in Carmel" award goes to **Lobos Lodge** (Monte Verde St. and Ocean Ave., 831/624-3874, www.loboslodge.com, $145–195), which is so close to the ocean (just a few blocks away) that the waves will lull you to sleep at night. Guests are treated to spacious rooms with gas fireplaces and a continental breakfast and newspaper delivered to your door in the morning. The 28 regular rooms are usually priced around $150; suites are more expensive, but these have living rooms as well as bedrooms, and some have kitchenettes. Even the regular rooms, which come with king or queen beds, are large enough to have sitting areas, so you aren't just getting a square box with a bed. Everything in Carmel is a short walk away; you can do without your car while you are here. The lodge decor is a bit dated, but everything is spotlessly clean and it's hard to beat the price.

A close second prize for "best value lodging" goes to **Carmel Village Inn** (Junipero Ave. and Ocean Ave., 831/624-3864 or 800/346-3864, www.carmelvillageinn.com, $135–195). Located a half mile from the beach, this 34-room inn is within easy walking distance of everything in Carmel village, so here, too, you can park your car and forget it. Parking and wireless Internet access are free, and a continental breakfast is served each morning by the stone fireplace in the lobby. Pay a little extra, and you can get a room with a fireplace (worth it for those chilly winter nights).

The Colonial Terrace (155 Highland Dr., 831/624-2741 or 800/345-8220, www.the colonialterrace.com, $170–220) is a great place to stay if you want to hear and see the ocean. While not on the beach, it's very close; the trade-off is that you'll have a longer stroll into town. This colonial-style collection of buildings has lovely landscaped common areas. Of the 26 rooms, some have ocean views and others overlook the courtyard and gardens. Most rooms have fireplaces and some have kitchens. The friendly hotel staff will lend you beach chairs and towels, and you can order a picnic lunch to take with you for the day.

The **Clarion Collection Carmel by the**

Sea (5th Ave. and Mission St., 831/624-5547 or 800/266-5547, www.clarionhotel.com, $150–200) is attractive, convenient, and a bargain by local standards. The Clarion is a typical chain motel in every way, and while the rooms won't win any awards for interior design, they work just fine for a decent night's sleep. Everything in Carmel is within walking distance, and you won't have to shell out your hard-earned cash for breakfast. A basket full of muffins, cereal, and goodies is delivered to your door each morning.

The Dolphin Inn (San Carlos St. and 4th Ave., 831/624-5356 or 800/433-4732, www.innsbythesea.com/dolphin, $140–190) provides a great value in an otherwise pricey area. Its location right in town allows you to access the best of Carmel. The balcony rooms near the reception area give you a view of the ocean on a clear day. A few pleasant extras include gas-burning fireplaces in many of the rooms and robes hanging in the closet. Pick up your map and discount book from the friendly front-desk folks before heading out for the day.

$200-300

◖ Mission Ranch (26270 Dolores St., 831/624-6436 or 800/538-8221, www.mission ranchcarmel.com, $220–300) has long been *the* place to stay in Carmel. What was once a pastoral dairy farm is now a quiet, B&B-style ranch owned by Clint Eastwood, who bought it in 1986 to save it from being turned into a condominium complex. The ranch overlooks the Carmel River and features views of the Carmel River wetlands and the coast at Point Lobos. Under Eastwood's ownership, the 1850s Victorian farmhouse and its outbuildings had an expensive makeover and together now resemble a Western village. The 31 guest rooms have

© KERRICK JAMES

Mission Ranch

UNIQUE ARCHITECTURE

The fairy tale-inspired architecture of Carmel is largely owed to the whimsical genius of local builder **Hugh Comstock,** who designed many of the town's quaintest structures in the 1920s. Comstock was not trained as an architect; he simply had a vivid imagination and a love of storybook-style elements like pitched gable roofs made of hand-cut redwood shake shingles, tall rock chimneys, hand-carved timbers, impractical nooks and crannies, diminutive windows and doors, and facades made of Carmel Valley chalk stone.

Comstock first practiced his charming "English countryside à la hobbit" style when building a house for his wife, a rag doll maker who wanted a home that would serve as a suitable showroom for her creations and reflect the whimsy of her profession. The tiny cottage was only 280 square feet, but its Hansel-and-Gretel charm quickly caught on in Carmel, and soon Comstock was designing and building similar structures all over town – often replacing the existing Craftsman and Victorian architecture – despite his lack of formal training. Comstock purposefully did not use a carpenter's level, so his cottages' lines were rarely straight and the chimneys crooked, but remarkably most were soundly built and withstood the test of time.

About 20 of Comstock's storybook cottages still stand on the east side of downtown Carmel, including his own studio at the corner of Santa Fe and 6th Avenues, and the Tuck Box Tea Room on Dolores Street between Ocean and 7th Avenues. The Carmel Chamber of Commerce Visitor Center (San Carlos btwn. 5th and 6th Sts., 800/550-4333, www.carmelcalifornia.org) provides a list of the Comstock building locations.

When the Great Depression hit in the 1930s, Comstock was forced to move to more economical construction methods and he started building structures out of adobe. In 1936 he created a waterproof formula for making adobe mud bricks. Rather than patenting his creation, which might have made him a small fortune, he freely shared his technology with the public.

© MONTEREY COUNTY CVB

Comstock's Tuck Box

More serious architects and builders also left an imprint on Carmel. In 1928, renowned California architect **Bernard Maybeck** designed the Harrison Memorial Library at Ocean Avenue and Lincoln Street. This open-to-the-public space is a prime example of the Arts and Crafts building style, and is a great place to hang out and read by the fireplace on winter days.

Julia Morgan was California's first renowned female architect and the genius who worked with newspaper magnate William Randolph Hearst on the design of Hearst Castle. Morgan built several private homes in Carmel, including one at 2981 Franciscan Way, overlooking the Carmel Mission. And perched above the ocean at Scenic Road at Martin Street is a **Frank Lloyd Wright**-designed home constructed in 1948. The stone building, known as the Walker House since it was built for Mrs. Clinton (Della) Walker, lies mostly below street level and takes full advantage of the view from its rocky promontory. Both of these famous structures are private residences and are not open for tours, but the architecturally curious are welcome to drive by.

fireplaces and whirlpool tubs, and are decorated here and there with props from Eastwood movies. Lodgings are available in the historic main house, the Hayloft, the Bunkhouse (which has its own living room and kitchen), and the Barn. The Meadow View Rooms feature, well, meadow views, complete with sheep ambling through the grass. Six championship tennis courts and a fitness facility provide ample opportunities for workouts. Another attraction is the excellent on-site Restaurant at Mission Ranch (26270 Dolores St., 831/625-9040, www.missionranchcarmel.com, daily 5–10 P.M., Sun. 10 A.M.–1:30 P.M., $18–30).

Vagabond's House Inn (4th Ave. and Dolores St., 800/262-1262 www.vagabonds houseinn.com, $215–275) is Tudor in style and built around a beautiful courtyard with an ancient oak and waterfalls. Its rooms provide many welcome luxuries such as fireplaces, large private baths, and private entrances. A wine-and-cheese reception is provided for guests in the courtyard in the evening. A light breakfast is delivered to your room at whatever time you specify. Concierge services are available, too, and pets are welcome for a small extra fee. The inn is within walking distance to all that matters in Carmel.

Horizon Inn and Ocean View Lodge (Junipero Ave. at 3rd Ave., 831/624-5327 or 800/350-7723, www.horizoninncarmel.com, $190–269) offers a range of rooms that may or may not include a whirlpool tub, fireplace, or kitchen, so be sure to ask for what you want when you book. The two properties are under one ownership and are located across the street from one another. Ocean View Lodge has a California-ranch style and is pet friendly at $20 a pet. Rooms and suites here have either a whirlpool tub or a fully equipped kitchen. The Horizon Inn is the fancier of the two properties and has a Mediterranean flavor, with private balconies outside of each room. Continental breakfasts are delivered in a basket to your door at both locations.

It's not in downtown Carmel, and you'll have to drive to most attractions, but the **Carmel Mission Inn** (3665 Rio Rd., 831/624-1841 or 800/348-9090, www.carmelmissioninncom, $190–240) is a great choice for travelers who want their lodgings to be less "vanilla" and more edgy/artsy/interesting. The inn is on the inland side of Highway 1. Rooms feature up-to-date upgrades, including iPod docks, 37-inch flat-panel televisions, wireless Internet, remodeled bathrooms, refrigerators, coffee makers, and more. A heated pool and two spas are on the grounds. A restaurant and bar, the Fuse Lounge café, serves breakfast and dinner daily. Immediately behind the hotel is the Barnyard shopping complex, with several more restaurants you can walk to.

Over $300

The **Tickle Pink Inn** (155 Highlands Dr., 831/624-1244 or 800/635-4774, www.tickle pink.com, $329–399), just four miles south of Carmel off Highway 1, offers spectacular views from 35 inviting rooms and suites, an ocean-view hot tub, continental breakfast, and wine and cheese at sunset. All rooms come with private balconies, flat-screen televisions, and a newspaper delivered to your door in the morning. Higher-priced rooms have fireplaces and/or whirlpool tubs. If you are wondering about the inn's name, the property once belonged to State Senator Edward and Mrs. Bess Tickle.

Featured in *Architectural Digest* magazine, **(The Tradewinds at Carmel** (Mission St. and 3rd Ave., 831/624-2776 or 800/624-6665, www.tradewindscarmel.com, $325–380) is a 28-room boutique hotel in downtown Carmel village that is luxuriously decorated in an Asian/Balinese theme. Expect the best of everything:

Egyptian cotton linens, down pillows, feather-beds, kimono robes and slippers, gourmet continental breakfast, attentive staff, and more. Many rooms boast ocean views, fireplaces, spa tubs, and/or private balconies. If you need extra space, several suites are available.

If you really want to splurge, book a room at the **Highlands Inn Hyatt** (120 Highlands Dr., 831/620-1234, www.highlandsinn.hyatt.com, $600–700) which, like the Tickle Pink Inn, is a few miles south of Carmel and just off Highway 1. This huge luxury resort has almost exclusively ocean-view rooms and suites that overlook the coast at Point Lobos State Reserve (five lower-priced rooms have garden views instead). Rooms are equipped with featherbeds, down pillows, soaking tubs, refrigerators, CD and DVD players, bathrobes, binoculars, and more. Most have wood-burning fireplaces and private patios or balconies. The *New York Times* is delivered to your room each morning. Nestled in the Monterey pines alongside the guest rooms is the resort's famous **Pacific's Edge** restaurant (120 Highlands Dr., 831/622-5445, www.pacificsedge.com, daily 5:30–9 P.M., $35–45), two cocktail lounges, a general store, a fitness room, an outdoor pool, and three outdoor spas.

BED-AND-BREAKFASTS

In Carmel, bed-and-breakfast inns are comparable in price to most area motels, and they're often much homier. The relaxed yet stylish **(Carmel Country Inn** (Dolores St. at 3rd Ave., 831/625-3263 or 800/215-6343, www.carmelcountryinn.com, $215–295) offers more than a typical B&B room; its 10 studios and suites feature private bathrooms (some with whirlpool tubs) and come with down comforters, country-pine furniture, gas fireplaces, color TV with cable, wireless Internet access, in-room coffeemakers, and refrigerators. A

continental breakfast is served in the kitchen each morning, and sherry is available in the evenings. This being Carmel, dogs and cats are welcome, too, for an extra $20 per night.

Another great Carmel B&B choice is the eight-room **(Sea View Inn** (Camino Real btw. 11th and 12th Aves., 831/624-8778, www.seaviewinncarmel.com, $110–185), just a few blocks from Carmel Town Beach and the downtown shopping area. The inn is tastefully decorated in a modern, breezy style, and there's a huge bonus here for the budget minded: The Sea View is much more affordable than other bed-and-breakfasts in town. The four rooms on the 3rd floor are the lowest priced; they are smaller, with slanted, attic-style ceilings, and two of them share a bath. Second-floor rooms are much larger (Room 7, with a four-poster canopy bed and a beguiling window seat, is the best of the lot). The 1st floor of this Craftsman-style building serves as common areas for the guests, including a living room/parlor, breakfast room, and front porch. The guest rooms don't have televisions or phones, but if you must stay connected to the outside world, there's free wireless Internet access. Breakfast and afternoon tea and wine are included in the deal.

The **Cobblestone Inn** (Junipero St. near 8th Ave., 800/833-8836, www.cobblestoneinncarmel.com, $260–325) is an exemplary B&B right in the heart of downtown Carmel. True to its name, it has a cobblestone courtyard and that classic Carmel English-Tudor style. Guest rooms are decked out with gas fireplaces, whirlpool tubs, sitting areas with window seats, and English country-house antiques. Beautifully prepared breakfasts are served in the sunny dining area, and guests look forward to afternoon wine and appetizers, plus daily homemade cookies.

Happy Landing Inn (Monte Verde St. btw. 5th and 6th Aves., 831/624-7917 or

800/297-6250, carmelhappylanding.com, $125–195) is situated near the heart of Carmel on a quiet side street and close to the beach. If your tastes run more toward storybook cottages than chic amenities, this is your place. The Great Room, with its vaulted ceiling and fireplace, will have you thinking that Hansel and Gretel might drop in momentarily. The award-winning gardens provide a romantic spot where you can wander the flagstone paths or join the garden gnomes at the small pond. Rates include a continental breakfast delivered to your room.

Carmel Wayfarer Inn (35 Mission St., 831/624-2711, www.carmelwayfarerinn.com, $139–189) is a small inn with 16 rooms located in a residential district within walking distance of shops, restaurants, and the beach. Park your car at the inn and you won't need it for the remainder of your stay. Both rooms and suites are available, some with kitchenettes. The buffet-style continental breakfasts are plentiful, and a wine-and-cheese reception is held each afternoon. Best of all, it's hard to beat the Carmel Wayfarer's prices.

Food

CASUAL DINING
American

A Carmel pooch and people pleaser, **The Forge in the Forest** (5th Ave. and Junipero St., 831/624-2233, www.forgeintheforest.com, Mon.–Thurs. 11:30 A.M.–9 P.M., Fri.–Sat. 11:30 A.M.–10 P.M., Sun. 11 A.M.–9 P.M. with brunch until 2:30 P.M., $20) is set in a one-time blacksmith shop, where outdoor garden tables are reserved for dogs and their people. You can dine alfresco year-round, as the patio is equipped with fireplaces, heaters, and big umbrellas. If it's pouring rain, the indoor dining rooms are equally charming and comfortable. Menu favorites include Reuben egg rolls with Russian dressing (really, they're good) and baked onion soup, but there's also an array of salads and sandwiches, plus steaks, ribs, and pastas. For dessert, it's hard to pass up the chocolate chip cookie dream or mocha mud pie. If Fido or Fifi are hungry, ask for the Dog Pound Menu, which features the Quarter Hounder.

Actor Clint Eastwood was once the owner of the **Hog's Breath Inn** (5th Ave. and San Carlos St., 831/625-1044, www.hogsbreathinn.net,

daily 11:30 A.M.–10 P.M., $15–25), and that's enough to inspire many Carmel visitors to stop in for a look-see or a meal. But regardless of its previous owner's fame, the Hog's Breath is

© ANN MARIE BROWN

Once owned by actor Clint Eastwood, the Hog's Breath Inn is the place for a classic Carmel patio dining experience.

CARMEL

a great place for a classic Carmel experience. The back patio, built with bricks and cobblestones and including a huge outdoor fireplace, is the kind of place where you'll want to linger all afternoon or evening. The indoor dining room has a cozy, pub-like ambience, with weathered wood, two fireplaces, and carved-wood animal heads mounted on the walls. Portions are hearty and the food is quintessentially American—cheeseburgers, cheese steaks, smoked brisket baby back ribs, pork chops, crab cakes, ahi tuna, and prime rib.

The star of *Dirty Harry* and *The Enforcer* still does own **The Restaurant at Mission Ranch** (26270 Dolores St., 831/625-9040, www .missionranchcarmel.com, daily 5–10 P.M., Sunday brunch 10 A.M.–1:30 P.M., $18–30), which serves "make my day" American fare at dinner—steaks, ribs, chicken, pasta, fresh local salmon and such—all served at tables near the wood-burning stove that starred in *The Unforgiven*. A children's menu is available, and the dining room has views of grazing sheep and the rocky Carmel coastline. The Sunday champagne brunch ($25 adults, $12.50 children), complete with live jazz, is worth a special trip.

Breakfast

Affordable and family-friendly **From Scratch,** at The Barnyard Shopping Center (3626 The Barnyard, 831/625-2448, daily 7 A.M.–8 P.M., $8–15), is a casual and eclectic place with local art on the walls. From Scratch delivers three great meals a day, but it is most popular for breakfast. The ambitious morning menu includes fresh-squeezed orange and grapefruit juice, smoothies, pancakes, and a wealth of egg dishes, including tasty huevos rancheros and corned beef hash. At lunch, choose from soups (the French onion is a specialty), salads, pastas, and sandwiches.

French

Head to **L'Escargot** (Mission St. btw. 4th and 5th Aves., 831/620-1942, www.escargot carmel.com, daily 5:30–9:30 P.M., $28–38) for classic French country cuisine such as coq au vin, marinated lamb, ratatouille, cassoulet, rabbit fricasse, and of course, the namesake escargot seeped in garlic-parley butter. This romantic, friendly restaurant serves up a three-course prix fixe dinner every night ($36), or you can choose from an à la carte menu. Whatever you order, save room for the crème brûlée, which is done to perfection here.

German

Le Coq d'Or (Mission St. btw. 4th and 5th Aves., 831/626-9319, www.lecoqdor.com, daily from 5 P.M., $24–34) has a menu with German dishes in one column and French in the other. This family-run restaurant has the homey feel of your German grandmother's house with cowbells hanging from the rafters. The average tourist will never find it, and those looking to be *seen* might turn and run. The lucky few who dine here will be captivated by the Sauerbraten, Jager Schnitzel, and Beef Rouladen. Outdoor seating and friendly service complete the dining experience. This being Carmel, dogs are welcome, too.

Italian

Little Napoli (Dolores St. near 7th Ave., 831/626-6335, www.littlenapoli.com, daily 11:30 A.M.–10 P.M., $23–30) is chef/owner Rick Pepe's tribute to Italy. This is the kind of Italian restaurant where folks sit side by side and get to know their neighbors as they drink chianti and eat bruschetta, pizza, pasta, cioppino, and risotto. Pepe's famous garlic bread is made from a 100-year-old family recipe; the olive oil comes in saucers for dipping. A great wine list, friendly service, and tiramisu for dessert (or a host of other traditional dolce offerings) make this a true Italian experience.

Restauranteur David Fink—the genius behind the Carmel dining empire that includes Bouchee and L'Auberge Carmel—also runs **Cantinetta Luca** (Dolores St. btw. Ocean and 7th Aves., 831/625-6500, www.cantinetta luca.com, Mon.–Fri. noon–2:30 P.M. and 5–9:30 P.M., Fri.–Sat. noon–2:30 P.M. and 5–10 P.M., $25), a casually elegant spot serving pizzas fired in their wood-burning oven, whole fish, roasted chicken, homemade pasta, and a dozen varieties of salumis. Many of the entrées are served family style, perfect for sharing. Try the pumpkin ravioli, a perennial favorite. For dessert, the chef takes panini bread, lathers it with chocolate spread, adds sliced bananas, and grills it until it's melted and gooey. It's like an adult version of s'mores.

On a sunny day, get a seat on the rooftop patio at **Piatti** (6th St. at Junipero, 831/625-1766, www.piatti.com, Sun.–Thurs. 11:30 A.M.–10 P.M., Fri.–Sat. 11:30 A.M.–11 P.M., $10–25) and you'll feel like an all-knowing Carmel local. Since it's off the main drag, most casual tourists never even find this restaurant, let alone know about its alfresco dining option. Yes, this Piatti is part of a chain, but the grilled asparagus appetizer, pizzas cooked in a stone hearth, fresh pastas (including cannelloni to die for), and local petrale sole are all specialties of this particular Piatti's executive chef. Everything is priced right, and families with kids are treated kindly here.

Japanese

A best bet in Carmel for ultra-fresh sushi and other Japanese specialties is The Barnyard's **Robata Grill & Sake Bar** (3658 The Barnyard, 831/624-2643, Mon.–Sat. 11:30 A.M.–2 P.M.

and 5–7 P.M., Sun. 5–7 P.M., $15–20), one of the locals' favorites since 1980. The Japanese food is expertly prepared—from the light golden tempura to the teriyaki beef—and the outdoor seating around the fireplace is a great spot to finish off your day in Carmel.

Mediterranan

Notably dog-friendly is the charming, quintessentially Carmel **Portabella** (Ocean Ave. btw. Lincoln and Monte Verde Sts., 831/624-4395, daily 11:30 A.M.–11 P.M., $22–33), which serves wonderful Mediterranean cuisine with dishes rich in color and flavor, such as fresh goat cheese ravioli, porcini-crusted dayboat scallops, Dungeness crab cakes, and their signature roasted corn and Dungeness crab bisque. If you are traveling with your canine friend, he or she can sit with you on the flagstone patio and enjoy the white-linen water dish treatment. The gardens surrounding the restaurant are as enjoyable as the food.

Seafood

❰ **Flying Fish Grill** (Mission St. btw. Ocean and 7th Aves., 831/625-1962, daily from 5 P.M., $19–33) serves up ample portions of innovative Asian grilled seafood—a fusion of Japanese and California influences. Tucked away on the basement level of Carmel Plaza, the creative dishes (try the peppered ahi, which is blackened and served with mustard and sesame-soy vinaigrette and angel-hair pasta, or the panfried almond sea bass with whipped potatoes, Chinese cabbage, and rock shrimp stir-fry) and first-rate service make it worth the effort to find. The ambiance created by the small booths, tight seating, and low lighting with no windows makes you feel like you've uncovered the locals' secret spot. You have.

CARMEL

CARMEL

Southwestern

One of Carmel's most long-lived restaurants, the **Rio Grill** in the Crossroads Shopping Village (101 Crossroads Blvd. at Hwy. 1 and Rio Rd., 831/625-5436, www.riogrill.com, lunch Mon.–Sat. 11:30 A.M.–4 P.M., dinner Sun.–Thurs. 4–10 P.M., Fri.–Sat. 4–11 P.M., Sun. brunch 11:30 A.M.–4 P.M., $25) is a dependable favorite for innovative Southwestern-style American fare, like grilled prawns on penne pasta or pumpkin-seed-crusted salmon. Many entrées are served straight from the oak wood smoker, like the chipotle chicken or the fire-roasted Castroville artichoke. Don't miss the Rio's famous ice-cream sandwich. The wine list is a winner, which is why this restaurant gets the nod from *Wine Spectator* year after year.

FINE DINING

California

The floor-to-ceiling windows at (**Anton and Michel** (Mission St. btw. Ocean and 7th Aves., 831/624-2406, www.antonandmichel.com, daily 11:30 A.M.–3 P.M. and 5:30–9:30 P.M., $25–39) overlook the Court of the Fountains patio, a Carmel landmark. The Old World dining room is decorated with original art, creating a regal setting for plates of Continental-California classics like rack of lamb, Chateaubriand, farmed abalone, Caesar salad, and flambé desserts such as cherries jubilee prepared at the table. The lengthy wine list includes over 800 selections. Add it all up and you have a perfect recipe for a romantic evening.

For dining with an ocean view, it's hard to beat the Highlands Inn's swanky restaurant, (**Pacific's Edge** (120 Highlands Dr., 831/622-5445, www.pacificsedge.com, daily 5:30–9 P.M., $35–45), which features contemporary California cuisine with a French influence—mushroom crepes, maple-glazed duck breast, roasted striped bass, and sautéed day boat scallops. Set high on a cliff overlooking the Pacific, this dining room has witnessed a lot of marriage proposals, anniversaries, and the like. Make sure you time your reservation so you can enjoy the spectacular sunset show (and pray that it's not obscured by fog). Executive chef Mark Ayers has won a long list of awards, and his five-course tasting menu ($90, or $150 with wine) changes nightly. For those so inclined, Pacific's Edge also offers caviar service and a cigar menu, plus a wine list with more than 1,000 choices.

French

(**Bouchée Bistro** (Mission St. btw. Ocean and 7th Aves., 831/626-7880, www.bouchee carmel.com, dinner Sun.–Thurs. 5:30–9:30 P.M., Fri.–Sat. 5:30–10 P.M., $22–28) and its adjacent wine shop are the sort of places you might expect to find in Paris, but here they are in downtown Carmel. The menu offers classic bistro dishes with a Monterey regional influence, which means local ingredients are prominently featured. Wine is a big part of the dining experience, with many wines offered by the glass as well as the bottle. Be sure to finish off your meal with Bouchée's selection of artisan cheeses and a glass of port. If you're a *Zagat* follower, Bouchée is one of the guide's favorite Monterey-area restaurants.

Bouchée's owner, restaurateur David Fink, is also the mastermind behind **L'Auberge Carmel** (Monte Verde St. at 7th Ave., 831/624-8578, www.laubergecarmel.com, Wed.–Sun. 6–9:30 P.M., $75–110), which has been named one of the top 50 restaurants in the U.S. by *Gourmet* magazine and is in proud possession of a Michelin star. With only 12 tables, it's not easy to get a reservation, but the intimacy of the space makes a meal here even more special.

A multicourse prix fixe menu is served nightly, with an optional wine pairing for an additional fee ($65–95). An underground wine cellar houses a 4,500-bottle collection. The daily changing menu is contemporary Californian with European influences, which could mean roast squab, strawberry soup with yogurt-mint sorbet, suckling pig with black truffle gnocchi, or big-eye tuna with blood orange.

Italian

Casanova (5th Ave. btw. Mission and San Carlos Sts., 831/625-0501, www.casanova restaurant.com, lunch daily 11:30–3 P.M., dinner daily 5–10 P.M., $20–30) is a Carmel classic in every way, from its charming exterior complete with brick patio, bistro tables, pots overflowing with flowers, and a sturdy-looking *bicyclette,* to its award-winning, hand-dug

wine cellar that has been excavated to 14 feet below the restaurant, and holds about 30,000 bottles. Casanova serves both Southern French and Northern Italian cuisine in its romantic Old World provincial-style dining rooms, plus has a heated garden for temperature-sensitive romantics. House-made pastas here are exceptional, as are the desserts.

Seafood and Steak

Immensely popular **Grasing's Coastal Cuisine** in the Jordan Center (corner of 6th Ave. and Mission St., 831/624-6562, www.grasings .com, daily 11:30 A.M.–2 P.M. and 5–9 P.M., $28) is the pet project of Kurt Grasing, one of the top chefs on the West Coast. At dinner, fish and seafood are the stars of the show, including crab risotto, seafood paella, and bronzed salmon with portabella mushrooms, roasted

Casanova is one of Carmel's most romantic restaurants.

garlic, and Yukon gold potatoes. Vegetarians won't starve, with choices such as lasagna with artichokes, tomatoes, spinach, Asiago cheese, and lemon vinaigrette.

Less fishy and more meaty is Grasing's up-beat **Carmel Chop House** (5th Ave. and San Carlos, 831/625-1199, www.carmelchophouse.com, daily 5–9 P.M., $20–35), a true steak house

featuring prime corn-fed meat—beef, lamb, pork, and veal—plus Maine lobster, Caesar salads, and other traditional American foods. Both of Grasing's Carmel restaurants come highly rated by *Zagat,* and at the Chop House, Grasing has teamed up with another contemporary food star, restauranteur and food critic Narsai David, so it's reasonable to expect greatness here.

CARMEL

Practicalities

INFORMATION AND SERVICES
Tourist Information
The **Carmel Chamber of Commerce** and visitors center is in the Eastwood Building (San Carlos St. btw. 5th and 6th Aves., 831/624-2522 or 800/550-4333, www.carmelcalifornia.org). Its annual *Guide to Carmel* includes information on just about everything—from shopping hot spots to accommodations and eateries. Another useful website is www.carmelcalifornia.com, which offers discount coupons for shopping, restaurants, and lodgings in Carmel, as well as general visitor information.

Media and Communications
The weekly *Carmel Pine Cone* (www.carmelpinecone.com) newspaper covers local events and politics. Two **post offices** are found in Carmel. One is located downtown at Dolores Street and 5th Avenue (831/624-3630, Mon.–Fri. 9 A.M.–4 P.M.). The other is located just off Rio Road (3845 Via Nona Marie, 831/625-9529) and is open on Saturdays (10 A.M.–1 P.M.) as well as weekdays (9 A.M.–5 P.M.).

Emergency Services
The nearest hospital is a few miles away in Monterey: **Community Hospital of the Monterey Peninsula** (CHOMP, 831/624-5311, www.chomp.org) is located on Monterey/Carmel hill west of Highway 1 just off Highway 68. The nearest **police** station (831/624-6403) is located on the southeast corner of Junipero and 4th Avenues.

GETTING THERE AND AROUND
In summer and on most warm-weather weekends, traffic on Highway 1 can back up for a mile or more in either direction due to the Carmel "crunch." At such times, parking is usually nonexistent. (Even if you do find a parking spot in downtown Carmel, don't dawdle; parking is limited to one hour, and you risk a steep fine if you're late getting back.)

To avoid the hassle and get to Carmel from Monterey without car or bike, take the **Monterey-Salinas Transit** bus 52 (831/899-2555, www.mst.org). Better yet, come to Carmel for a couple days and pretend you live here. Once you have arrived at your lodging, you can walk almost anywhere you want to go.

Carmel Valley

The sunny (and warmer), sprawling "village" of Carmel Valley stretches some 14 miles inland via Carmel Valley Road, a well-designed but curvaceous highway that runs between Highway 1 and the inland suburbs, wineries, and golf and tennis farms (including John Gardiner's Tennis Ranch). Affluence is the order of the day in most of Carmel Valley, at least until you drive farther back into the mountains, beyond the golf courses and vineyards, where there are a few surprises, like the Tassajara Zen Center and the Mira Observatory.

SIGHTS

(Tassajara Zen Mountain Center

Tassajara Hot Springs, beyond Carmel Valley Road in what is now the Ventana Wilderness, was established in 1869 and has been a respected area resort for over a hundred years. According to Native American legend, these curative springs first flowed from the eyes of a young chief seeking help for his dying sister. Offering himself as a sacrifice to the sun, he turned to stone, and his tears became the hot springs.

Today the hot springs are a part of the monastic Tassajara Zen Mountain Center (Tassajara Rd. turnoff at Cachagua Rd. near Tularcitos, www.sfzc.org/tassajara, 415/865-1899), affiliated with the San Francisco Zen Center, the first Soto Zen monastery outside of Asia. Casual visitors can come here for the day or stay overnight in spring and summer to enjoy the hot springs plus enjoy marvelous vegetarian meals. (From late Sept. to late Apr., Tassajara is closed to guests so that it can function fully as a monastery, with its monks in silent retreat.)

Guests are also welcome to join Tassajara's residents for meditation and chanting every morning and evening; free instruction is offered daily at 4 p.m. Hikers will also find a wealth of beautiful trails throughout the property.

Access to Tassajara isn't easy; guests arrive either by driving their own cars (four-wheel drive is strongly recommended as the last 14 miles are on a dirt road with steep drop-offs and a scary, narrow descent), or by driving to the junction at the hamlet of Jamestown and then taking "the Stage," an eight passenger van (reservations required, $45 round-trip). For hot springs lovers, the effort is more than worthwhile. The resort's bathhouse is Japanese style, with separate sides for men and women. Each side includes a tiled indoor hot plunge, an outdoor plunge, large decks for sunning and yoga, a steam room, showers, and a small private bath. Reservations are required for day guests, who can use all the resort's facilities between 9 a.m. and 9 p.m. ($25 adults, $12 children, call 831/659-2229 to reserve no more than two weeks in advance). Overnight guests are housed in cabins or dormitories ($90–160 per person includes three meals, call 415/865-1899 to reserve). There is a pay phone at Tassajara but no cell phone reception or Internet connection. Use of computers or any electronic equipment is discouraged. (Note: Although the area around Tassajara was badly burned in the summer 2008 Basin Complex Fire, including the region surrounding the access road, the resort and all its buildings were saved.)

MIRA Observatory

If for some reason you decide to drive the last six miles of unpaved Tassajara Road, this is

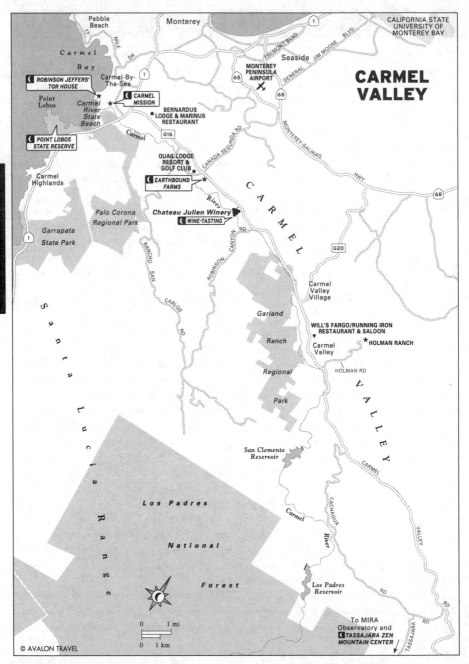

Pebble Beach

Monterey

CALIFORNIA STATE UNIVERSITY OF MONTEREY BAY

Carmel Bay

☾ ROBINSON JEFFERS' TOR HOUSE

Point Lobos

Carmel-By-The-Sea

☾ CARMEL MISSION

Carmel River State Beach

☾ POINT LOBOS STATE RESERVE

Seaside

MONTEREY PENINSULA AIRPORT

CARMEL VALLEY

BERNARDUS LODGE & MARINUS RESTAURANT

Carmel

G16

QUAIL LODGE RESORT & GOLF CLUB

☾ EARTHBOUND FARMS

Carmel Highlands

Palo Corona Regional Park

River

Chateau Julien Winery
☾ WINE-TASTING

C A R M E L

Garrapata State Park

ROBINSON CANYON RD

RANCHO SAN CARLOS RD

G20

Carmel Valley Village

S a n t a   L u c i a   R a n g e

Garland

Ranch

Regional

Park

WILL'S FARGO/RUNNING IRON RESTAURANT & SALOON

Carmel Valley

★ HOLMAN RANCH

HOLMAN RD

V A L L E Y

San Clemente Reservoir

CARMEL

CACHAGUA

VALLEY

L o s   P a d r e s

Carmel

River

N a t i o n a l

Los Padres Reservoir

RD

F o r e s t

TASSAJARA RD

To MIRA Observatory and
☾ TASSAJARA ZEN MOUNTAIN CENTER

0   1 mi

0   1 km

© AVALON TRAVEL

where you'll end up. Open to the public for tours in summer and on Sunday afternoons only in early fall, the Monterey Institute for Research in Astronomy (MIRA) Observatory is a barrel-shaped research station built atop Chews Ridge. Located high in the Santa Lucia Mountains and 12 miles inland from the coast, it is one of the best places in the continental United States for optical astronomy. Guests on the public tour (831/883-1000, www.mira.org, free tours on Sundays 2:30–4:30 P.M. by reservation only) get to see MIRA's 36-inch professional research telescope, learn some of the unique history that led to MIRA and its Oliver Observing Station, and discover how this high-tech research center runs on solar and wind power and collected rainwater. Even if you aren't captivated by astronomy, an afternoon spent at the observatory provides great views of the Ventana Wilderness (still beautiful even

after the 2008 wildfires), the Salinas Valley, the Monterey Peninsula, and on a clear day, all the way east to the Sierra Nevada mountains.

MIRA's earth-tone, two-story, corrugated Oliver Observing Station—named after a retired Hewlett-Packard vice president who kicked in some cash, some advanced electronics, and the 36-inch telescope—includes office and living space for its resident astronomers. It has a unique rooftop that slides in and out of place, exposing the telescope to the sky and quickly dissipating heat. The building has earned design awards from the American Institute of Architects.

◖ Earthbound Farms

Located 3.5 miles east of Highway 1 near Quail Lodge Resort, Earthbound Farms Farm Stand (7250 Carmel Valley Rd , 831/625-6219, Mon.–Sat. 8 A.M.–6:30 P.M.,

© ANN MARIE BROWN

Every season produces a bounty of organic produce at Earthbound Farms Farm Stand.

CARMEL

Sun. 9 A.M.–6 P.M.) is part of a 30-acre research and development organic farm that grows lettuce/salad mixes, heirloom potatoes, pumpkins, squash, raspberries, flowers, and more. Visitors can purchase vegetables, flowers, and farm-related gifts; enjoy a snack made in the farm's certified organic kitchen (the grilled vegetable lasagna with pesto is a winner, but if you just want dessert, go for the carrot cake); put together a salad from an all-organic salad bar; or take a stroll around the "cut your own" herb garden or chamomile aromatherapy labyrinth. For children, there is a kids' garden with lots of plants to touch and feel, plus an organic corn maze to navigate through in the autumn. On Saturdays from April to October, special events are often taking place, such as "bug walks" in which visitors help to release ladybugs into the farm fields.

◖ Wine-Tasting

Not surprising for such a moderate Mediterranean climate, vineyards do well in Carmel Valley—particularly with chardonnay and pinot noir grapes, but also cabernet sauvignon, merlot, syrah, and sauvignon blanc. Wine-tasting has become a major tourist attraction in the valley, starting with the fabulous **Château Julien Wine Estate** (8940 Carmel Valley Rd., 831/624-2600, www.chateaujulien.com, Mon.–Fri. 8 A.M.–5 P.M., Sat.–Sun. 11 A.M.–5 P.M.), which is housed in a French-style chateau set on a vineyard-covered hill. This boutique winery specializes in merlot, but chardonnay and cabernet sauvignon grapes are also grown. In addition to traditional wine-tasting, the estate offers free tours of its gardens and vineyards (by reservation only, Mon.–Fri. 10:30 A.M. and 2:30 P.M., Sat.–Sun. 12:30 and 2:30 P.M.).

© ANN MARIE BROWN

While wine-tasting in Carmel Valley, stopping at Château Julien is a must.

At posh **Bernardus Winery** (5 W. Carmel Valley Rd., 831/659-1900 or 800/223-2533, www.bernardus.com, daily 11 A.M.–5 P.M.) wine is elevated to the level of art. You can sample that art—Bordeaux-style varietals, chardonnay, pinot noir, and sauvignon blanc—at its swanky tasting room. Those with excess cash burning a hole in their pockets can also stay at the associated Bernardus Lodge (415 Carmel Valley Rd., 831/659-3247 or 888/648-9463, www.bernardus .com, $475–675), and/or dine at the lodge's highly lauded Marinus restaurant (Bernardus Lodge, 415 Carmel Valley Rd., 831/658-3595, www.bernardus.com, daily 6–10 P.M., $50).

Also check out other premium, small-production wineries in Carmel Valley, such as **Heller Estate Organic Vineyards** (831/659-6220, 69 W. Carmel Valley Rd., www.hellerestate.com, Mon.–Thurs. 11 A.M.–5:30 P.M., Fri.–Sun. 11 A.M.–6 P.M.), which produces cabernet sauvignon, chenin blanc, merlot, pinot noir, port, late harvest reisling, and chardonnay. Or visit the **Parsonage** tasting room and art gallery, located right in Carmel Valley Village, a half mile from the Parsonage vineyard and winery (19 E. Carmel Valley Rd., 831/659-7322, www.parsonagewine.com, Thurs.–Mon. 11 A.M.–6 P.M.). This tiny, seven-acre vineyard produces small batches of syrah, cabernet sauvignon, and merlot.

Although you can drive the winery-laden Carmel Valley Road on your own, a better option is to ride the Monterey-Salinas Transit **Carmel Valley Grapevine Express** (888/678-2871, www.mst.org, $4.50 to ride all day), which departs daily from the Barnyard Shopping Center (3626 The Barnyard) and the Crossroads Shopping Center (Hwy. 1 and Rio Rd.), then stops at Rancho Cellars, Boete Winery, Château Julien, Heller Estate, Jouillian, Bernardus, and other tasting rooms.

If you're thinking of wine-tasting in Carmel Valley, leave the driving to the Grapevine Express.

Visitors coming from Monterey can board the **Grapevine Express** at the Monterey Transit Plaza (at Jules Simoneau Plaza at the intersection of Munras Ave., Pearl St., and Tyler St. near the southern end of Alvarado St. in downtown Monterey) every hour at 15 minutes past the hour, starting at 9:15 A.M. daily. Or, Monterey visitors can take a guided five-hour tour on the **Wine Trolley** (831/624-1700, www .winetrolleytours.com, $49). The trolley picks up passengers at 11 A.M. daily at the Portola Plaza bus stop (off Del Monte Ave.); advance reservations are required.

RECREATION
Hiking
If you don't care for golf courses or wineries, you'll be glad to know that some notable Carmel Valley traditions remain, like wide-open

spaces. Outdoorsy types will appreciate **Garland Ranch Regional Park** (700 W. Carmel Valley Rd., 831/659-4488 or 831/659-6065, www.mprpd.org), 8.6 miles east of Highway 1. The park offers hiking trails on 4,500 hilly acres; the best place to start your exploration is at Garland Ranch's excellent visitors center (pick up a free trail map while you are there). The center serves as the trailhead for a 3.2-mile loop on **Lupine, Waterfall, and Mesa Trails.** Lupine Trail meanders along the open floodplains of the Carmel River, and yes, it is resplendent with blooming lupine in the spring. Waterfall Trail travels past the park's small waterfall, which flows only in the wettest months of the year (usually Dec.–Mar.), then heads uphill to a high mesa which offers views of Carmel Valley and beyond. Connect to Mesa Trail near Mesa Pond; then follow it back to Lupine Trail and the visitors center.

For a longer hike of 5.6 miles round-trip, you'll gain an astounding view from the top of **Snivley's Ridge.** Getting there requires a healthy climb of 1,600 feet, so this trip is best saved for a cool day. Take Lupine Trail from the visitors center, then continue uphill on Mesa Trail to Sky Trail, always heading uphill. Many hikers stop at the point where Sky Trail reaches Snivley's Ridge Trail, at a bench with a panoramic view of Carmel Valley, the forested Santa Lucia Mountains, and the Pacific Ocean. But those determined to reach the park's highest point should turn right on Snivley's Ridge Trail and walk another 0.75 mile west. Here you'll find a side trail leading left to a 2,038-foot-high point, offering spectacular views of Carmel, the Monterey Peninsula, and the ocean.

Horseback Riding

Once a hideaway for Hollywood celebrities, the 400-acre **Holman Ranch** (60 Holman Rd., 831/659-6054, www.holmanranch.com) is now a popular spot for weddings, family reunions, and corporate events. Its sun-baked vineyards produce pinot noir grapes, and the Holman Ranch Equestrian Center provides one- and two-hour guided scenic trail rides, horse boarding, English and Western riding lessons, and gentle pony rides for children. On weekends, the "Pastures of Heaven Picnic Ride" is offered. This three-hour ride departs at 11 A.M. and includes a picnic lunch ($60). Holman Ranch's rides are the only publicly accessible trail rides in Carmel Valley. The ranch is located 12 miles from Highway 1 off Carmel Valley Road.

Off-Roading

And now for something completely different...You can experience off-road driving in a Land Rover vehicle and in the company of a professional Land River Driving Instructor at **Quail Lodge Resort** (8205 Valley Greens Dr., 831/620-8854 or 800/239-0533, www.landroverusa.com). A variety of tour packages are available, from one- or two-hour sessions ($225–325) to full-day adventures ($850). All participants start on a dedicated "lesson" course, then progress to double-track trails that wind around the resort's 850 acres. The lesson courses allow participants to learn the basics of off-road driving in a controlled environment, covering driving challenges such as how to handle steep ascents and descents, log crossings, creek crossings, and rock and boulder crawls.

ACCOMMODATIONS
Camping

Tent campers don't have many options in Carmel Valley, but can always head south to

Andrew Molera State Park north of Big Sur. RVers have a couple parks to choose from within about five miles of downtown Carmel. **Carmel by the River RV Park** (27680 Schulte Rd. off Carmel Valley Rd., 831/624-9329, www.carmelrv.com, $56) offers 35 attractively landscaped RV sites right on the Carmel River, with full hookups, cable TV, laundry facilities, a recreation room, and other amenities. No tents are permitted. Nearby, **Saddle Mountain RV Park and Campground** (end of Schulte Rd., 831/624-1617, $30–50) offers 50 sites for tents or RVs (reservations accepted for weekends only), with restrooms, showers, picnic tables, a swimming pool, and a playground.

Resorts and Lodges

To see how the other one percent lives, book at stay the **Bernardus Lodge** (415 Carmel Valley Rd., 831/659-3247 or 888/648-9463, www .bernardus.com, $475–675) in Carmel Valley, a fine resort affiliated with the Bernardus Winery. Crafted from limestone, logs, ceramic tiles, and rich interior woods, the nine village-style buildings feature 57 suites that come with a bounty of amenities, including feather beds, limestone fireplaces, oversized bathtubs for two, French doors that open onto private terraces, a different wine-and-cheese tasting every night and a full-service spa. Educational forums on gardening, the culinary arts, and viticulture are held on a regular basis. There's an on-site ballroom, the celebrated Marinus restaurant (Bernardus Lodge, 415 Carmel Valley Rd., 831/658-3595, www.bernardus.com, daily 6–10 P.M., $50), and the more casual Wickets bistro. Outdoor recreation options include tennis and bocce ball, croquet, swimming, hiking and horseback riding on adjacent mountain trails, and golfing at neighboring resorts.

Another great choice for luxury accommodations, especially for golfers, is the five-star **Quail Lodge Resort & Golf Club** (8205 Valley Greens Dr., 831/624-2888 or 888/828-8787, www.quaillodge.com, $380–575) at the Carmel Valley Golf and Country Club. The lodge features elegant contemporary rooms and suites, some with fireplaces, plus access to private spa, tennis, and golf facilities. Even the smallest rooms are 450 square feet and feature private patios or balconies, plasma-screen televisions, and bathrooms with granite countertops. Many rooms have golf course views; the lodge is set on 850 acres of fairways and greens. If you don't want to wander far from your room, fine dining is available on-site at **The Covey** (831/620-8860, Tues.–Sat. 6–9 P.M., $35–50). Canines are welcome too, for an extra $35 per night; doggy beds and a Carmel doggie travel guide are provided.

FOOD

A must-visit for the serious epicurean, **Ⓒ Marinus** at Bernardus Lodge (415 Carmel Valley Rd., 831/658-3595, www.bernardus .com, daily 6–10 P.M., $50) can boast of having one of the country's best wine cellars, European master chef Cal Stamenov in charge of the kitchen, and four-star service. With all that going for it, it's no wonder the restaurant has been the frequent recipient of accolades from *Zagat, Wine Spectator,* and *Gourmet* magazine. Much of the produce used in the kitchen comes from the resort's own garden or from nearby organic farms. Meats and seafood are sustainably raised and/or harvested. The dinner menu changes nightly but might include Scottish partridge, Monterey red abalone, Dungeness crab, portobello mushroom soup, or a black truffle banana split.

A Carmel Valley Village institution, **Will's Fargo** (16 E. Carmel Valley Rd., 831/659-2774, www.willsfargo.com, daily from 4:30 P.M., $40) is the place to go for a classic Western prime- and choice-cut beef dinner. You can even have your red meat raw, if you so choose, as in steak tartar, but the rib-eye porterhouse is the most popular cut here. And if your dining partner is watching his or her cholesterol, a few fish and pasta entrées on the menu will serve that purpose.

Also located in Carmel Valley Village, the **Running Iron Restaurant and Saloon** (24 W. Carmel Valley Rd., 831/659-4633, Mon.–Thurs. 11 A.M.–9 P.M., Fri. 11 A.M.–9:30 P.M., Sat. 10 A.M.–9:30 P.M., Sun. 9 A.M.–9 P.M., $30) takes a page out of the Wild West. As you drive through town on Carmel Valley Road, you can't help but notice its wooden storefront with the antique bicycles perched on the rooftop. As you order a beer at the long wooden bar, you might find yourself wondering, where's the marshal and Miss Kitty? Plain old American home cooking is on the bill here, with big, fatty portions of everything: burgers, steaks, onion rings, fries, calamari, and pasta. On weekends, plenty of Harley riders drop in for a bite. Unlike the vast majority of Carmel and Carmel Valley, there is absolutely nothing about this place that would qualify as "gourmet," and plenty of locals like it that way.

PRACTICALITIES
Information and Services

For more information about Carmel Valley and vicinity, contact the **Carmel Valley Chamber of Commerce** (13 W. Carmel Valley Rd., 831/659-4000, www.carmelvalleychamber .com, daily 10 A.M.–4 P.M.). Carmel Valley has its own **post office,** located at 11 Via Contenta (off Carmel Valley Rd., 12 miles from Hwy. 1, 831/659-8839). The nearest hospital is in Monterey: **Community Hospital of the Monterey Peninsula** (CHOMP, 831/624-5311, www.chomp.org), located on Monterey/Carmel hill west of Highway 1 just off Highway 68. The nearest **police** station (831/624-6403) is in downtown Carmel on the southeast corner of Junipero and 4th Avenues.

Getting There and Around
Carmel Valley is accessed from Highway 1 near the town of Carmel by heading east on Carmel Valley Road. Once you cross Carmel Rancho Boulevard, you are officially in Carmel Valley. Exactly 12 miles inland is Carmel Valley Village, an area of shops and restaurants. Beyond the Village, Carmel Valley Road winds uphill to the vineyards of Cachagua and beyond to the famous Tassajara Hot Springs and Zen Center, plus MIRA Observatory.

BIG SUR

Poet and Big Sur resident Robinson Jeffers described this redwood and rock coast as "that jagged country which nothing but a falling meteor will ever plow." Another Big Sur resident, writer Henry Miller, said Big Sur was "the face of the earth as the creator intended it to look." A favored spot for painters, poets, and creators of all kinds, Big Sur is a place where sandstone and granite, surly waves, and the sundown sea come together in a never-ending dance of creation and destruction.

Still, Big Sur as a specific *place* is difficult to locate. It is not only a town, a valley, and a river, but the entire coastline from just south of Carmel to somewhere north of San Simeon—a distance of about 85 miles. Most would argue that Big Sur starts at the Bixby Bridge and stretches south past the post office and Big Sur Station to Julia Pfeiffer Burns State Park. This "downtown" part of Big Sur includes the area's most famous and fabulous inns and restaurants: the Ventana Inn, the Post Ranch Inn, Nepenthe, and Deetjen's.

Only one major road accesses Big Sur, and that is California's Coast Highway (Hwy. 1), the state's first scenic highway and one of the world's most spectacular roadways. A far cry from the eight-lane freeways that California is famous for, this two-lane road snakes alongside the precipitous coastline, slips around the

HIGHLIGHTS

◖ **Big Sur Scenic Byway:** This spectacular coast drive twists and winds through gorgeous scenery with breathtaking views. This is classic Big Sur at its most beautiful (page 145).

◖ **Point Sur Lightstation:** Listed on the National Register of Historic Places, the 1889 Point Sur Lightstation overlooks a shipwreck site once known as the Graveyard of the Pacific (page 146).

◖ **Pfeiffer Beach:** Due to the steep cliffs that line the Big Sur coast, the area's only easily accessible beach is this mile-long stretch of sand highlighted by offshore rock formations. It's a gold mine for photographers and beach lovers (page 147).

◖ **McWay Falls:** The short walk along McWay Creek leads through the tunnel under the road to Saddle Rock and the cliffs above Waterfall Cove, where you'll see California's only perennial waterfall that plunges directly into the sea (page 148).

◖ **Pfeiffer Big Sur State Park:** Redwoods, sycamores, big-leaf maples, cottonwoods, and willows hug the river here, a perfect place for family camping (page 153).

◖ **Hearst Castle:** Once media magnate William Randolph Hearst's castle, this oceanview, Spanish Renaissance – style palace was designed by Julia Morgan, then filled with European art and finery (page 167).

◖ **Piedras Blancas Elephant Seals:** Nowhere else in California can you so easily get so close to so many "e-seals" than on the beaches of Piedras Blancas, a few miles north of San Simeon. It's a wildlife show you'll never forget (page 170).

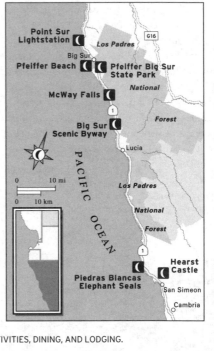

LOOK FOR ◖ TO FIND RECOMMENDED SIGHTS, ACTIVITIES, DINING, AND LODGING.

prominent ribs of the Santa Lucia Mountains, slides into dark wooded canyons, and soars across graceful bridges spanning the void. This is the kind of road that convertibles were made for. It's a marvelous drive, but for the uninitiated, it can be a bit nerve-racking.

Once "in" Big Sur, wherever that might be exactly, visitors notice a markedly different ambience from the coastal areas to the north and south. The vibe is decidedly laid-back, as evidenced by an abundance of unusual dwellings that were likely never visited by a county building inspector—hand-hewn redwood cabins, glass tepees, geodesic domes, and even round huts that look like wine barrels ready to roll into the sea. These structures were built

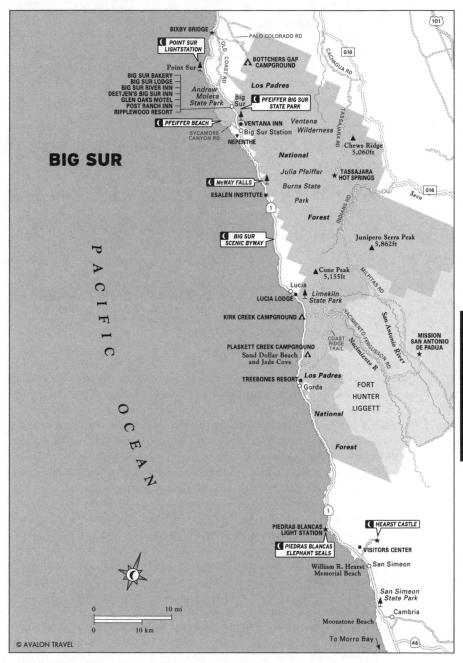

both to fit the limited space available alongside the cliff-hanging highway and also to express that elusive sense of Big Sur *style*.

Because the terrain itself is so tormented and twisted, broadcast signals rarely arrive here. In the days before satellite dishes, there was virt' ally no TV or Internet service. Electricity aı telephones have been available in Big Sur on since the 1950s, and some people along tl stretch of coast still have neither—often by choice. Big Sur is a very different California, a throwback to an earlier and simpler time and place.

PLANNING YOUR TIME

Many casual tourists do little more thaı "drive-through" of Big Sur, perhaps stc ping for lunch at Nepenthe, or for a short stretcher to see famous McWay Falls cascaı ing to the sea. Even a visit of this brief dura tion can be rewarding—the coastal scenery glimpsed from a car window while touring Highway 1 is nothing short of spectacular. But if you are a hiker or a nature lover, the urge to linger in this landscape will be strong. A half-dozen state parks plus thousands of acres of federal lands laced with trails traversing the redwood forests and coast will tempt you to stay a while. Rustic cabins, picturesque campsites, and luxurious resorts provide a wide variety of overnight options, and a dozen or so restaurants offer surprisingly fine dining for this still-remote area. To really "see" Big Sur on its own terms—and that means at its own languorous and leisurely pace—plan on at least two nights and two days. And, in summer and during the winter holidays, be sure to make lodging reservations well in advance, as places to stay are limited. Gasoline, too, is scarce and priced exhorbitantly, so fill up *before* you drive to Big Sur.

© ANN MARIE BROWN

Rugged and untamed, Big Sur dazzles with its tall headlands and sparkling waters.

HISTORY

The name "Big Sur" was derived in the late 18th century, when settlers knew little about the unexplored and unmapped wilderness area found along the coast south of Monterey. It was simply called El Sur Grande, or "the Big South." Although two Mexican land grants were awarded in the 1830s, which included most of the area north of the Big Sur Valley, neither grantee settled on the land. The first permanent white settlers arrived in Big Sur only a little more than a century ago, and those hardy souls had to adapt to a life of relative isolation. Local landmarks bear the names of some of the early settlers: Mt. Manuel, Pfeiffer Ridge, Post Summit, Cooper Point, Partington Cove, and others. Many of their descendants still live in Big Sur.

In the late 1800s, Big Sur sustained a larger population than it does today, due to its prospering redwood lumbering industry. The coastal Highway 1 did not yet exist, so steamers transported heavy goods and supplies to and from the Big Sur coast. In 1937, the present highway was completed after 18 arduous years of construction, making it possible for Big Sur to be "united" with the rest of California.

Sights

◖ BIG SUR SCENIC BYWAY

One of the world's truly spectacular coastal drives, Highway 1 through Big Sur is both a California Scenic Highway and an American National Scenic Byway. Constructed between 1922 and 1937, the road was built by Chinese laborers and California state prisoners, and sadly, many lives and much equipment were lost to the sea. Maintaining this remote ribbon of highway and its 29 bridges is still a treacherous year-round task, with landslides common during winter storms.

Driving this famous road, which is flanked on one side by the majestic Santa Lucia Mountains and on the other by the rugged Pacific Coast, means gliding around tight turns with steep drop-offs and striving to keep your eyes on the road, despite the fact that some of the most breathtaking scenery anywhere is calling your name. To live to tell about your Big Sur adventure, go slowly, drive defensively, and use the roadside pullouts when you want to gawk at the scenery.

© DAVID GUBERNICK/MONTEREY COUNTY CVB

Highway 1 along the Big Sur coastline

BIXBY BRIDGE

Thirteen-and-a-half miles south of Carmel is the famous Bixby Creek Bridge, 260 feet high and 716 feet long, the highest single-arch bridge in the world when constructed in 1932 and still one of the most photographed bridges in California. This bridge was one of the most important steps in the building of Highway 1 along the Big Sur coast. Before the road was constructed, coastal travelers had to endure rough wagon roads that made the 30-mile journey from Monterey to Big Sur as long as three days round-trip. The bridge's construction left a legacy of mind-boggling statistics. It required 600,000 pounds of reinforcing steel and 6,600 cubic yards (825 truckloads) of concrete. The wood framework needed to create the arch consumed 300,000 board feet of lumber (all milled locally from Big Sur's forests). Sightseers can park in pullouts on the north side to get a good look at the scenic bridge and the mouth of Bixby Creek below. One mile north of the Bixby Bridge is the Rocky Creek Bridge, a similar but smaller single-arch bridge. There are a total of 33 bridges in the stretch of Highway 1 between Carmel and San Simeon.

◖ POINT SUR LIGHTSTATION

Atop Point Sur stands the Point Sur Lightstation, an 1889 stone sentinel presiding over the shipwreck site once known as the "Graveyard of the Pacific." Perched 361 feet above the point's jutting volcanic rock outcrop—the nemesis of generations of sailors—the 50-foot-high lightstation pierces the dark with a million-candlepower beam every 15 seconds. The lightstation is accessible to visitors only by hiking one mile and then ascending a 65-step staircase. But it's much easier now than it used to be. Back in the days when the only

At 260 feet high and 716 feet long, the single-arch Bixby Bridge required an incredible feat of engineering in 1932.

© ANN MARIE BROWN

way to get here was on horseback, 395 wooden steps led to the light, originally a giant multi-wick kerosene lantern surrounded by a Fresnel lens with a 16-panel prism.

This 34-acre area and its central rocky mound is now a state historic park, and a great place for enjoying coastal views and spotting gray whales during their winter and spring migration. Besides the lightstation building, the park also features a carpenter/blacksmith shop, a barn, assistant keepers' quarters, the head keeper's house, and a large water cistern.

Entrance to the park and lightstation is by guided tour only; three-hour walking tours are offered on Wednesday, Thursday, and weekends in summer; Saturday and Sunday only in winter, usually starting at 10 A.M. and 2 P.M. From April to October, moonlight tours are offered during full moon nights; starting times vary. Reservations are not accepted; arrive early

to get a spot. Tours meet on the west side of Highway 1 at the farm gate, 0.25 mile north of the old Point Sur Naval Facility. The fee is $8 adults, $4 children ages 6–17, free for children 5 and under. For a current schedule, phone 831/625-4419 or visit www.pointsur.org or www.parks.ca.gov.

◖ PFEIFFER BEACH

Due to the precipitous cliffs and rocky shores that line the Big Sur coast, the only easily accessible beach in Big Sur proper is Pfeiffer Beach, a mile-long stretch of sand that is bounded by a forest of cypress trees and offshore rock formations with craggy caves, blowholes, and arches. Not surprisingly, this is a popular spot for photographers. Its soft, white sand is streaked with mauve and black, resulting from eroding minerals in its bluffs. Accessing Pfeiffer Beach requires a little detective work; the two-mile-long

BIG SUR

© ANN MARIE BROWN

Pfeiffer Beach is a popular spot for photographers because of its offshore rock formations pocketed with caves and arches.

access road is signed only as Sycamore Canyon Road, which is found about one mile south of Pfeiffer Big Sur State Park (look for some mailboxes and a narrow road heading sharply west and downhill). The road is extremely narrow in places, so trailers and RVs are not recommended. Neither is swimming: the water is cold, the surf capricious, and riptides deadly. Pfeiffer Beach is open to the public from sunrise to sunset (831/667-2315, www.campone .com, $5 parking).

ART GALLERIES

South of Deetjen's Big Sur Inn is the noted **Coast Gallery** (831/667-2303, www.coast galleries.com, daily 9 A.M.–5 P.M.) at Lafler Canyon. Rebuilt from redwood water tanks in 1973, the Coast Gallery offers fine local arts and crafts, from jewelry and pottery to paintings—including watercolors by Henry Miller—plus sculpture and woodcarvings.

More or less across the street from Nepenthe is the **Hawthorne Gallery** (48485 Hwy. 1, 831/667-3200, www.hawthornegallery.com, daily 10 A.M.–6 P.M.), featuring the art of various members of the Hawthorne family, Albert Paley forged metal sculptures, Max DeMoss bronze castings, Jesus Bautista Moroles granite sculptures, and the landscape creations of Frederick L. Gregory, among others.

HENRY MILLER MEMORIAL LIBRARY

North of Deetjen's and south of Nepenthe is the Henry Miller Memorial Library (831/667-2574, www.henrymiller.org), a collection of friendly clutter about the writer and his life's work. The remarkably talented and prolific Miller is probably best known for his novel *Tropic of Cancer,* which was banned in the U.S. for decades because of its sexually frank material. He lived,

wrote, and painted in Big Sur from 1944 to 1962. The library is housed not in Miller's former home but in that of the late Emil White, a good friend of Miller's, who started the library "because I missed him." Now a community cultural arts center, the library celebrates not just Miller but also the work of many other writers who called Big Sur home, including Robinson Jeffers, Lawrence Ferlinghetti, and Jack Kerouac. Exhibits, poetry readings, concerts, and special events are held throughout the year. In summer the library is open 11 A.M.–6 P.M. daily except Tuesday; Wednesday–Sunday only the rest of the year.

◖ MCWAY FALLS

About five miles south of Nepenthe is the stone marker for **Julia Pfeiffer Burns State Park** (831/667-2315, www.parks.ca.gov, $10 day-use), where you can take a short stroll to an overlook of one of California's most spectacular waterfalls, which plummets to the sea at McWay Cove. A wheelchair-accessible trail (signed as "Overlook") leads from the park restrooms, through a culvert under the highway, and out to the cliffs near **Saddle Rock,** where oft-photographed McWay Falls takes the plunge. The 0.25-mile walk takes about 10 minutes. Be sure to continue all the way to the trail's end, where the ruins of Waterfall House, the 1940s home of Lathrop and Helen Hooper Brown, can be seen. All that is left are a few foundations and palm trees, but oh, what a view this place had. In 1962 Helen Brown donated this land to California State Parks and insisted that it be named in honor of Julia Pfeiffer Burns, the daughter of a Big Sur pioneer family.

From December to April, the bench at the end of the Waterfall Overlook Trail is a great spot to see migrating gray whales pass by the

A wheelchair-accessible trail leads to spectacular McWay Cove at Julia Pfeiffer Burns State Park, where McWay Falls cascades to the sea.

coast. Occasionally, one will enter into the mouth of McWay Cove and spend an hour or so splashing around in the relatively calm waters.

NEW CAMALDOLI HERMITAGE

South of Lucia, at the large wooden cross, the road heading inland leads to the New Camaldoli Hermitage (831/667-2456, www .contemplation.com, hours vary), a small Benedictine monastery at the former Lucia Ranch. A sign says that the monks "regret we cannot invite you to camp, hunt, or enjoy a walk on our property" due to their customary solitude and avoidance of "unnecessary speaking." But visitors *can* come to buy homemade fruitcake, candles, and crafts, and to attend daily mass. In addition, the hermitage is available for very serene retreats of up to two weeks, although few outsiders can stand the no-talk rules for much longer than a few days.

OLD COAST ROAD

To get off the highway and get a taste of the inland valleys of Big Sur without lacing up your hiking boots, take a drive on the Old Coast Road (north end is across Hwy. 1 from the entrance to Andrew Molera State Park; south end is just north of the Bixby Bridge). Before the long, single-arch span of the Bixby Bridge was finally completed in 1932, the only thoroughfare that ran from Carmel to Big Sur was this road, which had to negotiate a long arc inland before it could cross the deep gorge of Bixby Creek. Much of the 10-mile-long road is open and exposed, providing great views of the coast, but in its farthest inland reaches it travels through a three-mile stretch of redwoods and ferns. The Old Coast Road connects to Highway 1 on both ends, so it's easy enough to make a 19-mile driving (or mountain biking) loop, or just drive it one way as an alternative to Highway 1.

BIG SUR

VENTANA WILDLIFE SOCIETY

The Ventana Wildlife Society (www.ventana ws.org), a 30-year-old nonprofit organization dedicated to preserving and protecting the natural resources of the Big Sur coast, has its main office in Andrew Molera State Park. Much of their efforts focus on reintroducing California condors and bald eagles to the area, but the society also operates an ornithology lab (831/624-1202, www.ventanaws.org, Apr.– Oct. Tues.–Sat. sunrise–noon, Nov.–Mar. days vary so call ahead, free but donations are accepted). Visitors can show up in the morning and observe the fascinating process of bird banding, in which songbirds are captured in mist nets and then identified, banded, and released. Spring is the busiest time of year at the lab, as that is when the greatest variety of birds pass through the area. Serious birders might also consider signing up for one of the fascinating bird tours led by Ventana Wildlife Society biologists; the most popular is the California Condor Viewing Tour (second Sun. of every month, $50), a two-hour tour along the coast designed for spotting endangered California condors. Tour leaders use radio telemetry to track the magnificent wild birds, so there's a near guarantee of seeing them.

MOLERA RANCH HOUSE

Located within Andrew Molera State Park, once part of the historic El Sur land grant, the Molera Ranch House is the former home of the dairy ranch foreman. The Big Sur Cultural and Natural History Center (831/602-0541, www .bigsurhistory.org) operates the ranch house on weekends only (11 A.M.–3 P.M.), allowing visitors to view exhibits on Big Sur artists, authors, early pioneers, and indigenous peoples, plus displays on the coast's rich diversity of flora and fauna. A small gift shop includes a selection of books about Big Sur. Entry to the museum requires paying an $8 parking fee at Andrew Molera's main entrance. From the entrance kiosk, head through the arch toward Molera Trail Rides, then turn left at the first driveway. Drive through the gate, past the Ventana Wildlife Society Barn and bird lab, and follow the Ranch House signs.

ESALEN INSTITUTE

Perhaps most coveted for its hot springs, the Esalen Institute (55000 Hwy. 1, 831/667-3000, www.esalen.org) is also considered to be the spiritual center of the human potential movement. Since the 1970s, Esalen has offered public workshops, conferences, and residential work-study programs to the general public, many featuring famous speakers such as Aldous Huxley, Hunter S. Thompson, Carlos Castaneda, and Alan Watts. Attending one of the hundreds of multiday workshops offered each year doesn't come cheap (rates are $1,200

THE MAGIC OF ESALEN

The Esselen and Salinan peoples frequented the hot springs here, supposedly called *tok-i-tok*, or "hot healing water." In 1939, Dr. H. C. Murphy (who officiated at John Steinbeck's birth in Salinas) opened Slate's Hot Springs resort on the site. In the early 1970s, the hot springs were transformed by grandson Michael Murphy into the famed Esalen Institute, the Cadillac of New Age retreats, according to absurdist/comedian/editor Paul Krassner. Even writer Alice Kahn, who, before arriving at Esalen, considered herself the "last psycho-virgin in California" and "hard-core unevolved," eventually admitted that there was something about the Esalen Institute that defied all cynicism.

and up for a five-day retreat), but hot springs enthusiasts can visit for a few hours instead and "take the cure" in Esalen's healing waters. These include a geothermally heated swimming pool and a bounty of hot tubs perched on a rocky ledge just 50 feet above the Pacific. At Esalen, natural hot springs flow from the ground at 119°F at the rate of 80 gallons per minute. The water is diverted into the pools and tubs of the institute's oceanfront bathhouse, an architectural marvel that was completely rebuilt after a 1998 landslide wiped out the original. Designed by architect Mickey Muennig, the Esalen baths seem to "float" above the ocean, thanks to an engineering feat that required driving 34 piers and horizontal anchors into 25 feet of rock. One caveat for hopeful visitors: the pools are only open to nonworkshop guests during the ungodly hours of 1–3 A.M. each morning, and reservations are required (831/667-3047, $20). Be forewarned: the springs are clothing optional. You can also come to Esalen as a nonworkshop guest to enjoy one of their famous massages (831/667-3002, $165 for 75 minutes, reservations required), which are given in the bathhouse area and accompanied by the soothing sounds of the ocean.

Recreation

HIKING

The best single source for hiking information at any of Big Sur's parks and public lands is **Big Sur Station** (831/667-2315, daily 8 A.M.–4:30 P.M.). The station is located just south of Pfeiffer Big Sur State Park on Highway 1.

Garrapata State Park

Garrapata State Park (831/624-4909, www.parks.ca.gov, free) stretches north along the coast for more than four miles from Soberanes Point, where the Santa Lucia Mountains dive into the sea. The park's name is Spanish for "tick," but you won't find any more of those pesky creatures here than anywhere else along the California coast. Park lands span both sides of Highway 1, beginning just seven miles south of Carmel Valley Road, with short, easy walking trails lacing the bluffs on the ocean side of the road, and more strenuous trails on the inland side. Access is easy but not clearly marked; look for the dirt pullouts by a metal-roofed barn alongside Highway 1, four miles south of Point Lobos State Park. There are no services available in the park.

Unlike most Big Sur parks, Garrapata is not known for its dense redwood forests or gurgling watercourses (although it possesses both of these), but rather for its inland grass-covered hills that are peppered with colorful wildflowers in the spring. In fact, Garrapata State Park is considered to be one of the best wildflower-viewing areas along the entire Monterey coast. Getting to those blossom-covered hills, however, requires a bit of a workout. Those seeking easier walks will want to stick to the coastal side of the park, west of Highway 1, where the paths are more level.

Those looking for an aerobically challenging workout should head for the inland seven-mile **Soberanes Canyon and Rocky Ridge Loop,** which travels through a remarkable variety of coastal terrain. In spring, hikers flock to this trail to witness the colorful wildflower displays. Follow Soberanes Canyon Trail from

BIG SUR

Garrapata State Park is known for its inland grass-covered hills.

the parking area into the creek canyon, where shortly beyond stands of cactus and coastal scrub, a surprising grove of redwoods grows along both sides of the creek. Beyond the lush redwoods the trail steepens harshly, but along these sharp slopes is where the wildflower show bursts into view. You'll climb 1,850 feet in just under three miles to a junction with Rocky Ridge Trail. Go left to loop back, enjoying stellar costal views all the way.

From the same roadside parking area, a much easier trail leads southwest for 0.75 mile to **Soberanes Point,** its sandstone bluffs riddled with arches and caves. You can circle around the bluff top (a great place to spot whales) or take a side trail to the top of 280-foot Whale Peak.

Three miles south of the trailhead for Soberanes Canyon and Soberanes Point and a quarter-mile north of the Garrapata Creek Bridge is the trailhead for **Garrapata Beach.** A

short walk along the wildflower-covered bluff top leads to a staircase that drops down to the beach, a half-mile-long crescent of sand. The beach has long been favored by "clothing optional" bathers, although technically that sort of behavior is not permitted, this being a state park beach.

Andrew Molera State Park

Once a part of the Mexican land grant "Rancho El Sur" belonging to Yankee fur trader Juan Bautista Roger Cooper, then passed on to his grandson, dairy farmer Andrew Molera, Andrew Molera State Park (831/667-2315, www.parks.ca.gov, $10 day-use) is comprised of seven square miles of windswept hills perched above the sparkling Pacific coastline and wide-open oceanside meadows ideal for grazing cows. The Big Sur River cuts through the middle of it all, completing its headlong march to the sea. Molera's beaches are dotted with driftwood shelters constructed by beachgoers attempting to flee from the frequent blustery breeze, which can elevate to a howling roar on many days.

Located two miles north of "downtown" Big Sur and with an entrance right off Highway 1, the park has little in the way of development except for the neighboring offices of the **Ventana Wildlife Society** and their bird ornithology lab (831/624-1202, www.ventanaws .org, Apr.–Oct. Tues.–Sat. sunrise–noon, Nov.–Mar. days vary, free) and the **Molera Ranch House** (831/602-0541, www.bigsur history.org, Sat.–Sun. 11 A.M.–3 P.M.), but plenty to offer for hikers, campers, equestrians, and beach lovers. An easy 1.25-mile trail leads from the main parking lot to **Molera Point,** where you can watch for passing whales and dolphins or look down on Molera Beach and count the sea lions lying on the rocks.

© ANN MARIE BROWN

Solitude is often possible on the driftwood-laden beaches of Andrew Molera State Park.

a junction with Panorama Trail, a short cut-off signed as Spring Trail leads to an exquisite stretch of driftwood-laden beach. Some people try surf fishing here.

For an all-day adventure, an eight-mile tour of the entire park is possible on River Trail, Hidden Trail, Ridge Trail, Panorama Trail, and Bluffs Trail. Trail maps are available at the park entrance station.

◖ Pfeiffer Big Sur State Park

One of the most densely wooded parks in the Big Sur area, 821-acre Pfeiffer Big Sur State Park (831/667-2315, www.parks.ca.gov, $10 day-use) is situated along the banks of the Big Sur River and boasts groves of redwoods, Douglas firs, oaks, sycamores, cottonwoods, maples, alders, and willows. Although many acres of the inland region of the park were badly burned in the July 2008 Basin Complex wildfire, closing the park's campground and surrounding areas for several months, the region of the park west of Highway 1 was untouched. The 821-acre park still has plenty to offer for campers, hikers, and those seeking relief from the summer heat in the cool pools of the Big Sur River. An excellent visitors center, plus the popular Big Sur Lodge (47225 Hwy. 1, 831/667-3100 or 800/424-4787, www.bigsurlodge.com), a restaurant, and a gift shop are also found on the property.

Most visitors walk all or part of the two-mile **Pfeiffer Falls and Valley View Loop** to enjoy the redwood forest and get a look at the park's 60-foot waterfall, a fern-lined cataract at its best in spring and early summer. For more exercise, backtrack about 100 feet from the falls and follow Valley View Trail as it climbs up and out of the canyon to a high overlook of the Big Sur Valley and Point Sur.

(Following the devastating wildfires of

Take the Molera Point Trail from the north side of the parking lot. The path stays on the north side of the Big Sur River and winds past the park's walk-in camp and historic Cooper Cabin, built in 1861 and the oldest structure on the Big Sur coast. At the river's mouth, the trail forks to the right, heading out to Molera Point. The hike's biggest reward is the view from this windswept promontory, a great spot for whale watching in winter. If the tide is low, go play on the beach at the river's edge.

Or, for a short out-and-back hike, cross the footbridge over the Big Sur River at the main parking lot and follow Beach Trail toward **Molera Beach.** It's one easy mile to the beach. For a longer trip, just before reaching the beach turn left on **Bluffs Trail** and follow it as far as you wish. You'll parallel the coast on a nearly level course, enjoying nonstop ocean views. About 2.5 miles out, near

BIG SUR

2008, all of Pfeiffer Big Sur State Park was closed, including this hiking trail to Pfeiffer Falls. At this book's press time, park officials expect that the park and trails will re-open by summer 2009. Expect to see fire-scarred foliage along the trail.)

If you'd rather have less company along the trail, follow the two-mile **Buzzards Roost Overlook Trail** along the Big Sur River, then ascend out of the redwoods and onto higher, chaparral-covered slopes. From high on Pfeiffer Ridge, you'll enjoy a 360-degree view of the Pacific Ocean, the Big Sur River gorge, and the Santa Lucia Mountains.

Ventana Wilderness

Local lore has it that a natural land bridge once connected two mountain peaks at Bottchers Gap, creating a window (or *ventana* in Spanish) until the 1906 San Francisco earthquake brought it all tumbling down. Crisscrossing this vast 240,000-acre federally protected wilderness area are the Big Sur, Little Sur, Arroyo Seco, and Carmel Rivers, as well as nearly 400 miles of backcountry trails. This is a land of diversity—elevations range from 600 feet, where the Big Sur River leaves the Wilderness, to 5,750 feet at the highest peaks. Grassy meadows, chaparral-covered slopes, and open stands

COMEBACK OF THE CONDOR

For birders, one of the most exciting parts of a visit to Big Sur is the chance to spot a California condor in the wild. The condor, a member of the vulture family and genetically related to the stork, is the largest North American land bird and one of the largest flying birds in the world. An adult weighs about 22 pounds. Having a wingspan of more than nine feet, a condor can fly more than 100 miles in a single flight. The birds possess a remarkable ability to soar on thermals, allowing them to fly for long distances without even flapping their wings.

Due to lead poisoning and hunting, the California condor was listed as endangered under the Federal Endangered Species Act in 1967. (Condors are scavengers, so they are often poisoned by feeding on the carcasses of animals that have been shot by hunters with lead bullets.) In 1987, the last wild condor in existence was taken into captivity to join 26 others. Through successful captive breeding during the following decade, the condor population increased significantly. In January 2000, the total population of California condors was 158 birds – but only 53 of those were in the wild. As of 2008, the population of California condors has grown to nearly 300. Of those, about 125 live in the wild, including 28 in Big Sur and

16 at Pinnacles National Monument. The other wild condors live in Ventura County and the Grand Canyon, with a few in Baja California, Mexico. The rest live in captivity.

It's not uncommon for visitors in Big Sur to spot condors. A favorite roost site, especially in the winter months, is at Pfeiffer Big Sur State Park. There are pullouts on Highway 1 on either end of the bridge over the Big Sur River, just south of the entrance to the park. Walk to the center of the bridge and look back inland (east), north of the river, for the roost trees, which are used both by turkey vultures and condors. Many visitors mistake the former for the latter, but condors are about twice as large as vultures.

The nonprofit **Ventana Wildlife Society** (www.ventanaws.org), based at Andrew Molera State Park in Big Sur, began releasing condors into the wild in 1997, in conjunction with the U.S. Fish and Wildlife Service's California Condor Recovery Program. Many of the released birds did not survive, but overall the program has been successful. For more information about the condor recovery program, consider signing up for one of Ventana Wildlife Society's California Condor Viewing Tours ($50), offered on the second Sunday of every month.

of pines are interspersed with virgin stands of coastal redwoods along the river and stream canyons, and scattered groves of bristlecone firs on the highest rocky slopes.

Hardy day hikers will want to summit 3,379-foot **Mount Manuel,** one of the best vantage points in the Ventana Wilderness, from which Big Sur, the Santa Lucia Mountains, and the Pacific Ocean are spread out below. The trailhead is located by the picnic areas and softball field at Pfeiffer Big Sur State Park ($10 day-use). The path climbs a hearty 3,100 feet to Manuel Peak's summit, so carry plenty of water. This trail is notoriously hot, so pick a cool day in winter or spring.

(Following the devastating wildfires of 2008, all of Pfeiffer Big Sur State Park was closed, including this hiking trail to Mount Manuel in the Ventana Wilderness. At this book's press time, park officials expect that the park and trails will re-open by summer 2009. Expect to see extensive fire damage along the trail, but Mount Manuel's summit view will be as sublime as ever.)

One of the most popular weekend backpacking trips on the Central Coast is the hike to undeveloped **Sykes Hot Springs,** accessible via a nine-mile one-way trek on the **Pine Ridge Trail** from the trailhead at Big Sur Station. Depending on current conditions, two or three hot springs pools can be found on a terrace alongside the Big Sur River. The largest of the group averages 100°F, although the other pools are slightly cooler.

For up-to-date trail information on Ventana Wilderness trails, check with the Monterey Ranger District of Los Padres National Forest (831/385-5434, www.fs.fed.us/r5/lospadres) or visit the website of the Ventana Wilderness Alliance (www.ventanawild.org).

Julia Pfeiffer Burns State Park

Compared to the other state parks along the Big Sur coast, Julia Pfeiffer Burns State Park (Hwy. 1, 831/667-2315, www.parks.ca.gov, $10 day-use) is tiny—only four square miles—but its relatively small acreage packs a powerful visual punch. Home to the only major California waterfall to descend into the Pacific Ocean, plus dramatic coastal vistas and a dense redwood and tanoak forest, the park is named for Big Sur pioneer woman and cattle rancher Julia Pfeiffer Burns, who lived just south of here in the early 20th century.

Everybody who visits this park should take the short stroll to see **McWay Falls** plunge into the sea. But after you do so, consider a longer hike at the same park on the spectacular **Ewoldsen Trail,** which heads inland from the main parking lot. The trail begins with an easy saunter along McWay Creek and its spectacular redwood forest, then climbs moderately to a fork at 1.5 miles in. This is the start of a loop; head right and in another mile you'll reach a spur trail to an overlook. Here, on a wide, grassy ridge, is a sweeping view over McWay Canyon and out to the ocean. Pull out your lunch and your camera, then hike the opposite side of the loop back to your starting point. The total distance is 4.3 miles.

(Following the devastating wildfires of 2008, the inland side of Julia Pfeiffer Burns State Park was closed to hiking, including the Ewoldsen Trail. The west side of the park, including McWay Falls, was untouched by the fire and remained open to visitors. At this book's press time, park officials expect that all of the park's trails will re-open by summer 2009.)

One of the best places for spotting sea otters and admiring the jagged Big Sur Coast up close is found at **Partington Cove** at Julia Pfeiffer Burns State Park, but not at the park's main entrance. Rather, it is 2.2 miles north at a sharp horseshoe bend in the highway. Look

© ANN MARIE BROWN

The beach at Partington Cove is a great place to look for sea otters or watch the sun set.

for pullouts alongside Highway 1 and a gated dirt road leading west. From the gate, the **Partington Point Trail** leads a steep half-mile down to an obvious fork. The right fork leads to a tiny rock-strewn beach at Partington Creek's mouth; the left fork leads into the redwoods, across a wooden footbridge, and through a rock tunnel built in the 1880s by pioneer John Partington. On the tunnel's far side is the remains of an old port on Partington Cove, where lumber was loaded onto seagoing freighters.

Limekiln State Park

About 2.5 miles south of Lucia is a 700-acre state park (831/667-2403, www.parks.ca.gov, $6 day-use) tucked into a steep coastal canyon, which preserves some of the oldest, largest, and most vigorous redwoods in Monterey County. The park is named for its 1880s wood-fired kilns, which smelted quarried limestone into

powdered lime, a critical ingredient for bricks and cement. The four still-standing kilns can be seen via a one-mile walk through the redwoods. In the wet months, be sure to take the right fork just beyond the second footbridge, which leads to Limekiln Falls, a spectacular 100-foot waterfall that drops over a limestone face. Getting to the waterfall requires some boulder hopping, and in spring, you may end up with wet feet, but it's good fun.

Brazil Ranch

Previously the property of Alan Funt, creator and host of the long-running *Candid Camera* television show, the spectacular lands of the 1,200-acre Brazil Ranch are open for guided hikes every Saturday. Hikes are led by naturalists from the Big Sur Environmental Institute (831/385-5434, reservations required), a nonprofit organization that has its headquarters on the property. On most Saturdays, the hike is an easy two-mile leg stretcher on a paved trail/road that offers spectacular views of the Bixby Bridge and Sierra Creek. On the last Saturday of every month, the guided hike is longer and more strenuous, heading up to Sierra Hill and back for even bigger views. The entrance to Brazil Ranch is approximately 100 feet beyond the south end of the Bixby Bridge, on the inland side of the highway (just past the Old Coast Hwy. junction with Hwy. 1). Hikers meet at 9:30 A.M. at the ranch gate on the morning of their scheduled hike.

Mill Creek Redwood Preserve

Mill Creek Redwood Preserve is a special place on the Big Sur Coast—so special, in fact, that you have to obtain a permit in order to visit it. Only eight permits per day are given out for this trail, with a maximum of five people allowed per permit. (To obtain a permit, submit an application at least 48 hours in advance of your visit to www.mprpd.org, or phone the Monterey Peninsula Regional Park District at 831/659-4488.) Although Mill Creek canyon was partially logged in the early 20th century and many stumps are apparent, some of the redwoods remaining here are impressive old growth. The preserve is also home to many special creatures, including a few magnificent owl species: great horned, northern saw-whet, and spotted.

The 2.5-mile Mill Creek Trail, constructed in 2006, provides access to this seldom-traveled canyon. The path laterals across the Mill Creek canyon, traveling under a dense canopy of tanoaks, madrones, and redwoods, and crossing over cascading streams on sturdy footbridges. In the wettest months of the year, these small streams produce lovely waterfalls. The trail very gradually gains 250 feet in elevation until it tops out at a high viewpoint that overlooks the Santa Lucia Mountains and the coast. A few wooden benches are in place here, inviting hikers to linger a while over the extraordinary view. This is the kind of place you'll want to share with someone you love.

To reach Mill Creek Redwood Preserve, drive north on Highway 1 from Andrew Molera State Park, then take Palo Colorado Road east for 6.8 miles to the trailhead.

BEACHES

Accessible beaches are in short supply in Big Sur, due to the region's steep cliffs and rocky shoreline. In "downtown" Big Sur, **Pfeiffer Beach** (Sycamore Canyon Rd., 831/667-2315, www.campone.com, $5 parking) is a photogenic spot for beach walks and admiring the coastal scenery, but not for swimming. If you're looking for a wind-protected spot, your best bet is five miles north at Andrew Molera State

Park, where a mile-long trail paralleling the Big Sur River leads to long, sandy **Molera Beach** (831/667-2315, www.parks.ca.gov, $10 day-use). Still farther north is no-fee and sometimes no-clothing **Garrapata Beach** (831/624-4909, www.parks.ca.gov), 16 miles north of Big Sur Station near the Garrapata Creek Bridge.

Or, take a drive south to Kirk Creek Beach or Sand Dollar Beach. The small sandy cove at **Kirk Creek Beach** is accessed via a short trail from Kirk Creek Campground, 27 miles south of Big Sur. It's popular for surfing and surf fishing. **Sand Dollar Beach** is a large, horseshoe-shaped cove across the highway from Plaskett Creek Campground, 32 miles south of Big Sur. Park in the lot across from the campground ($5 fee) and follow the short trail across the bluffs and down a stairway to the beach. This is the widest expanse of sand found along the Big Sur coast, and it usually has the best weather. The beach is also a designated hang glider landing site. About a mile south is **Jade Cove,** a popular spot for rock hounds and skilled divers to hunt for jade. (The best hunting is at low or minus tides, or just after storms.) In 1971, three divers excavated a world-record hunk of jade here—a huge boulder weighing 9,000 pounds.

HORSEBACK RIDING

In the summer months at Andrew Molera State Park, visitors can saddle up and go for one- to three-hour rides along the beach and through the park's meadows and redwood groves with **Molera Horseback Tours** (831/625-5486 or 800/942-5486, www.molerahorsebacktours.com). Guides explain the history, flora, and fauna of the area. Private rides are also available by appointment. Scheduled rides are $25–59, depending on length; custom rides start at $36 per hour.

WHALE-WATCHING

Since there is no harbor in Big Sur, there are no whale-watching boat tours, but that doesn't mean you won't spot whales. In the winter and spring months, from any high point along Highway 1 the distinctive "puffs of smoke" from spouting whales can be seen out to sea, especially on calm days when their spouts are not obscured by whitecaps and choppy water. Here are a few of the best places to spot whales from relatively close-up: **Andrew Molera State Park** (Hwy. 1, 831/667-2315, www.parks.ca.gov, $10 day-use) at Molera Point or on the Bluffs Trail; **Garrapata State Park** (831/624-4909, www.parks.ca.gov, free) at Soberanes Point or the Waterfall Overlook Trail; and **Julia Pfeiffer Burns State Park** (Hwy. 1, 831/667-2315, www.parks.ca.gov, $10 day-use). On weekends in January and February, ranger-led whale-watch programs are held at various state parks; contact Big Sur Station (831/667-2315) for a current schedule. Lastly, if you sign up for the docent-led tour to Point Sur Lighthouse during the winter months, your chance of seeing whales is first-rate.

Accommodations and Food

CAMPING

Camping is *very* popular in Big Sur, so make camping reservations early (where applicable; some campgrounds do not take reservations) and stock up on groceries and sundries in Monterey up north or in San Luis Obispo to the south. The following campgrounds in the Big Sur area are arranged from north to south.

The U.S. Forest Service operates a drive-in campground on Palo Colorado Road, a few miles north of the Bixby Bridge, and eight miles inland from Highway 1. **Bottchers Gap Campground** (831/667-2315, www.campone.com, $12) has 12 first-come, first-served tent sites with picnic tables, but no drinking water. The camp offers convenient access to the Skinner Ridge Trail, but it's a long way from the coast.

Andrew Molera State Park (831/667-2315, www.parks.ca.gov, $10 day-use) has 24 walk-in tent sites set about 250 yards from the parking lot. There is very little privacy, as the sites are set side by side in the middle of a large meadow, but the location is perfect if you want to hike, beach-comb, or surf fish at Andrew Molera's lovely beaches. Sites are first-come, first-served, with a three-night limit and four people maximum per site.

The private **Big Sur Campground** (Hwy. 1, 831/667-2322, www.bigsurcamp.com, $32–58), offers tent and RV sites with hookups located in the redwoods along the Big Sur River. Tent cabins and cabins are also available, as well as hot showers, laundry facilities, a store, telephone access, and a playground. Just downstream along the Big Sur River, with similar facilities and prices, is the **Riverside Campground** (Hwy. 1, 831/667-2414, www.riversidecampground.com) with 45 tent or RV sites plus rustic cabins. Ditto for the **Fernwood Resort** (831/667-2422, www.fernwood bigsur.com), which is adjacent to Pfeiffer Big Sur State Park and home to the strange "albino" redwood tree.

Pfeiffer Big Sur State Park (831/667-2315, www.parks.ca.gov, $20–35) boasts Big Sur's largest car campground with 218 sites with picnic tables and hot showers. All sites are in

© ANN MARIE BROWN

Kirk Creek Campground offers spacious sites perched on a grassy oceanfront bluff.

the redwoods or alongside the Big Sur River. RV sites are available, but there are no hookups. Reservations are essential in summer (800/444-7275, www.reserveamerica.com). If you get tired of eating blackened hot dogs at your campsite, you can always walk over to the park's restaurant for a great meal.

The private **Ventana Campground** (Hwy. 1, 831/667-2712, www.ventanacampground.com, Mar.–Oct., $30–45), managed by the Ventana Inn, has 80 very private, pretty sites in a scenic 40-acre redwood setting along Post Creek. Some RV hookups are available, plus hot showers (three bathhouses), fire grills, and picnic tables.

Julia Pfeiffer Burns State Park (Hwy. 1, 831/667-2315, www.parks.ca.gov, $20–25) has year-round camping at two hike-in environmental sites, Saddle Rock and South Garden. The sites are suitable for up to eight people and

offer spectacular coastal views, plus frequent wind. Reaching the sites requires a half-mile hike. Reserve sites in advance (800/444-7275, www.reserveamerica.com).

Campsites at **Limekiln State Park** (63025 Hwy. 1, 831/667-2403, $20–25), a few miles south of Lucia, are set in the redwoods alongside Limekiln Creek and near the mouth of the creek at the beach. RV sites are available, but there are no hookups. Reserve sites in advance (800/444-7275, www.reserveamerica.com).

The Forest Service–run **Kirk Creek Campground** is far south of Big Sur proper and just north of the intersection with Nacimiento-Ferguson Road. It consists of 34 first-come, first-served sites ($22) for tents and RVs, all situated on a grassy seaside bluff, plus some walk-in/bike-in tent sites ($5). Wind is frequent at this ocean-top perch, but the views are sublime. Also run by the Forest Service and even farther south is the forested, parklike **Plaskett Creek Campground,** 3.5 miles north of Gorda. Its 44 sites are on the inland side of Highway 1, but still provide easy access to Sand Dollar Beach. The first-come, first-served sites are $22 (hike-in/bike-in sites $5). A group site for up to 40 people is available by reservation (877/444-6777). For information on Kirk Creek or Plaskett Creek campgrounds, call 831/667-2315 or visit www.campone.com.

Lastly, **Treebones Resort** (877/424-4787, www.treebonesresort.com) near Gorda has five ocean-view campsites in addition to its 16 yurts. Camping rates are steep at $65 for two, but you get access to all of the resort's facilities and a complimentary breakfast.

CABINS AND RESORTS
$100-150

The **Big Sur River Inn** (Hwy. 1, 831/667-2700 or 800/548-3610, www.bigsurriverinn.com, $125–150) is a good choice for a budget stay in Big Sur, especially on weekdays in the winter months when "meals for two included" specials are often available for the price of just a room in summer. All 20 guest rooms are decent enough, but be forewarned that most are across the highway from the main lodge, so you'll have to dodge traffic if you want to eat at the inn's restaurant. The best rooms are the two-room suites with balconies that overlook the inn's big lawn and the Big Sur River. A heated swimming pool is positioned right at the river's edge.

Always a best bet for its affordable cabins is the charmingly rustic **Ripplewood Resort** (46840 Hwy. 1, 831/667-2242, www.ripplewoodresort.com, $140–160), about a mile north of Pfeiffer Big Sur State Park. The best units, some with fireplaces and kitchens, are

numbers 1–9 located along the Big Sur River. The sound of the water will lull you to sleep each night. The only cabins to avoid are numbers 10 and 11, both situated too close to the road. An on-site café is open for breakfast and lunch.

$150-250

The **Glen Oaks Motel** (Hwy. 1, 831/667-2105, www.glenoaksbigsur.com, $175–225) is the sort of homey lodging that belies the name "motel." It's the kind of place where you want to hang out in your room in the evening with a Scrabble game and someone you love. Although the motel's two freestanding cottages offer the most seclusion, they come with the highest price tags. For budget-watchers, the motel has 15 standard rooms with queen or king beds. Many rooms have gas fireplaces, and all offer wireless Internet service (no TVs or phones, though). Unlike many other lodgings in Big Sur, this one has been recently remodeled and is a big step above "rustic."

The 61 cottage-style rooms at **Big Sur Lodge** (47225 Hwy. 1, 831/667-3100 or 800/424-4787, www.bigsurlodge.com, $179–229) boast a hiker-friendly location inside Pfeiffer Big Sur State Park. This is a great option for families traveling to Big Sur who want activities right outside their front door. Each unit has its own porch or deck; some have wood-burning fireplaces or fully stocked kitchens. A pool, sauna, and restaurant are on-site. A stay at the lodge includes a complimentary pass to all Big Sur state parks.

Just south of Nepenthe is the landward, Norwegian-style **Deetjen's Big Sur Inn** (48865 Hwy. 1, 831/667-2377, www.deetjens.com, $135–185), Big Sur's most famous lodging. This rambling series of redwood buildings

BIG SUR

is listed on the National Register of Historic Places. The 20 eccentric rooms and cabins are chock-full of bric-a-brac and have thin walls, front doors that don't lock, and reasonably functional plumbing. Some have wood-burning fireplaces, but forget about trendy creature comforts like telephones or televisions. Nonetheless, people love this place—and have ever since it opened in the 1930s—because it has *soul*. If you opt for a room with a shared bath and no fireplace, you can save a bundle of money ($80–95 instead of about double that). Whatever room you get, make sure you eat at least one meal in the inn's wonderful restaurant (daily 8–11:30 A.M. and 6 P.M.–close, $25).

Cabins of a different kind are available at **(Treebones Resort** near Gorda (71895 Hwy. 1, 877/424-4787, www.treebonesresort .com, $155–185), where you can choose from 16 yurts, many with sweeping ocean views. For the uninitiated, a yurt is a circular canvas tent that is rustic in style but far more luxurious than a traditional tent. Although the yurt exteriors are nothing to write home about, the interiors are warm and inviting, with polished pine floors, ultracomfy quilt-covered beds, and a vanity sink so you can wash your face and hands without having to walk to the communal bathrooms. If you are visiting in the cooler months, reserve a yurt with a gas fireplace. Treebones also has a swimming pool, hot tub, restaurant, and main lodge, all set on a grassy bluff 500 feet above the Pacific Ocean. Even though the resort is on the inland side of

BIG SUR

© ANN MARIE BROWN

At Treebones Resort you can spend the night in a yurt perched high above the Pacific.

the highway, this is some piece of real estate, with knockout views everywhere you look. A continental breakfast is included in the price of your stay.

Not far from Treebones, **Lucia Lodge** (62400 Hwy. 1, 831/667-2391 or 866/424-4787, www.lucialodge.com, $195–255) rents 10 rustic cabins that occupy a daring perch a few hundred feet above the crashing Pacific surf. This 1930s-vintage lodge offers outstanding ocean views, especially from the Honeymoon Cabin, unit 10. The on-site restaurant serves lunch and dinner year-round, breakfast in summer. A small grocery store is also on-site, and they can charge whatever they want for potato chips, because it's a long drive to everywhere from Lucia.

Over $250

The woodsy, world-class **Ventana Inn** sits high up on the hill in Big Sur (Hwy. 1, 831/667-2331 or 800/628-6500, www.ventana inn.com, $550–650) and offers luxurious and contemporary lodgings on 240 acres overlooking the sea, outdoor Japanese hot baths, heated pools, the Restaurant at Ventana (daily noon–3:30 P.M., 4:30–5:30 P.M., and 6–9 P.M., $25–40), and a full-service spa. This hand-built hostelry comprises 12 separate buildings with rooms filled with down-home luxuries like queen- or king-sized beds with hand-painted headboards, handmade quilted spreads, and an abundance of pillows. Rates vary according to what size and type of accommodation you choose (rooms, suites, villas, or cottages), but in general, this is the kind of place where if you have to ask what it costs, you can't afford it.

The same holds true for the environmentally conscious **(Post Ranch Inn** (Hwy. 1, 831/667-2200 or 800/527-2200, www

.postranchinn.com, $700–900). Perched on a ridge overlooking the grand Pacific, the inn is priced for Hollywood celebrities and Silicon Valley survivors at a price range of $700–2,000 per night (but hey, you get a free breakfast). Developer Myles Williams and architect Mickey Muennig took the Big Sur region's rugged land to heart when they built the inn's 30 redwood-and-glass guest houses, which are intended to harmonize with, and almost disappear into, the hilltop landscape. The triangular "tree houses" are built on stilts to avoid damaging the roots of the oaks with which they intertwine, and the spectacular sod-roofed "ocean houses" literally blend into the ocean views. The emphasis here is on understated luxury and absolute privacy. Each house includes a wood-burning fireplace, a two-person spa tub, a sound system, an in-room refrigerator stocked with complimentary snacks, a king-sized bed, a private deck, and unforgettable views. Guests can also enjoy a massage, wrap, or facial at the Post Ranch Spa and exceptional dining at the California-style Sierra Mar restaurant (lunch daily noon–5:30 P.M., dinner seatings daily at 5:30 P.M., 6 P.M., or 8:45 P.M., lunch $12–20, dinner $120). When you add it all up, there couldn't be a better place for a honeymoon or a romantic getaway.

FOOD
Casual Dining

Dining at **(Deetjen's** (48865 Hwy. 1, 831/667-2377, www.deetjens.com, daily 8–11:30 A.M. and 6 P.M.–close, $25) is always a special event. The open-beamed redwood dining room is sized for hobbits, with cozy low ceilings and occasionally a kitty sleeping on a chair (he is grateful if you order the ahi). Breakfast is popular, with eggs Benedict and huevos rancheros luring repeat customers.

© ANN MARIE BROWN

Highly recommended for either a fine dinner or a rustic overnight stay, Deetjen's is famous for its Norwegian-style buildings tucked into the redwood forest.

Dinner is somewhat more formal, with a fireplace blazing to ward off the chill mist, classical music, and elegantly prepared food. Entrées are based on the season and include sustainably farmed meats and fishes, plus a few vegetarian options.

At least once in a lifetime, everyone should sample the view from famed **◖ Nepenthe** (48510 Hwy. 1, 831/667-2345, www.nepenthe bigsur.com, daily 11:30 A.M.–10 P.M., $20). At one time owned by director Orson Welles and his wife, actress Rita Hayworth (although they never spent a single night here), Nepenthe is the perfect place to relax on the outdoor terrace with a drink in hand to salute the sea and setting sun. The fare at Nepenthe is fair to good, but nowhere near as spectacular as the sweeping ocean view from this perch 800 feet above the water. Try the homemade soups, the hefty chef's salad, or the world-famous Ambrosia burger accompanied by a basket of fries. If you show up at sunset and can't get a table for an hour, order a South Coast margarita and soon you will "surcease from sorrows"—the Greek root of the name "Nepenthe," from *The Odyssey*. On the Nepenthe grounds, but one level lower on an outdoor terrace, is the even more casual **Café Kevah** (8 A.M.–3 P.M. Mar.–Dec., $8–13), a good option for breakfast or lunch. The place is locally famous for its croissant sticky buns and other freshly baked treats, but non-sugar-eaters can enjoy eggs Benedict with blue crab, a breakfast burrito, cobb salad, or a reuben Panini. The entire menu is served all day, so you can have scrambled eggs in the middle of the afternoon if you wish.

NEPENTHE

Nepenthe (48510 Hwy. 1, 831/667-2345, www. nepenthebigsur.com), perched atop a bluff 800 feet above the turquoise sea, was built almost exactly on the site of the cabin Orson Welles bought for Rita Hayworth. So, it's not too surprising that the restaurant is almost as legendary as Big Sur itself.

In 1944, Welles purchased what was then the Trails Club Log Cabin in Big Sur for his wife, Rita Hayworth. Orson Welles was persona non grata just down the coast at San Simeon (for his too-faithful portrayal of William Randolph Hearst in *Citizen Kane*), and this purchase would allow him to haunt W. R. Hearst from the north. However, the Welles-Hayworth marriage was ill fated, and the famous Hollywood couple never spent a single night there. The property was sold three years later while Hayworth and Welles divorced. The new owners were Lolly and Bill Fassett, parents of five children, who envisioned turning the place into an open-air pavilion with food, wine, and dancing, with that unforgettable South Coast view for all to behold. They worked with a student of Frank Lloyd Wright to design and build their dream on the Trails Club cabin site.

A striking multilevel structure complete with beautiful gardens, outdoor sculptures, and an arts and crafts gift shop, Nepenthe was named for an ancient drug mentioned in Homer's *The Odyssey*, taken to help people forget their grief. The Greek translation is roughly "isle of no cares" or "a place to surcease from sorrows." Naturally enough, the bar here does a brisk business.

The building, with its unique redwood architecture and unforgettable view, has been visited by many celebrities over the years. In 1963 Elizabeth Taylor and Richard Burton filmed the folk dancing scenes of the movie *The Sandpiper* in Big Sur. Lolly and Bill Fassett's son Kaffe choreographed the dances. Writer Henry Miller visited Nepenthe often during his years in Big Sur; he was a close friend to the entire Fassett family.

As is tradition at Nepenthe, relax on either of the upper decks perched above the Pacific (the "gay pavilion," presided over by a sculpted bronze and redwood phoenix) with drink in hand. Even the seats in the indoor dining room boast an incomparable view. On rainy days, secure a spot near the indoor, circular fireplace and prepare to relax and linger. During daylight hours, visit *The Phoenix* gift shop (daily 10:30 A.M.-7 P.M.) downstairs for a wide selection of local and international arts and crafts, plus books, candles, jewelry, and apparel. This is a store to get lost in.

To avoid the worst of the tourist traffic and to appreciate Nepenthe at its best, visit October to April, and *not* during holidays. And although Nepenthe is casual any time of year (shorts and flip-flops are just fine), it's not *too* casual. Local lore has it that John F. Kennedy was once turned away because he showed up barefoot.

And, if you can't be here in person, you can be here in spirit much more easily now that Nepenthe has an online weather camera pointing south over the back deck. To see what's happening along Nepenthe's coastline, visit the restaurant's website (www.nepenthebigsur.com).

© KERRICK JAMES

If the view is the thing at Nepenthe, the food is the thing at the [(**Big Sur Bakery and Restaurant** (Hwy. 1, 831/667-0520, www.bigsurbakery.com, breakfast and lunch daily 8 A.M.–3 P.M., dinner Tues.–Sat. 5:30–9:30 P.M., $22), near the post office. Dinner entrées include wild salmon, Niman Ranch ribeye, duck breast, and seared sea scallops, all served with a creative mélange of vegetables, or more casual choices like a glorious array of pizzas. Since this is also a bakery, don't miss the chance to order dessert. If you have dinner here, you will surely return for breakfast the next morning, and if you arrive at the right moment, the day's bread will just be coming out of the oven.

You don't have to stay at Pfeiffer Big Sur State Park's **Big Sur Lodge** (47225 Hwy. 1, 831/667-3100, www.bigsurlodge.com, daily 7:30 A.M.–9 P.M., $22–29) to enjoy a meal in its window-lined dining room. The restaurant serves three casual meals per day, and is one of the most kid-friendly eating places in the Big Sur area, complete with a children's menu for all three meals. But that doesn't mean that childless adults will be unhappy here; the menu is also suited to sophisticated appetites, with dinner entrées like panko-crusted chicken breast, grilled New Zealand rack of lamb, and pan-seared crab cakes. Breakfasts are hearty (huevos rancheros, omelettes, eggs Benedict) and a good bargain ($9–12).

Another great choice for three meals a day is the **Big Sur River Inn** (Hwy. 1, 831/667-2700 or 800/548-3610, www.bigsurriverinn.com, daily 7:30 A.M.–9 P.M., $18–32), where on warm days you can sit out on the patio and watch the Big Sur River roll by. When it's cool and foggy, the nostalgic, 1930s-era dining room is warmed by a cozy fire. The dinner menu includes some interesting surprises, like

filet of organic New Zealand ostrich, miso-glazed wild king salmon, and grilled tofu salad. If you don't want to order a big entrée, you can always settle on a hamburger or veggie burger and enjoy all the same ambience for about $12. On Sunday afternoons (May–Oct.) there is usually live music happening on the riverside deck.

Ultra casual, order-at-the-counter dining is what you get at **Fernwood Resort's Redwood Grill** (47200 Hwy. 1, 831/667-2422, www.fernwoodbigsur.com, daily 11:30 A.M.–9 P.M., $13–25), and it's the best place to go to meet Big Sur locals and enjoy first-rate barbecue. The burgers come in all varieties here, and that means turkey, ostrich, buffalo, salmon, and veggie in addition to the standard black angus. Plenty of diners order the blackened wild salmon ($19) or the Big Sur Barbecue Plate ($17), which includes chicken, pulled pork, and tri-tip. On Saturday nights, there is usually live music playing at Fernwood, and it's a big party.

Fine Dining

The finest of fine dining is served at Big Sur's poshest resorts, including the Post Ranch Inn's ocean-view [(**Sierra Mar** restaurant (Hwy. 1, 831/667-2800, www.postranchinn.com). Prime-time seatings are reserved for guests, but nonguests can dine earlier or later, which means lunch and "snacks" ($12–20) from noon –5:30 P.M., and a four-course prix fixe dinner ($120) with seatings at 5:30 P.M., 6 P.M., or 8:45 P.M. The menu changes daily and is comprised of organic, seasonal fare. But really, who cares what you are eating when the ocean vista is this sublime? One look at the crashing Pacific and no one ever complains about the food or the exorbitant prices. Just make sure you get here before dark.

For drinks with an ocean view or an al fresco lunch on the patio, Ventana Inn's lovely two-tiered Cielo restaurant (Hwy. 1, 831/667-2331 or 800/628-6500, www.ventanainn.com, daily noon–3:30 P.M., 4:30–5:30 P.M., and 6–9 P.M., $25–40) was the place to go. Following a structure fire in August 2008, the restaurant closed with plans to re-open in July 2009 with a new look and a new name: **The Restaurant at Ventana.** Loyal fans will surely return to see if certain well-loved standards remain the same, like the oak-grilled Kansas City steak, and a strangely delicious cocktail that tastes just right on a sunny Big Sur afternoon—beer with a scoop of sorbet. One thing certainly will not change, and that is Ventana's outstanding coastal view. Show up before sunset to make the most of it.

Practicalities

INFORMATION AND SERVICES

Beyond Big Sur proper (most of the "town" is clustered along a five-mile stretch of Hwy. 1), there is little in the way of services to be found along the Big Sur coast. The small hamlet of Gorda, 36 miles south of Big Sur, has a small gas station, cabin resort, and restaurant; and the even smaller hamlet of Lucia, 11 miles north of Gorda and 25 miles south of Big Sur, has a lodge and restaurant. But that's it. It's best to stock up on groceries, gasoline, and supplies in Carmel or Monterey to the north or San Simeon or Cambria to the south. A few gas stations and small grocery stores exist in Big Sur, but you will have to pay a premium for purchases made there.

Tourist Information

For general information about the area, contact the **Big Sur Chamber of Commerce** (831/667-2100, www.bigsurcalifornia.org). Another great source of information, especially for outdoor activities, is **Big Sur Station** (831/667-2315, daily 8 A.M.–4:30 P.M.) on the south side of Pfeiffer Big Sur State Park on Highway 1. This is the place to go in search of maps, permits, and hiking and camping information.

Media and Communications

The best place to go for free, wireless Internet access is the Henry Miller Library (831/667-2574, June–Aug. Wed.–Mon. 11 A.M.–6 P.M., Sept.–May Wed.–Sun. 11 A.M.–6 P.M.). Pfeiffer Big Sur State Park also has free Wi-Fi access within 150 to 200 feet of the park's camp store. Several of the lodgings in town also offer free Internet access for their guests.

Cell phone service is nonexistent in some areas of Big Sur, so be prepared to drive a few miles before being able to catch a signal. The best spots for cell service are around Point Sur, in the Big Sur Valley, and near the Post Ranch Inn. Also note that many cabins and rural resorts come sans phone.

The Big Sur **post office** (47500 Hwy. 1, 831/667-2305, Mon.–Fri. 8:30–11 A.M. and noon–4 P.M.) is located in a small strip mall next to the Big Sur Deli.

Emergency Services

The nearest hospital to Big Sur is the **Community Hospital of the Monterey Peninsula** (23625 Holman Hwy./Hwy. 68, 831/624-5311, www.chomp.org), approximately 30 miles to the north. To get there from Big Sur, follow Highway 1 to Carmel, then take the Highway 68 exit (west) to the hospital. For nonemergency health issues, visitors can go to the **Big Sur Health Center** (47600 Hwy. 1, 831/667-2580, Mon.–Fri. 10 A.M.–5 P.M.). **Police** service is provided to Big Sur through the Monterey County sheriff's office and California Highway Patrol. Call 911 for police.

GETTING THERE AND AROUND
Car
It's all about the car in Big Sur. When most visitors consider driving the Big Sur coast, they think of the entire 90-mile stretch from just south of Carmel to just north of San Simeon. This winding, curvy, two-lane road has many tight turns with precipitous dropoffs. To live to tell about your Big Sur adventure, go slowly, drive defensively, and use the roadside pullouts when you want to gawk at the scenery.

Bus
The only public transportation in these parts is **Monterey-Salinas Transit** (831/899-2555, www.mst.org), which runs to and from Big Sur daily Memorial Day to Labor Day and weekends only the rest of the year, stopping at Point Lobos, Andrew Molera State Park, the Big Sur River Inn, and Nepenthe.

Bike
Bicycling along the coast may seem like a great idea, until you find yourself wrestling with RVs and weekend speedsters for road space. If you must ride, it's best to head from north to south to take advantage of the tailwind. Most vistas and turnouts are seaward.

San Simeon and Cambria

In most visitors' minds, San Simeon and Cambria are synonymous with Hearst Castle, the ultraextravagant palace built by newspaper magnate William Randolph Hearst. Hearst's "Enchanted Hill" is a must-see when touring the Central Coast, but many first timers are surprised to find that this region offers other delights as well, including the bulbous, blubbery elephant seals that haul out on the beaches just north of San Simeon, rocky tidepools at Leffingwell Landing, the easy-walking village of Cambria with its many shops and restaurants, and William R. Hearst State Beach's gorgeous stretch of sand and surf.

SIGHTS
◖ Hearst Castle
This rich man's palace ranks right up there with Disneyland as one of California's premier tourist attractions, and rightly so. On top of "The Enchanted Hill" or *La Cuesta Encantada,* media magnate William Randolph Hearst built himself a castle filled to overflowing with furnishings, antiques, and art collected from around the world, including silk banners, fine Belgian and French tapestries, Norman fireplaces, Spanish choir stalls, and ornately carved ceilings.

As the owner of a wildly successful chain of newspapers and other media, Hearst was one of the most wealthy and powerful men in America in the first half of the 20th century. He even made an attempt at a career in politics. Hearst's life was loosely the subject of one of the greatest American movies ever made, Orson Welles' 1941 *Citizen Kane.* (Although some of

BIG SUR

TOURING HEARST CASTLE

In spring, when the hills are emerald green, Hearst Castle appears as if by magic up on the hill from the faraway highway. Before the place opened for public tours in 1958, the closest view commoners could get was from the road, with the assistance of coin-operated telescopes.

Today visitors can choose from five separate tours (four daytime and one evening) of Hearst Castle, each lasting about two hours, including a bus ride to and from the visitors center to the castle. Theoretically, you could accomplish several tours in a day, but don't try it. A dosage of two tours per day makes the trip here worthwhile, but not overwhelming. Visitors obsessed with seeing it all should plan a multiday stay in the area. Whichever tour, or combination of tours, you select, be sure to wear comfortable walking shoes, as there are lots of stairs. An "Accessibly Designed Tour" is available for individuals in wheelchairs or those who have difficulty with stairs, walking, or standing for lengths of time. Visitors may use their own wheelchairs or borrow one at no charge; trams are used to escort visitors along the tour route. Reservations for the accessibly designed tour are a must and can be made by calling 866/712-2286.

For everyone else, the **Experience Tour,** or Tour One, is the recommended first-time visit, taking in five rooms on the castle's ground floor (the grand assembly room, medieval-looking refectory or dining room, morning room, billiard room, and theater), the 18-room guesthouse overlooking the sea known as Casa del Sol, and gardens dotted with priceless marble sculptures. The tour begins with a showing of the large-format film *Hearst Castle: Building the Dream,* presented on the visitors center's huge National Geographic Theater five-story screen. This 40-minute film chronicles the building of Casa Grande (the main castle) and includes aerial footage of Hearst's estate and surrounding coastline. Completing the tour requires negotiating a total of 170 steps and a walk of about two-thirds of a mile. A highlight for many is a six-minute showing in the castle's theater (the largest room in Casa Grande) of some of Hearst's "home movies." This tour, as well as all the other tours, visits the outdoor Greco-Roman "Neptune Pool," which holds 345,000 gallons of water, and the indoor Roman Pool with blue Venetian glass and gold-leaf tiles, which took five years to build.

Tour Two, or **Casa Grande,** visits the upper floors of the main castle, including several guest rooms, a library filled with more than 4,000 books, Hearst's private "Gothic Suite" with its own library and adjoining office, and

Welles' biographers argue that the movie was more about Welles himself than Hearst.) The amazing coastside property where he chose to build his castle had belonged to his father, millionaire George Hearst, who raised cattle on the land. The castle's construction began in 1919, and since Highway 1 was not yet in existence, all materials had to be brought in by boat to the pier at San Simeon and then hauled up the hill over six miles of poor road. The process was slow, arduous, and costly. Hearst spent $3 million in 1930s dollars to build the main structure alone; it is estimated that the entire estate cost closer to $10 million. The building process continued for nearly 30 years, until 1947. To landscape the 127-acre grounds, a 20-man crew hauled in topsoil to create five levels of terraces on the hill, then planted 3,000 rosebushes and more than 100,000 trees.

Whatever else you think about it, Hearst Castle (750 Hearst Castle Rd., San Simeon) is certainly a monument to one man's monumental ego and impressively ostentatious taste. Designed by Berkeley architect Julia Morgan, the buildings themselves are handsome hallmarks of Spanish Renaissance architecture.

the huge kitchen and pantry area where food was prepared for the Castle's glittering parties. This tour requires a walk of about 0.75 mile and climbing and descending a total of about 400 stairsteps.

Tour Three, or **Casa Grande North,** tours the north wing of Casa Grande (three floors of guest suites) and the North Terrace, an unfinished area that was originally intended to be the castle's main entrance. The tour also visits Casa del Monte, a 10-room guesthouse overlooking the mountains. Tour guests watch a short video that utilizes vintage footage from the 1920s and 1930s to show the complexities of constructing Hearst Castle. This tour requires a walk of about 0.75 mile and climbing and descending a total of about 350 stairsteps.

Tour Four, or **The Garden Tour,** is offered only April through October, and shows off many of the estate's extensive gardens, terraces, and walkways, as well as the 17 colorfully painted dressing rooms that surround the Neptune Pool. A highlight is the "Hidden Terrace" – an early staircase, pond, and terrace that was completely concealed by later construction and rediscovered as the castle was being restored. The tour also visits the wine cellar of Casa Grande, and the largest and most elaborate of the estate's guest houses, Casa del Mar (where Hearst chose to live during his final years on the estate). This tour requires a walk of a little more than a mile and climbing and descending a total of about 240 stairsteps.

Tour Five, or **The Evening Tour,** is offered most Friday and Saturday evenings from March to May and September to December, plus some additional weeknights during the winter holidays. It includes highlights from several of the other tours, but the castle looks completely different – even more glamorous – at night. Docents dressed in 1930s attire act out roles as guests and staff of the castle – lounging by the Neptune Pool, playing poker in the Assembly room, preparing dinner in the castle kitchen. This tour requires a walk of about 0.75 mile and climbing and descending a total of about 300 stairsteps.

Perhaps the toughest decision to make is not which tour to take but what time of year to visit. The estate's spectacular gardens are at their best in the late spring and summer, but many repeat Hearst Castle visitors time their trips for the holiday season (mid-Nov.-Jan. 2), when the the main house and all three guest houses are festively decorated for Christmas, as they were in Hearst's time.

The centerpiece, "La Casa Grande," boasts 100 rooms, including a movie theater, a billiards room, two libraries, and 31 bathrooms—one of the West's most theatrical temples to obscene wealth. It was here and in three neighboring guest houses that Hearst entertained famous guests such as Winston Churchill, Charles Lindbergh, Joan Crawford, and Harpo Marx.

Visitors can choose from four different daytime tours ($24 adults, $12 children 6–17, under 6 free) and one evening tour ($30 adults, $15 children 6–17, under 6 free). Daytime tours are discounted by a few dollars in the off-season (Sept. 16–May 14). Tours last about two hours and include a five-mile bus ride to and from the visitors center to the castle. One thing visitors don't see on a tour of the enchanted hill is William Randolph Hearst's 2,000-acre zoo, once the country's largest private collection of exotic animals, featuring more than 70 species. The animals have long since been dispersed, although survivors of Hearst's elk, zebra, and Himalayan goat herds still roam the grounds. It's not uncommon to spot a zebra or two as you drive along Highway 1 in San Simeon.

Even if you decide not to take a tour, stop in

the Neptune Pool at Hearst Castle

at the visitors center and watch the large-format film *Hearst Castle: Building the Dream,* presented on the visitors center's (805/927-6811, free admission) huge **National Geographic Theater** five-story screen. The center also contains a large gift shop, a museum shop with reproductions of Hearst Castle art pieces, several food and beverage concessions, and interpretive exhibits that spotlight Hearst's life and accomplishments, the work of architect Julia Morgan, and the film career of actress Marion Davies, who was in a relationship with the married Hearst during his time at the castle. Hearst Castle is open daily except Christmas, Thanksgiving, and New Year's Day; make tour reservations in advance at 800/444-4445 or www.hearstcastle.com. Limited walk-up tickets are available on a first-come, first-served basis, but especially during the summer high season and winter holiday season, advance reservations are the smart way to go.

(Piedras Blancas Elephant Seals

If elephant seals were people, we'd think they were loud, obnoxious, and obscenely fat. But since they are pinnipeds, we think they are cute. And nowhere else in California can you so easily get so close to so many "e-seals" than on the beaches of Piedras Blancas, a few miles north of San Simeon. The huge males can weigh up to 5,000 pounds and put on a tremendous show as they bellow, roar, and fight each other for the best spots on the beach. When there is nothing to fight about, the seals lay like giant slugs on the beach, flipping sand over their backs every few minutes.

Although the elephant seals are most plentiful from November to March, some type of pinnipeds (sea lions or seals) can be seen almost any day of the year on the Piedras Blancas beaches. All you have to do is drive up, park, and walk a few yards to the overlook area on a bluff above the beach. The seals are usually less than 30 feet away—ideal for taking photographs. Docents are often on hand, especially on weekends and during the birthing and breeding season (Jan.–Feb.). The Elephant Seal Overlook is located on Highway 1, four miles north of the entrance road to Hearst Castle. The nonprofit group Friends of the Elephant Seal also runs an information center and gift shop at Plaza del Cavalier (250 San Simeon Ave., 805/924-1628, www.elephantseal.org, daily 9 A.M.–5 P.M.).

Piedras Blancas Light Station

Just up the coast from San Simeon is one of California's historic lighthouses. The Piedras Blancas Light Station (805/927-7361 or 805/927-3719, www.piedrasblancas.org, $15 adults, free for children under 16), built in 1874, is open for tours every Tuesday and Thursday, plus the third Saturday of each month. During

the 90-minute tour, docents dressed in period clothing give visitors a glimpse of the lonely life of the 19th-century light keeper. During the winter and early spring months, gray whales sometimes migrate so close to the lighthouse that visitors can not just see but *hear* their spouts. Reservations for the Saturday tour can be made at the Hearst Castle Visitor Center (805/927-6811). For Tuesday and Thursday tours, participants simply meet at the former Piedras Blancas Motel site, one mile north of the light station.

Downtown Cambria

The artsy coastal town of Cambria is like the poor cousin to Monterey County's Carmel, with dozens of art galleries, antique malls, restaurants, and come-hither shops, but without the high prices and overwhelming crowds. The entire village area is easily visited on foot with a stroll along Main Street; it's informally divided

BIG SUR

© ANN MARIE BROWN

It's easy to get up close with the elephant seals at Piedras Blancas, but don't forget that these are wild, unpredictable creatures.

© ANN MARIE BROWN

Start your exploration of downtown Cambria with a visit to the 1870 Guthrie-Bianchini house, which serves as the local historical museum.

into West Village and East Village, with just under a mile of walking in between. You can concentrate your efforts on one end or the other if you wish, but make sure you wander the side streets for a block or so off Main Street as well. Several of the town's historic buildings remain, including the 1870 Guthrie-Bianchini house at the corner of Burton Drive and Center Street, and the restored 1871 Santa Rosa Chapel on Bridge Street, both in the East Village. Thanks to the Friends of the Piedras Blancas Lighthouse, the restored original Fresnel lens from the local light station stands enthroned in its own "lantern room" directly on Main Street. For more information on Cambria's historic buildings, visit www.cambria historicalsociety.org.

Nitt Witt Ridge

The beautifully bizarre Nitt Witt Ridge (881 Hillcrest Dr., 805/927-2690, $10 adults, $5

children) is an eccentric "middle-class Hearst Castle" and a state historical monument. This multilevel, sandcastle-like cement structure was lovingly built by local garbage man Arthur Beal (also known as Captain Nitt Witt), who sought to construct the cheapest, most elaborate castle possible. He began in 1928 with a one-room shack, which he enhanced over the next 60 years with cement, abalone shells, glass, discarded car parts, toilet seats, and beer cans, then added some driftwood, feathers, and rock for good measure. Beal died in 1992, but his three-story masterpiece still stands and is open for private tours by appointment. Or, just drive by and take a look: From Main Street in the West Village, take Cornwall Street to 881 Hillcrest Drive.

Wine-Tasting

Head east on scenic Highway 46 from Cambria and you'll soon find yourself in wine country (www.paso46westwineries.com). Most

© ANN MARIE BROWN

A monument to eccentricity, the three-story Nitt Witt Ridge was built by Cambria's local garbage man, Arthur Beal.

BIG SUR

wineries are located on the far eastern end of the highway near Paso Robles, but right in downtown Cambria you can sample a few vintages at **Moonstone Cellars** (801 Main St., 805/927-9466, www.moonstonecellars.com) and **Fermentations** (4056 Burton Dr., 805/927-7141, www.fermentations.com). In the tiny hamlet of Harmony, just four miles south of Cambria on Highway 1, is **Harmony Cellars** (3255 Harmony Valley Rd., 805/927-1625, www.harmonycellars.com), with a tasting room and gourmet gift shop. Most tasting rooms are open daily 11 A.M.–5 P.M.

RECREATION
William Randolph Hearst Memorial State Beach

If you've had enough of the pompous circumstance on display at Hearst Castle, head across the highway for a long coast walk on this sandy white crescent beach (805/927-2010 or 805/927-2145, www.parks.ca.gov, $8 day-use), or a swim in San Simeon Bay. This is a family-style stop with a picnic area, restrooms, a public pier popular for fishing, plus kayak and boogie board rentals. The **Coastal Discovery Center** (www.coastaldiscoverycenter.org, Fri.–Sun. 11 A.M.–5 P.M.), a small visitors center, offers exhibits on local wildlife and history.

For a 2.5-mile hike, walk the **San Simeon Bay Trail** that begins at the beach and leads along the bluff tops to the tip of dramatic **San Simeon Point.** The trail passes through a classic coastal forest of Monterey pines and cypress trees. Lined with secluded coves and tide pools, San Simeon Point extends nearly a half-mile into the ocean. Nude sunbathers sometimes congregate on the more remote stretches of sand.

In the summer months, **Sea for Yourself Kayak Outfitters** (805/927-1787 or 800/717-6226, www.kayakcambria.com)

operates a touring and rental center at William R. Hearst Memorial State Beach. Kayak rentals ($20 per hour, $50 all day) include paddle gear and a free lesson. They also offer guided tours of San Simeon Cove and the kelp forest off the coast of Cambria, plus guided kayak fishing trips ($45–110). Wildlife such as sea otters, harbor seals, whales, and dolphins are often seen in San Simeon Cove. Surf boards, body boards, and skim boards are also available for rental.

Pier fishing is allowed at the William R. Hearst State Beach pier; no fishing license is required. Anglers pull in barred surf perch year-round, with the best numbers in December and January. Smelt and mackerel are also common.

Hearst San Simeon State Park

The beaches at Hearst San Simeon State Park (805/927-2020, www.parks.ca.gov, $10 day-use), midway between San Simeon and Cambria, are large and rocky. The best access is at the Washburn Day Use Area off Highway 1, just south of San Simeon Creek Road. To stretch your legs on land, not the beach, walk the 3.3-mile **San Simeon Creek Trail,** which travels across a diverse landscape of wetlands, meadows, and coastal scrub. From the Washburn parking area, head to your right on the boardwalk and then bear right on the trail at its end. The path climbs into a Monterey pine forest, then drops into a lush, fern-filled gully. Continue on the loop to the edge of Washburn Campground, then bear right to follow the trail as it parallels San Simeon Creek, eventually returning to the boardwalk. Interpretive signs along the way explain the natural and human history of the area.

Moonstone Beach

Any time of year is a good time to walk the boardwalk trail that leads from the parking lot at Leffingwell Landing along the bluffs above Moonstone Beach in Cambria (off Moonstone Beach Dr., across from Moonstone Gardens, 805/927-2020). Leffingwell Landing is in the middle of the trail, so you can walk out-and-back in either direction, enjoying nonstop coastal views. This isn't entirely a nature experience, since a row of colorful motels and inns frames the inland view, but no matter, since all your attention will be drawn to the sea. Most of the trail is wheelchair-accessible, and benches are in place to encourage lingering. Every half-mile or so, the trail drops down to the beach via wooden staircases. Right below Leffingwell Landing are some extraordinary tide pools, where at low tide you'll be able to observe a variety of intertidal creatures. It's not uncommon to see a sea otter float by on his back, often using his paws to crack open a sea urchin or crab. Rock hounds can search for moonstones (white agates), jasper, chert, and jade from the mouth of Santa Rosa Creek north to San Simeon.

Moonstone Beach is also a popular place for rock and surf fishing, with surf perch being the common catch.

Fiscalini Ranch Preserve

Another great place for a short walk or hike in Cambria is the Fiscalini Ranch Preserve (www .ffrpcambria.org), particularly the 364-acre parcel on the ocean side of Highway 1. Here, 11 separate trails crisscross the oceanfront bluff tops, allowing for a multitude of loops and out-and-back walks. For the best ocean views, start your exploration at the parking lot at the end of Windsor Boulevard. Follow the one-mile Bluff Trail south as it curves along the coastal bluffs to just above Otter Cove, then loop back on the Marine Terrace Trail for an easy two-mile round-trip hike.

ACCOMMODATIONS
Camping
Hearst San Simeon State Park (San Simeon Creek Rd. and Hwy. 1, btw. San Simeon and Cambria, www.parks.ca.gov, $11–25) has the closest camping facilities to Hearst Castle. Fully developed San Simeon Creek Campground has 115 sites for tents or RVs, with fire rings, picnic tables, water spigots, and restrooms with flush toilets and coin-operated showers. Adjacent Washburn Campground, located on a hill above San Simeon Creek Campground, is smaller (70 sites) and more primitive (chemical toilets and no shower facilities). From mid-March to the end of September, reserve in advance (800/444-7275, www.reserve america.com); the rest of the year sites are first-come, first-served.

Hotels and Motels
UNDER $100
A good choice for budget travelers in San Simeon is the remarkably affordable **Silver Surf Motel** (9390 Castillo Dr., San Simeon, 805/927-4661 or 800/621-3999, www.silver surfmotel.com, $59–106). Some rooms feature ocean views, balconies, and fireplaces; all have phones, TV, free wireless Internet access, and complimentary coffee and tea. The bathrooms and furniture are older in style, but you get what you pay for. After a busy day touring Hearst Castle, you can relax in the heated pool and spa or on the rooftop sundeck. Pets are welcome here, too, for an extra $10 fee.

In the same minimalist-but-easy-on-the-wallet category is the **Motel 6 San Simeon** (9070 Castillo Dr., 805/927-8691, www.motel6 .com, $50–75), where you can count on a decent room of the usual Motel 6 chain standard. Hearst Castle is just six miles away; the ocean

is across the street. You can find food at the on-site Castle Café, or head to other restaurants in San Simeon or Cambria. And like at all Motel 6s across the country, your dog is welcome to stay here with you at no extra charge.

For warm, welcoming, and affordable European-style lodging (translation: you'll have to share a bathroom), head for Cambria's charming **Bridge Street Inn** (4314 Bridge St., Cambria, 805/927-7653, www.bridge streetinncambria.com). This small, homey hostel offers private bedrooms ($40–70), or, for those who are really pinching pennies, bunk beds in a shared bunkroom (about $22 each). Some bedrooms are configured for families, with a larger bed plus one or two bunk beds. All guests share two bathrooms upstairs and a half bath downstairs.

The bluebird of budget happiness has also been known to alight downtown at the **Bluebird Motel** (1880 Main St., Cambria, 805/927-4634 or 800/552-5434, www.blue birdmotel.com), where standard rooms are $65–110. If you want a fireplace and a patio or balcony, you'll have to spring for a deluxe room or suite ($110–220). No matter what room you get, you'll be able to enjoy the sight and sound of Santa Rosa Creek, which runs through the property, and the glorious array of flowers that bloom in the gardens year-round.

$100-150
San Simeon's only oceanfront motel is the **⟨ Best Western Cavalier Oceanfront Resort** (9415 Hearst Dr., San Simeon, 805/927-4688 or 800/826-8168, www.cavalier resort.com, $125–175). This 90-room lodging offers everything from family-friendly rooms with two double beds to romantic oceanfront rooms with wood-burning fireplaces. All rooms come with a refrigerator, coffeemaker, minibar,

© ANN MARIE BROWN

Cambria's Bridge Street Inn hostel is within walking distance of downtown shops and restaurants.

television, and voicemail, but you won't care much about these amenities, because it's the seaside location that steals the show. Expect to find a few nice extras, from whale-watching telescopes to evening bonfires at the beach fire pits.

Over in Cambria, the charming **Fogcatcher Inn** (6400 Moonstone Beach Dr., 805/927-1400 or 800/425-4121, www.fogcatcherinn.com, $129–169) is just two minutes from downtown and right across the street from Moonstone Beach. The inn bears a Carmel-style Old English countenance, with a thatched roof and flower-lined brick walkways. All rooms have fireplaces; a pool and hot tub are on the grounds. The best rooms have the ocean views, but even the "garden view" rooms are lovely. Little extras like cookies at check-in and a complimentary continental breakfast turn many new guests into repeat guests.

OVER $150

Visitors seeking a secluded beach getaway should reserve a night or two at **Moonstone Cottages** (6580 Moonstone Beach Dr., Cambria, 805/927-1366, www.moonstonecottages.com, $229–289). Tucked away in a grove of cypress trees, these three cottages are as close to the beach as you can get in Cambria. Each unit has an ocean view, fireplace, and whirlpool tub. This is a prime spot for honeymoons or romantic getaways.

For boutique-style lodging with a perfect location across from Moonstone Beach, book a stay at the 29-room ◖ **Moonstone Landing** (6240 Moonstone Beach Dr., Cambria, 805/927-0012 or 800/830-4540, www.moonstonelanding.com, $145–195). All rooms have fireplaces, mission-style furniture, refrigerators, microwaves, coffeemakers, and DVD players. Ten oceanfront rooms ($200–295) also have whirlpool tubs and private patios. A continental breakfast is served each morning, and snacks in the afternoon.

The 17-room **Little Sur Inn** (6190 Moonstone Beach Dr., 866/478-7466, www.littlesurinn.com, $175–225) is another choice lodging among the many lined up along Moonstone Beach. Rooms are surprisingly large, with a king bed and two cozy chairs next to a gas fireplace, and a large tub and separate shower in the bathroom. Many rooms have whirlpool tubs, garden patios, or decks with ocean views. Guests look forward to afternoon snacks in the lobby and a continental breakfast in the morning.

On the same stretch of lovely Moonstone Drive is the 20-room **(Sand Pebbles Inn** (6252 Moonstone Beach Dr., 805/927-5600 or 800/222-9970, ww.cambriainns.com, $160–200). Each room has a gas fireplace, king or queen bed, refrigerator, microwave, and large bathroom—many with whirlpool tubs. The nice folks at the front desk will loan you DVD movies and board games. The continental breakfast served here is surprisingly generous, with fresh waffles, bagels and bread for toasting, cereals, fresh fruit, juice, yogurt, and hard-boiled eggs.

Another local classic is **Cambria Pines Lodge** (2905 Burton Dr., Cambria, 805/927-4200 or 800/966-6490, www.cambriapineslodge.com, $160–240), tucked into 25 acres of Monterey pines and flowery gardens on a hill above downtown Cambria. The lodge, which is popular for conferences and family reunions, offers everything from 1920s-vintage cabins to two-bedroom suites. Most rooms have wood-burning fireplaces. A heated Olympic-size pool is on site. Breakfast is included in the room rate, and it's a huge buffet-style affair with pancakes, eggs,

potatoes, granola, and the like. You won't go away hungry. The only downer here is that the walls are a bit thin, so you might hear your neighbors.

Bed-and-Breakfasts

Cambria offers some fine selections for the bed-and-breakfast set. The two-story **(J. Patrick House** (2990 Burton Dr., 805/927-3812 or 800/341-5258, www.jpatrickhouse.com, $165–215) was Cambria's first B&B, and specializes in warm Irish hospitality. All eight guest rooms in this log-style home have Irish place names and feature private baths and fireplaces. A gourmet breakfast and afternoon wine and hors d'oeuvres are served in the comfortable garden room. Chocolate chip cookies and a glass of milk are provided before bedtime.

The top-drawer **Blue Whale Inn** (6736 Moonstone Beach Dr., 805/927-4647 or 800/753-9000, www.bluewhaleinn.com, $295–450) features six striking European country-style mini-suites with ocean views and separate entrances, plus canopy beds, gas fireplaces, whirlpool tubs, and in-room refrigerators. This place has won all kinds of accolades, and it deserves them all.

Another noteworthy B&B is the historic, 12-room **Burton Inn** (4022 Burton Dr., 805/927-5125 or 800/572-7442, www.burtoninn.com, $159–350), where guests carefully plan their days so they can return in time for the bountiful wine-and-cheese hour. It's not much of a problem, though, because everything in Cambria is within walking distance. Breakfast is a carb-loaders dream: hot oatmeal, pastries, waffles, scones, and fruit. Guest rooms and bathrooms are lavishly decorated and include a few surprising little extras, like personal voicemail service. If you are traveling with a family, rent the inn's 2,000-square-foot suite.

BIG SUR

Furnished with Victorian florals, lace, and turn-of-the-last-century antiques is the charming, two-story, 1870s Greek revival **Olallieberry Inn** (2476 Main St., 805/927-3222 or 888/927-3222, www.olallieberryinn.com. $135–225). Sure, it's a little noisy in this old house situated on Cambria's main drag, but the great breakfast, warm hospitality, and afternoon wine and hors d'oeuvres more than make up for it. Most of the nine guest rooms have fireplaces; all have private baths. The innkeepers are amazing cooks who make good use of the Central Coast's bountiful produce.

FOOD
Casual Dining

Great for lunch or dinner is warm, welcoming **Robin's** (4095 Burton Dr., Cambria, 805/927-5007, www.robinsrestaurant.com, lunch daily 11 A.M.–4:30 P.M., dinner daily 5–9:30 P.M., Sunday brunch 11 A.M.–3 P.M., $12–19), where you can settle in near the fireplace and contemplate the international menu choices. Tasty vegetarian entrées include grilled eggplant sandwiches, avocado croissant melt, marsala mushrooms, and black bean surprise, but you can also get a hefty beef burger here along with curried chicken salad, salmon fettuccine, and tandoori prawns.

Famous for its upscale comfort food is the intimate **Sow's Ear Cafe** (2248 Main St., Cambria, 805/927-4865, www.thesowsear.com, dinner daily from 5 P.M., $13–20), serving peppercorn pasta, fresh salmon in parchment, lobster potpie, and even chicken and dumplings. As soon as you are seated, you'll be served delicious fresh-baked bread in a terra-cotta flowerpot. Don't worry about eating like a pig, either. The place is full of them—pig figurines, pig woodcuts, paintings of pigs, and so on.

If you're craving something Asian inspired,

Wild Ginger Cafe (2380 Main St., Cambria, 805/927-1001, www.wildgingercambria.com, lunch Fri.–Wed. 11 A.M.–2:30 P.M., dinner Fri.–Wed. 5–9 P.M., $11–15) is an intimate spot with a creative, Pacific Rim—influenced menu. The foods of many different countries are presented here—Thai bouillabaisse, Korean barbecue beef short ribs, crispy Vietnamese rolls—and all are done well. Whatever you order, be sure to save room for dessert, especially the house-made sorbets.

Linn's Main Bin Restaurant (2277 Main St., Cambria, 805/927-0371, www.linnsfruit bin.com, daily 7 A.M.–9 P.M., $5–12) is the favored stop of tour buses heading to or from Hearst Castle. It's a good bet for breakfast or lunch, which includes potpies, soups, salads, and sandwiches. The house-made olallieberry pie is a winner. To sample and/or shop for Linn's jams, jellies, and gift baskets, try Linn's Fruit Bin Farmstore just east of town on Santa Rosa Creek Road.

Fine Dining

The most epicurean place to eat in Cambria is **☙ Black Cat Bistro** (1602 Main St., Cambria, 805/927-1600, www.blackcat bistro.com, dinner Thurs.–Mon. from 5 P.M., $16–32). With a chef who isn't afraid to take a few culinary risks, this place is worth a special trip. Consider an appetizer of sautéed shrimp and beet gnocchi with brandied lobster vanilla cream, or for an entrée, breast of pheasant stuffed with caramelized apple. Chef/owner Deborah Scarborough is an ex-film and television producer who has clearly found her calling in the food biz.

PRACTICALITIES
Information and Services

For general information about the area,

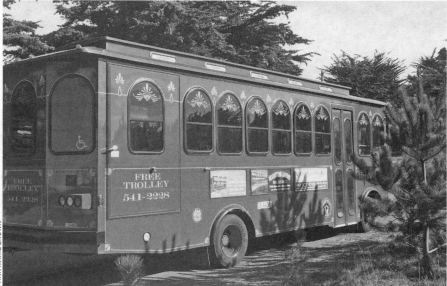

© ANN MARIE BROWN

If you don't want to drive or walk around downtown Cambria, just hop on the free Cambria Village Trolley.

contact the **Cambria Chamber of Commerce** (767 Main St., 805/927-3624, www.cambria chamber.org, Mon.–Fri. 9 A.M.–5 P.M., Sat.– Sun. noon–4 P.M.).

Cambria's **post office** is located at 4100 Bridge Street (Mon.–Fri. 9 A.M.–5 P.M.). San Simeon's post office is located at 444 San Luis Obispo-San Simeon Road (Mon.–Fri. 8:30 A.M.–noon and 1–5 P.M.).

The closest hospital to either town is **Twin Cities Hospital** (1100 Las Tablas Rd., 805/434-3500, www.twincitieshospital.com), located off U.S. 101 in Templeton, about 25 miles east of Cambria/San Simeon via Highway 46 or 41. Two more hospitals are located in San Luis Obispo, about 35 miles from Cambria/ San Simeon.

Getting There and Around

Cambria and San Simeon are located directly on Highway 1, approximately 240 miles north of Los Angeles and 240 miles south of San Francisco. You can also reach the two towns, which are six miles apart from each other, from U.S. 101 near Paso Robles by taking Highway 46 or Highway 41 west, then heading north on Highway 1.

It's easy enough to walk around Cambria, but if you'd like to get off your feet, try the free **Cambria Village Trolley** (805/541-2228, www.cambriacsd.org), also known as the "Otter Bus." The trolley route makes 24 stops, beginning and ending at San Simeon Pines Resort on Moonstone Beach Drive. The trolley operates from 9 A.M.–6 P.M. year-round (June 1–Sept. 4 Thurs.–Mon., Sept. 5–May 31 Fri.–Mon.).

SANTA CRUZ

In tune with its gracefully aging boardwalk, Santa Cruz is a middle-class tourist town enlightened and enlivened by retirees and the local University of California campus. It's made more colorful by a sizeable population of folks who lead a left-of-the-norm lifestyle, whether they are aging hippies, unemployed musicians, surfers living only for the next big wave, bohemian street performers, or those who are simply down-and-out. The town's lodging, restaurant, and tourism businesses don't particularly like it, but the "People's Republic of Santa Cruz" is a way station for the homeless, and the city's progressive politics are firmly entrenched on that issue.

Although it's not inexpensive to live here, Santa Cruz is far less hoity-toity than the more affluent and staid Monterey Peninsula. No one notices if you wear your most colorful tie-dyed clothes, or stand on a street corner and stage a one-person protest against…well, just about anything. When the city council tried to propose laws to regulate street performers and musicians, the owner of a local bookstore waged a massive campaign against the politicians, creating bumper stickers and T-shirts that read: "Keep Santa Cruz Weird." For years, the downtown area has been home to a resident whom everyone calls the "Umbrella Man." He walks very slowly up and down Pacific Avenue

© ANN MARIE BROWN

HIGHLIGHTS

◖ Santa Cruz Beach Boardwalk: This is the West Coast's answer to Atlantic City, an authentic amusement park complete with a classic wooden roller coaster (page 184).

◖ Monarch Butterflies at Natural Bridges State Beach: From mid-October to mid-February, see thousands of orange and black lepidoptera flitting about the eucalyptus grove at Natural Bridges (page 186).

◖ Santa Cruz Museum of Art and History: Leave it to Santa Cruz to come up with the most creative combinations – including the art of exhibiting history and the history of regional art (page 189).

◖ West and East Cliff Drive Beaches: For swimming, surfing, or just relaxing around a campfire, the beaches lining West and East Cliff Drives are the place to be. Don't miss a visit to the Surfing Museum at Lighthouse Point to brush up on your surfing history (page 195).

◖ Wilder Ranch State Park: With miles of coastline and tons of trails for bikers, hikers, and equestrians, this is a great place to explore the scenic coast. Be sure to check out the Victorian ranch house, barns, and workshop of this former dairy farm (page 202).

◖ Año Nuevo State Reserve: This reserve is a breeding ground and rookery for thousands of northern elephant seals. A visit here provides a close-up wildlife experience you'll never forget (page 225).

◖ Big Basin Redwoods State Park: Big Basin, California's first state park, is a haven for coast redwoods and hikers alike (page 227).

◖ Elkhorn Slough National Estuarine Research Reserve: The second-largest salt marsh in California, Elkhorn Slough is 2,500 acres of marsh and tidal flats. This protected wildlife sanctuary is prime territory for birding, kayaking, and nature walks (page 228).

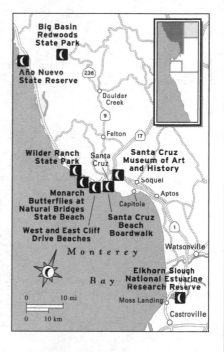

LOOK FOR **◖** TO FIND RECOMMENDED SIGHTS, ACTIVITIES, DINING, AND LODGING.

wearing pink clothing and carrying a pink parasol. In Santa Cruz, dreams and dreamers run the show.

This town saw its heyday in the 1890s, when trainloads of Bay Area vacationers in their finest summer whites stepped out to enjoy the Santa Cruz waterfront and its landmark boardwalk amusement park. The young and young-at-heart headed straight for the park's classic wooden roller coaster, pleasure pier, natatorium (indoor pool), and dance-hall casino. More decadent fun lovers visited the ships anchored offshore to gamble.

Santa Cruz still welcomes millions of visitors each year, and it does have its share of tacky and tawdry shops aimed at the lowest common denominator of tourist, yet it somehow manages to

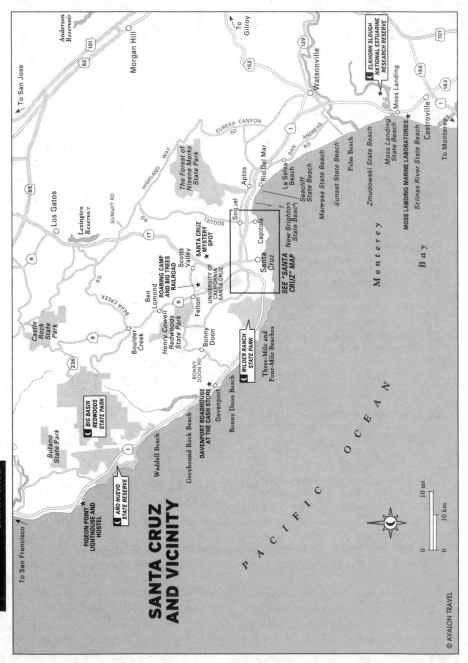

SANTA CRUZ

SANTA CRUZ AND VICINITY

To San Francisco

★ PIGEON POINT LIGHTHOUSE AND HOSTEL

◼ AÑO NUEVO STATE RESERVE

Butano State Park

To San Jose

Anderson Reservoir

Morgan Hill

To Gilroy

82

101

Los Gatos

85

9

Castle Rock State Park

236

Boulder Creek

BEAR CREEK RD

SUMMIT RD

Lexington Reservoir

17

HIGHLAND WAY

EUREKA CANYON RD

The Forest of Nisene Marks State Park

Ben Lomond

ROARING CAMP AND BIG TREES RAILROAD

Scotts Valley

★ SANTA CRUZ MYSTERY SPOT

Henry Cowell Redwoods State Park

Felton

9

★ UNIVERSITY OF CALIFORNIA SANTA CRUZ

Bonny Doon

BONNY DOON RD

DAVENPORT ROADHOUSE AT THE CASH STORE

Davenport

◼ WILDER RANCH STATE PARK

Three-Mile and Four-Mile Beaches

Soquel

SOQUEL RD

Capitola

Santa Cruz

SEE "SANTA CRUZ" MAP

New Brighton State Beach

Aptos

Rio Del Mar

La Selva Beach

Seacliff State Beach

Manresa State Beach

Sunset State Beach

Palm Beach

SAN ANDREAS RD

1

129

152

Watsonville

101

156

183

◼ ELKHORN SLOUGH NATIONAL ESTUARINE RESEARCH RESERVE

★ Moss Landing

Zmudowski State Beach

Moss Landing State Beach

★ MOSS LANDING MARINE LABORATORIES

Salinas River State Beach

Castroville

1

To Monterey

Monterey Bay

Big Basin Redwoods State Park

◼ BIG BASIN REDWOODS STATE PARK

Greyhound Rock Beach

Waddell Beach

Bonny Doon Beach

1

9

Boulder Creek

PACIFIC OCEAN

10 mi

10 km

0

0

© AVALON TRAVEL

retain its dignity. Despite the town's fairly blatant commercialism, some of the best things to do here are free: surfing or watching the surfers at Steamer Lane, tide pooling or butterfly-watching at Natural Bridges, strolling or pedaling the West Cliff Drive recreation trail, and beachcombing and sunbathing all along the coast.

PLANNING YOUR TIME

You'll need a minimum of two days in Santa Cruz to allow enough time to explore some of its natural wonders—the redwood groves at Henry Cowell Redwoods State Park, the coastal bluffs at Wilder Ranch State Park, or the bird-rich tidal marshes of Moss Landing's Elkhorn Slough. More urban attractions may tempt you as well, like scoring a few cheap thrills on the Santa Cruz Boardwalk's roller coaster or riding the steam trains of the Roaring Camp Railroad, each of which can easily fill another half or full day. And if you want to learn to surf, go sailing or kayaking, or just lounge all day on the beach and swim in the ocean, well, it seems like there are never enough days in a summer for that.

HISTORY

In 1769 the Spanish explorer Don Gaspar de Portolá discovered the area that is now known as the city of Santa Cruz. Portolá named the river flowing through the region "San Lorenzo" in honor of St. Lawrence, and the hills above the river "Santa Cruz," meaning "holy cross." Two decades later, in 1791, Father Fermin de Lasuen came to the area and established Misión Exaltación de la Santa Cruz, the 12th in the chain of 21 California missions.

Meanwhile, across the San Lorenzo River, in what is now known as East Santa Cruz, Villa de Branciforte was established, a Spanish civil settlement like those founded in San Jose and Los Angeles. This neighboring settlement made life hard for the mission. The rowdy, quasi-

Brussels sprouts thrive in the area's mild climate.

criminal culture of Branciforte so intrigued the native peoples that Santa Cruz men of the cloth had to use leg irons to keep the Ohlone Indians working at the mission. While the mission community faltered, Branciforte prospered, and it eventually became the heart of what is now known as the city of Santa Cruz.

By the 1820s Mexico had won its independence from Spain and assumed control of the area. The Mexican government handed out many land grants, and more than a dozen ranchos were established. Within the next 20 years, settlers from the East began to arrive in great numbers. California became a state in 1849, and Santa Cruz County was created in 1850 as one of the state's 27 original counties. By the late 1800s, logging, lime processing, and commercial fishing industries prospered in the area. The area's mild climate gave rise to commercial farms growing strawberries, artichokes, brussels sprouts, and flowers. With the area's sunny beaches and warm weather, Santa Cruz also became a prominent resort community, and that tradition has continued to this day. Olympic swimmer and epic surfer Duke Kahanamoku visited Santa Cruz in 1912 and helped popularize it as a world-class surfing destination.

Sights

◖ SANTA CRUZ BEACH BOARDWALK

The Santa Cruz Beach Boardwalk (400 Beach St., 831/423-5590, www.beachboardwalk.com) may be more than a century old, but it's certainly lively, playing host to over one million visitors per year. The original wood planking is now paved over with asphalt, stretching from 400 Beach Street for a half mile along one of northern California's finest swimming beaches. Open daily from Memorial Day to Labor Day and on weekends the rest of the year, the boardwalk is an authentic old-time amusement park, with dozens of carnival rides, assorted shops and eateries, good-time arcades, and even a big-band ballroom. Its most famous attraction is the **Giant Dipper,** a gleaming white wooden roller coaster that has been making riders scream out of a mixture of fear and delight since 1924. Both the Dipper and the 1911 **Charles Looff carousel,** with its 70 handcrafted horses, two chariots, and a circa-1894 Ruth Band pipe organ, are designated National Historic Landmarks. In addition to rides, the boardwalk also has an 18-hole miniature golf course, bowling lanes, laser tag, and an old-fashioned arcade.

Admission to the boardwalk is free, but enjoying its amusements is not. If you'll be staying all day, the best deal is the all-day unlimited rides wristband ($29.95 summer, $16.95 winter). You can also just buy tickets for individual rides, such as the Giant Dipper, for $2.25–$4.50.

SANTA CRUZ WHARF

The half-mile-long pier at the western end of Beach Street, within walking distance of the boardwalk, did a booming business during

The 1935 fishing boat *Marcella* is on display at Santa Cruz Wharf.

California's steamship heyday. Today, the Santa Cruz Wharf (831/420-5273 or 831/420-6025, www.santacruzwharf.com) is packed instead with tourists, and most fish markets, seafood restaurants, and shops here charge a pretty penny. Events such as the March "Jazz on the Wharf" and June "Woodies on the Wharf" are held here annually, but on any day the wharf is worthy of a sunset stroll. There is no charge for walking onto the pier, but you pay for parking if you drive your car ($2 for one hour, $9 for four hours, $21 for eight hours). Check out the historical interpretive signs near the 1935 fishing boat *Marcella,* and peer down into the fenced-off "holes" at the end of the wharf to watch the sea lions, who haul out on the piers. You might plan to have at least one meal on the wharf, since all of its dozen or so restaurants have an ocean view. (Try Carniglia's, 831/458-3600, www.carniglias.net, lunch 11:30 A.M.–3 P.M. and dinner from 5 P.M., $14–32.)

SANTA CRUZ SURFING MUSEUM

Cowabunga! Instead of cutting a ribbon, they snipped a hot pink surfer's leash when they opened the world's first surfing museum here at Lighthouse Point in June 1986. The Santa Cruz Surfing Museum (701 West Cliff Dr., 831/420-6289, www.santacruzsurfing museum.org, July–mid-Sept. Wed.–Mon. 10 A.M.–5 P.M., mid-Sept.–June Thurs.–Mon. noon–4 P.M., free admission) interprets 100 years of surfing history with displays on the evolution of surfboards and equipment, including the Model T of boards, a 15-foot redwood plank weighing 100 pounds, and an experimental Jack O'Neill wetsuit made of nylon and foam. The museum's gift shop is a great place to get one-of-a-kind T-shirts and other emblems of California cool.

The museum is located on the ground floor of the Mark Abbott Memorial Lighthouse on

© ANN MARIE BROWN

The Santa Cruz Surfing Museum at Lighthouse Point interprets 100 years of surfing history.

SANTA CRUZ

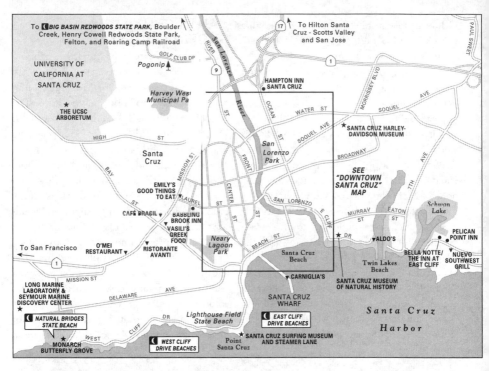

To █ *BIG BASIN REDWOODS STATE PARK*, Boulder
Creek, Henry Cowell Redwoods State Park,
Felton, and Roaring Camp Railroad

UNIVERSITY OF
CALIFORNIA AT
SANTA CRUZ

GOLF CLUB DR
Pogonip

Harvey West
Municipal Pa

★ THE UCSC
ARBORETUM

17   To Hilton Santa
Cruz - Scotts Valley
and San Jose

HAMPTON INN
● SANTA CRUZ

WATER ST

★ SANTA CRUZ HARLEY-
DAVIDSON MUSEUM

HIGH   ST

Santa
Cruz

San
Lorenzo
Park

BROADWAY

SEE
"DOWNTOWN
SANTA CRUZ"
MAP

EMILY'S
GOOD THINGS
TO EAT

CAFÉ BRACIL   BABBLING
BROOK INN

VASILI'S
GREEK
FOOD

To San Francisco   O'MEI
RESTAURANT   RISTORANTE
AVANTI

Neary
Lagoon
Park

MISSION ST

SAN LORENZO

MURRAY   EATON

Schwan
Lake

Santa Cruz
Beach

DR   ▼ALDO'S

Twin Lakes
Beach

PELICAN
POINT INN

BELLA NOTTE/
THE INN AT
EAST CLIFF

NUEVO
SOUTHWEST
GRILL

LONG MARINE
LABORATORY &
SEYMOUR MARINE
DISCOVERY CENTER

DELAWARE   AVE

▼ CARNIGLIA'S

SANTA CRUZ MUSEUM
OF NATURAL HISTORY

SANTA CRUZ
WHARF

★ NATURAL BRIDGES
STATE BEACH

MONARCH
BUTTERFLY GROVE

WEST   DR   Lighthouse Field
State Beach

CLIFF

█ EAST CLIFF
DRIVE BEACHES

Santa Cruz

Harbor

█ WEST CLIFF
DRIVE BEACHES

Point
Santa Cruz

★ SANTA CRUZ SURFING MUSEUM
AND STEAMER LANE

West Cliff Drive, overlooking the prime surf turf of Steamer Lane, considered to be the Holy Grail of Santa Cruz surfing spots. (And don't call it *Steamer's* Lane or the locals will know you aren't from around here.) It's a fitting place for official homage to the pursuit of the perfect wave. Just outside the museum you can join the crowds along the bluff-top fence and watch surfers scamper down the cliffs, plunge into the ocean, and join their comrades shooting the curls at the Lane.

█ MONARCH BUTTERFLIES AT NATURAL BRIDGES STATE BEACH

Located farther southwest, at the end   West Cliff Drive, the eucalyptus grove at   atural Bridges State Beach (831/423-4609, www

.parks.ca.gov, daily 8 A.M.–sunset, $8 parking) is the winter home for thousands of orange and black monarch butterflies from mid-October through mid-February. Although Pacific Grove near Monterey proudly proclaims itself "Butterfly City USA," Natural Bridges claims the bigger numbers (the winter population is often more than 10,000 butterflies). Visitors can walk the 0.25-mile wheelchair-accessible trail to the grove's observation deck on their own, or attend a free, docent-led butterfly tour Saturday or Sunday at 11 A.M. or 2 P.M. Warm, sunny days are the best times to view the monarchs as they flit about the trees. When the temperature is below 55°F they can't fly, and below 45°F they can't move at all.

A year-round highlight at the same park is

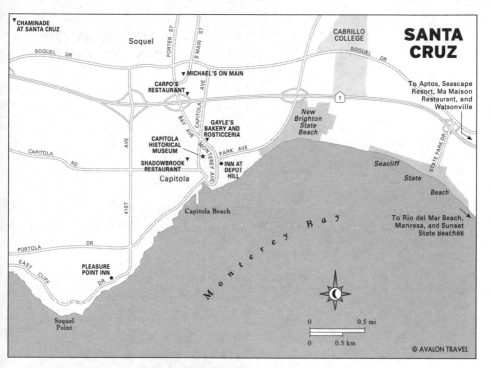

SANTA CRUZ

Monarch butterflies cluster in the eucalyptus grove at Natural Bridges State Beach.

© ANN MARIE BROWN

the sandstone "natural bridge" that makes a photogenic arc over the ocean. At one time the beach had two bridges, but the second one collapsed in 1980 under assault from a winter storm. In the winter months, the bridge is often covered with perching brown pelicans, which can be viewed close-up from the overlook area right by the park entrance kiosk. The north side of Natural Bridge's beach is lined with critter-rich tidepools, inviting exploration at low tide. Red or ochre sea stars, turban snails, limpets, and hermit crabs are easily spotted.

LONG MARINE LABORATORY

Well worth a stop for ocean lovers, the Joseph M. Long Marine Laboratory conducts research on subjects ranging from plankton to

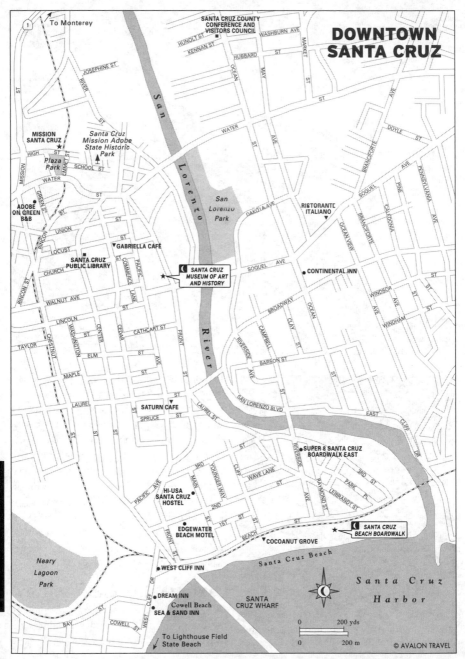

DOWNTOWN SANTA CRUZ

Pelicans find a rocky perch across from Long Marine Laboratory and the Seymour Marine Discovery Center.

blue whales, from cold water ecology to tropical coral reefs. To help interpret the lab's work, the **Seymour Marine Discovery Center** (831/459-3800, www2.ucsc.edu/seymourcenter, Tues.–Sat. 10 A.M.–5 P.M., Sun. noon–5 P.M. $6 adults, $4 students, seniors, and children under 16) features exhibit halls, touch tanks, and an aquarium. Visitors can marvel at the world's largest displayed whale skeleton (Ms. Blue, as she is called, is 87 feet long) or cradle a sea star in their hands. Docent-led tours of the lab are offered at 1, 2, and 3 P.M. The Ocean Discovery Shop sells a variety of natural history books, marine science kits for children, cards, prints, handmade pottery, and ocean-inspired jewelry. Take Highway 1 (Mission St.) north, turn left on Swift Street, then right on Delaware Avenue. Continue on Delaware to the Long Marine Lab entrance at the end of the road, near Natural Bridges State Beach.

◖ SANTA CRUZ MUSEUM OF ART AND HISTORY

Traveling exhibits and local artists get prominent play at the Museum of Art and History (705 Front St., 831/429-1964, www.santacruz mah.org, Tues.–Sun. 11 A.M.–5 P.M., $5 adults, $3 seniors, $2 youth, free for children under 12) at the McPherson Center. The museum's permanent exhibitions are a fascinating smattering of this and that: a Santa Cruz High School yearbook from 1917, a tablecloth that traveled with the Gold Rush pioneers through Death Valley in 1849, colorful etchings and pottery from Santa Cruz artists, and the first portable baseball pitching machine. Even if you aren't a museum person, you'll probably find something to interest you here.

Up on the roof is the **Mary and Harry Blanchard Sculpture Garden,** a showcase for outdoor sculptures from the museum's permanent collection, and a fine spot to admire the view of Santa Cruz and the surrounding mountains. Adjacent to the museum is The Octagon, an eight-sided 1882 brick building that serves as the museum store, filled with one-of-a-kind art earthenware from local artists, prints of pieces showcased in the museum's exhibitions, cards, and hand-crafted jewelry. Admission to the museum is free on the first Friday of the month.

SANTA CRUZ MUSEUM OF NATURAL HISTORY

The city's natural history museum (1305 E. Cliff Dr., 831/420-6115, www.santacruz museums.org, Tues.–Sun. 10 A.M.–5 P.M., $2.50 adult, $1.50 seniors 60 and up, children under 18 free) is located in Tyrell Park across the street from Seabright Beach. This building anchors the park's southern edge, overlooking Monterey Bay, and features exhibits on the native Ohlone Indians, wildlife of the Santa Cruz region, and marinelife of Monterey Bay. There's a tide pool "touch tank" full of intertidal creatures; fossils of whales, dolphins, and a sea cow; a live honeybee hive; and other fascinating natural history exhibits. Kids enjoying digging for 10-million-year-old sand dollars in the museum's fossil dig. The museum also sponsors a year-round schedule of classes and events.

MYSTERY SPOT

The bumper-sticker ballyhooed Mystery Spot (465 Mystery Spot Rd., 831/423-8897, www.mysteryspot.com, June–Aug. daily 9 A.M.–7 P.M., Sept.–May daily 9 A.M.–5 P.M., $5 admission, $5 parking) is a "gravitational anomaly" where "every law of gravitation has gone haywire." Or has it? Within about 150 feet of the Mystery Spot, the laws of gravity

don't seem to apply. Trees, people, and even the Mystery Spot's rustic shack and furnishings appear spellbound by a lack of basic physics principles. During the 45-minute guided tour, Mom, Dad, and the kids can *literally* climb the walls. Balls roll uphill. The Mystery Spot has been perplexing visitors since 1940, although some cynics do leave wondering why they spent $5 to get in, plus another $5 to park their car.

If you have your heart set on visiting the Spot, purchase tickets in advance for summer or holiday visits. Believe it or not, the Mystery Spot does sometimes sell out for the entire day's tours. To get there, follow Market Street north from Water Street for 2.5 miles. Market Street becomes Branciforte Drive; turn left on Mystery Spot Road.

ROARING CAMP AND BIG TREES RAILROAD

During the logging heyday in Santa Cruz in the early 1900s, 20 or more trains pushed through the redwood forests every day. Today you can visit historic Roaring Camp (831/335-4484, www.roaringcamp.com, $6 parking) and ride the rails on one of two different trips. Hop aboard a 100-year-old steam engine and make a 75-minute loop around a virgin redwood forest ($19.50 general, $13.50 youth 3–12), or for a three-hour excursion, take a 1940s-vintage passenger train out-and-back to the Santa Cruz Boardwalk ($21.50 general, $16.50 youth 3–12). The railroad offers daily runs from spring through fall (usually just one train per day on nonsummer weekdays) and in winter operates only on weekends and major holidays. Roaring Camp is located six miles north of Santa Cruz in Felton (exit Hwy. 17 at Mt. Hermon Rd.). A bonus for dog lovers: Fido is allowed to ride the train, too.

© ANN MARIE BROWN

The Roaring Camp Covered Bridge, the shortest covered bridge in the United States, welcomes visitors to Roaring Camp and Big Trees Railroad.

CAPITOLA VILLAGE

Home to the colorful Mediterranean-style Venetian Court seaside motel and residences, which was the first condominium project in California, Capitola (800/474-6522, www .capitolavillage.com) lies a few miles south of, but psychologically a world apart from, downtown Santa Cruz. This charming village is a throwback to a more genteel time, when travelers came by train to spend their summer holidays at this coastal resort. Starting at or near the wharf, today's visitors can easily spend a day meandering through Capitola's downtown, which is filled with shops tucked into narrow rows of storefronts painted in soothing shades of terra cotta, blue, and green. Or wander the town's quaint beach cottage—filled neighborhoods, follow the footpath alongside Soquel Creek, or play on the white-sand beach, which is generally calm enough for swimming.

The **Capitola Historical Museum** (420 Capitola Ave., 831/464-0322, www.capitola museum.org., Wed. and Fri.–Sun. noon–4 P.M.) provides a map of 12 historic sites in the village. More than a dozen restaurants are found along the beachfront Esplanade, most with lovely ocean views. A highlight for many visitors is dinner or Sunday brunch at the 1940s-era **Shadowbrook Restaurant** (1750 Wharf Rd., Capitola, 831/475-1222, www .shadowbrook-capitola.com, dinner Mon.–Fri. 5:30–9 P.M., Sat.–Sun. 4:30–9:30 P.M., Sun. brunch 10 A.M.–2:15 P.M., $25–35) alongside

© ANN MARIE BROWN

Capitola is home to the Venetian Court seaside motel and residences, the first condominium project in California.

the river, accessed by cable car from Wharf Road. To get to Capitola, take the 41st Avenue exit off Highway 1 and follow it to the coast.

HARLEY DAVIDSON MUSEUM

Motorcycle fans will want to make a stop here to check out the vintage wheels, memorabilia, and photo displays. The Harley Davidson Museum (1148 Soquel Ave., 831/421-9600, www.santa cruzharley.com, Tues.–Fri. 10 A.M.–6 P.M., Sat. 9 A.M.–5 P.M., and Sun. 10 A.M.–5 P.M.) houses some exquisitely restored machines, including a Harley bicycle (no engine) that was first introduced in 1917, as well as motorbikes from the 1920s and 1930s. Not surprisingly, the museum is located inside the Harley Davidson shop, so if you get inspired, you can buy yourself a brand new set of wheels, or at least a leather keychain.

SANTA CRUZ MISSION STATE HISTORIC PARK

The restored **Santa Cruz Mission adobe** (144 School St., 831/425-5849 or 831/429-2850, www.parks.ca.gov, Thurs.–Sun. 10 A.M.–4 P.M., free), just off Mission Plaza, is one of the county's last remaining original adobes, built from mud and straw bricks by and for Native Americans who were "employed" at Mission Santa Cruz in 1824. It is the last of the original 32 mission buildings that stood on or near this spot. The adobe's 17 rooms were used as homes for the hardest-working Indians at the mission; seven of these have been restored and are open to the public, illustrating how Native American, Californio, and Irish American families once lived. Call for current information about guided tours and living history demonstrations (usually offered Sun., the latter in Mar. only).

The original site of the **Misión de Exaltación de la Santa Cruz** (126 High St., 831/426-5686, Tues.–Sat. 10 A.M.–4 P.M., Sun. 10 A.M.–2 P.M.) was at High and Emmet Streets, too close to the San Lorenzo River, as it turned out. The move to higher ground left only the garden at the lower level. The original Santa Cruz mission complex was established in 1791—the 12th link in the chain of 21 historic Spanish Franciscan missions—but was completely destroyed by earthquakes in the mid-19th century. The replica church, scaled down by half and built in 1931 based on the only painting ever made of the original building, seems to have lost more than just stature.

UNIVERSITY OF CALIFORNIA AT SANTA CRUZ

The city on the hill just beyond town is the U.C. Santa Cruz campus (1156 High St., 831/459-0111, www.ucsc.edu), planned by architect John Carl Warnecke and landscape architect Thomas Church—a total of 10 clustered colleges and associated buildings overlooking the Pacific Ocean. Campus buildings were designed by noted architects such as Charles Moore, William Wurster, Joseph Esherick, Ernest Kump, Antoine Predock, Hugh Stubbins, Ralph Rapson, William Turnbull, and Kathy Simon. When the doors of U.C. Santa Cruz opened in the 1960s, few California students could gain admission to the close-knit, redwood-cloistered campus. The selection process was weighted in favor of students with unusual abilities, aptitudes, and attitudes—those not likely to thrive within the traditional university structure. So many children of movie stars and other members of California's moneyed upper classes have attended U.C. Santa Cruz that it has been playfully dubbed "California's public finishing school."

The University of California regents set about transforming the redwood-forested rangeland here, once the Henry Cowell Ranch, into California's educational Camelot in 1961. Designs ranged from modern Mediterranean to "Italian hill village" (Kresge College). The official explanation for the Santa Cruz "college cluster" concept was to avoid the depersonalization common to large U.C. campuses, but another reason was alluded to when then-Governor Ronald Reagan declared the campus "riot proof."

To truly appreciate this place, wander the campus hiking trails and paths. Some of the old converted ranch buildings are worth noting: the lime kilns, blacksmith's shop, cookhouse, horse barn, bull barn, slaughterhouse, cookhouse, workers' cabins, and cooperage. On a clear day, the view of Monterey Bay from the top of the hill on the 2,000-acre campus is marvelous.

One sight not to miss is **The Arboretum at UC Santa Cruz** (831/427-2998, www.arboretum.ucsc.edu, daily 9 A.M.–5 P.M., $5 adults, $2 youth 6–17), a great spot year-round for nature lovers, gardeners, and bird-watchers. Located on the west side of the campus near the intersection of Empire Grade and Western Drive, the arboretum specializes in conifers, primitive angiosperms, and plant families of the Southern Hemisphere. The arboretum had its beginnings in 1964 with a gift of about 90 species of eucalyptus. Today it is divided into four main geographical sections and their associated plants: California, Australia, South Africa, and New Zealand. Also on-site is Norrie's, a great gift shop filled with garden-related items. And serious birders know that a walk through the arboretum may yield sightings of Anna's, Allen's, and rufous hummingbirds; California quail; seasonal warblers, flycatchers, and sparrows; American and lesser goldfinches; and various raptors.

WINE-TASTING

The coastal mountains near Santa Cruz are well known for their redwoods. But since as far back as the late 1800s, they have also been known for their vineyards. The Santa Cruz Mountains appellation applies to wine grapes grown in the region defined by Half Moon Bay in the north and Mount Madonna in the south. More than 70 small, family-owned wineries now produce Santa Cruz Mountains wines.

North of Santa Cruz, the eclectic **Bonny Doon Vineyard** (10 Pine Flat Rd., 831/425-3625, www.bonnydoonvineyard.com, daily 11 A.M.–5 P.M.) specializes in Rhône and Italian varietals, although wine lovers and critics are also smitten with the winery's worldly, witty, and wickedly entertaining website.

Nearby in Felton is the award-winning and historic **Hallcrest Vineyards** (379 Felton Empire Rd., 831/335-4441, daily noon–5 P.M.), noted for its cabernet sauvignon, chardonnay, merlot, and zinfandel. Hallcrest is also home to **The Organic Wine Works** (379 Felton Empire Rd., 800/699-9463, daily noon–5 P.M.), producing the nation's first certified organic wines. Using certified organically grown grapes, the wine-making process itself is also organic, taking place without the use of sulfites.

Also in Felton is the renowned **Zayante Vineyard** (420 Old Mount Rd., 831/335-7992, www.zayantevineyards.com, open by appointment only), makers of award-winning merlot, syrah, zinfandel, and chardonnay.

Closer to downtown Santa Cruz is **Pelican Ranch Winery** (402 Ingalls St., 831/426-6911, www.pelicanranch.com, Fri.–Sun noon–5 P.M.), specializing in pinot noir, zinfandel, and chardonnay.

There are dozens more. For more information about area wineries, including a current wineries map and upcoming events, contact the **Santa Cruz Mountains Winegrowers Association** (7605 Old Dominion Ct., Ste. A, Aptos, 831/685-8463, www.scmwa.com). For guided tours of Santa Cruz Mountains wineries (so you can taste to your heart's content and not worry about driving), contact one of the following companies: **Santa Cruz Wine Tours** (301 Sea Ridge Rd., Aptos, 800/910-2136, www.santacruzwinetours.com) or **Santa Cruz Experience Wine Tours** (1114 Pacific Ave., 831/421-9883, www.thesantacruz experience.com). Tour rates are typically $70–90 per person, depending on your itinerary and length of trip.

Recreation

BEACHES
Santa Cruz Main Beach and Cowell Beach

The in-town Santa Cruz Main Beach (831/420-6015, www.santacruzparksandrec .com) on Beach Street by the boardwalk and extending to the wharf, with fine white sand and towel-to-towel baking bodies in summer, is "the scene"—especially for weekend visitors from San Jose. This is the place to go play (or watch) beach volleyball, or to buy yourself an ice cream cone and plop down in the sand for an afternoon of people watching. Lifeguards are on duty.

To get away from the biggest crowds, head east to the mouth of the San Lorenzo River.

Southwest of the wharf, Cowell Beach (101 Beach St.) is a famous surfing beach, where Huey Lewis and the News filmed one of their music videos. This is the best place in Santa Cruz to take your first surfing lesson; the waves are tame and generally consistent. Lessons and equipment rentals are available daily in summer.

◖ West and East Cliff Drive Beaches

Skirting alongside West Cliff Drive and its parallel walking/biking path, **Lighthouse Field State Beach** (831/420-5270, www.santacruzstateparks.org) is home to Lighthouse Point and its surfing museum and the world-famous surfing spot, Steamer Lane (at Mark Abbott Memorial Lighthouse on West Cliff Drive). There are several places to access the beach from wooden staircases on West Cliff Drive. Locals call the north side of this beach "Its Beach."

On the far northwest end of West Cliff Drive at Swift Street is a fine crescent of sand at **Natural Bridges State Beach** (831/423-4609), as well as the park's namesake "natural bridge" arched rock formation, an excellent visitors center, and a grove of eucalyptus trees that is home to wintering monarch butterflies (mid-Oct.–mid-Feb.). The tidepools and underwater reefs just north of the beach are considered so ecologically valuable that they were named a state marine reserve.

A popular locals' beach, **Twin Lakes State Beach** (831/427-4868, www.santacruzstateparks.org) is found near the Santa Cruz Small Craft Harbor on the eastern extension of East Cliff Drive (near Seventh Ave.). A good visual landmark for this stretch of sand is the **Walton Lighthouse**, Santa Cruz's "other"

© ANN MARIE BROWN

A bike ride or stroll along the recreation trail on West Cliff Drive between Natural Bridges State Beach and Lighthouse Point provides nonstop views of Monterey Bay.

SANTA CRUZ

© ANN MARIE BROWN

Only one of the sandstone natural arches remains at Natural Bridges State Beach.

lighthouse (not the one with the Surfing Museum). Constructed in 2002, this 41-foot-tall lighthouse sits on a manufactured rock jetty at the harbor entrance (end of Atlantic Ave.) It is easily visible from many points in town and along the beach. Twin Lakes Beach is usually quite warm and sunny, and great for swimming with relatively calm surf. Outdoor showers and restrooms are available. This beach, which also includes the stretch of sand between the harbor and the San Lorenzo River known as **Seabright Beach** (foot of Seabright Ave.), is a good place to have an evening campfire on the sand in designated rock-lined pits; campfires are not permitted on most Santa Cruz beaches, but this is a rare exception to the rule. Schwann Lake, on the easternmost end of the beach, is a popular spot with birds and bird-watchers.

Beyond the Santa Cruz Yacht Harbor, various small beaches line East Cliff Drive. The unofficially named **26th Street Beach** (at the end of 26th St., naturally enough) is tops among them.

Wilder Ranch State Park Beaches

Just a few miles north of Santa Cruz, Wilder Ranch State Park (1401 Old Coast Rd., 831/423-9703 or 831/426-0505, www.santa cruzstateparks.org or www.parks.ca.gov, $8 per vehicle entrance fee) is a playground for mountain bikers, hikers, and equestrians. But beach lovers will find plenty to enjoy as well, such as the small pocket beaches found along the park's Old Landing Cove Trail and Ohlone Bluff Trail—**Fern Grotto Beach, Sand Plant Beach,** and **Strawberry Beach.** Fern Grotto Beach, accessible via an easy one-mile walk or bike ride, is a small, sandy cove with a shallow cave tucked into its back wall. The cave is lined with sword and bracken ferns; water drips from its ceiling. Sand Plant Beach lies less than a half-mile farther north by trail and continuing north, another half-mile of travel brings you to Strawberry Beach, the largest of the three cove beaches.

At the northwest edge of the park's coastline lie **Three-Mile** and **Four-Mile Beaches,** long strips of sand well known for their excellent surfing and clothing-optional tendencies (not the surfers—they usually wear wetsuits). Park rangers sometimes patrol and issue warnings or citations to the unclothed, but nonetheless, don't be surprised if you get an anatomy lesson here. Three-Mile and Four-Mile beaches are 2.6 miles and 3.8 miles from the main trailhead at Wilder Ranch, but you can also walk to them via a much shorter route from Highway 1, four miles north of Santa Cruz (hence the name Four-Mile Beach), where the highway crosses Baldwin Creek.

Davenport Beaches

North of Wilder Ranch on Highway 1, the beaches surrounding the small hamlet of Davenport are less "civilized" than those in Santa Cruz proper. You won't find any official signs or parking lots, and you won't pay any parking fees. If you tire of the crowds at Santa Cruz beaches, you can probably find your own private stretch of sand here.

Bonny Doon Beach at the intersection of Highway 1 and Bonny Doon Road, just south of Davenport, is popular with surfers and nude sunbathers. (The beach is under the control of the California State Parks Department, and it is possible that at any time rangers may prohibit nudity on this and neighboring beaches. Nudists, keep your clothes within arm's reach, just in case.) Park in the large paved parking lot (there is room for about 50 cars) and then walk to the beach by crossing the railroad tracks and following any one of several use trails. This

beach is nicely tucked in at the base of steep cliffs, so it's fairly wind protected. While this beach is usually well populated with a happy, mellow crowd in the daytime, there has been some trouble here at night, including a few assaults, so go home when the sun goes down.

South of Bonny Doon Beach is a long stretch of sand lined with stunning sandstone cliffs and rock arch formations known as **Panther Beach** (between milepost 26.86 and 26.4, park on the dirt on the west side of the highway), accessible via a short hike across the railroad tracks and down a steep, narrow trail. This is a great beach for long walks and precious solitude. From the south side of Panther Beach, you can access

SURVIVING THE SURF

Every year along the California coast, people drown because they do not understand the dangers of the Pacific Ocean. With a little awareness, these accidents are easily preventable. First, understand that sleeper waves, or rogue waves, can hit the shore without warning. These giant waves are much larger than normal waves, and crash much farther up the beach or cliffs. A sleeper wave can knock down children or adults and drag them into deep water. Always keep an eye on the surf, especially if you are standing near the cliffs, rocks, or crashing waves to take a photograph.

And second, be aware of rip currents, which are a common occurrence along the California coast. These are swift "rivers" of backwash that surge through the surf, pulling swimmers away from the beach and farther out to sea. If you find yourself caught in a rip current, do not try to swim to shore – your efforts will be useless and you will just wear yourself out. Instead, swim parallel to the beach until you are free of the current, then head for shore.

SANTA CRUZ

neighboring **Hole in the Wall Beach** at low tide. The two beaches are separated by a rock arch formation (a "natural bridge"), which you must pass through. Keep an eye on the tide so you don't become stranded.

Right across the highway and the railroad tracks from the Davenport Post Office, **Davenport Landing Beach** (831/454-7956, www.scparks.com) is a great spot for a picnic. The beach has some interesting geological features, including sea caves on its northern edge, and an ocean-bound stream that carves a sculpted canyon through the bluffs on its southern edge. From the bluff tops above the beach, it is often possible to spot migrating gray whales from December to April. This protected cove was the original site of Davenport Landing, a thriving whaling port.

Six miles north of Davenport is **Greyhound Rock Beach** (831/454-7956, www.scparks.com), with great surf fishing, tide pools, and a picnic area. Massive Greyhound Rock, a sea stack of Santa Cruz mudstone, can be easily seen from the overlook at the Greyhound Rock parking area. A paved trail leads to the beach.

Still farther north is **Waddell Beach** (7.5 miles north of Davenport on Hwy. 1, 831/427-2288, www.santacruzstateparks.org,), a world-famous kiteboarding and windsurfing beach. This is no place to get in the water unless you are an expert, but it's great fun to park your car alongside the beach and watch the colorful wind-and-waves action. Some of the best kiteboarders will lift off the cresting waves and grab as much as 40 feet of air. A nature center is located across the highway at Rancho del Oso.

Capitola Beach

The charming coastal village of Capitola, just four miles south of Santa Cruz, has its own sparkling coastline, including its downtown beach, white-sand Capitola Beach (Cliff Dr. and Whard Rd.). Surfers find nice wave breaks close to shore at Capitola's East Jetty, and rentals and lessons are available. This is generally a good place to learn to surf, with gentle but consistent waves. Swimming is also generally safe. To get to Capitola, take the 41st Avenue exit off Highway 1 and follow it to the coast. In summer, parking can be difficult, so arrive early in the day.

New Brighton, Seacliff, and Rio del Mar State Beaches

About five miles down the coast from Santa Cruz and just south of the Capitola suburbs is popular New Brighton State Beach (1500 Park Ave., 831/464-6330, www.santacruzstateparks.org, $8 day-use). Its 93 often-sunny acres are protected by pine-, cypress-,

© ANN MARIE BROWN

A paved recreation trail runs between Seacliff State Beach and Rio del Mar Beach, and it's suitable for two wheels or even just one.

© ANN MARIE BROWN

The SS *Palo Alto*, also known as "the cement ship," has found a permanent resting place at Seacliff State Beach.

and eucalyptus-shaded headlands that shelter a great family campground and nature trails, and provide a dazzling nighttime view of Monterey Bay. Picnicking, fishing, hiking, and swimming are popular activities here, and bonfire pits are located on the beach. The **Pacific Migrations Visitor Center** (831/464-5620, www.santacruzstateparks.org, Tues.–Sun. 10 A.M.–4 P.M.) interprets the migrations of creatures that pass by the Central Coast, including gray whales and monarch butterflies. Access New Brighton State Beach by taking the Park Avenue exit off Highway 1 just south of Capitola.

A few miles farther south, two-mile-long Seacliff State Beach (201 State Park Dr., Aptos, 831/685-6440, www.santacruz stateparks.org, $8 day-use) is so popular that in summer, you may not be able to park. The only camping at Seacliff is for self-contained

RVs, so this is primarily a day-use park. A visitors center has exhibits on local geology and fauna, a wheelchair-accessible fishing pier is popular with anglers, and a paved recreation trail runs alongside the sand and connects to Rio del Mar Beach to the south. The small village of Rio del Mar, with a strip of restaurants and coffeehouses, sits right next to the beach. But the real draw for curiosity seekers is the concrete carcass of the doomed World War I–vintage SS *Palo Alto,* which was sunk here after seeing no wartime action. In the 1930s the pier was built to extend out to the cement ship, and entrepreneurs converted it into an elegant ballroom, restaurant, and amusement center. Today the ship is gated off to the public and has gone to the birds, literally— pelicans and cormorants perch on its bow. Access Seacliff State Beach by taking the State Park Drive exit off Highway 1 in Aptos.

SANTA CRUZ

Campfires are permitted in designated rings at both Sunset and Manresa State Beaches.

© ANN MARIE BROWN

Manresa and Sunset State Beaches

The farther south you go from Santa Cruz, the more rural the landscape becomes, and the less crowded the beaches. Manresa and Sunset state beaches are both located off San Andreas Road, approximately 14 miles south of Santa Cruz, and offer a more "natural" and less urban beach experience. Manresa State Beach (206 Sand Dollar, La Selva, 831/761-1795, www.santacruzstateparks.org) has a popular walk-in tent campground at Manresa Uplands and a separate day-use area just north of the camp. Swimming is not recommended at Manresa because of dangerous rip currents, but beach walking and beachcombing are first-rate. Picnic tables are perched along the bluff tops and offer panoramic ocean views. Another mile farther south is Sunset State Beach (831/763-7063), a safer bet for swimming and other water sports, and a popular

spot for camping and picnicking in the pine forest above the beach. Sunset Beach is well named—sunsets are often spectacular here. The beach lies at the foot of tall bluffs and has 200-foot-tall sand dunes that give it a secluded feel. Campfires are permitted at both Manresa and Sunset State Beaches. To reach the beaches from Highway 1, take the San Andreas Road exit and follow the signs.

HIKING AND MOUNTAIN BIKING

Although Santa Cruz is first and foremost a beach town, there are wonderful hiking and mountain biking trails to be found within a few miles of the hustle-bustle of downtown. Bike rentals are available at several local bike shops, including the **Family Cycling Center** (914 41st Ave., 831/475-3883, www.familycycling.com, Mon.–Sat. 10 A.M.–6 P.M., Sun. 10 A.M.–5 P.M., $25–75 per day depending on type of bike rented) and **Electric Sierra Cycles** (302 Pacific Ave., 831/425-1593, www.electricrecbikes.com, Mon.–Sat. 10 A.M.–6 P.M., Sun. 10 A.M.–5 P.M., $35 per day for electric bikes, $25 per day for pedal-powered bikes). If you want to hit the trails on two wheels or on foot, the following parks and paths are definitely worth a visit.

West Cliff Drive Recreation Path

Natural Bridges State Beach is connected to Lighthouse Point, the Santa Cruz Surfing Museum, and the Santa Cruz Wharf by a 2.5-mile recreation trail that runs parallel to West Cliff Drive. A walk or ride here provides nonstop views of Monterey Bay's crashing surf and a chance to see some of Santa Cruz's best sights without having to drive or park your car. The path is popular for jogs, bike rides, and romantic sunset strolls.

Henry Cowell Redwoods State Park

Just "up the hill" six miles from Highway 1 is Henry Cowell Redwoods State Park (101 North Big Trees Park Rd., Felton, 831/335-4598 or 831/438-2396, www.santacruzstateparks.org or www.parks.ca.gov, $7 per vehicle entrance fee), a 1,700-acre parkland celebrated for its ancient groves of coast redwoods, or *Sequoia sempervirens*. The tallest tree in the park is about 285 feet tall and about 16 feet wide; the oldest trees are about 1,400–1,800 years old. Henry Cowell Redwoods is also famous for its Roaring Camp Railroad steam trains (831/335-4484, www.roaringcamp.com, $6 parking), and for the San Lorenzo River, which provides cool swimming holes for park visitors in summer and rushing waters for salmon and steelhead trout in winter. With all these natural resources, it's not surprising that the park's campground (800/444-7275, www

.reserveamerica.com, $25) is one of the most popular in the state park system.

The 0.8-mile, wheelchair-accessible **Redwood Grove Nature Trail** through the old-growth redwood grove in dark San Lorenzo Canyon is this park's showpiece. The well-named Neckbreaker, Giant, and Fremont Trees are all standout redwood specimens, but it's the peaceful ambience of the entire grove that impresses most visitors. The trail begins near the park visitors center (daily 10 A.M.–4 P.M.). Pick up an interpretive brochure at the trail's start to get a quick lesson in redwood ecology.

More serious hikers can follow a 6.5-mile loop from the same trailhead to the Observation Deck, Big Rock Hole, and Cathedral Redwoods, or drive over to the park's northern **Fall Creek Unit,** which comprises another 2,300 acres of parkland and where the ruins of 1870s lime kilns can be seen alongside Fall Creek. An eight-mile loop through the Fall Creek Unit shows off all of its best features, including the old kilns, a massive redwood called the Big Ben Tree, and a remarkably beautiful mixed forest alongside crystal-clear Fall Creek. The Fall Creek Unit is found on Felton Empire Road off Highway 9, a few miles from Henry Cowell's main entrance.

Bicyclists on fat or skinny tires can pedal the closed-to-cars **Pipeline Road** from the main park entrance and visitors center. Except for a few short hills, the paved road is an easy cruise and suitable for families. Fat-tire riders can make longer loops by combining the paved road/trail with some of the park's dirt fire roads.

To get to Henry Cowell Redwoods State Park, take Highway 9 north from Highway 1 for six miles. The main park entrance is on the right. You can also reach the park via Highway 17 and Mount Hermon Road and Graham Hill Road.

SANTA CRUZ

The Forest of Nisene Marks State Park

Two major forces have shaped the land at The Forest of Nisene Marks State Park (Aptos Creek Rd. and Soquel Dr., Aptos, 831/763-7063, www.santacruzstateparks.org or www.parks .ca.gov, $6 per vehicle entrance fee): the railroad and unstable geology. Old-growth redwoods remained untouched in this steep and winding canyon for hundreds of years until the Loma Prieta Lumber Company came into ownership in 1881. Teaming up with Southern Pacific, they built a railroad along Aptos Creek and worked the land with trains, oxen, skid roads, inclines, horses, and as many men as they could hire, removing 140 million board feet of lumber over the course of 40 years. In 1922, when the loggers finally put their saws down, there were no trees left.

Luckily, Mother Nature has taken over since then. Today the canyon is filled with second- and third-growth redwoods and Douglas firs. The park's higher ridges are lined with oaks, eucalyptus, and madrones. Mother Nature was especially busy on October 17, 1989, when the epicenter of the famous Loma Prieta earthquake occurred in the park. The quake forcefully shook the entire San Francisco Bay Area and did extensive damage to downtown Santa Cruz. It took nearly a decade for the town's economy to recover.

In this redwood-lined park, mountain bikers ride the wide **Aptos Creek Road,** an old railroad grade, under a dense canopy of shade to sunny Sand Point, which overlooks Monterey Bay, the city of Santa Cruz, and the forested ridges of Big Basin Redwoods State Park. This is a good intermediate level ride with lots of aerobic work but little or no technical challenges over its 8.8-mile distance. Hikers usually prefer to leave the wide dirt roads behind

and follow the park's narrower trails instead, where bikes aren't permitted. One popular trip is the eight-mile loop on Loma Prieta Grade and Bridge Creek Trail to see 30-foot **Maple Falls.** Reaching the waterfall requires a final half-mile scramble up Bridge Creek. Pick up a park map at the entrance station; there are dozens more trail options available in this huge, 10,000-acre park.

To get to The Forest of Nisene Marks State Park, take Highway 1 south from Santa Cruz for six miles to the State Park Drive exit. Go east on State Park Drive to Soquel Drive. Turn right and go one mile to Aptos Creek Road; turn left and enter the park.

◖ Wilder Ranch State Park

This 7,000-acre state park, a favorite of mountain bikers, is also a California coastal dairy farm museum, a remnant of the days when dairies were more important to the local economy

© ANN MARIE BROWN

Farm animals greet visitors to the historic ranch buildings at Wilder Ranch State Park.

The preserved Victorian ranch house at Wilder Ranch State Park helps to tell the story of California's coastal dairy operations in the 1890s.

than tourists. The historic dairy buildings at Wilder Ranch State Park (1401 Old Coast Rd., 831/423-9703 or 831/426-0505, www.santa cruzstateparks.org or www.parks.ca.gov, $8 per vehicle entrance fee), located three miles north of Santa Cruz on the west side of Highway 1, include a Victorian ranch house decked out in period furnishings, an elaborate 1890s stable, a dairy barn, and a bunkhouse/workshop with water-driven machinery. Ranch tours, led by docents dressed in period attire, are offered on occasional weekend afternoons. A variety of other history- and natural history—oriented events are sponsored throughout the year, from demonstrations on making corn-husk dolls to mastering cowboy-style roping. The interpretive center and park store are generally open Thursday–Sunday 10 A.M.–4 P.M. in summer; Friday–Sunday only in winter.

For outdoors enthusiasts, Wilder's biggest appeal is its miles of coastline and thousands of acres of grassland-covered hills, laced with trails for bikers, hikers, and equestrians. A great place to start exploring is on the 2.5-mile **Old Landing Cove Trail,** which passes alongside agricultural fields and wetlands and over wave-cut terraces that tower over the crashing surf. Highlights along the trail include a seal rookery, sandy coves, and a hidden fern grotto. You can hike or bike this trail—it's an easy cruise no matter how you do it. More serious riding and hiking is possible on the inland side of the park (from the historic dairy buildings, go through the tunnel underneath Hwy. 1, then follow wide Wilder Ridge Trail uphill).

Pogonip

The land known as Pogonip (333 Golf Club Dr., 831/420-5270, www.ci.santa-cruz.ca.us) was once part of the extensive Henry Cowell

SANTA CRUZ

Ranch, home to a successful lumber business and later a productive livestock operation. In 1961, the western portion of the ranch was sold to the University of California to become U.C. Santa Cruz and the remaining acreage became known as Pogonip. This 640-acre expanse of open meadows, woods, and creeks is managed by the City of Santa Cruz and features eight miles of hiking trails. In the northernmost portion of Pogonip, a one-mile multiuse trail (U-Con Trail, which is open to bikers and horses as well as hikers) connects the lands of the U.C. campus to Henry Cowell Redwoods State Park. Pogonip has several walk-in entrances, but no on-site parking. Visitors may park on Golf Club Drive off Highway 9 (less than a mile from Hwy. 1) and walk to the main entrance gate at the end of Golf Club Drive, or access the park from the east end of the U.C. campus (at the end of East Drive or near the junction of McLaughlin Drive and Glen Coolidge Drive). Access is also possible from Harvey West Park via the Harvey West Trail; park at the end of Evergreen Street in Santa Cruz or along Harvey West Boulevard.

And what's the meaning of the word "Pogonip"? It's a dense winter fog consisting of ice crystals that are frozen in the air. You may find fog here in Santa Cruz, but it's darn rare to find ice crystals.

FISHING

For Monterey Bay fishing charters, contact **Stagnaro's Sportfishing** at the Santa Cruz municipal wharf (831/427-2334, www.stagnaros.com), or **Scurfield's Landing/Shamrock Charters** (831/476-2648, www.scurfslanding.com) at the yacht harbor. Trips vary throughout the year, but the usual catch is sand dabs (Dec.–Apr.), salmon (Apr.–Sept.), snapper or cod (May–Dec.), and albacore (July–Nov.).

Charter fishing rates are typically $50–75 per adult, $40 for kids under age 16. Most trips leave very early in the morning (6 A.M. or earlier) and return in early afternoon.

Pier fishing is popular at Seacliff State Beach (201 State Park Dr., Aptos, 831/685-6440, www.santacruzstateparks.org, $8 day-use) at the pier by the sunken cement ship. For surf fishing, head south to Manresa (206 Sand Dollar, La Selva, 831/761-1795, www.santacruzstateparks.org) or Sunset State Beaches (one mile south of Manresa, 831/763-7063), where big catches of surf perch, striped bass, and starry flounder are common.

KAYAKING

Venture Quest (125 Beach St., 831/427-2267 or 831/425-8445, www.kayaksantacruz.com) offers kayak rentals at Santa Cruz Wharf ($20 for two hours or $35 all day), plus guided sunset, moonlight, half-day, and all-day paddle tours ($40). Tours typically explore the coves and kelp forests near the wharf and Lighthouse Point area. **Kayak Connection** (831/479-1121, www.kayakconnection.com) at the Santa Cruz Yacht Harbor also rents and sells kayaking equipment, and offers guided three-hour naturalist tours ($50). Reservations are required.

SAILING

For an unusual view of the boardwalk and the bay, take a boat ride. One of the best going is the 70-foot *Chardonnay II* (reservations required, 831/423-1213, www.chardonnay.com, $49 and up), an ultralight sailing yacht that departs from Santa Cruz Yacht Harbor. Relax on the deck or in the spacious cabin while the crew dispenses tidbits about local wildlife and ecology. Excursions are often based on "themes" such as astronomy, wine tasting, beer brewing, or whale-watching. This sleek, white sailboat can hold up to 49 passengers and is also available for private charters. The Saturday Sunset Sails, complete with wine and appetizers, are the most popular, but the best deal is the Thursday Night Special—bring your own snacks and the fee is discounted.

SURFING
Surf Breaks

Santa Cruz has many hot spots for surfing, but the two most famous are Steamer Lane and Pleasure Point. Neither are suitable for beginners, and both are subject to a strong dose of "localism," i.e. if you aren't from around here, you better be an expert surfer and extremely polite to boot. **Steamer Lane** is just off Lighthouse Point on West Cliff Drive, right below the Santa Cruz Surfing Museum. It's the most dangerous place to surf in Santa Cruz (deaths happen every year) and the swell can get huge, as in triple overhead. No

matter what, Steamer Lane always provides a great show—crowds gather along the blufftop fence on West Cliff Drive to watch those brave comrades in wetsuits shooting the curls at the Lane. Nearing Capitola farther to the south, **Pleasure Point** (831/454-7956, www .scparks.com), also known as "The Hook," is found at East Cliff Drive and Pleasure Point Drive. Technically, the Hook comprises the very southern tip of Pleasure Point and it is most easily accessed by taking the stairs from the end of 41st Avene. It's not quite as dangerous as Steamer Lane, but still, it's rocky out here. The centerpiece of Pleasure Point lies around 36th Avenue and East Cliff Drive (use the 36th Ave. stairs for access), and depending on the tides and swell, waves here come in all shapes and sizes. Jack O'Neill, inventor of the wetsuit, still lives in the Pleasure Point neighborhood and surfs here.

If you want to get out of town a bit, head

© ISTOCKPHOTO.COM

A surfer catches some air off Steamer Lane.

south to **Manresa State Beach** (206 Sand Dollar, La Selva, 831/761-1795, www.santacruz stateparks.org) near Aptos. You won't find nearly the crowds that throng to Santa Cruz, especially on weekends, and this classic beach break is remarkably consistent as long as it doesn't get blown out. The downer here is riptides, so pay attention to how far you are from shore.

Surf Lessons

Beginners on longboards generally fare well at **Cowell Beach** (101 Beach St.) on the north side of the Santa Cruz Wharf. The waves are gentle and consistent, and rentals are available right on the beach. If you want some instruction, the masters at **Club Ed** on Cowell Beach (831/464-0177 or 800/287-7873,

---

A LEXICON OF SURFING

Spend any time around surfers and you soon realize they have their own language to describe their sport and the watery world they inhabit. This terminology varies widely depending on what region of the coast the surfers hail from, and how old they are. Many of the terms below would be considered "old school" by 20-somethings, but they are included here anyway, if only for their color value.

- **backdoor:** to enter a barreled wave from behind its peak (typically occurs when a surfer is late to catch a wave)

- **bailing out:** deciding not to go for a wave, usually at the last moment

- **barrel:** the hollow section of a wave, also called the tube or pipe; to be "barreled" is to ride inside the barrel

- **blown out:** when the wind stirs up the waves too much, ruining the surfing conditions

- **Dawn Patrol:** serious surfers think nothing of getting up at 5 A.M. to surf; these hardy souls comprise the Dawn Patrol

- **dropping in:** ruining another surfer's ride by taking a wave they have already caught; also called "snaking"; this is very bad form and could land you a black eye at many surf spots

- **glassy:** the opposite of "blown out" – when there is little or no wind and the ocean is smooth

- **goofy:** surfing with the right foot forward on the board (most surfers put their left foot forward)

- **grommet:** very young surfers (usually teens or younger)

- **kook:** a surfer that can't surf well and is rude or offensive to other surfers; nobody likes a kook

- **left:** a wave that breaks to the surfer's left when he/she is in the water and looking at the shore

- **lineup:** the calmer water beyond the break where surfers hang out and chitchat, waiting for the next wave

- **localism:** when local surfers become territorial about their surf spots and are unfriendly to nonlocals

- **offshore:** winds that blow away from the shore and toward the ocean, creating ideal surfing conditions

- **rag dolled:** when a surfer gets tossed off a wave and his/her body is tossed around like a rag doll

- **set:** a group of larger-than-normal waves rolling into shore

- **stalling out:** losing momentum on the board by putting too much weight on the tail

- **swell:** a long series of waves caused by an ocean disturbance, usually a storm, which can occur thousands of miles away from the actual event

- **take-off:** when a surfer paddles into a wave, grabs the rails of his or her board, and assumes a standing position

www.club-ed.com) can show you the way. A two-hour beginner group lesson with all equipment included (wetsuit and board) costs $85 per person; semiprivate lessons are $120 per person. After a few hours with the pros, you'll be able to take your "big stick" and head out in search of the perfect wave.

Probably the most famous surfing instructor in Santa Cruz is **Richard Schmidt** (849 Almar Ave., 831/423-0928, www.richardschmidt .com), a Santa Cruz local who made his name surfing the big waves on Oahu's North Shore in the 1980s. Schmidt, together with his wife Marisa, run weeklong, overnight surf camps in Santa Cruz during the summer, and Costa Rica in the winter. If you don't have a whole week to devote to surfing, Schmidt's staff of instructors provide two-hour group lessons ($80). If you want private lessons with Richard, they'll cost $130 per hour. All classes come with the same guarantee: that you will stand up and ride down the face of a wave in your first lesson. Alternatively, just skip the lessons altogether and instead purchase Richard's "Learn to Surf" DVD, which *Surfer* magazine calls "the best how-to video ever released."

Surf lessons are also available from **Santa Cruz Surf School** (322 Pacific Ave., 831/426-7072, www.santacruzsurfschool .com). A two-hour group lesson ($80–85) will get you started, but most people sign up for a follow-up lesson as well ($60). Private lessons are available for those who want more individualized training. Classes meet at the surf school's shop, then head to Cowell Beach or another suitable location, depending on the day's swell and tide.

Another great spot for novice surfers is **Capitola Beach** (Cliff Dr. and Whard Rd., Capitola), just to the left of its small rock jetty. There are generally a lot less surfers here than at Cowell's, but then again, the break doesn't accommodate as many comers. **Capitola Beach Company** (131 Monterey Ave. in Capitola Village, 831/462-5222, www.capitolabeach company.com) offers surfboard rentals right at Capitola Beach at Esplanade Park (June–Aug. daily 10 A.M.–6 P.M.; Apr.–May and Sept. Sat.–Sun. 11 A.M.–5 P.M.). Typical rates for surfboards are $9 per hour or $25 per day; wetsuits are $6 per hour or $15 per day. Private and group lessons are also offered almost every day from May to September, depending on tides and swell; reservations are required.

Entertainment and Shopping

NIGHTLIFE
Bars and Clubs
It's hard to resist a neighborhood pub called **99 Bottles of Beer** (110 Walnut Ave., 831/459-9999, www.99bottles.com, daily 11:30 A.M.–1:30 A.M.). Forty of the more than 100 different beers available here are on tap, so this place is serious about its barley and hops. If you come here often enough to drink all 99 varieties, you can get your name on the wall

and join others who have likewise made Santa Cruz history. And if you don't like beer, you can sample their selection of California wines and fermented ciders, but really, you'll feel out of place. There's a food menu, too, and it's typical bar fare—buffalo wings, salads, burgers, and the like.

For the younger crowd, the **Blue Lagoon** (923 Pacific Ave., 831/423-7117, www.the bluelagoon.com, daily 4 P.M.–2 A.M.) is where it's at. Don't come here unless you are planning to dance and drink cheap well drinks ($2–4 on weeknights). Live bands appear on some nights, smoking-hot DJs on other nights, and the music is decidedly young—goth rock, hip hop, and industrial. One night a week (usually Wed.) is reserved for the sounds of the '80s and '90s, which, in case you haven't heard, is now considered "retro." On most nights there is no cover charge.

Located upstairs in the historic Santa Cruz Hotel downtown, **Red Restaurant and Lounge** (200 Locust St., 831/425-1913, www.redsantacruz.com, daily 5 P.M.–2 A.M.) is the place where the ultra-sophisticated, and those just hoping to look hip, go to meet each other and clink martini glasses. Think plush Parisian nightclub and you've got the picture here, complete with lots of dark wood paneling and seductive lighting. This is definitely a cocktail kind of place, although the wine and beer selection is good, too. Get a seat near the fireplace, or on one of the velvet couches. Downstairs is the **Red Room,** where for some reason patrons are still allowed to smoke cigarettes indoors.

Live Music

The **Catalyst** (1011 Pacific Ave., 831/423-1338, www.catalystclub.com) is the main event for nightlife in Santa Cruz, featuring live acts from around the world, including some big names like Neil Young, No Doubt, Red Hot Chili Peppers, and Pearl Jam. The main dance floor can hold 800 people over its 5,000-square-foot expanse. Six pool tables, a jukebox, arcade games, and a 100-foot-long bar round out the scene.

Almost any night of the week you might find live music at **Moe's Alley** (1535 Commercial Way, 831/479-1854, www.moesalley.com), and it could be blues, salsa, reggae, roots,

or anything else. The dance floor is always packed with people finding their groove, and the dress code is definitely "jeans." A local Indian restaurant serves Indian food at most weekend shows, and a full bar is available. The outdoor patio is the place to be on warm summer days.

At **Kuumbwa Jazz Center** (320-2 Cedar St., 831/427-2227, www.kuumbwajazz.org) top-notch jazz artists perform each week in a small, intimate setting. World-renowned artists that have graced the bill here include Dave Brubeck, Diane Schuur, Ottmar Liebert, Joshua Redman, Marian McPartland, and Christian McBride. Dinner is served one hour before showtime, but you don't choose from a menu. Only one entrée is prepared each night, and that's what everyone eats, along with salad, bread, and bowls of chili (vegetarian options are always available).

For a classic Santa Cruz experience, head to **The Attic** (931 Pacific Ave., 831/460-1800) on the second floor above the Blue Lagoon bar. Music at The Attic is usually the acoustic variety—folk, jazz, and bluegrass—but it happens more rarely since new owners took over in early 2008 (they are focusing more on the coffee/tea aspect of the business and less on the live music end). If no one is performing, a full restaurant menu and an amazing tea bar makes this the place to order a hot chai and argue about Hegel or Kant with your neighbors. Plenty of couches and tables set against walls decorated with colorful local artwork invite you to linger.

PERFORMING ARTS

Contemporary theater is alive and well in Santa Cruz at the nonprofit **Actors' Theatre** (1001 Center St., 831/425-7529 or 831/425-1003, www.actorssc.org). A variety of new plays are performed year-round, but one of the most popular events is the "Eight Tens at Eight" series (usually performed in midwinter), in which eight different 10-minute plays are performed, one after the other.

It's all about music and arts at **Cayuga Vault** (1100 Soquel Ave., 831/421-9471, www.cayuga vault.com). The Vault is set in an old bank building circa 1915, with high ceilings, hardwood floors, and fabulous acoustics. Concerts, recitals, and performances take place here on a regular basis, and although the acts are not exactly world renowned, the historic ambience is ultracool. Families are welcomed with open arms at most events here; children get in free with their parents. In addition to performances, salsa dance lessons are offered several nights a week, plus yoga, martial arts, and other types of dance/movement classes.

It's always worth checking out what's on the marquee at the **Rio Theatre for the Performing Arts** (1205 Soquel Ave., 831/423-8209, www.riotheatre.com). The Rio showcases both live performances (music, dance, lecture series, and more) and films.

CINEMA

Santa Cruz has more than its fair share of movie theaters and film series. The historic 1936 **Del Mar Theatre** (1124 Pacific Ave., 831/469-3220, www.thenick.com) has been lovingly renovated and shows great art house and independent films. If it's not playing at the Del Mar, then it's probably showing at the associated **Nickelodeon Theatre** (210 Lincoln St., 831/426-7500, www.thenick.com).

For first-run films, see what's playing at downtown's **Santa Cruz Regal Cinema 9** (1405 Pacific Ave., 831/457-3505, www.mr movietimes.com) or **Regal Cinema Riverfront Stadium Twin** (155 S. River St., 831/429-7250, www.mrmovietimes.com).

FESTIVALS AND EVENTS

Spring

Indie film fans flock to Santa Cruz in mid-May for the **Santa Cruz Film Festival** (831/459-7676, www.santacruzfilmfestival .com), held at various theaters throughout town over a 10-day period. More than 100 films are shown in a typical year. Later in May, usually on Memorial Day Weekend, is the annual **Santa Cruz Blues Festival** in Aptos (831/479-9814, www.santacruzbluesfestival .com), featuring nearly a dozen big-name performers playing outdoors in a redwood- and oak-bordered amphitheater. In past years, musicians have included Robert Cray, Bonnie Raitt, Ray Charles, and Buddy Guy.

A completely different kind of music can be heard at the **Santa Cruz Baroque Festival's Music in the Gardens Tour** (831/457-9693, www.scbaroque.org), also usually held on Memorial Day weekend. Patrons get to tour five private gardens at various locations in town while listening to different baroque musical groups and enjoying wine and food at each spot.

Summer

Fans of the Bard will find something to look forward to from mid-July to the end of August, when Shakespeare's plays are performed outdoors in the Festival Glen and on the U.C. Santa Cruz main stage at the annual **Shakespeare Santa Cruz Festival** (1156 High St., 831/459-2159, www.shakespeare santacruz.org). Also in August is the famed **Cabrillo Festival of Contemporary Music** (831/426-6966, www.cabrillomusic.org), which has been held for more than 40 years at various locations throughout Santa Cruz. The festival, which showcases the works of contemporary orchestral composers, runs for about two weeks.

Less highbrow but still plenty of fun is the **Woodies on the Wharf Festival** (Municipal Wharf, 831/420-6025, www.santacruz woodies.com), held every year in late June. Over 200 woodies (wood-bodied automobiles, usually dating from the 1920s–1960s) are on display, along with plenty of related surf-retro fun.

Only the most manly of men dare compete in the annual August **Mountain Men Gathering** (831/335-4484, www.roaringcamp .com) at Roaring Camp Railroads in Felton. Well, actually, there are a few women, too, and they all show up to relive the wild days of the 1830s with a variety of lumberjack contests and a musical saw concert.

Autumn

Early September is the time for Capitola's annual **Begonia Festival** (831/476-3566, www .begoniafestival.com), which celebrates that colorful shade-loving flower that was brought to Capitola in the 1930s. Besides showing off plenty of tuberous begonias (which flourish here in the cool, foggy climate), the festival also includes a sandcastle-building contest, a fishing derby, and a parade with dozens of begonia-covered floats drifting down Soquel Creek. A few weeks later is another local Capitola event, the annual **Art and Wine Festival** (Capitola-Soquel Chamber of Commerce, 831/475-6522, www.capitolachamber.com), which features all the usual trappings of such a weekend festival: wine, art, music, and fun. Typically over 150 artists and more than a dozen wineries participate in the festival.

The last week in October, Santa Cruz proves itself to be the real "Surf City" when the **O'Neill Cold Water Classic** (West Cliff Dr., 831/475-4151, www.oneill.com)—four days of competitive surfing—takes place at Steamer Lane.

Winter

There will be fungus among us come January, when the first rains have made the mushrooms appear and the annual **Fungus Fair** is held at the Louden Nelson Community Center (301 Center St., 831/684-2275, www.fungusfed .org). If you are a serious mycophile, or even a novice, you'll enjoy this celebration of the 'shroom, which includes cooking demonstrations, lectures, and identification workshops. Food aficionados will also enjoy the late-February **Clam Chowder Cook-off**, held at the Santa Cruz Wharf (831/420-6025, www.santacruz wharf.com). The event began in 1982 with a mere 30 entrants, and now has grown to more than twice that size. This being Santa Cruz, amateur and professional chowder chefs often come dressed in zany costumes and make a major production out of preparing their secret recipes.

SHOPPING

Santa Cruz has its own version of the traditional American mall, and it's a lot more hip. The outdoor **Pacific Garden Mall** (Pacific Ave. near River St., 831/429-8433, www.downtown santacruz.com) is the centerpiece of downtown Santa Cruz, its eight blocks filled with eclectic shops selling one-of-a-kind jewelry, clothes, art, books, and music. There are a few chain stores, such as The Gap and Starbucks, but also a bounty of smaller, homegrown shops. Basically, pedestrian-friendly Pacific Avenue extending from Water Street to the north to Laurel Street in the south *is* the mall, but the shopping district also extends for a block or so on either side of Pacific. A good landmark is the historic clock tower at the northern end of Pacific Avenue. The city of Santa Cruz has 17 parking lots in the downtown area, most of them free. (The most convenient lots for the Pacific Garden Mall are located at Church

browsing at Pacific Garden Mall

St. and Walnut Sts., Front St., Locust St., and Center St.)

Books and Music

There are several bookstores in the Pacific Garden Mall (Pacific Ave. near River St., 831/429-8433, www.downtownsantacruz .com), including the classic **Bookshop Santa Cruz** (1520 Pacific Ave., 831/423-0900, www.bookshopsantacruz.com, Sun.–Thurs. 9 A.M.–10 P.M., Fri.–Sat. 9 A.M.–11 P.M.), a community institution that offers a full calendar of author and reader events and is a great champion of the small presses. Have a seat in one of its overstuffed chairs and enjoy the long-standing success of this independent bookstore—one of the last and greatest of a dying breed.

But if your taste runs more toward mainstream best sellers, a unit of the behemoth **Borders** chain is nearby (1200 Pacific Ave., 831/466-9644, www.borders.com, daily 10 A.M.–9 P.M.). For used/recycled books, there's **Logos Books and Records** (1117 Pacific Ave., 831/427-5100, www.logosbooks records.com, Sun.–Thurs. 10 A.M.–10 P.M.,

Fri.–Sat. 10 A.M.–11 P.M.), which specializes in buying and selling used, collectible, and rare books and music. Their 11,000-square-foot, two-story building houses over a quarter of a million items for sale. Another great choice for CDs and records (both new and used) is **Streetlight Records** (939 Pacific Ave., 831/421-9200, www.streetlightrecords .com, daily 11 A.M.–10 P.M.).

The downtown area also draws musicians, not just music listeners, who head to **Union Grove Music** (1003 Pacific, 831/427-0670, www.uniongrovemusic.com, Mon.–Wed. 9 A.M.–6 P.M., Thurs. 10 A.M.–8 P.M., Fri. 10 A.M.–7 P.M., Sat. 10 A.M.–6 P.M., Sun. 11 A.M.–5 P.M.) or **Sylvan Music** (1521 Pacific, 831/427-1917, www.sylvanmusic.com, daily 11 A.M.–6 P.M.) to buy instruments—especially guitars, keyboards, and drums—or to get a string fixed or purchase sheet music.

Clothing and Jewelry

Apparel shops abound in and around downtown's Pacific Avenue, with choices as varied as the upscale **Vault Gallery** (1339 Pacific Ave., 831/426-3349, www.thevault gallery.com, Mon.–Fri. 11 A.M.–6 P.M., Sat. 10 A.M.–6 P.M., Sun. 11 A.M.–5 P.M.), noted for contemporary fine jewelry and wearable art; and the neoprene-happy **O'Neill Surf Shop** (110 Cooper St., 831/469-4377, Sun.–Thurs. 10 A.M.–9 P.M., Fri.–Sat. 10 A.M.–10 P.M.), the store that bears the name of Jack O'Neill, pioneer of the modern-day wetsuit. Anything you need for the beach, you'll find here. Another only-in-Santa-Cruz apparel shop is **Eco Goods** (1130 Pacific Ave., 831/429-5758, www.eco goods.com, Mon.–Sat. 10 A.M.–6 P.M., Sun. 11 A.M.–5 P.M.), home to all things hemp and/ or organic, including recycled and nontoxic T-shirts, jewelry, wallets, sandals, and bags.

SANTA CRUZ

SURF'S UP AT O'NEILL'S

A Santa Cruz phenomenon with considerable worldwide renown is **O'Neill Surf Shop** (www.oneill.com), the legendary business legacy of Jack O'Neill, a local surfer who in the 1950s created a wetsuit that protected surfers from Northern California's chilling waters. In 1952 O'Neill and friends were surfing the frigid Pacific off Ocean Beach in San Francisco, wearing little more than traditional bathing suits. O'Neill, who had served in the Army Air Corps, thought that maybe flexible plastic foam could be used to keep the body warm in the water. He stuffed it in his bathing trunks and found that it worked fairly well, cumbersome as it was. When he first saw neoprene foam used as carpet on the aisle of a DC-3 passenger plane, he knew he had found his magic material – one that could be shaped to fit the body and would move with a surfer's motions. He started making vests out of neoprene, and as these became popular, he expanded to designing full-body wetsuits.

O'Neill's business grew and flourished, becoming the world's number-one wetsuit manufacturer. The company also sells popular surfing-style sportswear. There are three O'Neill shops in Santa Cruz County, including one at the boardwalk (400 Beach St., 831/459-9230), one downtown (110 Cooper St., 831/469-4377), and one in Capitola (1115 41st Ave., 831/475-4151).

O'Neill's legacy is broader and deeper, however, especially since the O'Neill children are fully involved in the company's enterprises. The slogan "It's always summer on the inside" is not just a marketing slogan but a life philosophy. Come to Santa Cruz in late October for a literal test of the summer-inside lifestyle at the famed **O'Neill Cold Water Classic,** a contest held at Steamer Lane that attracts top surfers from around the world. The **O'Neill Sea Odyssey** (www.oneillseaodyssey.org) is an oceangoing environmental education program offered free for fourth- to sixth-grade children onboard the 65-foot Team O'Neill catamaran, a "living classroom." Follow-up lessons are held at the Education Center at the Santa Cruz Harbor. Although the program is free of charge, students have to earn their way into the program by performing a community service project.

Pacific Avenue also has plenty of thrift and vintage clothing shops, including **Cognito Clothing** (821 Pacific, 831/426-5414, www.cognitoclothing.com, Tues.–Sat. 11 A.M.–7 P.M., Sun.–Mon. 11 A.M.–6 P.M.), which sells offbeat apparel such as swing-dance fashions, two-toned panel shirts, and Hawaiian shirts.

Lastly, the only enclosed shopping mall in Santa Cruz County is found in Capitola at the **Capitola Mall** (41st Ave. and Capitola Rd., www.shopcapitolamall.com, Mon.–Fri. 10 A.M.–9 P.M., Sat. 10 A.M.–8 P.M., Sun. 11 A.M.–7 P.M.). The mall has a few big apparel names like Abercrombie and Fitch, Gap, Ann Taylor Loft, and Victoria's Secret, plus the typical mall-quality restaurants (Chili's and Marie Callender's).

Gift and Home

Barbra Streisand and Oprah Winfrey are among the big-name fans of Santa Cruz's **Annieglass** (110 Cooper St., 831/427-4260, www.annieglass.com, Mon.–Sat. 10 A.M.–6 P.M., Sun. 11 A.M.–5 P.M.) handcrafted glass tableware. These translucent, sculpturelike dishes and vases are fused with 24-karat gold and platinum rims, and are so unique that they are displayed in the permanent collection of the Smithsonian. And yes, they can even go in the dishwasher. Annieglass designer/founder Ann Morhauser also makes sculptural jewelry and handbags out of glass, precious gems, and metals. And if you like Annieglass, you'll want to pay a visit to L.H. Selman's **Glass Gallery** (103 and 123 Locust St., 831/427-1177, www

.theglassgallery.com, Mon.–Fri. 9 A.M.–5 P.M., Sat. 11 A.M.–5 P.M.) and its accompanying **Paperweight Museum.** This combined gallery/shop is all about the beauty of colored glass, fashioned into myriad shapes and forms.

Both decorative and practical kitchen supplies and accessories can be found at **Chefworks** (1527 Pacific Ave., 831/426-1351, www.chefworks-santacruz.com, Mon.–Thurs. 10 A.M.–6 P.M., Fri.–Sat. 10 A.M.–9 P.M., Sun. 11 A.M.–6 P.M.). This everything-for-the-chef store has over 18,000 cookware and bakeware items, wine accessories, culinary tools, small appliances, and kitchen accessories in stock.

Accommodations

SANTA CRUZ
Camping

There's a wide range of camping choices in the Santa Cruz area, but since most are state park campgrounds, advance planning is essential for the summer, when most, if not all, sites are booked six months in advance. For all state park or state beach campgrounds, reserve at 800/444-7275 or www.reserveamerica.com.

Campers who prefer the beach can choose from several campgrounds south of Santa Cruz at New Brighton State Beach, Manresa State Beach, or Sunset State Beach. At **New Brighton State Beach** (1500 Park Ave. in Capitola, 831/464-6330, $25–35), four miles south of Santa Cruz, 111 sites can accommodate tents or RVs. Flush toilets and coin-operated showers are available. "New Bright's" attractive sites are perched on the bluffs, with ample shade from Monterey pines. This area was once called China Beach or China Cove, after the Chinese fishermen who built a village here in the 1870s.

At **Manresa State Beach** (206 Sand Dollar, La Selva, 831/761-1795, www.santacruzstateparks.org, $25), Manresa Uplands Campground is set up for walk-in tent camping only; 64 sites are set on a high bluff overlooking the ocean. Many sites have ocean views; others are set in a shady cypress grove. From the loading zone where you unload your gear from your car, the walk to the sites is anywhere between 20 and 150 yards. Flush toilets and coin-operated showers are available.

At **Sunset State Beach** (one mile south of Manresa, 831/763-7063, $25), 90 sites for tents or RVs (no hookups) are set on a bluff top, a short walk from the beach (no ocean views from these sites). The three-mile-long beach is spectacular, with sand dunes reaching as high as 50 feet; The entire area is very bucolic; fields of brussels sprouts surround the campground for as far as the eye can see.

Heading farther south, RVers can camp at **Seacliff State Beach** (State Park Dr., Aptos, 831/429-2851, www.parks.ca.gov, reserve at 800/444-7275 or www.reserveamerica.com, $35), but no tents are permitted.

The only private campground near the beautiful beaches south of Santa Cruz is the **Santa Cruz KOA** (1186 San Andreas Rd., 831/722-0551 or 800/562-7701, www.santacruzkoa.com), which has 180 sites best suited for RVs, although tents are permitted. The camp is located on the inland side of San Andreas Road, a five-minute drive from either Manresa State Beach or Sunset State Beach. Campsites are a pricey $50 and up, but the best bet here are the 50 "Kamping Kabins" ($92–125) that are one- and two-room cabins with cots; you bring your own bedding. Restrooms and showers are a short walk away. More luxurious cabins that sleep up to six people and have private bathrooms are also available, as are a dizzying array of in-camp entertainment options, including mini golf, a small climbing wall for kids, a playground, horseshoes, volleyball, a heated swimming pool, and much more.

For camping in the redwood forest just a few miles uphill from Santa Cruz, head to **Henry Cowell Redwoods State Park** (off Hwy. 9 in Felton, 831/438-2396, reserve at 800/444-7275 or www.reserveamerica.com, $25). Its 120 sites are quite civilized and suitable for tents and RVs; flush toilets and coin-operated showers are available, plus free wireless Internet access. This is one of the most popular campgrounds in the state park system—thus campsites are extremely hard to come by; reserve yours way in advance.

Hostels

The **HI-USA Santa Cruz Hostel** (321 Main St., 831/423-8304, www.hi-santacruz.org, $25–55), downtown on Beach Hill, occupies the historic 1870s Carmelita Cottages. The hostel is just two blocks from the beach, wharf, and boardwalk, and features an Internet kiosk, laundry facilities, barbecue, lockers, and rose and herb gardens. Some private rooms and limited parking are available (extra fee for both). The large, fully stocked kitchen makes cooking meals a snap. Remember that this is a hostel, not a hotel, so you won't have a private bathroom, there are no locks on the doors, and you have to obey the curfew rules—in by 11 P.M. and out by 11 A.M. But you can't beat the price.

Hotels and Motels

$100-150

A converted motor inn, the family-owned and operated **Pelican Point Inn** (21345 E. Cliff Dr., 831/475-3381, www.pelicanpointinnsantacruz.com, $129–159) is a great choice for budget-priced accommodations in Santa Cruz, located within walking distance of Twin Lakes Beach and several restaurants. The rooms have marble baths, hardwood floors, and tasteful decor. Several units have kitchenettes and living rooms, and all have either one or two queen beds. Free wireless Internet access, as well as plug-in access, is available. If you are traveling with more than a few people in your party, consider renting the inn's separate beach house that is located in Aptos, across from Seacliff State Beach.

There are two Super 8 motels near the boardwalk, and they are distinguished only by "East" and "West." You want East—the **Super 8 Santa Cruz Boardwalk East** (338 Riverside Ave., 831/426-3707, www.super8.com, $100–150). Located less than two blocks from the beach and boardwalk, this Super 8 is run by a delightful family who wants to ensure that you enjoy your stay. For a low-budget chain motel, the place has some surprisingly plush amenities, like flat-screen televisions, refrigerators and microwaves, an outdoor pool, free wireless Internet, and a free continental breakfast. If you pay a little extra, you can get a room with a whirlpool tub.

Sometimes all you want is a clean, decent place to sleep after a full day of outdoor fun, and the **Hampton Inn Santa Cruz** (1505 Ocean St., 831/457-8000, www.hamptoninn.com, $135–165) provides that. This chain motel offers all the amenities you would expect, including a free continental breakfast, high-speed Internet access, and coffee and tea in the lobby 24 hours daily. The Santa Cruz Boardwalk is only one mile away—about a five-minute drive. A word of warning for light sleepers: The Hampton Inn is just a block off the 17 freeway and right next door to a busy Denny's restaurant. A pair of earplugs may help you get your rest.

The Continental Inn (414 Ocean St., Santa Cruz, 831/429-1221 or 800/343-6941, www.continentalinnsantacruz.com, $120–160) is an affordable lodging with a nice family feel to it. Children 12 and under stay free, which adds to the value. With its mural of the Santa Cruz surf on the front of the building, the inn is easy to recognize. Yes, the hotel straddles a street which runs down the middle of its two buildings, but get over it. If you've driven to every hotel and motel in Santa Cruz looking for a room on a busy weekend, you'll wish you went here first. The beach, boardwalk, and downtown are all walkable, and the inn offers plenty of amenities, including a continental breakfast and a pool.

$150-250

Close to the wharf and overlooking the bay is the small but immensely popular **Sea & Sand Inn** (201 W. Cliff Dr., 831/427-3400, www.santacruzmotels.com, $219–269). The inn sits atop a rocky cliff, so all 20 rooms can claim an ocean view. The more expensive suites have hot tubs set on private patios overlooking the ocean; some rooms have indoor spas as well. Free wireless Internet access and a continental breakfast are included in your stay.

The **Edgewater Beach Motel** (525 Second St., 831/423-0440 or 888/809-6767, www.edgewaterbeachmotel.com, $175–225) is situated in the heart of Santa Cruz on top of Beach Hill, surrounded by flower-filled gardens. You can easily walk to the wharf, the beach,

downtown restaurants, and anywhere else you want to go. The motel offers plenty of amenities, including fireplaces and whirlpool tubs in some rooms, free wireless Internet, a heated pool, and a barbecue area. Rooms are set up to accommodate 2–8 people; some suites even have fully equipped kitchens. Pets can be accommodated for a small extra fee.

The **Bella Notte/The Inn at East Cliff** (21305 East Cliff Dr., 831/600-0001 or 877/342-3552, $200–250) is a new and different kind of Santa Cruz lodging. It's located on the "quiet" south side of town, near Twin Lakes Beach and the Santa Cruz Yacht Harbor, so it's not right for people who want to spend their vacation partying at the boardwalk and wharf. But those who seek a more sedate stay in town will enjoy the high-ceilinged rooms, large bathrooms with heated tile floors, high-definition televisions, pillow-top mattresses, and bathrobes. Many rooms have fireplaces and/or whirlpool tubs and the amenities are in excellent condition. Free wireless Internet and a continental breakfast are included in the nightly rate.

OVER $250

Adjacent to the wharf and a block from the Santa Cruz Beach Boardwalk, the imposing **◖ Dream Inn** (175 W. Cliff Dr., 831/426-4330 or 866/774-7735, www.jdvhotels.com, $250–300), is right on Cowell Beach and adjacent to the Santa Cruz Wharf. You can take surf lessons right in front of the hotel. The Dream Inn is the latest incarnation of what used to be the Coast Santa Cruz Hotel. The multistory hotel's colorful, retro-chic decor is a perfect fit for the beach, and the place is hip enough to have iPod docking stations and flat-screen televisions with Xbox hookups in each of its 167 rooms, plus balconies and/or patios overlooking the deep blue sea. Try to reserve one of the rooms on the higher floors for the most impressive water vistas, but really, there are no disappointing views here.

Another great place for views of the long-distance variety is **Chaminade at Santa Cruz** (1 Chaminade Lane, 831/475-5600 or 800/283-6569, www.chaminade.com, $239–299). Occupying the old Chaminade Brothers Seminary and Monastery, this quiet resort and conference center set high on a hill overlooking Monterey Bay offers a wealth of amenities, including a fitness center, a spa, a jogging track, lighted tennis courts, a heated pool, saunas, and whirlpools. Rooms and suites are scattered around the 80-acre grounds in 11 "villas" that include shared parlors with refrigerators, wet bars, and conference tables. Decorated in a contemporary Spanish style, the guest rooms have king or queen beds, in-room coffeemakers, irons and ironing boards, and phones. Chaminade also boasts two good restaurants and a bar.

Bed-and-Breakfasts

The Mediterranean-style **((Pleasure Point Inn** (2-3665 E. Cliff Dr., 831/469-6161 or 831/475-4657, www.pleasurepointinn.com, $225–295) overlooks the ocean at Pleasure Point, one of the most famous surfing breaks on the Central Coast. If you came to Santa Cruz to enjoy the beach, this is the ideal place to stay. All four rooms offer fine ocean views and gas fireplaces, but the biggest draw at the inn is its rooftop deck, which provides a sweeping coastal vista. The deck is a popular spot for sunsets, with multiple seating areas, a gas-lamp heater for cool coastal evenings, and an eight-person hot tub. Guests are provided with a welcome basket filled with edible goodies on the first night of their stay, and a continental

breakfast is served each morning in the dining room overlooking Monterey Bay. You can take surfing lessons on the beach right in front of the inn, or, if you already know how to surf, board and gear rentals are available.

The downtown **((Adobe on Green** (103 Green St., 831/469-9866, www.adobeongreen.com, $99–205) is a very untypical B&B. Breakfast is not a lavish, made-to-order affair, but rather a simple buffet of local foods, including farm-fresh eggs and granola. The furnishings are modest and tasteful—the polar opposite of the cluttered "Grandma's house" style seen at too many inns. Flowery gardens can be viewed from every window, often with hummingbirds flitting about the blossoms. Many restaurants, theaters, and shops are within walking distance, so if you wish, you can park your car and leave it here for the duration of your Santa Cruz visit.

The **Babbling Brook Inn** (1025 Laurel St., 831/427-2437 or 800/866-1131, www.babblingbrookinn.com, $229–329) was once a log cabin, but was added to and otherwise spruced up by the Countess Florenzo de Chandler almost a century ago. All 13 rooms and suites are designed for romance, with many having full or partial ocean views, featherbeds, fireplaces, and spa tubs. Several are decorated to suggest the works of Old World artists and poets, from Cézanne and Monet to Tennyson. A full breakfast and afternoon wine and cheese (or tea and cookies) are included in the rate. Also here: a babbling brook (of course), waterfalls, and a garden gazebo.

The three-story Victorian **West Cliff Inn** (174 W. Cliff Dr., 800/979-0910, www.westcliffinn.com, $175–425) was built in 1877, but recently underwent a $2.5 million renovation to restore its intricate hardwood floors and Italianate cornices, and add modern amenities like spa tubs and wireless Internet access. This hilltop mansion overlooks Monterey Bay and is just a short walk from the Santa Cruz Boardwalk. Nine guest rooms have fireplaces and marble-tiled bathrooms. Breakfast and afternoon wine and hors d'oeuvres are provided. Since this is a member of the prestigious "Four Sisters" family of inns, you know that everything will be done just right. And as with all of the Four Sisters properties, a teddy bear is found in every room.

For a special stay in a redwood forest, book one of the three rooms at **Redwood Croft B&B** (275 Northwest Dr., 831/458-1939, www.red woodcroft.com, $150–230). A far cry from the touristy tackiness that often prevails in downtown Santa Cruz, this B&B is a stylish, tastefully decorated home with a wraparound porch, a swing and a hammock under the redwoods, beautiful gardens, and luxurious rooms. A favorite is the Garden Room, which has a wood-burning stove and a private deck with its own whirlpool tub. Breakfast is prepared and served by the cheerful innkeeper each morning, and it's a gourmet affair. Plan on about a 15-minute drive into downtown Santa Cruz, but then again, you may not want to leave this place.

CAPITOLA AND APTOS

Set on a bluff overlooking Monterey Bay in the small town of Aptos, **Seascape Resort** (1 Seascape Resort Dr., 831/688-6800 or 800/929-7727, www.seascaperesort.com, $325–375) provides its guests with access to 17 miles of beachfront. Compared to the busy city beaches of nearby Santa Cruz, the near solitude on this stretch of sand is a blissful respite. This is a condo-style resort, so even the least expensive accommodation is a small suite with a kitchenette and fireplace. The higher-priced "villas" are akin to having your own private

beach house. One caveat, though: make sure you reserve a unit with a "full" ocean view, as the partial views can be a disappointment. All the typical resort conveniences are provided, such as room service, high-speed Internet access, high-definition television with movies and games on demand, spa services, golf, and tennis. The beach is a five-minute walk from your room, but if you don't want to walk, a free golf cart shuttle travels the distance. On most evenings, the staff holds a sunset bonfire party on the beach, complete with s'mores. In the spring and summer months, "Camp Seascape" offers plenty of fun activities for kids, so parents can get away for a round of golf or a romantic walk on the beach.

For a memorable bed-and-breakfast stay in Aptos, the historic **Sand Rock Farm** (6901 Freedom Blvd., 831/688-8005, www.sand rockfarm.com, $175–275) is an exquisitely restored, turn-of-the-20th-century Craftsman-style home, complete with the original push-button light switches. The 10-acre setting includes country gardens, walking trails, and the ruins of the old Liliencrantz family winery. Sand Rock features five guest rooms and suites with in-room whirlpool tubs, cable TV, and private baths, plus a lounge, fireplace, hot tub, and room service. Well-informed food enthusiasts make a beeline to Sand Rock strictly for the wonderful breakfasts and winemaker dinners created by famed Chef Lynn Sheehan.

Capitola's ◖ **Inn at Depot Hill** (250 Monterey Ave., 831/462-3376 or 800/572-2632, www.innatdepothill.com, $239–299) is a luxurious bed-and-breakfast housed in a onetime railroad depot. This inn is popular for special getaways like anniversaries and honeymoons. Each of the eight rooms features its own unique design motif, inspired by international locales (Delft Room, Stratford-on-Avon, Paris Room,

Portofino), as well as a private garden and entrance, fireplace, and state-of-the-art television and stereo system. Bathrooms have double showers, so two isn't necessarily a crowd. Rates include a full breakfast, which you can have delivered to your room; afternoon tea or wine; and after-dinner dessert.

FELTON AND SCOTTS VALLEY

Nothing fancy, but fine for pine-paneled cabin ambience just five miles north of Santa Cruz, the **Fern River Resort Motel** (5250 Hwy. 9, Felton, 831/335-4412, www.fernriver.com, $75–155) rents 14 cabins with kitchens or kitchenettes, fireplaces, cable TV, and a private beach on the river. If you are planning to ride the train at Roaring Camp Railroad or pay a visit to Henry Cowell Redwoods State Park, this bargain-priced resort serves as a great base

camp. Don't expect the Ritz, but for a cozy cabin in the redwoods, this place is perfect.

From the outside, the **Hilton Santa Cruz-Scotts Valley** (6001 La Madrona Dr., 831/440-1000, www.hilton.com, $195–235) looks a lot like a castle, complete with flags flying over two towers flanking the front entrance. Although the hotel attracts a lot of business travelers, it's also well suited for Santa Cruz vacationers, being just two miles from Highway 1 and a 15-minute drive to local beaches and the boardwalk. The hotel boasts a heated outdoor pool, a spa, a fitness center, a guest laundry, and on-site dining for three meals a day at Café Max. Its 159 guest rooms and 18 suites come with high-speed Internet, speakerphones, microwave ovens, refrigerators, ergonomic desk chairs, and cable television. A newspaper is delivered to your room each weekday morning.

Food

FARMERS MARKETS

Santa Cruz hosts not one but three farmers markets weekly (and two of them year-round). The **Downtown Santa Cruz Market** (Lincoln and Cedar Sts., www.santacruzfarmersmarket .org) is held on Wednesdays 2:30–6:30 P.M. year-round. Farmers, bakers, egg producers, cheese makers, and an oyster cultivator from Marin County gather here to sell their goods directly to the public. The **Westside Market** (2801 Mission St., www.santacruzfarmersmarket .org) is also open year-round and is held on Saturdays 9 A.M.–1 P.M. The **Live Oak Market** (21509 East Cliff Dr., www.santacruzfarmers market.org) is held from May to November only on Sundays 10 A.M.–2 P.M.

In nearby **Felton,** a farmers market (St. John's

Catholic Church, Hwy. 9, 831/425-3331, www .feltonfarmersmarket.org) is held every Tuesday 2:30–6:30 P.M. from May to November.

Farther south in Aptos, the **Cabrillo College Farmers Market** (Soquel Dr., 831/728-5060) is held every Saturday morning 8 A.M.–noon.

SANTA CRUZ
Breakfast

Legendary for breakfast, **Café Brasil** (1410 Mission St., 831/429-1855, www.cafebrazil .us, $7–12) serves the real deal from *way* south of the border. This is the place to try a Brazilian omelette made with chicken and creamed corn, or traditional Brazilian *feijoada* (black bean stew with sausages). The breakfast polenta is far more intriguing than plain old oatmeal. Lunch options include chicken, beef, seafood, and tofu, all prepared in interesting ways. Wash it all down with a hot chai or a fresh choice from the juice bar. The only downer: Parking nearby is next to impossible.

NEWMAN'S OWN SANTA CRUZ

Nell Newman, Cool Hand Luke's daughter, is the farm-loving Santa Cruz resident posing with the famed actor on all those tongue-in-cheek, stylized *American Gothic* **Newman's Own Organics** (www.newmans ownorganics.com) product labels. And how appropriate, since it was a father and daughter so stoically represented in the original *American Gothic*.

Formerly a biologist with the Ventana Wilderness Sanctuary Research and Education Center down the coast in Big Sur, Nell Newman is an accomplished cook who in 1993 was inspired by the Santa Cruz area's love affair with "whole food" to add an organics division to her father's popular company, Newman's Own.

The point of Newman's Own Organics is producing "good tasting food that just happens to be organic." The brand focuses on what might be considered the nonessentials – snack foods, including chocolate bars, tortilla chips, pretzels, Pop's Corn, and several cookie varieties (from Fig Newmans to Oreo-like Newman-O's). But there's also organic premium pet foods, fair-trade coffee, tea, dried fruit, and olive oil and balsamic vinegar.

Like the first generation of Newman's Own, Newman's Own Organics – the second generation – donates 100 percent of after-tax profits to charitable causes. These have included the University of California Santa Cruz Farm and Garden Project, the Organic Farming Research Foundation, the Henry A. Wallace Institute for Alternative Agriculture, and the Western Environmental Law Center in Taos, New Mexico.

For seaside ambience, breakfast at **Aldo's** (616 Atlantic Ave. at the west end of the yacht harbor, 831/426-3736, www.aldoscruz.com, Mon.–Sat. 8 A.M.–8:30 P.M., Sun. 7 A.M.–1 P.M., $8–20) on the harbor is unforgettable. The menu features various egg and omelette combinations, including a creamy eggs Benedict. The best bet, though, is the raisin toast, made with Aldo's homemade focaccia bread. Breakfast is served until 1 P.M., and you can eat inside the restaurant, where family photographs decorate the walls, or outdoors on the picnic tables covered with checkered plastic tablecloths. At lunch and dinner, look for homemade pastas and plenty of seafood, including clam chowder, calamari, fish tacos, and crab louie.

If you're more of a muffin person than a full-on breakfast person, you'll be among friends at **Emily's Good Things to Eat** (1129 Mission St., 831/429-9866, www.emilysbakery.com, daily 7 A.M.–3 P.M., $5). Owner Emily Reilly, who has served two terms as Santa Cruz mayor, really knows how to bake. Just seeing the shop's motto above the door ("Relax…you have plenty of time") makes you feel good. You might as well slow down and enjoy a coffee and a few cookies on Emily's outdoor deck.

California

Colorful arts and crafts are for sale and accompany the outstanding meals at the **Davenport Roadhouse at the Cash Store** (31 Davenport Ave. at Hwy. 1, 831/426-8801, www.davenport roadhouse.com, Tues.–Sun. 8 A.M.–9 P.M., $18–24), located about 15 minutes north of Santa Cruz on Highway 1 in the small seaside hamlet of Davenport. The menu, like the dining room, is warm, unpretentious, and inviting, with pastas, pizzas, and comfort-food entrées like roasted chicken, rib-eye steak, cioppino,

OUTSTANDING IN THE FIELD

Outstanding in the field of foodie tourism is Outstanding in the Field (877/886-7409, www.outstandinginthefield.com), a hugely popular food, wine, and farm experience originally served up by Chef Jim Denevan of the Gabriella Café in Santa Cruz. Local organic farmers and winemakers joyfully get together with visiting chefs – some of Northern and Central California's most honored – to create unique regional dining events that combine a personal farm tour with a spectacular multicourse meal.

At each event, the inviting, well-laden tables are "outstanding" – literally standing out in the farmer's field – and become the "meeting place between the sky and the soil." Family-style, five-course meals, complete with a wine selected to accompany each course, salute the land from which the bounty comes. Tickets are a hefty $180-220 per person, but attendees are paying for an experience, not just a spectacular meal. Most events accommodate about 100-150 diners, and they are held at farms throughout the United States. About 10 dinners per year are held at farms in or near the town of Santa Cruz.

and stuffed pork chops. A kids' menu is always available, and live music usually happens on Tuesday, Thursday, and Saturday nights. If you enjoy yourself too much and need to spend the night, the Roadhouse has eight rooms for rent on the floor above the restaurant.

White linen–covered tables, colorful fresh flowers, and warm earth tones create an oasis of calm at ◖ **Gabriella Café** (910 Cedar St., 831/457-1677, www.gabriellacafe.com, lunch Mon.–Fri. 11:30 A.M.–2 P.M., dinner Sun.– Thurs. 5:30–9 P.M. and Fri.–Sat. 5:30–10 P.M., brunch Sat.–Sun. 11 A.M.–2 P.M., $24–30), so

it's no wonder that *Sunset* magazine calls this restaurant "the town's most romantic spot." If you are looking for a place to take your sweetie in Santa Cruz, this might be it. The eclectic menu changes daily, with the emphasis on locally produced organic produce and sustainably raised meats and dairy. Expect expertly prepared gourmet fare such as grilled quail, Sicilian swordfish, or grilled soft-shell crab, each presented so beautifully that it's painful to dig in with your knife and fork and ruin the artwork on the plate. The desserts and the wine list are also superb.

Chinese

The food critics at *Zagat* love **O'mei** (2316 Mission St., 831/425-8458, Tues.–Sun. 5–9 P.M., $15). This cutting-edge Chinese restaurant with a California twist has been around for more than 25 years, despite its off-putting location in an ugly strip mall. This is a far cry from "standard" Chinese food—it's more like a Chinese culinary adventure. Specialties include plump, red-oil dumplings, drunken mushrooms, tea-smoked sea bass, and chicken with black bean and garlic sauce. Desserts, such as the warm apple pastry, come as a complete surprise, and it's the good kind of surprise.

Greek

For great Greek food, **Vasili's Greek Food and Barbecue** (1501 Mission St., Ste. A, 831/458-9808, www.vasilisgreekrestaurant.com, Tues.–Sat. 11 A.M.–9 P.M., Sun. noon–9 P.M., $10–18) is the spot. The pita bread is handmade, the salads are fresh, and lemon and garlic flavors abound. From dolmas to moussaka eggplant to shish kebab to baklava, the menu offers it all. The lamb, beef, or chicken gyros ($6.50) are favorites among the collegiate crowd. There are plenty of vegetarian options, too.

Italian

For patio dining, it's hard to beat **Ristorante Italiano** (555 Soquel Ave., 831/458-2321, lunch 11:30 A.M.–2 P.M., dinner 5–9 P.M., $13–25), which has been serving traditional and more innovative Italian food in Santa Cruz for more than 25 years. The indoor dining room is warm and welcoming, but in summer, everyone wants to sit outside beneath the sycamore trees and be mesmerized by the patio's three-story-tall mural of an Italian street scene. Menu selections include cacciuco (seafood and fish stew in marinara sauce), prawns Parma, and dozens more Italian favorites. The motto here is "abbondanza," which roughly means "great food in huge portions," so come hungry.

Don't let its shopping center location dissuade you. **(Ristorante Avanti** (1711 Mission St., 831/427-0135, lunch daily 11:30 A.M.–2 P.M. and dinner daily 5–9 P.M., $13–25) delivers beautifully prepared food that is grown locally and organically. Dip their homemade bread in Kalamata oil, and then peruse the menu and choose between entrées like raviolis filled with asparagus, beets, or butternut squash (whichever is in season) or Mediterranean-style mussels and clams. The low-key, cozy environment here is perfect for enjoying both wonderful food and well-selected wines from the Santa Cruz Mountains, France, Italy, and Germany.

Located about three-quarters of the way down the wharf, **Carniglia's** (Santa Cruz Municipal Wharf, 831/458-3600, www.carniglias.net, lunch 11:30 A.M.–3 P.M. and dinner from 5 P.M., $14–32) lays claim to the best Santa Cruz real estate, giving diners a view of Monterey Bay while they enjoy classic Italian meals. The osso buco (veal shank), the ravioli dei funghi (with mushrooms, red onions, and ricotta cheese), and the gamberi (prawns, pancetta, and mushrooms tossed with linguini) create a near-perfect dining experience. If you would rather eat here in the daytime so you can enjoy the view, panini sandwiches and specialty entrées are served for lunch.

Southwestern

South of the wharf and boardwalk, **(Nuevo Southwest Grill** (21490 E. Cliff Dr., 831/475-2233, dinner Tues.–Sun. 5–9 P.M., lunch Thurs.–Fri. 11 A.M.–3 P.M., brunch Sat.–Sun. 9 A.M.–2 P.M., $5–12) offers healthy, reasonably priced fare that is a far cry from ho-hum. The Southwestern menu is creatively put together, including a tower of roasted vegetables, macadamia beet salad, barbecue chicken quesadilla, mango salad, crab cakes, and red potato enchiladas. The grill offers the best sangria in town, plus warm chips and guacamole—served indoors or out. Everything is fresh and served with a smile in this down-to-earth place. Be sure to order the flourless chocolate cake for dessert.

Vegetarian

An icon in vegetarian and vegan dining, downtown's **(Saturn Cafe** (145 Laurel St., 831/429-8505, www.saturncafe.com, 11:30 A.M.–3 A.M., $8), serves inexpensive meals for lunch, dinner, and beyond (they stay open until 3 A.M.). Two of the things they do best are french fries (made with trans fat-free oil, which is later recycled to fuel bio-diesel cars) and the FLT ("fake" bacon, lettuce, and tomato). The "Space Cowboy Burger" is also a source of restaurant pride (it's *sans* meat, of course). On the weekends, brunch is served 10 A.M.–4 P.M., so go ahead, sleep as late as you want. This place is quintessential Santa Cruz.

CAPITOLA, APTOS, AND SOQUEL

Casual Dining

Enjoying something like a cult following, **Gayle's Bakery and Rosticceria** (504 Bay Ave., 831/462-1200, www.gaylesbakery.com, daily 6:30 A.M.–8:30 P.M., $8–12) is consistently the busiest eatery in Capitola. The rosticceria has a wonderful selection of salads and homemade pastas, soups, sandwiches, pizza, spit-roasted meats—even dinners-to-go and heat-and-serve casseroles. But the aromas drifting in from Gayle's Bakery are the real draw. The bakery's breakfast pastries include various Danishes, croissants, muffins, and the like, and specialties such as a schnecken ring smothered in walnuts. The Jewish rye bread, sold in half loaves, is as good as you'll find in Manhattan. Apple crumb and ollalieberry pies are house specialties. This is no place for dieters.

If you want healthy fast food, head to **Carpo's** (2400 Porter St., Soquel, 831/476-6260, www.carposrestaurant.com, daily 11 A.M.–9 P.M., $5–16) where you can get your omega-3s dining on grilled salmon and assorted other treats from the sea. Carpo's is loved by Santa Cruz moms for its speedy service and its shrimp and crab sandwiches, great burgers and fries (or onion rings), seafood and bell pepper kebabs, and other kid-friendly but heart-healthy choices—if you stay away from the deep-fried stuff. This is how it works: You place your order at the counter, and they hand you a vibrating buzzer. When your food's up, you get the message. Carpo's is immensely popular, so be prepared to wait if you arrive at traditional dinner hours. For dessert, try the ollallieberry pie.

Fine Dining

Top of the food chain in Soquel is **Michael's on Main** (2591 Main St., 831/479-9777, www.michaelsonmain.net, Tues.–Fri. 11:30 A.M.–9 P.M., Sat.–Sun. 11 A.M.–9 P.M., $25) where "cutting edge comfort food" is the main event. This means pork chops, pot roast, and salmon served in fresh, creative ways. Be sure to try the crab and avocado tower or a bowl of Michael's famous chili. The best seats in the house are on the patio overlooking Soquel Creek, but you can also choose from the casual bar area or the more formal dining room.

The most famous dinner spot in Capitola is the **Shadowbrook Restaurant** (1750 Wharf Rd., Capitola, 831/475-1222, www .shadowbrook-capitola.com, dinner Mon.– Fri. 5:30–9 P.M., Sat.–Sun. 4:30–9:30 P.M., Sun. brunch 10 A.M.–2:15 P.M., $25–35). The kitchen's well-prepared variety of seafood, steaks, and pastas is only a small part of the Shadowbrook experience; the restaurant's setting overlooking Soquel Creek is what steals the show. Just getting to the dining room is fun—a cable car runs downhill from the parking lot on Wharf Road to the dining room at the water's edge. Many diners choose to walk for at least one leg of the trip, as the hillside gardens are exquisitely landscaped and worth lingering over. If you don't want to have a formal meal in the dining room, you can enjoy light entrées, pizzas, and desserts in the casual Rock Room Lounge. Brunch, with choices like apple and cheddar omelettes, is served on weekends.

If you've traveled to France and enjoyed the fabulous food and warm embrace of a family-owned French restaurant, you'll recognize the same at **Ma Maison** (9051 Soquel Dr., Aptos, 831/688-5566, www.mamaisonrestaurant.com, lunch Tues.–Fri. 11:30 A.M.–2 P.M. and dinner Tues.–Sun. from 5:30 P.M., $20–29). Owned

© ANN MARIE BROWN

Dinner or brunch at the 1940s-era Shadowbrook Restaurant is highlighted by a ride on the tram through lush gardens.

and operated by Chef Lionel LeMorvan and his wife, Janet, both from Paris, this French-meets-California restaurant offers specialties such as French onion soup, lamb shank, and filet mignon with marrow bone, served in one of two dining rooms or on the intimate patio.

Practicalities

INFORMATION AND SERVICES
Tourist Information

The best all-around source for city and county information is the **Santa Cruz County Conference and Visitors Council** (1211 Ocean St., 831/425-1234 or 800/833-3494, www.santacruz.org, Mon.–Sat. 9 A.M.–5 P.M., Sun. 10 A.M.–4 P.M.).

Media and Communications

Santa Cruz Good Times (www.gtweekly .com) is a long-running free weekly with an entertainment guide and sometimes entertaining political features. The *Santa Cruz County Sentinel* daily newspaper (www.santacruz sentinel.com) is another good source of current local information.

The main **post office** in town is found at 850 Front Street near Water Street (831/426-0144, Mon.–Fri. 9 A.M.–5 P.M.). For Saturday postal service, you'll need to go to the 120 Morrissey Boulevard location in east Santa Cruz (Sat. 9 A.M.–2 P.M., Mon.–Fri. 9 A.M.–5 P.M.).

SANTA CRUZ

Emergency Services

The largest public hospital in Santa Cruz is **Dominican Hospital** (1555 Soquel Dr., 831/462-7700, www.dominicanhospital.org). The main **police** station is located at 155 Center Street (831/420-5800, www.ci.santa-cruz.ca.us).

GETTING THERE AND AROUND

Air

Two large airports are found less than an hour's drive from Santa Cruz. **Monterey Peninsula Airport** (831/648-7000, www.montereyairport .com) provides service to and from San Francisco, Los Angeles, Phoenix, Denver, Las Vegas, Long Beach, Ontario, and San Diego. United Airlines, Allegiant, American Eagle, and American West all service this airport.

A much larger airport is located north in San Jose. **San Jose International Airport** (408/501-7600, www.sjc.org) is served by all major U.S. airlines and also provides flights to and from Mexico. The **Early Bird Airport Shuttle** (831/462-3933, www.earlybirdairport shuttle.com, $75–190) can get you to and from the airport and Santa Cruz.

Train

Amtrak's (800/872-7245, www.amtrak.com) Coast Starlight train stops in San Jose daily on its route between Seattle and Los Angeles. Bus service (Amtrak Hwy. 17 Express, $4 one-way) is provided from San Jose to Santa Cruz, less than an hour's ride. The bus makes a curbside stop at 920 Pacific Avenue.

Bus

A **Greyhound** (800/752-4841 or 800/231-2222 for travelers with disabilities, www.greyhound .com) bus terminal is located in Santa Cruz (425 Front St., 831/423-1800). Greyhound provides service from San Francisco to Santa Cruz, as well as connections south to L.A. via Salinas or San Jose.

To get around on public buses otherwise, **Santa Cruz Metro Transit** (370 Encinal St., 831/425-8600, www.scmtd.com) serves the entire county, including bus service to the beach, mission, lighthouse, university, and even neighboring towns like Bonny Doon, Davenport, Boulder Creek, Felton, Capitola, and Watsonville. Metro bus fares are $1.50 one-way or $4.50 for an all-day pass. Exact change is required when boarding the bus.

Car

Driving access to Santa Cruz from San Jose is via Highway 17, but this route can be very congested on summer weekends and at peak rush-hour times on weekdays year-round. For the easiest driving, travel this road very early in the morning on weekends (before 9 A.M.) or midday during the week (10 A.M.–3 P.M.).

The Coast Highway, or Highway 1, runs directly through Santa Cruz from San Francisco to the north or Monterey to the south. Highway 1 tends to back up as it travels through Santa Cruz, where there are several stoplights. Be patient, and don't expect to move anywhere fast.

Once you are in town, driving around Santa Cruz is easy enough, as long as you pay attention to which streets are one-way only. Parking, however, especially in summer and near the beach, is another matter. The city of Santa Cruz has 17 parking lots in the downtown (Pacific Ave.) area, most of them free, but this will mean a walk of about a mile to the beach, or catching a Metro bus. To get your own parking spot near the beach, you simply have to arrive very early in the day.

Bike

Bicyclists are among their ilk in Santa Cruz,

a town that has no shortage of wide bike lanes, bike racks, and buses that welcome bicyclists. Santa Cruz Metro Transit even has a "bike and ride" service for bicyclists who want to hitch a ride partway, then pedal on their own.

Vicinity of Santa Cruz

◖ AÑO NUEVO STATE RESERVE

A trip to Año Nuevo State Reserve (New Year's Creek Rd. off Hwy. 1, 650/879-0227 or 650/879-2025, www.parks.ca.gov, Dec.–Apr.) and an easy walk on the Año Nuevo Point Trail provides a wildlife show you'll never forget. The winter months are when more than 3,000 elephant seals—some as much as 18 feet long and weighing more than two tons—show up on the beaches to give birth and breed. During the peak elephant seal season (Dec. 15–Mar. 31), entry to Año Nuevo's beaches is by guided walk only; tours last about 2.5 hours. Although walks are held several times daily, advance reservations are strongly recommended, especially on weekends. Tickets go on sale as early as 56 days in advance (800/444-4445, $5 per person plus $8 parking fee). From April through November, you may visit the preserve and hike on your own. Although the elephant seals are not usually present during these months, California sea lions and harbor seals can be viewed year-round.

The pendulous proboscis of a two- to three-ton alpha bull dangles down like a fire hose, so

SANTA CRUZ

In the winter months, more than 3,000 elephant seals show up on the beaches of Año Nuevo.

the name is apt. Hunted almost to extinction for their oil-rich blubber, northern elephant seals numbered less than 100 at the turn of the 20th century. All these survivors lived on Isla de Guadalupe off the west coast of Baja California. Their descendants eventually began migrating north to California. In the 1950s, a few arrived at Año Nuevo Island, attracted to its rocky safety. The first pup was born on the island in the 1960s. By 1975 the mainland dunes had been colonized by seals crowded off the island rookery, and the first pup was born onshore. By 1990, 800 northern elephant seals were born on the mainland, part of a total known population of more than 80,000 and an apparent ecological success story. Although Año Nuevo was the first northern elephant seal rookery established on the California mainland, northern elephant seals have since established other colonies elsewhere along the state coastline, such as San Simeon and Point Reyes. From all appearances, their population is doing just fine.

It takes about 30 minutes to drive from downtown Santa Cruz to Año Nuevo; simply follow Highway 1 north for 21 miles. If you'd rather not drive yourself, organized bus excursions, which include walking tour tickets, are available through **San Mateo County Transit** (call 650/508-6441 or 800/660-4287 after November 1 for reservations, www.samtrans.com).

Pigeon Point Lighthouse and Hostel

A few miles to the north of Año Nuevo is a unique attraction that also serves as an unusual lodging option. **⟨ Pigeon Point Lighthouse** (210 Pigeon Point Rd., Pescadero, 650/879-0633 or 800/909-4776, www.norcalhostels.org, $20–24 for dorm beds, $55–100

for private rooms), one of the country's most photographed lighthouses, also operates year-round as a hostel. The rooms are former family residences for the U.S. Coast Guard—male or female bunkrooms, plus some couples' and family rooms. The old Fog Signal Building is now a rec room. Keep in mind that this is a hostel, not a Ritz-Carlton, so the rooms and bathrooms are basic at best, but the view from the lighthouse grounds, along with the windswept coast at neighboring Whaler's Cove, is unforgettable. To top it all off, the hostel's big claim to fame is its hot tub perched on the rocky cliffs above surging surf.

Even if you don't have reservations to stay here, it's worth stopping by for a look. The lighthouse stands 115 feet high—it shares the title of tallest lighthouse on the West Coast with Point Arena Lighthouse near

The Pigeon Point Lighthouse stands 115 feet high.

Mendocino—and has been in continuous operation since 1872. The first-order Fresnel lens is made of 1,008 separate prisms. Guided walks of the grounds are held Friday–Sunday 10 A.M.–4 P.M. (650/879-2120, www.parks.ca.gov), and the Keeper's Store sells educational books, posters, games, and apparel related to the light station, its history, and the area's flora and fauna. Both tide pooling and bird-watching in the vicinity are excellent.

【 BIG BASIN REDWOODS STATE PARK

Designated in 1902 as California's first state park, Big Basin Redwoods (21600 Big Basin Way, 831/338-8860 or 831/338-8861, www.santacruzstateparks.org or www.parks.ca.gov, $7 day-use fee) today is still one of the Golden State's most beloved parks. Comprised of more than 18,000 acres of redwoods, Big Basin contains the largest continuous stand of old-growth redwoods south of Humboldt State Park in the northwest corner of California. Many of the park's behemoth trees are as much as 2,000 years old. The coast redwoods grow so abundantly here because of two major factors: rain and fog. In the winter months (Dec.–Mar.), the park receives about 60 inches of rain per year. In the summer, cooling fog from the Pacific Ocean brings almost daily moisture to the mammoth trees. The park's 80 miles of trails are a wonderland for hikers, and a few additional miles of trail are open to mountain bikes. The park's campground (800/444-7275, www.reserveamerica.com, $25) is packed all summer long with visitors trying to escape the inland heat.

To reach Big Basin Redwoods State Park headquarters and its main trailhead from Santa Cruz, turn north on Highway 9 and drive 12 miles to Boulder Creek and Highway 236 (signed for Big Basin). Turn west on Highway 236 and drive nine miles to the park headquarters. These mountain roads are quite curvy; use caution and take your time. Another major trailhead for Big Basin is located at Rancho del Oso, across from Waddell Beach (7.5 miles north of Davenport on Hwy. 1).

Hiking and Mountain Biking

Although the main entrance to this fantastic redwood park is found inland near Boulder Creek, hikers and mountain bikers can access Big Basin from its western edge at Rancho del Oso off Highway 1, across from Waddell Beach (7.5 miles north of Davenport). Located here is the small **Rancho del Oso Nature and History Center** (3600 Hwy. 1, 831/427-2288, www.santacruzstateparks.org, Sat.–Sun. noon–4 P.M.), with exhibits on the natural and cultural history of Waddell Valley, as well as the western trailhead for the 30-mile **Skyline-to-the-Sea Trail.** It takes a few days and nights to hike the entire trail, which threads its way through the park along Waddell Creek to the Pacific Ocean, and it's well worth it. For those who only have a day, take a long day hike or short mountain bike ride (12.6-miles round-trip) on the first portion of this trail to **Berry Creek Falls.** This 70-foot-high waterfall is a roaring sight to behold in the winter and spring months, and bears a more delicate, misty countenance in the summer months. If you ride the trail, bring a bike lock; the last 0.7 mile to the falls is accessible on foot only, but a bike rack is in place where you can lock up your wheels.

If you approach Big Basin from its main entrance near Boulder Creek, as the majority of visitors do, you can still hike to Berry Creek Falls and its neighboring waterfalls, Silver Falls and Golden Falls, by following the opposite end of the **Skyline-to-the-Sea Trail** from Big Basin park headquarters (no bikes allowed on this stretch). The trip is about 4.7 miles one-way to Berry Creek Falls (9.4 miles round-trip), or 12 miles round-trip to see all three waterfalls and make a semiloop.

Another excellent and much easier walk from the headquarters area of the park is the 0.5-mile **Redwood Trail,** which shows off some of Big Basin's largest and oldest redwoods, including the Mother of the Forest (329 feet tall) and the Santa Clara Tree (17 feet in diameter). Nothing quite compares to the humbling feeling of walking in the shadows of these 2,000-year-old giants.

Camping

The campground at Big Basin Redwoods State Park (800/444-7275, www.reserveamerica.com, $25) has 31 sites for tents or RVs up to 27 feet long (or smaller trailers), plus 69 sites for tents only, and 38 walk-in tent sites, requiring a walk of about 100 feet from where you park your car. This camp is considered by many to be one of the best California state park campgrounds for tent campers, with sites sheltered by giant redwood trees. Flush toilets, drinking water, and coin-operated showers are available, and each site has a picnic table, fire grill, and food locker. Group sites are also available. Those who would prefer to backpack to their campsite instead of drive in can do so at one the park's of 52 hike-in campsites, including several that are set along the 30-mile Skyline-to-the-Sea Trail.

But the biggest attraction at Big Basin's campground is its 36 tent cabins, which can sleep a family of four and come equipped with cots and a small wood stove for keeping warm. This makes a camping trip possible for people who do not have camping gear available to them, or simply do not want to sleep on the ground. To reserve a tent cabin, phone 800/444-7275 or visit www.reserveamerica .com ($65 per night plus $7.50 reservation fee). For more information on the tent cabins, visit www.bigbasintentcabins.com.

MOSS LANDING

Near the mouth of Elkhorn Slough on the coast, about 30 miles south of Santa Cruz, the hamlet of Moss Landing is a cluster of unpretentious antique shops, homespun art galleries, roadside knickknack stands, marine research centers, and slapping-fresh seafood restaurants, all watched over by a towering steam power plant (built in 1948, it's the second largest in the world) and a Kaiser firebrick-making plant. First a Salinas Valley produce port, then a whaling harbor until 1930, Moss Landing is now surrounded by artichoke and broccoli fields. The town's busy fishing harbor and adjoining Elkhorn Slough are home to hundreds of bird and plant species, making this an important region for wildlife. The harbor area is one of the best places in all of California to see sea otters—sometimes dozens of them at one time—and the slough is considered one of the top 100 places in the United States to spot birds.

◖ Elkhorn Slough National Estuarine Research Reserve

This special place with a long and cumbersome name is a mecca for wildlife lovers. Here, in the largest tract of tidal salt marsh outside of San Francisco Bay, meandering river channels and wetlands are thick with an incredible variety of shorebirds, waterfowl, and wildlife. More than 300 bird species reside in or migrate through Elkhorn Slough Reserve (831/728-2822, www.elkhornslough.org, Wed.–Sun. 9 A.M.–5 P.M., $2.50), including endangered

© ANN MARIE BROWN

Kayakers at Elkhorn Slough can observe sea otters, harbor seals, and water birds at eye level.

and threatened birds such as the brown pelican, California clapper rail, peregrine falcon, and California least tern. In the peak of the migration season (usually Sept.–Oct.), more than 20,000 birds per day congregate here. In the spring months, birders head for the North Marsh to see great blue herons and great egrets nesting in a grove of Monterey pines. The reserve has a total of five miles of trails that pass by tidal mudflats, salt marshes, and an old abandoned dairy. The visitors center loans out binoculars and bird identification books. Free, docent-led walks are offered year-round (Sat.–Sun. 10 A.M. and 1 P.M.). To get there from Highway 1 at Moss Landing, turn east on Dolan Road by the power station. Drive three miles to Elkhorn Road, turn left (north), and drive two miles to the reserve entrance.

Kayaking and Boat Tours

The best way to explore the waterways of Elkhorn Slough is in a one- or two-person kayak, where you can observe sea otters, harbor seals, and water birds at eye level. Even if you've never paddled a kayak before, you can quickly master the basics necessary to propel yourself around the calm waters of the slough. Kayak rentals ($30–40 per day) are available in Moss Landing through **Monterey Bay Kayaks** (2390 Hwy. 1, 831/373-5357 or 800/649-5357, www.montereybaykayaks.com) or **Kayak Connection** (831/724-5692, www .kayakconnection.com). If you would rather not set out on your own, guided kayak tours are available; two- or three-hour tours typically cost $50 per person.

Another great way to see the slough is through a guided tour with **Elkhorn Slough Safari** (831/633-5555, www.elkhornslough .com, $32 adults, $30 seniors, $24 children 3–12) aboard their 27-foot pontoon boat. Tours can be scheduled every day of the week

SANTA CRUZ

(advance reservations required). Unlike kayaking, there's no work involved in this excursion, so all you have to do is sit back and enjoy the show. Plan on having this trip exceed your wildlife-sighting expectations. During the two-hour tour, it's not uncommon to see more than 100 harbor seals and a similar number of sea otters, plus up to 50 different species of birds. Often these creatures are within only a few feet of the boat, and the on-board naturalist guide and captain Yohn Gideon will help you spot and identify them all.

For year-round whale-watching tours, reserve a seat with **Sanctuary Cruises** (831/917-1042, www.sanctuarycruises.com, $40–46 adults, $30–36 children 3–12) out of Moss Landing Harbor. Cruises last 3–4 hours, and 90 percent of all trips report whale sightings. Gray whales and orcas are most often seen in winter. In spring, it's gray whales, humpbacks, and orcas. In summer and fall, look for humpbacks and blue whales. Dolphins—Risso's, Pacific white-sided, common, and bottlenose—are present year-round as well as harbor and Dall's porpoises. And if none of these larger creatures show up during your cruise, at least you have a near guarantee of spotting sea otters, sea lions, harbor seals, and seabirds.

Moss Landing State Beach

There may be no better place in all of California to observe sea otters playing, feeding, sleeping, and caring for their young than just off the parking lot at Moss Landing State Beach (Jetty Road, 831/649-2836, www.parks .ca.gov). Here, as you look inland toward the power plant smokestacks, is a calm lagoon of water that is particularly favored by these furry, frolicking creatures. On many days, it's not uncommon to spot 50 otters within a 200-yard stretch of water. Considering that only about 2,200 sea otters exist in all of California, having been hunted for their fur almost to extinction in the 18th and 19th centuries, this is an

Moss Landing State Beach is a great place to take a stroll with your dog.

© ANN MARIE BROWN

© ANN MARIE BROWN

Moss Landing is one of the best places in California to see sea otters up close.

amazing number to observe in one spot. This beach and neighboring **Zmudowski State Beach** (Giberson Rd., 831/649-2836, www.parks.ca.gov) further north are also great places for spotting birds—gulls, terns, snowy plovers, and shearwaters near the ocean, as well as American bitterns, snowy egrets, and night herons in the freshwater ponds.

Horseback Riding

There are only a few places in California that allow public horseback riding on the beach, and **Salinas River State Beach** (Monterey Dunes Way, 831/649-2836, www.parks.ca.gov) is one of them. **Monterey Bay Equestrian Center** (831/663-5712, www.montereybay equestrian.com) is based out of Salinas but will meet you at the beach for guided horseback rides. Reservations are required; rates are $70 per person for a one-hour ride, $85 per person for a 75-minute ride, and $115 per person for a two-hour ride.

To reach Salinas River State Beach, drive two miles south of Moss Landing on Highway 1, then turn right on Molera Road. Drive one mile and turn right on Monterey Dunes Way; follow the road to the end.

Accommodations

The 1906-vintage **(Captain's Inn B&B** (8122 Moss Landing Rd., 831/633-5550, www.captainsinn.com, $145–245), once home to the Pacific Coast Steamship Company, has been meticulously, creatively, and nautically restored, and now houses a unique B&B. From the cozy library and game area in the historic building to the classic "boat beds" in the newer boathouse, a stay here offers true Moss Landing ambience. All rooms have private baths and king or queen beds; many have fireplaces and "romance showers" or two-person tubs. Boathouse rooms face the river, with large windows for wildlife-watching. The "boat beds" are the real deal—converted fishing boats, canoes, and catamarans. Big breakfasts and other goodies are included in the rate.

SANTA CRUZ

ARTICHOKE 411

To most Americans, it's a distinctly Californian food, that prickly and loveable member of the thistle family, the artichoke. A native of the Mediterranean, where they have been considered a delicacy for 400 years, artichokes have been grown in the Monterey area since 1924. The part that we eat is the thistle's flower bud, or unripe head, which grows at the end of the plant's long central stalks. The bud is harvested in late April and May, but artichokes keep well, so they are available year-round.

The town of Castroville, just east of Moss Landing, is the undisputed artichoke capital of California, or possibly the world. Three-quarters of California's artichokes are grown here. The town's annual Artichoke Festival dates back to the late 1940s; the first "Artichoke Queen" to be crowned was a young Hollywood starlet named Norma Jean, who later became Marilyn Monroe.

If you're a novice, the most popular way to prepare artichokes is to boil them vigorously for 30 to 40 minutes. Then, using your fingers, you peel off the layers of fleshy bracts (they look like small leaves) and dip them in mayonnaise or dressing. Don't swallow them whole; rather, scrape off the "flesh" with your lower front teeth. The real prize comes after you've polished off all the bracts and can dig into the "heart," which is the soft bottom part of the artichoke bud. Nutritionally speaking, you're getting some good stuff here (if you don't count the artery-clogging sauce you've dipped the bracts into). The artichoke possesses potassium, calcium, phosphorus, and fiber.

The Monterey food scene being what it is, many local restaurants prepare the artichoke in creative and unusual ways. You can find it deep-fried, grilled, baked, broiled, or stuffed with couscous, rice, or bread crumbs. For breakfast, try artichoke Benedict and artichoke frittatas. A few brazen chefs have even come up with artichoke desserts, such as artichoke ice cream and artichoke mousse.

Just seven miles north of Moss Landing (and seven miles south of Capitola) is the beachfront condo/townhouse resort **Pajaro Dunes** (105 Shell Drive, Pajaro Dunes, 831/728-7400 or 800/564-1771, www.pajarodunes.com, $180–240), where you can rent one-, two-, or three-bedroom houses and condos right on the beach. Since these are privately owned homes, each unit comes with a fully equipped kitchen and is completely furnished. Most have fireplaces, decks, and barbecues. It's hard to find a spot on Monterey Bay where you can sleep closer to the crashing surf than at Pajaro Dunes.

If you are looking for a bargain stay near Moss Landing, there are two chain motels located right on Highway 1 that might fit the bill: the **Motel 6 Watsonville** (125 Silver Leaf Dr., 831/728-4144, www.motel6.com, $50) and the **Red Roof Inn Watsonville** (1620 West Beach St., 831/740-4520, www

.watsonvilleredroofinn.com, $75). The latter costs a little more but includes a few extras, like microwaves and refrigerators in each room and a free continental breakfast. Kids under 18 stay free. Both motels are north of the Moss Landing turnoff by about seven miles.

RVers can find a place to park their rig at **Moss Landing KOA** (7905 Sandholdt Rd., 831/633-6800, www.koa.com, $70). This is an RV-only campground, so tenters will have to head north to Sunset State Beach (one mile south of Manresa, 831/763-7063, $25) or the Santa Cruz KOA (1186 San Andreas Rd., 831/722-0551 or 800/562-7701, www.santacruzkoa.com, $50).

Food

Time-honored seafood eateries abound in Moss Landing, particularly near the harbor. **The Whole Enchilada** (Hwy. 1 and Moss Landing Rd., 831/633-3038, www

.wenchilada.com, Mon.–Tues. 5:30 A.M.–4 P.M., Wed.–Fri. 5:30 A.M.–8:30 P.M., Sat.–Sun. 6:30 A.M.–8:30 P.M., $10–20) appeals to the Highway 1 driving crowd with its obvious location right on the road, and specializes in Mexican seafood entrées. Breakfast, lunch, and dinner are served, but the place doesn't get packed until evening. The colorfully painted dining room puts diners in the mood to order margaritas, including their specialty made with pomegranate juice, but all of the restaurant's festive cocktails come in regular and super-gigantic sizes, and are served with a plastic mermaid figurine perched on the rim. The "whole enchilada" is a filet of red snapper wrapped in a corn tortilla and smothered in enchilada sauce and melted cheese, and it's a favorite among a long list of entrées. After your meal, head to the adjoining **Moss Landing Inn,** where thousands of dollar bills line the ceiling, and enjoy some rollicking live music and the most diverse

bar crowd you'll find anywhere. Grab a magic marker, pull a George Washington out of your pocket, scribble a message on it, and tack it to the ceiling. Then grab your partner and take a spin on the dance floor.

For a quieter, more intimate dining experience at breakfast or lunch, get a seat at the associated **Haute Enchilada Bistro** (7902 Moss Landing Rd., 831/633-5843, www.haute enchilada.com, daily 7 A.M.–6 P.M., $10–17), a folk art café located next door in a flowery courtyard. The salmon quesadilla is to die for, but there's also an array of tamales, tacos, burritos, sandwiches, salads, and bakery items. Count on great espresso, too.

Phil's Fish Market (7600 Sandholdt Rd., 831/633-2152, www.philsfishmarket .com, Sun.–Thurs. 10 A.M.–8 P.M., Fri.–Sat. 10 A.M.–9 P.M., $14–24) makes a great roadside stop when driving up or down the coast. Plenty of Moss Landing visitors miss out on Phil's

For fish as fresh as you can find it, Phil's Fish Market in Moss Landing is the place.

because it is tucked into an industrial-looking building a few blocks off the highway. But for the best variety of the freshest fish—both local catches and other species flown in from all over the world—this is the place. Artichokes are prepared in a multitude of ways, including fire roasted and stuffed with garlic. The food is served in ultracasual, order-at-the-counter style, and, if you like, you can carry your plate out the back door and onto Moss Landing's sandy beach. Live bluegrass music usually happens a couple nights of the week.

Also frequently missed by Moss Landing visitors is **Lemongrass** (413 Moss Landing Rd., 831/633-0700, Tues.–Sun. 11 A.M.–9 P.M., $10–18), a Thai restaurant that specializes in seafood and also boasts a full bar. Entrées include green tea salmon, salmon fried rice, shrimp curry, steamed mussels, and "crazy mad fish" (fish in a spicy apple sauce with chili and lime dressing). Lunch specials on weekdays are a steal ($7–11). The restaurant is on the southern outskirts of town, just before Moss Landing Road reconnects with Highway 1.

Probably the fanciest place to eat in Moss Landing—and it still isn't very fancy—is the casually upscale **Sea Harvest** (2420 Hwy. 1, 831/633-8300, www.seaharvest.com, daily 11 A.M.–8 P.M., $15–25), a member of the same chain found in Monterey and Carmel. This is the best choice in Moss Landing for open water views and the pleasure of watching wildlife—otters, pelicans, seals, and sea lions—while you dine. Get a table on the patio if you can, and order something fishy from the menu, because that's what they do best.

Practicalities

Moss Landing is located directly off Highway 1, 30 miles south of Santa Cruz. Look for the turnoff across from the obvious power plant with the two huge smokestacks. There is no visitors center in Moss Landing, but any of the shops in town will gladly provide you with information. The **Moss Landing Chamber of Commerce** (www.mosslandingchamber.com) maintains a website with information about local businesses.

In Moss Landing, sea lions are commonly seen hanging out on piers and docks.

RESOURCES

The Land

HISTORY

Juan Rodríguez Cabrillo, the first European explorer of the California coast, spotted Point Piños and Monterey Bay in 1542. Sixty years later, Spanish explorer Sebastian Vizcaíno sailed into the bay and named it for the viceroy of Mexico, the count of Monte-Rey. A century later, in 1769, along came explorer Gaspar de Portolá and Father Juan Crespi, who later, together with Father Junípero Serra, founded both Monterey's presidio and mission at Carmel.

Because of its isolation, the Monterey and central coast area remained undisturbed until the arrival of Portolá's expedition. The sickly Spaniards made camp in the Rancho del Oso section of what is now Big Basin Redwoods State Park, experiencing an almost miraculous recovery in the valley they called Cañada de Salud (Canyon of Health). A Spanish garrison and mission were soon established on the north end of Monterey Bay.

By the end of the 1700s, the entire central California coast was solidly Spanish, with missions, pueblos, and military bases or presidios

ON A MISSION

Anyone who went to grade school in California knows there were 21 missions founded in California, linked into a chain which stretched along the coast for 600 miles from San Diego to Sonoma, north of San Francisco Bay. Each mission was situated so as to be a day's walk (or horseback ride) apart from the next, via a road called the El Camino Real. It took 54 years to build the entire chain.

If you went to grade school anywhere else, you might not know that the missions were started because the Spanish king wanted to create permanent settlements in the part of the New World then known as Alta California. Father Junípero Serra, a well-respected Spanish Franciscan priest, was put in charge of the task. In 1769, Father Serra and Spanish explorer Gaspar de Portolá made their first expedition to establish the California missions.

In developing the mission system, Father Serra's main purpose was to convert the local Native Americans to Christianity. At each mission, the Spanish recruited neophytes from the local Indians, brought them to live at the mission, and taught them Spanish, farming, and other skills. Many Native Americans came willingly, but they were forced into slave labor and often cruelly treated by the Spanish soldiers. Many died of European diseases to which they had no immunity.

All of the Spanish missions were run as businesses, although some were more prosperous than others. Most raised wheat, corn, cattle, and sheep; some had vineyards and sold leather goods. Ultimately, Spain's plans for gaining a foothold in the New World were short-lived. When Mexico gained independence from Spain, they took over the Spanish landholdings in Alta California. The new Mexican government could not afford to support the California missions, and in 1834, they decided to secularize them and sell the land. Only a few missions remained in the hands of the Spanish Catholic fathers. In 1863, President Abraham Lincoln returned all the mission lands to the Catholic church. Many of them still operate as Catholic parishes today.

Following is a listing of all the California missions and where they are located, in order of founding:

- Mission San Diego de Alcalá (1769) – San Diego
- Mission San Carlos Borromeo del Río Carmelo (1770) – Carmel
- Mission San Antonio de Padua (1771) – Fort Hunter Liggett Military Reservation, near Jolon
- Mission San Gabriel Arcángel (1771) – San Gabriel, Los Angeles County
- Mission San Luis Obispo (1772) – San Luis Obispo

holding the territory for the king of Spain. With the success of the Mexican revolution in 1822, California's loyalty went with the new administration closer to home. But the people here carried on their Spanish cultural heritage despite the secularization of the missions, the increasing influence of cattle ranches, and the foreign flood that threatened existing California tradition. Along the rugged central coast, just south of the boisterous and booming Gold Rush port of San Francisco, the influence of this new wave of "outsiders"—European Americans who were miners, farmers, fishermen, whalers, and fur traders—was felt only later. It wasn't until 1850 that California officially became America's 31st state. California's first constitution was drawn up in Monterey's Colton Hall the year before, during the state's constitutional convention.

GEOGRAPHY

Much of the redwood country from Santa Cruz to Big Sur resembles the boulder-strewn, rough-and-tumble coast of far Northern California. Here the Pacific Ocean is far from peaceful;

- Mission San Francisco de Asís (1776) – San Francisco

- Mission San Juan Capistrano (1776) – San Juan Capistrano

- Mission Santa Clara de Asís (1777) – Santa Clara/San Jose

- Mission San Buenaventura (1782) – Ventura

- Mission Santa Barbara (1786) – Santa Barbara

- Mission La Purísima Concepción (1787) – Lompoc

- Mission Santa Cruz (1791) – Santa Cruz

- Mission Nuestra Señora de la Soledad (1791) – Soledad

- Mission San Jose (1797) – Fremont, San Francisco Bay Area

- Mission San Juan Bautista (1797) – San Juan Bautista

- Mission San Miguel de Arcángel (1797) – San Miguel, near Paso Robles

- Mission San Fernando Rey de España (1797) – Mission Hills, north Los Angeles county

- Mission San Luis Rey de Francia (1798) – Oceanside, north San Diego County

- Mission Santa Inés (1804) – Solvang

- Mission San Rafael (1817) – San Rafael

- Mission San Francisco Solano (1823) – Sonoma

© ANN MARIE BROWN

one of the bell towers of Carmel Mission

posted warnings about dangerous swimming conditions and undertows are no joke. On dry land to the east, the San Andreas Fault menaces, veering inland from the eastern side of the Coast Ranges, through the Salinas Valley, and on to the San Francisco Bay Area.

The Monterey Peninsula

Steinbeck captured the mood of the Monterey Peninsula in *Tortilla Flat:* "The wind . . . drove the fog across the pale moon like a thin wash of watercolor.... The treetops in the wind talked huskily, told fortunes and foretold deaths." The peninsula juts into the ocean 115 miles south of San Francisco and forms the southern border of Monterey Bay. The north shore sweeps in a crescent toward Santa Cruz and the Santa Cruz Mountains; east is the oak- and pine-covered Santa Lucia Range, rising in front of the barren Gabilan ("Sparrow Hawk") Mountains beloved by Steinbeck. Northward are the ecologically delicate Monterey Bay Dunes. To the south, the piney hills near Point Piños and Asilomar overlook rocky crags and coves dotted with wind-sculpted trees; farther south, beyond Carmel and the Pebble Beach golf mecca, is Point Lobos, said to be Robert Louis Stevenson's inspiration for Spyglass Hill in *Treasure Island.*

Monterey "Canyon"

Discovered in 1890 by George Davidson, Monterey Bay's submerged valley teems with sea life: bioluminescent fish glowing vivid blue to red, squid, tiny rare octopi, tentacle-shedding jellyfish, and myriad microscopic plants and animals. This is one of the most biologically prolific spots on the planet. Swaying with the ocean's motion, dense kelp thickets are home to sea lions, seals, sea otters, and giant Garibaldi—California's state saltwater fish. Opal-eyed perch in schools of hundreds swim by leopard sharks and bottom fish. In the understory near the rocky ocean floor live abalones, anemones, crabs, sea urchins, and starfish.

Students of Monterey Canyon geology quibble over the origins of this unusual underwater valley. Computer-generated models of canyon creation suggest that the land used to be near Bakersfield and was carved out by the Colorado River; later, it shifted westward due to plate tectonics. More conventional speculation focuses on the creative forces of both the Sacramento and San Joaquin Rivers, which perhaps once emptied at Elkhorn Slough, Monterey Canyon's principal "head."

However Monterey Canyon came to be, it is now centerpiece of the 5,312-square-mile **Monterey Bay National Marine Sanctuary,** which extends some 400 miles along the coast, from San Francisco's Golden Gate in the north to San Simeon in the south. Established in 1992 after a 15-year political struggle, this federally sanctioned preserve is protected from offshore

oil drilling, dumping of hazardous materials, the killing of marine mammals or birds, personal watercraft, and aircraft flying lower than 1,000 feet. As an indirect result of its federal protection, Monterey Bay now boasts a total of 18 marine research facilities.

Big Sur Coast

Farther south, the land itself is unfriendly, at least from the human perspective. The indomitable, unstable terrain—with its habit of sliding out from under hillsides, houses, highways, and hiking trails during winter rains and at the slightest provocation—has made the area hard to inhabit. But despite its contrariness, the central coast, that unmistakable pivotal point between California's north and south, successfully blends elements of both.

Although the collective Coast Ranges continue south through the region, here the terrain takes on a new look. Northern California's redwoods begin to thin out, limiting themselves to a few large groves in Big Sur country and otherwise straggling south a short distance beyond San Simeon, tucked into hidden folds in the rounded coastal mountains. Where redwood country ends, either the grasslands of the dominant coastal oak woodlands begin or the chaparral takes over, in places almost impenetrable. Even the coastline reflects the transition—the rocky, rough-and-tumble shores along the Big Sur coast transform into tamer beaches and bluffs near San Simeon.

Another clue that the north-south transition occurs here is water—or, moving southward, the increasingly obvious lack of it. Though both the North and South Forks of the Little Sur River, the Big Sur River a few miles to the south, and other northern waterways flow to the sea throughout the year, as does the Cuyama River in the south (known as the Santa Maria

© MONTEREY COUNTY CVB

surf crashing against rocks in Big Sur

River as it nears the ocean), most of the area's streams are seasonal. But off-season hikers, beware: even inland streams with a six-month flow are not to be dismissed during winter and spring, when deceptively dinky creek beds can become death-dealing torrents overnight.

CLIMATE

The legendary California beach scene is almost a fantasy here—almost, but not quite. Surfers ply the waters of the Pacific year-round, but usually clad in wetsuits. Sunshine warms the sands (between storms) from fall to early spring, but count on fog from late spring well into summer. Throughout the Monterey Bay area, it's often foggy and damp, but clear summer afternoons can get hot. The warmest and least foggy months along the coast are September and October. (Sunglasses, suntan lotion, and hats are prudent, but always bring a sweater.) Inland, expect hotter weather in

summer, colder weather in winter. Rain is possible as early as October, although big storms don't usually roll in until December.

FLORA

California's central coast region, particularly near Monterey, exhibits tremendous botanic diversity. Among the varied vascular plant species found regionally is the unusually fast-growing **Monterey pine,** an endemic tree surviving in native groves only on hills and slopes near Monterey, Santa Cruz, Cambria, and Año Nuevo, as well as on Guadalupe and Cedros Islands off the coast of Baja, Mexico. It's now a common landscaping tree and the world's most widely cultivated tree, grown commercially for its wood and pulp.

The **Bishop pine** is found only on poor serpentine soil, favoring swamps and the slopes from "Huckleberry Hill," near Monterey, south to the San Luis Range near Point Buchon and

the classic icon of the 17-Mile Drive, the native Monterey cypress

Monte Forest and at Point Lobos are as old as 2,000 years. The soft, green **Sargent cypress** is also fairly common in the Monterey area, ranging south to Santa Barbara along the coast and inland.

Coastal redwoods thrive near Santa Cruz and south through Big Sur. Not as lusty as those on the north coast, these redwoods often keep company with Douglas firs, tanoaks, and a dense understory of shade-loving shrubs. The fog-loving coastal redwoods are known for growing to tremendous heights, and for the dense, shady canopy they create over the forest floor.

Other regional trees include the California wax myrtle, the aromatic California laurel or bay tree, the California nutmeg, and the tanoak (and many other oaks), plus alders, big-leaf maples, and madrones. Many of these tree species, especially the tanoaks and madrones around Big Sur, are afflicted with **sudden oak death,** a fast-moving, fungus-like brown alga that

Santa Barbara County. A fairly common tree in the hotter inland hills is the chaparral-loving **knobcone pine.** Both the Bishop pine and knobcone pine are closely related to the Monterey pine, and the three can hybridize. All three pines are known as fire-climax pines, because they bear tenaciously closed cones that will open and release their seeds only with the intense heat of a forest fire.

The unusual **Monterey cypress** is a relict, a specialized tree that doesn't occur naturally beyond the Monterey Peninsula, although it has been planted at many other places along the coast. This wind-sculpted tree with its hard, roundish cones is the classic icon of the 17-Mile Drive and Point Lobos State Reserve. These are the only two places in the world where this tree still grows as a native, although at one time the Monterey cypress ranged across the West Coast. Some of the Monterey cypresses in Del

at the base of a coastal redwood

was first identified in Marin County in 1994. Sudden oak death thrives in cool, moist, and foggy conditions. It spreads through soil and root systems, and easily travels from place to place on hiker's boots and mountain bike and car tires. If you hike in any of the redwood- and tanoak-forested lands managed by the Monterey Peninsula Regional Park District (like the Mill Creek Redwood Preserve in Big Sur), you will see a cleaning station at the start of the trail for cleaning your shoes with bleach when you have finished your hike.

FAUNA
Whales, Dolphins, Porpoises, and Sharks

The annual migration of the California **gray whale,** the state's official mammal, is big news all along the coast. From late October to January, these magnificent 20- to 40-ton creatures head south from the Arctic seas toward Baja (pregnant females first). Once the mating season ends, males, newly pregnant females, and juveniles start their northward journey from February to May. Females with calves, often traveling close to shore, return a bit later.

Humpback whales and **blue whales** (the largest animal on earth, weighing about 40 tons) also make an appearance around Monterey Bay and the coast, usually in the summer months. Smaller whale species such as fin, minke, and killer whales (orcas) can be seen sporadically at any time of year. Thousands of dolphins and porpoises frolic in Monterey Bay and off the coast of Big Sur year-round. **Pacific white-sided dolphins** often travel in very large groups and will come quite close to boats. They are known for their impressive performance of leaps and aerial flips. Often traveling with the Pacific white-sided dolphins are **northern rightwhale dolphins.** The **Dall's porpoise, common dolphin,** and **Risso's dolphin** are also frequently seen.

A wide variety of **sharks** are common in Monterey Bay. Occasionally, 20-foot-long great white sharks congregate here to feed on sea otters, seals, and sea lions. Unprovoked attacks on humans do occur (to surfers more often than scuba divers), but are very rare. The best protection is avoiding ocean areas where great whites are common, such as Año Nuevo Island at the north end of the bay.

Seals and Sea Lions

The **California sea lion** is frequently heard and seen in these parts; the females are the barking pinnipeds (fin-footed mammals) popular in aquatic amusement parks, and are commonly seen hanging around Fisherman's Wharf in Monterey. True seals don't have external ears, whereas sea lions—the gregarious, fearless creatures swimming in shallow ocean waters or lolling on rocky jetties and docks—usually do. Also here in Monterey are northern, or Steller's, sea lions, which roar instead of bark and are usually lighter in color. Chunky **harbor seals** (no ear flaps, usually with spotted coats) commonly haul out on sandy beaches, since they're awkward on land.

The massive **northern elephant seals**—the largest pinnipeds in the Western Hemisphere—are rapidly increasing in numbers along the California coast, and can be seen during the winter mating and birthing season at the Año Nuevo State Reserve rookery near Santa Cruz and the Piedras Blancas rookery near San Simeon. One look at the two- or three-ton, 18-foot-long males explains the creatures' common name: their long, trunklike noses are used to create roaring noises that express their territoriality.

CALIFORNIA GRAYS

A close-up view of the California gray whale, the state's official (and largest) mammal, is a life-changing experience. As those dark, massive, white-barnacled heads shoot up out of the ocean to suck air, a spray with the force of a firehose blasts skyward from their blowholes. During the peak migration season (Dec.-Apr.), you have a good chance of seeing California gray whales at many spots along the California coast.

Despite the fascination they hold for Californians, little is yet known about the gray whale. Once endangered by whaling – as so many whale species still are – the grays are swimming steadily along the comeback trail. Categorized as baleen whales, which dine on plankton and other small aquatic animals sifted through hundreds of fringed, hornlike baleen plates, gray whales were once land mammals that went back to sea. In the process of evolution, they traded their fore and hind legs for fins and tail flukes. Despite their fishlike appearance, these are true mammals: warm-blooded, air-breathing creatures who nourish their young with milk.

Adult gray whales weigh 20-40 tons, not counting a few hundred pounds of parasitic barnacles. Calves weigh in at a hefty 1,500 pounds at birth and can expect to live for 30-60 years. They feed almost endlessly from April to October in the arctic seas between Alaska and Siberia, sucking up sediment and edible creatures on the bottom of shallow seas, then squeezing the excess water and silt out their baleen filters. Fat and sassy with an extra 6-12 inches of blubber on board, early in October they head south on their 6,000-mile journey to the warmer waters of Baja in Mexico.

Pregnant females leave first, traveling alone or in small groups. Larger groups make up the rear guard, with the older males and nonpregnant females engaging in highly competitive courtship and mating rituals along the way – creating quite a show for human voyeurs. The rear guard becomes the frontline on the way home: males, newly pregnant females, and young gray whales head north from February to June. Cows and calves migrate later, between March and July. The greatest number of whales are usually passing by the Monterey and Central Coast between December and April, although there are always a few stragglers who can be seen earlier or later. For your best chance at spotting whales from land, head to any high point directly above the ocean, such as the rugged coastal bluffs at Big Sur. To get a close-up view of whales, head out to sea on a whale-watching tour in Monterey Bay.

Brown pelicans gather at Natural Bridges State Beach.

near piers in and around harbors—are incredibly graceful when soaring only inches above the tops of waves or diving for their dinners. A squadron of 25 or more pelicans can often be seen skimming above the water; then, one by one, the birds plunge dramatically—bill first—into the sea. Brown pelicans are another back-from-the-brink success story. Their numbers have increased dramatically since DDT (highly concentrated in fish) was banned in 1972. California's pelican platoons are often accompanied by greedy gulls, somehow convinced they can snatch fish from the fleshy pelican pouches if they just try harder.

Seabirds are the most obvious seashore fauna; besides brown pelicans, you'll see long-billed curlews, ashy petrels nesting on cliffs, surf divers like grebes and scooters, and various gulls. Pure white California gulls are seen only in winter here (they nest inland), but yellow-billed western gulls and the scarlet-billed,

The elephant seal's presence in California is a remarkable testament to the healing power of nature. By the year 1900, less than 100 elephant seals were left in the world; the rest had been killed for the oil contained in their blubber. Miraculously, one small surviving group of seals located on an island west of Baja, California, slowly began to multiply. By the 1920s, elephant seals were occasionally seen off the coast of Southern California, and in 1955 they returned to Año Nuevo Island, one of their traditional breeding grounds. -Since then, their numbers have increased dramatically along the beaches of Año Nuevo, Piedras Blancas, and Point Reyes National Seashore (north of San Francisco).

Pelicans and Other Seabirds

The ungainly looking, web-footed **brown pelicans**—often seen perched on pilings or

A white pelican and a great egret feast on the nutrient-rich waters of Monterey Bay.

white-headed Heermann's gulls are common seaside scavengers. Look for the hyperactive, self-important sandpipers along the shore, along with dowitchers, plovers, godwits, and avocets. Killdeers—so named for their "ki-dee" cry—lure people and other potential predators away from their clutches of eggs by feigning serious injury.

Tidepool Life

The twice-daily ebb of ocean tides reveals an otherwise hidden world. Tidepools below rocky headlands are nature's aquariums, sheltering abalone, anemones, barnacles, mussels, hermit crabs, starfish, sea snails, sea slugs, and tiny fish. Four distinct zones of marine life are defined by the tides. The first is the low intertidal zone, which is underwater 90 percent of the time, so you get to see its inhabitants only during the lowest tides of the year (called "minus" tides). This is where the most interesting creatures are: eels, octopus, sea hares, brittle stars, giant keyhole limpets, sculpins, and bat stars. The second area is the middle intertidal zone, which is underwater only 50 percent of the time, so it's in between the low and high tide line. This area has the creatures we usually associate with tidepools: sea stars or starfish, purple sea urchins, sea anemones, gooseneck

© ANN MARIE BROWN

a starfish, one of the inhabitants of the Monterey area's tidepools

barnacles, red algae, and mussels. In the high intertidal zone (underwater only 10 percent of the time), you'll see common acorn barnacles, shore crabs, black tegulas, and hermit crabs. These creatures can live out of water for long periods of time. The final tidepool region is the splash zone, where you'll find rough limpets, black turban snails, and periwinkles.

Getting There and Around

AIR

Not far from Santa Cruz, **San Jose International Airport** (408/501-7600, www.sjc.org) is the closest major airport. The airport is served by all major U.S. airlines and also provides flights to and from Mexico. The Monterey-Salinas Airbus (831/373-7777, www.montereyairbus.com) provides 14 trips daily to

the San Jose and San Francisco international airports from downtown Monterey ($30–40 per person one-way).

You can also fly directly into the Monterey Peninsula area. The **Monterey Peninsula Airport** (200 Fred Kane Dr. #200, 831/648-7000, www.montereyairport.com) provides service to and from San Francisco,

Los Angeles, Phoenix, Denver, Las Vegas, Long Beach, Ontario, and San Diego. United Airlines, Allegiant, American Eagle, and American West service this airport. Taxi service is available through Central Coast Taxi (831/626-3333). Limousine service is available through Arrow Luxury Transportation Company (831/646-3175). Rental cars are available at the airport through the following companies: Alamo (800/327-9633, www.alamo.com), Avis (800/831-2847, www.avis.com), Budget (800/527-0700, www.budget.com), Enterprise (800/736-8222, www.enterprise.com), Hertz (800/654-3131, www.hertz.com), and National (800/227-7368, www.nationalcar.com).

For private pilots, there is **Marina Municipal Airport** (831/582-0102, www.airnav.com/airport/oar), north of Monterey proper on Neeson Road in Marina, and the **Salinas Municipal Airport** (831/758-7214, www.salinasairport.com).

TRAIN

Amtrak's Coast Starlight (800/872-7245, www.amtrak.com) runs from Los Angeles to Seattle, with central coast stops in Oxnard, Santa Barbara, San Luis Obispo, Salinas, and Oakland. Monterey-Salinas Transit buses can get you to and from the Amtrak station in Salinas (30 Station Place, 831/422-7458). Check the website for reservations and schedule information, including details on Amtrak's bus connections from Monterey.

If heading to the San Francisco Bay Area from the Monterey Peninsula—or vice versa—keep in mind that Amtrak also connects in San Jose with the San Francisco–San Jose **Caltrain** (650/817-1717 or 800/660-4287, www.caltrain.com). For help in figuring out the way to San Jose—and how to get around the entire Bay Area by rapid transit—visit www.transit.511.org.

Another way to get out of town is via Santa Cruz Metro's **Highway 17 Express** buses (831/425-8600, www.scmtd.com). The bus travels to the San Jose train station (65 Cahill St.), which connect directly with Caltrain to San Francisco and with Amtrak to Oakland, Berkeley, and Sacramento. The fare is just $4 one-way or $8 for an all-day pass.

BUS

Greyhound (800/752-4841 toll free or 800/345-3109 TDD/TTY, www.greyhound.com) has bus terminals in Santa Cruz (425 Front St., 831/423-1800) and Salinas (19 W. Gabilan St., 831/424-4418). Greyhound provides service from San Francisco to Santa Cruz, as well as connections south to Los Angeles via Salinas or San Jose. Check the website for current route details and fares. Bus connections also serve Amtrak (800/872-7245, www.amtrak.com) and the Bay Area's Caltrain system (650/817-1717 or 800/660-4287, www.caltrain.com).

CAR

Direct driving access to Monterey is provided from San Jose and San Francisco via Highway 156 off Highway 101. Access from Los Angeles is easiest via Highway 101 and Highway 68. The Coast Highway, or Highway 1, runs from San Francisco to Los Angeles, passing directly through Big Sur and Santa Cruz, and also provides access to Monterey via Highway 68. Driving access to Santa Cruz from San Jose is via the twisting Highway 17.

Suggested Reading

The following listings represent a fairly basic but useful introduction to relevant area books. The interested reader can find many other titles by visiting good local bookstores and/or Monterey-area state park visitors centers.

MONTEREY-RELATED LITERATURE

Brautigan, Richard. *A Confederate General from Big Sur, Dreaming of Babylon, and the Hawkline Monster.* New York: Mariner Books, reissue edition, 1991. Did you miss the 1960s? If so, you probably also missed Richard Brautigan, whose literary star flamed out too quickly. He was one of the most quirky and humorous writers of the Beat generation.

Jeffers, Robinson. *Selected Poems.* New York: Random House, 1965. The poet Robinson Jeffers died in 1961 at the age of 75, on a rare day when it actually snowed in Carmel. One of California's finest poets, classically sophisticated yet accessible, Jeffers composed many poems that paid homage to the beauty of his beloved Big Sur coast. Pieces collected here are selections from some of his major works, including *Be Angry at the Sun, The Beginning and the End, Hungerfield,* and *Tamar and Other Poems.*

Jeffers, Robinson. *Stones of the Sur.* Stanford, CA: Stanford University Press, 2001. A coffee-table book for people who don't even have coffee tables, this stunning work is crafted from the words of the Carmel poet Robinson Jeffers and the brilliant black-and-white photos of Morley Baer. As a general introduction to the significance of Jeffers's work and his connection to Carmel, scholar James Karman's contribution is invaluable.

Karman, James. *Robinson Jeffers: Poet of California.* Brownsville, OR: Story Line Press, Inc., revised second edition, 1994. This marvelous critical biography details the life and times of the reticent poet Robinson Jeffers, for whom the Big Sur coast was once named. "It is not possible to be quite sane here," Jeffers wisely observed. Karman also sympathetically introduces us to Jeffers's wife, Una; of additional interest to Jeffers fans is Story Line's *Of Una Jeffers* by Edith Greenan.

Kerouac, Jack. *Big Sur.* New York: Penguin USA, reprint edition, 1992. Here is Kerouac's hellish Big Sur hike into the dark side of manic depression, paranoia, and alcoholism, as experienced by his alter ego Jack Dulouz, now a writer experiencing fame. A sobering follow-up to Kerouac's more optimistic *On The Road* and *The Dharma Bums.*

Miller, Henry. *Big Sur and the Oranges of Hieronymus Bosch.* New York: W.W. Norton & Co., 1978. First published in 1957, this volume includes the famed writer's impressions of art and writing, along with his view of life as seen from the Big Sur coastline—the center of his personal universe in his later years, and the first real home he had ever found.

Miller, Henry. *Tropic of Capricorn.* New York: Grove Press, 1994. Although fairly tame by today's standards, this cornerstone of modern literatures was banned in the United States for almost 30 years because of its explicit sexual content. The companion volume to Miller's *Tropic of Cancer,* this book chronicles Miller's life in New York City in the 1920s.

Steinbeck, John. *Cannery Row.* New York: Penguin USA, centennial edition, 2002. Here it is: A poem, a stink, a grating noise, told in the days when sardines still ruled the boardwalk on Monterey's Cannery Row. Also worth an imaginative side trip on a tour of the California coast is Steinbeck's *East of Eden,* first published in 1952, the Salinas Valley version of the Cain and Abel story. Steinbeck's classic California work, though, is still *The Grapes of Wrath.*

Stevenson, Robert Louis. *The Complete Short Stories of Robert Louis Stevenson: With a Selection of the Best Short Novels.* New York: Da Capo Press, 1998. It's hard to know where to start with Stevenson, whose California journeys served to launch his literary career. Da Capo's collection is as good a place as any.

Stevenson, Robert Louis. *The Complete Short Stories of Robert Louis Stevenson: Strange Case of Dr. Jekyll and Mr. Hyde and Nineteen Other Tales.* Modern Library, 2002. Leading Stevenson scholar Barry Menikoff arranges and introduces this complete selection of Stevenson's brilliant stories.

GENERAL TRAVEL

Chiang, Connie. *Shaping the Shoreline: Fisheries and Tourism on the Monterey Coast.* University of Washington Press, 2008. This academic study looks at the ways in which Monterey has been shaped by the tension between work and leisure. The author examines Monterey's development from a seaside resort to a working-class fishing town and then back again.

Clark, Donald Thomas. *Monterey County Place Names: A Geographical Dictionary.* Carmel Valley, CA: Kestrel Press, 1991. This marvelous resource, meticulously researched and guaranteed to enlighten all who dip into it, is a gift from the U.C. Santa Cruz University Librarian, Emeritus. Also well worth searching for is the same author's *Santa Cruz County Place Names* (2008).

Gudde, Erwin G., and Bright, William O. *California Place Names: The Origin and Etymology of Current Geographical Names.* Berkeley: University of California Press, 2004. Did you know that *Siskiyou* was the Chinook word for "bobtailed horse," as borrowed from the Cree language? More such complex truths await every time you dip into this fascinating volume—the ultimate guide to California place names (and how to pronounce them). This convenient, alphabetically arranged pocketbook—is perfect for travelers, explaining the names of mountains, rivers, and towns throughout California.

WPA Guide to the Monterey Peninsula. Introduced by Page Stegner (son of Wallace Stegner). Tucson: University of Arizona Press, 1990. A Federal Writers Project guide, long out of print in its original version. This more recent paperback version is also out of print, but finding a used copy would be well worth it.

HISTORY AND PEOPLE

de la Pérouse, Jean François. *Life in a California Mission: Monterey in 1786, The Journals of Jean François de la Pérouse.* Berkeley: Heyday Books, 1989. On September 14, 1786, two ships sailed out of the fog and into Monterey Bay. The ships were French, *L'Astrolabe* and *La Boussole,* the first foreign vessels to visit the Spanish colonies in California. Onboard, as Malcolm Margolin tells us in his introduction, "was a party of eminent scientists, navigators, cartographers, illustrators, and physicians," sent by King Louis XVI to explore the western coast of North America, look for sea otters (for the fur trade), and report on Spain's colonies. Leader of the expedition was Jean François de la Pérouse, whose journal describes the presidio at Monterey, the mission at Carmel, Indian customs, and the land and its abundant plant and animal life. Reading his journals, as Margolin points out, allows to unfold before us "not a tale of a distant fantasy land, but the far more gripping story of our place, of our times, the story of us." The journals are greatly enhanced by Margolin's historical introduction and careful annotations.

Gutiérrez, Ramon A., and Richard J. Orsi, eds. *Contested Eden: California Before the Gold Rush.* Berkeley: University of California Press, 1998. Various essays explore California before the gold rush.

Heizer, Robert F., and Albert B. Elsasser. *The Natural World of the California Indians.* Berkeley: University of California Press, 1981. As an adjunct to the rest of Heizer's work, this fact-packed volume provides the setting— the natural environment, the village environment—for California's native peoples.

Holiday, James. *The World Rushed In: The California Gold Rush Experience: An Eyewitness Account of a Nation Heading West.* University of Oklahoma Press, 2002. A reprint of a classic history made while new Californians were busy creating American California—and ending the Spanish-Mexican era over which Monterey presided.

Margolin, Malcolm. *The Way We Lived: California Indian Stories, Songs & Reminiscences.* Berkeley: Heyday Books, 2001. A wonderful collection of California native peoples' reminiscences, stories, and songs. Also by Margolin: *The Ohlone Way,* about the life of California's first residents of the San Francisco–Monterey Bay Area.

McCaffery, Jerry. *Lighthouse: Point Piños.* Pacific Grove, CA: Jerry McCaffery, 2001. This gem of a book tells the story of the lighthouse at Point Piños, starting in 1855 and continuing to the present. The story is particularly strong on Emily Fish, principal keeper from 1893 to 1914, sometimes known as the "socialite lightkeeper." Yet Emily, in the author's view, was the lighthouse's hero—"not a heroine in the fainting but persistent Scarlett O'Hara fashion" but a straight-on heroine, who battled on behalf of the lighthouse for 21 years. Great black-and-white photos, lighthouse plans, a timeline, and a map of nearby shipwreck locations are included, along with select lightkeeper log entries.

McDonald, Linda, and Carol Cullen. *California Historical Landmarks.* Sacramento, CA: California Department of Parks and Recreation, 1997. Revised edition. Originally compiled in response to the National Historic Preservation Act of 1966, directing all states to identify all properties "possessing historical, architectural, archaeological, and cultural value," this updated edition covers more than 1,000 California Registered Historical Landmarks, organized by category—sites of aboriginal, economic, or government interest, for example—and indexed by county.

Nasaw, David. *The Chief: The Life of William Randolph Hearst.* New York: Mariner Books, 2001. *The Chief* draws on papers and interviews that were previously unavailable, including documentation of Hearst's interactions with such figures as Hitler, Mussolini, Churchill, every president from Grover Cleveland to Franklin Roosevelt, and movie giants Louis B. Mayer, Jack Warner, and Irving Thalberg. David Nasaw completes the picture of this colossal American "engagingly, lucidly and fair-mindedly," according to Arthur Schlesinger, Jr.

Paddison, Joshua, ed. *A World Transformed: Firsthand Accounts of California Before the Gold Rush.* Berkeley: Heyday Books, 1999. According to popular California mythology, the Golden State was "born" with the onrushing change that accompanied the gold rush of 1848. But this collection of earlier California writings gathers together some intriguing precedent observations—from European explorers and visitors, missionaries, and sea captains—that reveal pre–Gold Rush California.

Santa Cruz Seaside Company. *The Santa Cruz Beach Boardwalk: A Century by the Sea.* Ten Speed Press, 2007. Attracting three million visitors per year, the Santa Cruz Boardwalk is known as the "Coney Island of the West." This book, filled with 500 full-color and archival photos, details 100 years of boardwalk history, 1907-2007.

Wall, Rosalinde Sharp. *A Wild Coast and Lonely: Big Sur Pioneers.* Wide World Publishing, 1993. Read all about the rugged individuals—primarily ranchers and lumbermen—who settled the Big Sur coast in the days before the Coast Highway was built.

NATURE AND NATURAL HISTORY

Bakker, Elna. *An Island Called California: An Ecological Introduction to Its Natural Communities.* Berkeley: University of California Press, 1984. Expanded, revised edition. An excellent, time-honored introduction to the characteristics of, and relationships between, California's ecological communities.

Barbour, Michael, Bruce Pavlik, Susan Lindstrom, and Frank Drysdale. *California's Changing Landscapes: Diversity and Conservation of California Vegetation.* Sacramento: California Native Plant Society Press, 1991. This well-illustrated, well-indexed guide to California's astonishing botanical variety is an excellent introduction for the layperson. For more in-depth study, the Native Plant Society also publishes excellent regional flora keys.

Henson, Paul, Donald J. Usner, and Valerie Kells (illustrator). *The Natural History of Big Sur.* Berkeley: University of California Press, 1996. Both a useful guide to Big Sur's public lands and a fascinating natural—geology, climate, flora, and fauna—and human history, this user-friendly book includes color photographs, drawings, maps, species lists, and a bibliography.

Langstroth, Lowell, Libby Langstroth, and Todd Newberry. *A Living Bay: The Underwater World of Monterey Bay.* Berkeley: University of California Press, 2000. A stunning introduction to the complexity of life in Monterey Bay, organized by habitat and complete with 200 color photos.

Orr, Robert T., and Roger Helm. *Marine Mammals of California.* Berkeley: University of California Press, 1989. Revised edition. A handy guide for identifying marine mammals along the California coast, with practical tips on the best places to observe them.

Rigsby, Michael A. (ed.), and Lawrence Ormsby (illus.). *A Natural History of the Monterey Bay National Marine Sanctuary.* Monterey: Monterey Bay Aquarium Press, 1999. Here's a look-see beneath the waters of the nation's largest marine sanctuary, the first complete natural history of one of the most popular dive and tourist meccas in this country.

Schoenherr, Allan A. *A Natural History of California.* Berkeley: University of California Press, 1995. With introductory chapters on ecology and geology, *A Natural History* covers California's climate, geology, soil, plant life, and animals based on distinct bioregions, with almost 300 photographs and numerous illustrations and tables.

Schoenherr, Allan A. and C. Robert Feldmeth. *A Natural History of the Islands of California.*

Berkeley: University of California Press, 2003. A comprehensive introduction to California's Año Nuevo Island, Channel Islands, Farallon Islands, and the islands of San Francisco Bay—living evolutionary laboratories with unique species and ecological niches.

RECREATION

California Coastal Commission, State of California. *The California Coastal Access Guide.* Berkeley: University of California Press, 2003. Sixth revised edition. According to the *Oakland Tribune,* this is "no doubt the most comprehensive look at California's coastline published to date."

Emory, Jerry. *The Monterey Bay Shoreline Guide.* Berkeley: University of California Press (Monterey Bay Aquarium Series in Marine Conservation), 1999. A great guide to what to see and do.

Kirkendall, Tom, and Vicky Springs. *Bicycling the Pacific Coast.* Seattle: Mountaineers Books, 2005. Fourth edition. A very good, very practical, mile-by-mile guide to the tricky business of cycling along the California coast (and north).

Lorentzen, Bob, and Richard Nichols. *Hiking the California Coastal Trail, Volume One: Oregon to Monterey.* Mendocino, CA: Bored Feet Publications, 2002. Second edition. The first comprehensive guide to the work-in-progress California Coastal Trail, America's newest and most diverse long-distance trail. Published in conjunction with Coastwalk—which receives a hefty percentage of the proceeds to support its efforts to complete the trail—this accessible guide describes 85 sections of the California Coastal Trail's northern reach.

Soares, Marc J. *Best Coast Hikes of Northern California: A Guide to the Top Trails from Big Sur to the Oregon Border.* San Francisco: Sierra Club Books, 1998. There's something for everyone here: 75 scenic trails, organized north to south, suited for all skill levels (including mention of those that allow dogs). Two more good guides from Soares: *75 Year-Round Hikes in Northern California* and *100 Classic Hikes in Northern California,* the latter coauthored with John R. Soares.

Stienstra, Tom. *Moon California Camping.* Berkeley, CA: Avalon Travel, 2009. 16th edition. This is undoubtedly the ultimate reference to California camping and campgrounds, public and private. In addition to a thorough, practical introduction to the basics of California camping—and reviews of the latest high-tech gear for hiking and camping comfort and safety—this guidebook is meticulously organized by area, starting with the general subdivisions of Northern, Central, and Southern California.

Stone, Robert. *Day Hikes Around Monterey and Carmel.* Day Hikes Books, 2002. This regional guide includes 77 day hikes that stretch along 100 miles of California coast, from Monterey Bay through Big Sur. Trails of varying lengths lead to waterfalls, tidepools, marine terraces, beaches, redwood groves, and great coastal viewpoints. The same author also has written *Day Hikes Around Big Sur.*

Taber, Tom. *The Santa Cruz Mountains Trail Book.* Oak Valley Press, 2006. 10th edition. Trail lovers (beachcombers, off-road bicyclists, equestrians, and hikers): this book will keep you busy, with descriptions of more than 1,000 miles of trails weaving through some 153,000 acres of mountains, forests, and coastline. The most popular coastal access guide to the Santa Cruz County coast and area parks and trails.

Index

IJK

itineraries: general discussion 10, 12-14; beaches 15; historical architecture 11; Pacific Coast Highway 14-17
Jacks Peak County Park: 46
Jade Cove: 157
Jeffers, Robinson: 22, 110-111
Jouillian Vineyards: 19, 137
Julia Pfeiffer Burns State Park: 16, 18, 148, 155-156, 158
kayaking: Elkhorn Slough 229-230; Monterey 47; Pacific Grove 78; Santa Cruz 204; William Randolph Hearst Memorial State Beach 173-174
Kelp Forest: 34
Kirk Creek Beach: 157

L

La Mirada: 42
Larkin House: 38
Lewis, Sinclair: 111
Lighthouse Field State Beach: 195
lighthouses: Piedras Blancas Light Station 171; Pigeon Point Lighthouse and Hostel 226-227; Point Piños Lighthouse 73, 75; Point Sur Lightstation 146-147; Walton Lighthouse 195-196
Limekiln State Park: 20, 156
Links at Spanish Bay, The: 12, 87
literary figures: 22, 110-111
live music: Monterey 51; Santa Cruz 208
Live Oak Market: 19, 218
London, Jack: 111
Lone Cypress: 73
Long Marine Laboratory: 187, 189
Lover's Point Beach Park: 72, 77
Lower Presidio Historic Park: 43
Lupine Trail: 138

M

Manresa State Beach: 200, 206
Marina International Festival of the Winds: 52
Marina Municipal Airport: 245
Marina State Beach: 15, 45
Mary and Harry Blanchard Sculpture Garden: 189-190
Maybeck, Bernard: 124
McAbee Beach: 20, 48
McWay Falls: 16, 148-149, 155
Mesa Trail: 138

Middle Beach: 114
Mill Creek Redwood Preserve: 156-157
Miller, Henry: 22
MIRA Observatory: 133, 135
missions: general discussion 236-237; see also specific place
Mission San Juan Bautista: 11, 102-103
Mission Santa Cruz: 11, 192-193
Molera Beach: 153, 157
Molera Point: 152
Molera Ranch House: 150
monarch butterflies: 21-22, 75-76, 186-187
Monarch Butterfly Grove Sanctuary: 22, 75-76
Monarch Madness: 79
Monastery Beach: 20, 114-115, 116-117
Monterey: 25-70; accommodations 56-60; entertainment/nightlife 50-53; food 61-67; information and services 68; maps 2-3, 29, 57; recreation 45-50; shopping 53-56; sights 28, 30-31, 33-44; transportation 68-70
Monterey Bay Aquarium: 10, 15, 28, 30-31, 33-34
Monterey Bay Birding Festival: 53
Monterey Bay Blues Festival: 52
Monterey County Fair: 53
Monterey cypress: 240
Monterey Institute of International Studies: 43
Monterey Jack cheese: 62
Monterey Jazz Festival: 53
Monterey Live: 51
Monterey Maritime and History Museum: 10, 35
Monterey Museum of Art: 41-42
Monterey Museum of the American Indian: 37
Monterey Peninsula Airport: 68, 244-245
Monterey Peninsula College: 19, 61
Monterey Peninsula Recreation Trail: 20, 45-46, 77-78
Monterey Sports Car Championships: 53
Monterey State Beach: 45
Monterey State Historic Park: 10, 35-41
Monterey Wine Festival: 53
Moonstone Beach: 15, 17, 174
Moonstone Cellars: 173
Morgan, Julia: 124
Moses Spring Trail: 99
Moss Landing: 14-15, 228-234
Moss Landing State Beach: 15, 230-231
Mountain Men Gathering: 210
Mount Manuel: 155
Mystery Spot: 190

List of Maps

www.moon.com

DESTINATIONS | ACTIVITIES | BLOGS | MAPS | BOOKS

MOON.COM is all new, and ready to help plan your next trip! Filled with fresh trip ideas and strategies, author interviews, informative blogs, a detailed map library, and descriptions of all the Moon guidebooks, Moon.com is all you need to get out and explore the world—or even places in your own backyard. As always, when you travel with Moon, expect an experience that is uncommon and truly unique.

MAP SYMBOLS

▦ Expressway		**◖** Highlight		✗ Airfield		⚲ Golf Course	
Primary Road		○ City/Town		✗ Airport		**P** Parking Area	
Secondary Road		◉ State Capital		▲ Mountain		⬟ Archaeological Site	
▦ Unpaved Road		⊛ National Capital		✛ Unique Natural Feature		⚑ Church	
Trail		★ Point of Interest				⚑ Gas Station	
Ferry		• Accommodation		🐾 Waterfall		⬯ Glacier	
Railroad		▼ Restaurant/Bar		▲ Park		Mangrove	
Pedestrian Walkway		▪ Other Location		▣ Trailhead		Reef	
Stairs		∧ Campground		�skiing Skiing Area		Swamp	

CONVERSION TABLES

$$°C = (°F - 32) / 1.8$$
$$°F = (°C \times 1.8) + 32$$
1 inch = 2.54 centimeters (cm)
1 foot = 0.304 meters (m)
1 yard = 0.914 meters
1 mile = 1.6093 kilometers (km)
1 km = 0.6214 miles
1 fathom = 1.8288 m
1 chain = 20.1168 m
1 furlong = 201.168 m
1 acre = 0.4047 hectares
1 sq km = 100 hectares
1 sq mile = 2.59 square km
1 ounce = 28.35 grams
1 pound = 0.4536 kilograms
1 short ton = 0.90718 metric ton
1 short ton = 2,000 pounds
1 long ton = 1.016 metric tons
1 long ton = 2,240 pounds
1 metric ton = 1,000 kilograms
1 quart = 0.94635 liters
1 US gallon = 3.7854 liters
1 Imperial gallon = 4.5459 liters
1 nautical mile = 1.852 km

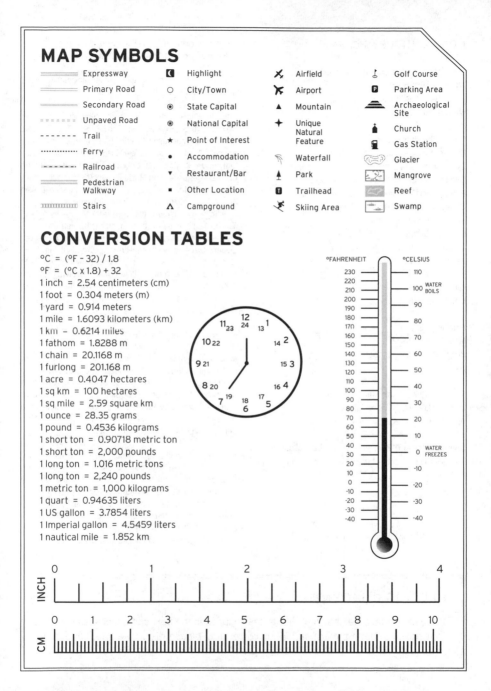

MOON MONTEREY & CARMEL

Avalon Travel
a member of the Perseus Books Group
1700 Fourth Street
Berkeley, CA 94710, USA
www.moon.com

Editor: Sabrina Young
Series Manager: Kathryn Ettinger
Copy Editor: Kia Wang
Graphics Coordinator: Elizabeth Jang
Production Coordinator: Elizabeth Jang
Cover Designer: Elizabeth Jang
Map Editor: Albert Angulo
Cartographers: Chris Markiewicz,
 Kat Bennett, and Mike Morgenfeld
Indexer: Greg Jewett

ISBN: 978-1-56691-995-1
ISSN: 1539-9656

Printing History
1st Edition – 2002
3rd Edition – September 2009
5 4 3 2 1

Front cover photo: Sea Otter, *Enhydra lutris*
© Bradley Ireland; DanitaDelimont.com

Title page: Monarch Butterfly Grove Sanctuary, Pacific
Grove © Ann Marie Brown

Interior photos: pg. 4 Big Sur coast © Ann Marie
Brown; pg. 5 (left) Pacific Grove in spring © Julie
Armstrong/Monterey County CVB; (center) marbled
godwits © Ann Marie Brown; (top right) Point Pinos
Lighthouse © Monterey County CVB; pg. 6 (thumbnail)
Carmel Mission © Ann Marie Brown; (bottom) elephant
seal © Ann Marie Brown; pg. 7 (top left) pelican © Ann
Marie Brown; (top right) whale watching expeditions
© Ann Marie Brown; (bottom left) Monterey Wharf
© Ann Marie Brown; (bottom right) horseback riding
on the beach in Carmel © Jeffrey Greenberg/Monterey
County CVB; pg. 9 © Monterey County CVB; pg. 10–11
© Ann Marie Brown; pg 12 © Monterey County CVB;
pg. 13 (top left and right) © Ann Marie Brown; (bottom)
Deborah Jesch; pg. 14 –21 © Ann Marie Brown; pg. 22
© Kerrick James; pg. 23 © Ann Marie Brown; pg. 24
Paul Ratcliffe/OceanFriendsImages.com

Printed in Canada by Friesens

KEEPING CURRENT

If you have a favorite gem you'd like to see included in the next edition, or see anything
that needs updating, clarification, or correction, please drop us a line. Send your
comments via email to feedback@moon.com, or use the address above.